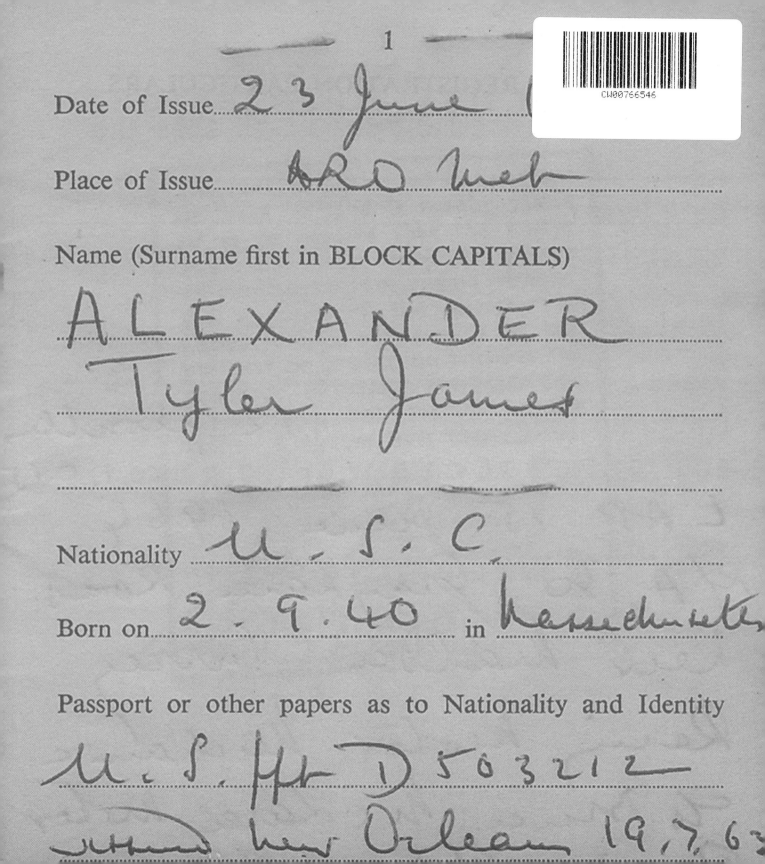

1

Date of Issue 23 June

Place of Issue ARO Meh

Name (Surname first in BLOCK CAPITALS)

ALEXANDER

Tyler James

Nationality U.S.C.

Born on 2.9.40 in Massachusetts

Passport or other papers as to Nationality and Identity

U.S.H. D503212

New Orleans 19.7.6

**TYLER ALEXANDER**
**A LIFE AND TIMES**
**WITH McLAREN**

# TYLER ALEXANDER
## A LIFE AND TIMES WITH McLAREN

**BY TYLER ALEXANDER**
FOREWORD BY BERNIE ECCLESTONE

 **DAVID BULL** PUBLISHING

Library of Congress Control Number: 2014955991

ISBN: 978 1 935007 21 0

*David Bull Publishing,* logo, and colophon are trademarks of David
Bull Publishing, Inc.

Book and cover design: Tom Morgan, Blue Design, Portland, Maine

Printed in China

10  9  8  7  6  5  4  3  2  1

David Bull Publishing
4250 East Camelback Road
Suite K150
Phoenix, AZ 85018

602-852-9500
602-852-9503 (fax)

www.bullpublishing.com

Page 2: Tyler Alexander aboard the 1974 McLaren M16 C/D at the
McLaren Engines facility in Livonia, Michigan.  Earlier that year
Johnny Rutherford had driven the car to victory at the Indianapolis
500. (GARY KNUTSON)

Right: From left to right, John Barnard, Niki Lauda, Ron Dennis, and
Tyler Alexander confer during practice for the 1982 United States
Grand Prix West at Long Beach, California. (LAT PHOTOGRAPHIC)

Page 6: Tyler confers with a thoughtful Bruce McLaren before the
1969 South African Grand Prix at Kyala. (LAT PHOTOGRAPHIC)

# CONTENTS

Tyler Alexander catches up with his old friend Bernie Ecclestone before the 2008 Hungarian Grand Prix in Budapest. (TYLER ALEXANDER COLLECTION)

# Foreword by Bernie Ecclestone

Looking back over the years there has been only a handful of special people who have lasted a really long time in the fascinating but dog-eat-dog world of top-level motor racing, including Formula One, Indy cars, and the original Can-Am series. Even fewer have been able to operate effectively in all three forms of motorsport. And, contrary to appearances, they were not all New Zealanders, Australians, or Englishmen!

One was Teddy Mayer, who helped me to sort out the early days of the Formula One Constructors' Association (FOCA), and the other was his close friend, Tyler Alexander. Both are Americans. They were an integral part of the very small group of people who in 1963 helped Bruce McLaren start up Bruce McLaren Motor Racing.

For all but a few years Tyler was a key part of McLaren—from that very beginning until he retired in early 2009. Despite this length of time I have always noticed that his passion, commitment, and focus in racing never really changed. He never pushed himself forward and never felt the need to say much, but he was always there, keeping in touch with a certain group of like-minded people, doing good work.

He's witnessed and been at the epicenter of a lot of good things that have happened in this sport, and he was also there for some of the bad things, yet he never appeared to let

Bruce McLaren wears the winner's wreath as his teammate Phil Hill looks on after the final race of the 1965 Tasman series at Longford, Australia. (TYLER ALEXANDER)

them get to him. Whatever was needed to keep a team going, Tyler made sure it happened most of the time, regardless of the circumstances or his personal emotions. That was never more evident than in the days, weeks, and months following Bruce McLaren's death in 1970, and again, when Ayrton Senna was killed in 1994. Tyler was the background person who could marshal the troops and keep them going, even when they probably didn't want to.

The things that have always appealed to me about Tyler? He knew what he was talking about; and, more than anything, he was, and still is, a racer.

And as you'll see from this unique story, he always tells it like it is.

—Bernie Ecclestone

# Prologue: March 1964, Vermont

It's minus 15 degrees outside, but right now I'm feeling warmer and more comfortable than I have all day. I'm sitting in a nice soft chair, which is a good thing, since my ass and several other parts of my body are black and blue. Even though I grew up in New England, I've never been downhill skiing before, and today I've been learning the hard way on the icy slopes of Mount Mansfield in Stowe, Vermont.

My instructor is a woman named Garrill Mayer. Even though she's about my age—23—she's now a widow after her husband, Timmy Mayer, was killed in an accident less than two months ago. Timmy was a promising race-car driver who'd been getting ready for his first season in Formula One. In the last few months I'd been his mechanic, preparing his car for races in Europe, the United States, the Bahamas, and, most recently, Australia. It was there that Timmy died in a practice accident before the last race of the 1964 Tasman Series.

Along with several other people, Garrill and I are the guests of Timmy's older brother Teddy, who owns the ski house we're staying in. Teddy has a law degree from Cornell University, but instead of pursuing a legal career, he's been managing his brother's racing activities—until now. Teddy was with Garrill and me in Tasmania when Timmy's accident occurred. In the weeks since returning to the States he's been dealing with Tim's estate and, like me, thinking about the future. Though it may not have been a conscious decision on Teddy's part, I think that's one reason he invited me to join him in Vermont.

To ease my pain and clear my mind, I've been working my way through a small glass of Teddy's rather nice single malt scotch whisky. Then the telephone rings, with a call that would ultimately send me on a journey that would last for decades, span the globe more times than I can remember, and allow me to meet a remarkable group of people in and around the world of motor racing.

Peter Revson looks on as I explain something to Dick Gail of Champion Spark Plugs before the 1972 Can-Am race at Mosport. Engineer Gary Knutson is to the right of Chris. The arrival of Porsche was about to end McLaren's run of success in the Can-Am series. (TYLER ALEXANDER COLLECTION)

# 1940–1960: Growing Up in New England

**B**efore we get into that phone call to Vermont, I should take you back a bit further. My own story started on September 2, 1940, when I was born in Weymouth, Massachusetts, near Boston. During my early years, I lived in northern Maine near Presque Isle with some of my mother's relatives and her parents, who probably came to Maine from New Brunswick, Canada, after leaving Ireland.

My mother, Joan Hargrove, was Irish, and my father, James D'Allessandro, was Italian, which probably explains a lot! In 1958 my father legally changed his last name to Alexander to avoid confusion, since there were some immigration documents done with the name D'Allessandro and others with Alexander.

It is difficult to remember things from 65 years ago, but my grandparents on both sides were hard workers, and I'm sure this is what helped them to survive when they first came to the United States. All their children had the same hardworking attitude.

Two of my mother's brothers owned a couple of large potato farms in Maine, and it was on one of these that I lived for a while. Later I went to live on another farm with one of my mother's sisters, where they raised cows, pigs, and chickens. You learned to think quickly when you were chased by a large pig across the farmyard. It was also not unusual in the winter to have three or four feet of snow closing the road, which meant no school bus or school, sometimes for more than a week at a time.

One of my mother's brothers, Jimmy Hargrove, taught me how to fish, something I have never forgotten. He also made some beautiful model ships inside bottles. Sadly, he was in the hospital for long periods and died quite young from tuberculosis.

My father served in the Marines during World War II, and found himself in a few nasty places in the Pacific. When he came back (thankfully), we went to live for a while in a cottage on a 12-mile-long lake near a little town called Naples, Maine. This was not far from Portland, where his sister, my aunt Rhetta, lived with her husband, Gus Bove, who owned a gas station and a restaurant alongside it. My father worked for a while in the gas station before he moved our family to Hingham, Massachusetts, where one of my mother's sisters lived. That's where the next part of the journey slowly began.

We were now only a few miles from the town of Weymouth, where my father's mother (Virginia Mary, who was born in New York City in 1885, although her family came from Florence, Italy) and father (Raphael, who came from Naples, Italy) lived with two of his sisters. My Italian grandfather came to the United States through Ellis Island, New York, in the late 1800s. He met some people in New York City who had information about jobs in Weymouth. My grandfather was a master cobbler, having learned his trade in Italy. He went to Weymouth and got a job with the Stetson Shoe Company. He also had a workshop at home, and usually gave me a pair of his very nice handmade Italian shoes for Christmas.

The one thing I will never forget about Weymouth is the fantastic meals prepared for Easter and Christmas by my father's sisters. There was everything from antipasto to home-made ravioli made on the kitchen table, and a large pot of tomato sauce with meatballs and sausage slowly simmering for hours. This was followed by roast chicken and salad, and finished off with chocolate and vanilla ricotta cheese pies! I always sat by my grandfather, who kept "his" bottle of red wine on the floor by his chair. He made this wine from the grapes in the backyard, and always gave me a small glass.

Before my interest in race cars began, I liked to build and fly model airplanes. Then in high school I met up with Larry Cronin Jr., who lived across the street from Hingham harbor. Along with fishing, we also did a fair amount of photography, developing the film and printing the photos ourselves.

We were also into scuba diving and snorkeling at a time when there were not many

Here I am with my father and mother sometime during the 1940s. I'm not sure what the occasion was, but we're all dressed up rather nicely. (TYLER ALEXANDER COLLECTION)

people doing it. We belonged to a scuba diving club, and went to scuba competitions up and down the New England coast, doing rather well. Larry and I even helped with some rescue operation tests for cars that had gone into the water. This involved going down in all your scuba gear to the car and pulling a steel cable that you hooked to the car so it could be pulled to the surface. Recovering the people in the car—if there were any—was usually something for the people onshore to deal with.

Whether it was fishing, photography, or scuba diving, most of the time Larry and I were joined by one more good friend: Paul Wuori, known by everyone as Batt.

When I graduated from high school, my father bought me a really nice black Austin-Healey 100 with an aluminum body. It sure would have been nice to have kept this, along with a couple of other special things, such as a 1939 Chevrolet Coupe and an 1863 Springfield

# Paul Wuori

It was in the mid-1950s when Tyler, Larry Cronin Jr., and I became friends in high school. After high school Tyler went to Wentworth Institute to study aeronautical engineering and Larry and I developed our own businesses. But we were always friends, and spent much of our early days together.

Tyler really got involved in motor racing because of his friend John Ffield, who was racing a Cooper Formula 3 car. This led to his becoming friends with various people involved in racing, and a year or so later, led him to England and the start of Bruce McLaren Motor Racing.

As the racing grew in popularity, so did the McLaren company. Tyler would ask Larry and I to come along and lend a hand at various races in the United States. It was a great experience for the three friends from Hingham to all be involved in some way at the races, although Tyler was naturally a great deal more involved than Larry and I.

I felt very close to the team, and even today I consider myself most fortunate to have known Bruce McLaren and played a small part in his career. Although Tyler was and still is very private, to this day he still makes certain that the current McLaren team is introduced to Larry and I when we attend an F1 race.

And whenever the three of us get together—either at the track or away from it—you can see the ease and understanding that fifty-plus years of friendship has created.

musket rifle that we used to shoot. We would use black powder and cast the lead bullets ourselves.

I then went to Wentworth Institute in Boston, taking their aircraft engineering course. Besides the very interesting classroom work, there were real airplanes and engines that we were required to service. I learned a lot of practical things and got an A&E (airframe and engine) license, allowing me to work on airplanes.

During this time, the small group of guys that I hung around with—several living in the same old house—would buy an old car, never paying more than $50. Plymouths were the best, since they were pretty hard to break. The dirt roads in the local woods were fun, as was driving on the beach. When the tide was out you could actually pull a water-skier behind the car.

There were several times when the car became stuck in soft sand as the tide started to come in. I vividly recall waiting on one occasion for the Coast Guard truck to pull us back to a dry bit of the beach. One of the guys was casually sitting on the right front fender drinking a large bottle of beer, with the waves breaking over him and the side of the car!

What about the world of motor racing? Well, I guess we should really start back in the years from 1960 to 1962. You think that's a long time ago? It's a long time ago for me, too! But I was there, so best we get on with it.

I was lucky to catch this image of my friend John Ffield having a shunt in his Cooper Formula 3 car at Connecticut's Lime Rock Park. John was bruised up pretty well, but otherwise came out okay. (TYLER ALEXANDER)

# 1960–62: Aircraft and Racecraft

John Ffield was one of my early friends in motor racing. He was in the process of graduating from the Massachusetts Institute of Technology, and one of the first things I did with him was to build a smoke generator. He used it to demonstrate airflow over different shapes, taking photographs that were included in his thesis on aerodynamics.

John was into a lot of things—cars and airplanes in particular. His first plane was a classic Piper Cub. We tested its rebuilt engine by tying it to a post between the garage doors at his home. John, you might have gathered, lived in a rather large house in Hingham. His father, who was English, worked for Bethlehem Steel Company, developing antirust paint for oil tankers, which meant he took many trips to Monaco to meet with the people who owned them.

John bought this very nice 1939 BMW 328 and turned it into a "special" by throwing away the original bodywork and replacing it with sheets of aluminum. I think he tried to race this car at some early Sports Car Club of America (SCCA) races. It was certainly quick in a straight line, but I don't remember it liking corners very much!

John also raced an MGB a few times before buying a Cooper Formula 3 car, along with several Norton motorcycle engines. The F3 car was powered by the 500cc Norton single-cylinder, in both long- and short-stroke versions. The Cooper was a very popular car in England, and if you look at the reports and records, you'll see that a Mr. Ecclestone and Ken Tyrrell were a couple of the people racing them at the time.

John, being the practical type, and clever, got rid of the single disc brake at the rear of the car and replaced it with—believe it or not—a pair of Studebaker drum brakes. These were actually quite a bit lighter and made the braking much more stable. Another vivid memory I have of John is of rebuilding the engines at his dining-room table while a still that produced hard apple cider was set upon the kitchen stove. The alcohol content of hard apple cider is about 8.5 percent, so it definitely made engine rebuilds more appealing.

By this time John had also bought a very nice single-engine low-wing Swift airplane. He flew it down to Sebring, Florida, where I met up with him after seeing some friends from school in Miami. It was a good thing that I had an A&E (airframe and engine) license. Together we did some work on the engine magnetos, which I then legally signed off on in the logbook. After the Sebring 12 Hours, we flew back north to Hingham.

On another occasion we came pretty close to crashing the Swift on a lake in Vermont during the winter. We had gone up there to see some friends who were in college. It was very cold, so the lakes in the area were frozen. Choosing one to land on, we went down to do a "touch and go," to make sure. When the wheels just touched the surface, the nose of the plane pitched forward. John immediately eased back on the controls and we went across the lake, desperately trying to get enough speed to clear the tall pine trees at the other end. Which we did—just barely!

When we did a low pass over the lake to have a look, we could see marks from the wheels and propeller in the snow. After that, we flew over the college and tossed out a note in a film canister, telling our friends to pick us up at the real airport!

The Formula 3 car was taken to the races on a trailer behind the MG, which proved much more useful as a tow vehicle than as a race car. In 1961 John won 15 of 17 races in the SCCA series for Formula 3 cars, which was run with other classes, including Formula Junior and sports cars.

While John was winning his class, the likes of Timmy Mayer, Peter Revson, and Bill Smith Jr. were winning theirs, along with Roger Penske, Dan Gurney, Jim Hall, and Hap Sharp. Also on hand was Teddy Mayer, who helped out his brother at the races. Many of these people were to play a major part in my life, and have remained friends ever since.

It was around this time that John Ffield became interested in other things, although he was still living in Hingham. This was when my friendship with the Mayers started. I was just a young guy with a couple of Nikon F cameras who they asked to come to a few races when I wasn't going anywhere else with John Ffield. I had no idea that this would be the beginning of a very long relationship with Teddy Mayer. I didn't actually "work" for Teddy; I just went along to help out, and in return my expenses were looked after.

Teddy and his brother Timmy must have realized that my experience with John Ffield, as well as my A&E license, meant I was capable of doing a variety of things to help out with the race car. I think Teddy wanted me along because the others knew even less than I did at the time. Whatever the reason, he was willing to take a chance on me.

At the end of the 1961 season, when Timmy had to go into the army, Teddy said he would cover our expenses if John Ffield and I would take Timmy's Cooper Formula Junior car to Nassau for Roger Penske to drive. Timmy had won the SCCA Formula Junior Championship, which got him the invitation to Nassau, but the army call-up prevented him from going. With its BMC engine the Cooper was not really quite as quick as some of the Ford-powered Lotus cars, but Roger still managed to finish third.

In early 1962 Teddy set up a new team called Rev-Em Racing. It was made up of Timmy Mayer, Peter Revson, and Bill Smith Jr., working out of Bill's Ford dealership in Norwich, New York. I stayed at Bill's house, where I spent a lot of time on the phone with his ex-wife. Bill didn't really want to talk to her. She wasn't sounding off about him—she just wanted someone to talk to. Adding a bit more interest, Bill's girlfriend was also staying at the house! Bill remains a remarkable friend and a splendid guy who has helped me with a great many things along the way.

The service manager at Bill's dealership was a very good Canadian mechanic named Bill Barnard. He also was part of the racing team and helped me with various things. The worst part of the job was the late-night drives to and from the race tracks. Sometimes I got so tired trying to stay awake that I started seeing mirages in the middle of the road—not a pleasant experience!

The relationship with Roger Penske got started on that trip to Nassau at the end of 1961. I had also spent some time at Roy Gane's workshop, helping out on Roger's Cooper Monaco, as well as the single-seat Zerex Special, which we later turned into a quasi-two-seater.

I'm not quite sure why I went down to Florida in February 1962, but I guess it must have been to help Roy Gane with Roger's Cooper Monaco at the inaugural three-hour Daytona

# Roger Penske

I first met Tyler Alexander in the early 1960s, when I was still driving cars before becoming a team owner. I had a little race shop in Bryn Mawr, Pennsylvania, called Updraft Enterprises, run by a guy named Roy Gane. Roy worked on my Birdcage Maserati, Cooper Monaco, and the Zerex Special as we moved up from racing Porsche RSKs. I sold the Zerex to Bruce McLaren, who rebuilt the car with an Oldsmobile engine. It became the first McLaren race car.

Well, one day a guy came into our shop wearing his denims with tennis shoes and no socks. It was Tyler, and we became friends from that point on.

Tyler already had a real keen eye for motorsport and was a very good friend of Teddy Mayer's. Together they helped form Bruce McLaren Motor Racing, with Tyler eventually becoming the "glue" that held the team together. He was an ace technician with impressive mechanical knowledge, and as the sport became more technical, he really drove that process for McLaren. In those days many people were just backyard mechanics, but Tyler had some engineering sophistication. When you look at his record of championships and wins in the Can-Am, Formula One, and Indy cars, it really is incredible. There's no doubt that he's one of motor racing's most successful people.

Tyler and McLaren loved to beat us back in the Can-Am days with Bruce, Denny Hulme, and Peter Revson. Peter had a really strong relationship with Tyler because they had gone racing together with Teddy and Timmy Mayer in the early 1960s. In those days, McLaren was a very small, very tight family of totally committed people.

Later, Ron Dennis took over McLaren. Ron could be a tough guy to work for, but he got results, and after returning to the team, Tyler had a place there, which was very important to McLaren. He was very well respected up and down the pit lane in Formula One. His personality and character were also very important. I think that when the team was down, Tyler was one of those people in the background who gave the team the support it needed.

I regard Tyler as a great friend. He and Teddy Mayer, who worked for many years at Penske Cars in the UK, had a bond that went beyond their years together at McLaren. When Teddy passed away a few years ago, both Tyler and I felt we had lost a super friend who was instrumental to our success in racing.

One regret I have is that Tyler never came to work for the Penske team. This almost happened in the mid-1970s when Heinz Hofer, who ran our Formula One team, was killed in an automobile accident. In the end Derrick Walker took over the job, but before that I talked to Tyler about joining us. He had such a loyalty to McLaren that it would have been tough for him to leave. That's the kind of guy Tyler was, and is.

I'm sure Tyler would have had a big impact on our company. He's a good people person, but he also understood the rules and the cars, and was a great strategist. In the early days everybody was a specialist. It was rare to find someone like Tyler, who had the range and experience to understand all the different aspects of the car and how to go racing. He's a great friend, and I've always had great respect for him. Like I said before, Tyler is one of motor racing's most accomplished men.

From left to right, Roger Penske, Dan Gurney, and Bruce McLaren at Sebring in 1962. Roger and Bruce finished fifth overall driving a Cooper Monaco entered by Briggs Cunningham. (TYLER ALEXANDER)

Continental on February 11. Teddy Mayer's Formula Junior car was also there for Roger to drive. Whatever the reason, I'm damn glad I went. The race had a classic ending, as Dan Gurney coasted his Lotus 19 down the banking and across the finish line to win the race. The Cooper Monaco ran 60 of the 70 laps until it had an engine oil pressure problem. The other real pleasure for me was the photos that I took at Daytona.

A few months later, Peter Revson and I drove to Canada with his Formula Junior car for a race at Mosport on June 6, 1962. There were a few problems in practice, the main one being a broken distributor, but we sorted everything out for the race, and Peter won the Formula Junior class. The two of us then loaded the car back onto the trailer and drove back down to Bill Smith's place in Norwich, New York. Writing about this now makes it sound like a piece of cake, but somehow, I don't think it was that easy! Neither were any of the other Formula Junior races that Rev-Em Racing did.

On July 29, 1962, Indianapolis Raceway Park held an "Intercontinental" race called the Hoosier Grand Prix, which was run in two heats. It was a pretty major event, attracting cars and drivers from England. Roger Penske was concerned about the pits, which were located at the edge of the track. At the drivers' meeting just before the race he asked just what constituted the track. The answer came from Innes Ireland, who told him simply, "Just keep it between the bits of grass."

Roger kept it between the bits of grass and won the first heat; an engine problem meant he didn't finish the second heat, which was won by Hap Sharp. Timmy Mayer stalled the Cooper Monaco he'd rented from Roger in the first heat and finished 18th in the second. Teddy had a deal with Roger that allowed us to use his Cooper Monaco in several other races as well.

I also recall a race on October 14 at Riverside, California. I went there with Roger and Roy Gane, who had entered Roger's Zerex Special on behalf of the Updraft Enterprises shop. Roger won the race, while Bruce McLaren—driving a works Cooper Monaco, looked after by his Formula One mechanic, Mike Barney—finished fourth.

Another two-heat event at Laguna Seca in Monterey, California, followed on October 21. We actually worked on the cars in Carmel Valley and drove or towed them to the race track. This was a really nice area made even better by a great steak house called Will's Fargo. It was next to the garage where we worked, and is still there today. The thing I remember most about this place was the counter displaying the cuts of steak: They would cut your choice of steak to a size you thought you could eat. There were only two other things on the main menu at the time—fish and chicken.

As for the race, Roger finished second in both heats, while Timmy didn't have a good time due to engine problems, which forced him out of the first heat and prevented him from starting the second.

Timmy's luck improved in Puerto Rico on November 11, when there were races for Sports Cars and Formula Junior on the Caguas circuit. Despite having to make a pit stop for a punctured tire, Timmy finished second in a Cooper Monaco sports car rented from Roger Penske, who won the race in his Zerex Special. Timmy then won the Formula Junior race from H. W. Smith and Peter Revson.

Aside from the racing, there were quite a few incidents that weekend. I remember working on the cars on race morning when someone yelled, "Get a big stick!" A spider a bit bigger than your hand had been found in the cockpit of one of the Formula Junior cars.

More serious—for some of us, anyway—was an incident after the racing had finished. We had permission from the governor of the island to drive the sports cars to the airport from the circuit once the race was over. Our progress was slow because we had to tow the Formula Junior cars with one of the rental cars, and we needed to stick together.

We got stopped at a police inspection roadblock quite near the airport and, of course, they found our transport didn't comply with the various aspects of a proper car. Roy Gane, Hap Sharp's mechanic Don Allen, and myself, who were driving the sports cars, were taken off to court. At least the other guys were left to deal with the cars. We were found guilty of driving improper cars on the road in Puerto Rico. And to make matters worse, the judge said he didn't really care what the governor of the island had said!

We were taken to the old San Juan prison, lined up in the courtyard with all the rest of the great unwashed, and told to go inside. We answered quite loudly, "No! We are not going to do that." After a lot of words in both English and Spanish, we were put on some old wooden benches in a corner of the yard and allowed to talk to the prison doctor, who fortunately spoke quite good English.

Of course, neither Teddy nor any of the others from the race team knew what had happened to us. After a while, Teddy, Timmy, and some people from the race track showed up and got us out of the prison. It was none too soon; our reception from the inmates hadn't been helped by the fact that Roy had on one of those giant straw hats, and Don was wearing shorts!

Despite being in the army, Timmy had won the SCCA Formula Junior Championship, thanks to getting leave on race weekends. His performance had been good enough to win him a drive with Ken Tyrrell's works Cooper Formula Junior team. So early in 1963, Timmy and Teddy moved to England.

Wally Willmott (left) and I pose with one of the two cars built for the 1964 Tasman Series. (TYLER ALEXANDER COLLECTION)

# 1963: From Mecom to McLaren

**B**ecause the Mayers had buggered off to England, I was kind of left standing in an open field, as it were. I drove down to Pennsylvania to see Roger Penske, who was driving for John Mecom Jr.'s team. John Jr. lived in Houston, Texas. His father was an independent oil executive with his own wells near Galveston, along with interests in others all over the world. He also owned the *Houston Chronicle*, several hotels, and many other properties.

Roger sorted out a place for me on Mecom's team in Houston (thank you, Roger!), in a workshop set up in one of his father's airplane hangars at the airport. I worked there with an Australian, Neil Robinson, on the modified Zerex Special (now converted to a quasi-two-seater) and a Ferrari 250 GTO.

We raced these two cars at various events, including the 1963 Sebring 12 Hours, where Roger Penske and Augie Pabst (yes, the beer scion) finished fourth overall, and first in class with the Ferrari GTO.

Traveling across the Deep South had some drawbacks at that time, mainly because the people there had a pronounced dislike for anyone they didn't know. This made it a bit awkward when we stopped to get something to eat. A couple of times it became unpleasant enough for us to get up and leave before a fight was served instead of our hamburgers. One does have to remember that the redneck locals didn't like us purely because we were not locals!

The neat thing with the Ferrari was that when we brought it back to Houston, we just changed the spark plugs to normal ones for the road, which allowed Little John to drive the car around Houston.

John and his wife Katsy were genuinely nice people. They collected various forms of wildlife, and I remember riding in the backseat of John's car with his pet cheetah. Fortunately, the cat was very well behaved, thank you, as I'm still here.

John would invite us down to the family ranch in Galveston, where we had the oil wells in the background for the company barbecues and a bit of shooting at coyotes. I'm not sure we actually shot any, but we did have a fantastic time, with a large selection of guns to choose from. John had a very special gun collection, including very old matched dueling pistols and automatic rifles that spanned a great many years. One of John's friends spent a fair bit of time during his travels around the world looking for more special items to add to John's already very special collection.

At one point during 1963 we acquired a Lotus 19 with a 2.0-liter Coventry Climax engine for Augie Pabst to drive. On June 1 at Mosport Park in Canada Roger finished fourth in the Zerex Special and Augie was 18th. I don't recall why Augie was so far behind, because the Lotus 19 was a good car. Maybe it had something to do with Augie's comment about the handling of the car, which he described as "chocolate ice cream." I took this to mean it was okay. Maybe not!

On the way back into the United States, Neil Robinson was stopped by the immigration people and basically deported. I think their reasoning went a bit like this, "Sir, you are working in the United States, getting paid in the United States, and there's no paperwork." We set off from the border in the transporter and stopped for something to eat about an hour or so later, having left Neil with the nice immigration people.

As we stopped, a car pulled up beside the transporter and, just like in the movies, a couple of guys jumped out and wanted to search the transporter. It was fairly pathetic, really; they wanted to see if we had hidden Neil somewhere. There was a motel near the immigration building, and it's possible they thought Neil had jumped in the transporter after checking into the motel. We gave them the keys and told them to do whatever the hell they wanted. We said we were going to get something to eat, and to please give us the

Team owner John Mecom Jr. (right) with Jackie Stewart at the 1966 Indianapolis 500. Jackie was leading the race when a broken scavenge pump forced him out with just eight laps to go. (TYLER ALEXANDER)

keys back before they left. Neil was later let into the States to collect his personal stuff and then sent on his way.

Early in August, a trip to England was organized, as Penske and Mecom had been invited to Brands Hatch for the Guards Trophy sports-car race. Mecom had bought a Lola GT car for Pabst to drive, which meant we had a place to work at the Lola factory in nearby Bromley.

For my first visit to the UK, we stayed in the Hilton Hotel on Park Lane. Looking out of the hotel-room window, one of the first things we noticed was some blokes putting tar down on the roof of a building, all of them dressed in suits and ties. It certainly seemed fairly strange to us, particularly to me as a complete stranger to those shores. It was my first introduction to English formality and customs.

The first real challenge for us was learning how to drive from the center of London to Bromley. Getting from there to Brands Hatch wasn't quite so bad, because we could at least follow someone from Lola. Once we got to the circuit, the English scrutineers didn't like the way the Zerex Special was built: As a former single-seat car built for Formula One, it didn't really comply with the "letter of the law" in the regulations.

This is when I first met Don Beresford, who, along with a few other blokes at Lola, worked several very long nights with us to get the car into a fit state to pass scrutineering. It paid off when Roger won the race, although poor Augie failed to finish. This was really something quite special, because Roger competed against all of the really big-name drivers around at that time—Graham Hill, Innes Ireland, and Roy Salvadori, among others. I guess Roger was not called "The Captain" for nothing. Timmy Mayer rounded off the weekend for us by finishing third in a Cooper Monaco.

While we were at Brands Hatch, Teddy Mayer had asked if I would help build Timmy's Tasman car. It seemed that Teddy and Timmy had done a deal with this guy—who just happened to be Bruce McLaren—to build two cars to run in what was called the Tasman Series. These races were to start in January 1964, with four weekly races in New Zealand, then a two-week break before three races, a week apart, would be held in Australia. A week after that the last race would be held in Tasmania.

The next step changed my life and upset John Mecom Jr. To this day, I feel sorry about leaving John's team and staying in the UK. I'm not sorry for what I did, but I do regret not having the chance to actually tell John what I was planning to do, and why I had to do it. I had been given an opportunity to work with some interesting people, so I said to myself, "What the hell—let's just get on with it."

The Tasman cars were based on a Cooper Formula One car, since Bruce was driving for the Cooper F1 team. Bruce changed quite a bit of the car to suit what he wanted and to better align with the nature of the Tasman races, which were not very long. One change that resulted was the replacement of the Cooper car's side fuel tanks with one under the driver's seat. The cars were built in Cooper's F1 workshop in Surbiton. The floor there was two-thirds concrete and one-third hard-packed dirt. You can guess which bit of the floor we were told to use. The real dirt floor part was quite common at the time.

Wally Willmott, a good friend of Bruce's, came over from New Zealand to help build Bruce's car. The Mayers had me, sometimes known as "The Ugly American." But unlike some of the English, we at least weren't wiping our asses with wax paper, and I knew what a shower was. As soon as I got the chance I brought a showerhead with rubber hoses back from the States to attach to the British bathtub taps. And once the Cooper blokes—a very talented bunch, I might add—realized that I could weld and machine things (and work just as hard as they could, without getting upset by their suggestions and comments), I started to fit in.

I stayed in Teddy's rented house on an island in the river Thames, just by the village of Thames Ditton. I remember you had to pay two (old) pence to cross the bridge to get to his house! It was at a Sunday lunch party there that I first met this McLaren chap. There must have been something about him. I remember thinking this guy with one leg a bit shorter than the other (the result of an illness in childhood) seemed to know a lot about motor racing, and perhaps I'd better tag along to find out more about it myself. I wasn't wrong. I learned a lot of things in a very short period of time working with Bruce, Wally, and the Cooper F1 mechanics.

One day, as we were working away, a loud voice from outside the workshop said, "Tyler! What the hell are you doing in there?" It was Dan Gurney, who was driving a Formula One car for Jack Brabham and lived just up the road from the Cooper workshop. Of course, I had known Dan from some of the early racing in the United States, and it was nice to have a few minutes to chat and catch up with him.

Both Tasman cars were duly finished and sent off to New Zealand by boat, along with crates of spares. They would end up in the garage owned by Bruce's father, Les McLaren, in Auckland, where we would prepare the cars for the first couple of races.

Before that trip down under, however, there were some sports-car races in the United States. Teddy had bought a Lotus 23 for Timmy to drive at Riverside and Laguna Seca in California. All of this happened on rather short notice. The car was air-freighted to New York City and arrived a bit late. Having picked up the truck and trailer from Bill Smith's place in Norwich, New York, Teddy and I drove down to Idlewild Airport (now John F. Kennedy International Airport) to collect the car and the spare bits and pieces.

Then we set off, driving to Riverside, just outside Los Angeles. It was nonstop, except for one night. What the hell—it's only the odd 3,000 miles. When we got there, we went to the airport and picked up Walter Boyd, a really good mechanic and engineer who was going to be working with us.

The Lotus 23 had a 2.0-liter engine, which meant it was in a different class, but still in the same race as cars with bigger engines. Since they all ran together, there were quite a few cars in the field. We had a properly serious problem in the race when the engine's crankshaft broke for some strange reason. But things went a lot better in the next race at Laguna

The 1964 Tasman car with its bodywork removed. Though based on the 1963 Cooper T61 Formula One car, it featured extensive modifications specified by Bruce McLaren. (TYLER ALEXANDER)

Seca, where Timmy finished first in class and sixth overall; this really was an achievement.

The car was taken back to Walter Boyd's place in Litchfield, Connecticut, before going to Nassau for the annual Bahamas Speed Week. It was while working on the car in Walter's workshop that we heard President Kennedy had been shot dead in Dallas, Texas. It was November 22, 1963.

Wally Willmott came from England to Nassau to give us a hand. We had quite a reasonable time there, with Timmy finishing third overall in the Nassau Trophy race. While Walter Boyd took the car back to his place in Connecticut, Wally and I stayed in Nassau for a few days before the start of our long trip to New Zealand. In terms of the time required, this was an especially long journey in those days. But at least we were able to stop off in Fiji and spend the night there before catching another flight to take us down to Auckland.

# 1964: Tragedy in Tasmania and a New Beginning

Once we arrived in New Zealand, one of the first things to learn, of course, was the timing of the opening—but really the closing—of the local pubs. Generally speaking, there was a fair bit of serious drinking. People getting out of work only had about an hour for a few beers before the pub closed. In the last half-hour or so, the casual partaking of beer rapidly changed to something more serious, and patrons were allowed to order a case of large bottles of beer to take away before the bell rang. Best of all was the pub where someone wandered around in the main room, refilling people's glasses with a long garden hose, which would later be connected to a water tap to rinse off the floor after the pub closed.

Meanwhile, we got back to the business of unpacking and sorting out how to transport the cars and spares around New Zealand and Australia. Bruce and Wally had rounded up several friends who were damn good at practically anything, from working on the race cars to driving the trucks and trailers here, there, and everywhere.

The first race of the Tasman series was at Levin, close to Wellington in the southern part of New Zealand's North Island. Denny Hulme won, with Timmy Mayer second and Bruce

McLaren third. The second race was at Pukekohe near Auckland on the North Island, and was won by Bruce, followed by Denny and Timmy.

At a prize-giving party and dinner after one of the first Tasman races, there was a whole roasted pig on the table, one with a strange hint of a smile on its well-cooked face. Lenny Gilbert, one of Bruce's commandeered friends, explained it this way, "You'd look like that too if you had an apple in your mouth and a loaf of bread stuffed up your ass!"

It took someone quite good to pull up the engine cover in our old Thames van and adjust the spark and fuel mixture in an attempt to get more speed, with the trailer and race car attached. This was done on a downhill run on the way to the next race at the old Wigram airfield, near Christchurch on the South Island of New Zealand. Bruce won the race, with Jack Brabham second, Denny Hulme third, and Timmy Mayer eighth.

The last of the four races in New Zealand was in Teretonga at the very bottom of the South Island, not that far from the South Pole. Bruce won the race there, and Timmy was a very, very close second. Almost as memorable was a remark from Timmy during breakfast at the hotel with Bruce's wife Pat. Exasperated by her distracted approach to eating, he exclaimed, "Could you please stop beating the hell out of your plate and eat your breakfast?"

We had a couple of weeks' break before going off to Australia for the last few races, which started with Sandown Park in Melbourne and then up to Sydney for a race at Warwick Farm. This was a road-racing circuit built in and around a horse-racing track. The area was also noted for producing some of the best-looking girls (or sheilas, to use the Australian term) in the world. The weather was so hot that fuel for the race cars was kept in big containers with dry ice before being put into the fuel tank. Since the tank in the Tasman car was literally part of the driver's seat, the fuel helped to keep the driver cool, at least during the first part of the race.

Brisbane was the next stop, where we stayed in a very small motel right near the ocean. There really wasn't much there at all—just the beach, ocean, and some scorpions. Today it's called the Gold Coast, and there are high-rise hotels and apartments everywhere, but it certainly wasn't like that in 1964.

Timmy was getting better with every race. He probably would have won the race in Brisbane had a connecting rod not broken in the engine, but either way, he was looking forward to the next race in Tasmania.

Before that, we first had to make an epic journey to Melbourne, where we planned to change the engines in the two race cars before shipping them to Tasmania. We left the

Preparing the engine on Timmy Mayer's car before one of the early races in the 1964 Tasman series. (TYLER ALEXANDER COLLECTION)

Brisbane track after the race and drove until about midnight, when we found a place to stay. The next part of the trip down to Melbourne was nonstop. How we managed to make it without a major accident I don't know, because there were several off-road moments. But we got the job done in time to get the cars to the docks and onto a boat bound for Davenport, in Tasmania.

Practice at Longford began very well, with both cars being quite quick. We stopped to change the gear ratios in Timmy's car and off he went again. He was pretty much the quickest at that point. Timmy then had an accident on the part of the road circuit where the cars became airborne. The car landed badly and went into a tree, making a direct hit on the cockpit. Timmy died straightaway, virtually on impact. It was February 28, 1964.

Timmy was a very low-key, quiet guy who was becoming very interested in driving racing cars. At some point, he and Teddy had set their sights on professional careers in racing, with Timmy driving and Teddy as his manager. During the short time I knew him, Timmy was easier going than Teddy, but this doesn't imply that he was soft on or off the race track.

Timmy and I certainly got on very well, and I liked his wife, Garrill. He was a serious, yet funny, happy-go-lucky person. He also knew how to cleverly use those traits at the right time and place.

I don't know if Timmy knew how good he was at the time, but he did know he needed to be better. Timmy and Peter Revson were very close in ability in the early Formula Junior races, but we will never know if he could have been as good as Peter, or perhaps even better.

Certainly, as the 1964 Tasman Series progressed, Timmy had been getting closer to Bruce in several of the races. I don't really know exactly how Bruce felt when Timmy passed away. But without realizing it at the time, I learned a lot from Bruce that day, and the next. You have to realize that this was a time in motor racing when many drivers were losing their lives—and Bruce was racing with and against them.

Because Bruce didn't do the qualifying session that afternoon, he had to start the race the next day from the back of the grid. Did he want to race that day? Well, I guess you could have asked him at the time . . . but actually, we know the answer. Despite the tragedy, Bruce drove very well. By finishing second to Graham Hill, he won the Tasman Series for 1964. I don't quite know how to explain this quality, but I think it's called "Fucking tough!"

I don't think that I had a gut reaction about the real impact of the accident. This is not meant as a callous comment, or to claim that I was at a loss for words. We all just got stuck into what actually needed to be done at that time; this ability to focus and cope was something I was learning from both Bruce and Teddy.

I'm not sure how all of this sank in at the time. I do remember having a quiet dinner and a few drinks at the hotel that evening after the accident. Garrill was a very strong person and kept control of things; she did a superb job under the circumstances. Teddy chartered an airplane to take Timmy, Garrill, himself, and me to Sydney, the first leg of a long trip back to the States. We had to stop in Hawaii and again in San Francisco, where we stayed overnight at the airport hotel. Then it was on to New York, where Teddy's uncle, Bill Scranton, the ex-governor of Pennsylvania, had his private plane waiting to take us to Scranton, Pennsylvania, where the Mayer family lived, and the wealthy Scrantons had been so influential that the city carried their name.

We went to Happy Apple Farm, where Teddy's mother (affectionately referred to as M) lived. The next day the house was filled with friends and relatives. I was left to explain just what the hell their relative was doing in someplace called Tasmania, and how he got killed. It certainly was a challenge to use the little knowledge I had at the time to explain the basic things about motor racing and how dangerous it really was. I had to try to get across that Timmy was doing something that he really enjoyed.

You can imagine the mixed emotions I was experiencing at this point. Here I was, a 23-year-old, having to explain—and, in a way, defend—a sport Timmy had suddenly found himself pursuing at a fairly high level. At the same time, I still hadn't become fully engaged with racing as a possible long-term career. I'm not sure I realized at the time that this was just the beginning of something very significant in my life.

Bruce summed up his feelings this way in an article he wrote not long after Timmy's passing, "To do something well is so worthwhile that to die trying to do it better cannot be foolhardy. It would be a waste of life to do nothing with one's ability, for I feel life is measured in achievement, not in years alone."

Once various things in Scranton had been dealt with, I went back to my parents' house in Hingham, where I spent quite a bit of time working in my friend Larry Cronin Jr.'s darkroom.

Several weeks later, Teddy called me about coming up to Stowe, Vermont, where he had a house with Tommy Bryant, whose sister Sally would become the future Mrs. Teddy Mayer. Garrill Mayer, Timmy's widow, was going to be up there as well, and had promised to teach me to ski—or at least try to. All of which brings us back to where we began, with me sipping scotch after a day on Mount Mansfield.

Then the phone rang.

Working on Timmy's car in the pit lane at New Zealand's Teretonga Park in January 1964. He would finish a very close second to his teammate Bruce McLaren. (TYLER ALEXANDER COLLECTION)

The person on the other end was Bruce McLaren. He said there were several sports-car races coming up in England, and he was thinking about buying the Zerex Special from John Mecom Jr. and Roger Penske. Teddy had told Bruce that I was there with him, and that we would have a chat about it before Bruce called back later.

Did we ever think about quitting motor racing because of what had happened to Timmy? It sure doesn't look like it. There may have been some thought of it, but the phone call from Bruce in England seemed to change all that, creating what would become the path forward—and why not? One has to do something with one's life.

Teddy called Bruce back the next day, saying that it sounded like a reasonable idea, and agreeing we should go ahead with it. Teddy gave me a check and I went down to Bill Smith Jr.'s place in Norwich to pick up a trailer to tow behind the station wagon. Then I set off for Corry Field in Pensacola, Florida, to collect the Zerex Special after a race that weekend. After Roger had finished second, the Mecom Racing mechanics removed the engine and helped me load the car onto the trailer and several boxes of spares into the station wagon.

A couple of Oldsmobile V8 engines were also part of the deal, but these were sent later.

I set off for the nonstop drive to New York's John F. Kennedy International Airport. (Idlewild had been renamed after the president's death the year before.) After the NoDoz tablets and Pepsi-Cola started to wear off, I thought I'd better stop beside the road somewhere in Virginia and have a nap. But the nightmares—I would guess from lack of sleep and traffic noise—were worse than trying to stay awake. So I set off again, holding my head out the window like a damn dog every once in a while to help keep me awake.

Teddy had sorted out the shipping with Pan-American. I dropped off the race car and spares very late in the afternoon, leaving the station wagon and trailer in the parking lot for one of Mr. Smith's guys to collect. After a night in the airport hotel, the next morning I caught a Pan-Am flight to London.

I was picked up at Heathrow that evening by Eoin Young. Eoin was a former bank clerk from New Zealand. He was also a motorsport fan, and had met Bruce while writing race reports for his local newspaper. When Bruce invited Eoin to come to Europe to be his secretary, he jumped at the chance. Eoin took me to nearby Hounslow where Bruce had rented space in a workshop. The car was already there, and several people—including Wally Willmott, Bruce Harry, and Howden Ganley (a mechanic and aspiring driver lately arrived from New Zealand)—were working on it. I don't remember getting much sleep because we were racing at Oulton Park on April 11, which was the following weekend.

Eoin had sorted out somewhere for Wally and I to stay in the place where he was living in New Malden. There would be a couple of epic journeys between Hounslow and New Malden as I tried to get home without really knowing the way. Decades later I'm still trying to understand the English road system!

We reached Oulton Park on time and were doing okay in the race until the freshly rebuilt gearbox had a problem and we didn't finish. But at least we were there. From Pensacola, Florida, to Oulton Park in England in the space of a single week was a pretty damn good effort for all of those who made it happen. Today it's called "back-to-back races"; in those days it was just what you did.

While we were at Oulton Park, Ken Tyrrell introduced me to a young Scottish driver who had rolled one of Ken's Formula 3 Coopers into some bushes during practice on Saturday. He then took over John Love's car to win the race on Sunday.

This was John Young Stewart, now Sir Jackie Stewart. He and I have been friends ever since.

# Sir Jackie Stewart

Tyler Alexander became one of the best-known and most respected engineers in the world of motorsport. It was remarkable that Tyler, as an American, was so revered, when Britons, Australians, and New Zealanders were so prominent among the top people in the world of motor racing from the 1960s through the present day.

Tyler was a man for all seasons; whether it was Formula One, Indy car racing, or Can-Am, Tyler was at the forefront. His relationship with Bruce McLaren created that versatility of skills and depth of knowledge that Tyler applied to all three categories. In addition, Tyler's social skills—including an ability to fit into almost any circumstance, or with any group of people—were also a reflection of Bruce's diplomatic and charming personality.

Tyler worked with a great many drivers, and sadly, I wasn't one of them. But I would love to have had Tyler Alexander as part of my life while I was racing. I first met Tyler in 1964, when I was driving for Ken Tyrrell's Formula 3 Team. In those days, F3 was quite often the support race at the Formula One grand prix meetings. I used to hang out with Bruce and Pat McLaren, often staying with them in their apartment in Surbiton, attending parties with them after race weekends at

Silverstone, Brands Hatch, and Goodwood. These were held in Surbiton in a very large house shared by a bunch of McLaren folk, such as Tyler, Eoin Young, Wally Willmott, Howden Ganley, Bruce Harry, Chris Amon, Peter Jackson, and, of course, Bruce and Pat McLaren. They produced some great nights—what fun those times were!

Sadly, when Bruce McLaren died at Goodwood in 1970, we lost one of the world's great ambassadors for motorsport. Bruce's dignity and style had a huge impact on the quality people that he had carefully chosen to work for him. Tyler was a perfect example. As time progressed Tyler moved on to work for the McLaren Indy car team, and later returned to the new-generation McLaren International Formula One Team, before finally retiring from the sport with the same dignity, reputation, and style that he's always had.

Like his late mentor, Tyler Alexander has served as an ideal ambassador to represent the community of motorsport. In all of his dealings he was soft-spoken but firm in his commitments, socially capable in every respect. He dressed well, behaved well, spoke well, and engineered well. There's much to be learned from Tyler's life and example.

We were back in the same part of northwest England a week later for the next race at Aintree, near Liverpool. Derelict and bombed-out buildings were signs that the city still showed a great many marks from World War II. Thick fog and the cold and damp didn't help much either. Bruce won the race and beat some of the best people there, including Jimmy Clark in a new Lotus 30 sports car.

I'm not sure if it was on the return from Oulton Park or from Aintree, but we were stopped by the police on the M1, thankfully close to the London end of the motorway. We

Future world champion Jackie Stewart was still driving for BRM when I caught him on the grid before the 1967 British Grand Prix at Silverstone. (TYLER ALEXANDER)

had been trying to get the old Ford Zephyr and trailer to hit 100 mph on a long downhill stretch. This didn't go over particularly well with the police. The penalty was that we had to leave the M1. I have no idea how long it took us to get home, but it sure as hell wasn't the shortest or the quickest way.

Three alloy-block Oldsmobile engines were part of the Zerex Special deal. The V8s were rebuilt from a GM production engine by Traco in Culver City, California, turning them into something you could use in your race car. In the end, the GM program to build alloy cylinder blocks proved too costly and was canceled.

We had now moved to our own workshop in New Malden. This was actually just a corner space in a building that we shared with some road-building machinery. Looking back now at the part-dirt floor, you wouldn't really believe it. And we probably should have had a tetanus shot after going to the loo.

As all of this was going on, Bruce was still driving for Cooper in Formula One. Before leaving for the Belgian Grand Prix, he made a wire model of the mods he wanted for the Zerex chassis before we installed the Oldsmobile engine. (This was classic Bruce, although we didn't really know it at the time.) He gave the four of us the model and set off, saying, "I'll be back on Monday to see how the Oldsmobile engine fits."

The welding of the new tubes in the chassis was finished by Sunday morning, and Eoin Young was dispatched to find some paint for the chassis. He had a hard time finding what was needed on a Sunday morning, but when he did, it happened to be a very dark green paint used for garden fences, ensuring that the car looked ugly. It quickly became known as the Jolly Green Giant.

I did the rebuilding of the engine because it was American, and I was an American—so it was my job! Once that was done, it was run on someone's dynamometer; I have no idea who owned it or where it was. Fortunately there were no real problems, other than a mistake I made with the rocker-arm pushrods. They had a different size on each end. It was only a small amount, but I put a couple of them in upside down, and it was enough to split the rocker adjuster. We were not sure of the cause of the problem until Bruce checked some dimensions carefully and then organized better and stronger rocker adjustors. These were used for the rest of the time we raced the Oldsmobile engine.

Having run out of time to do a proper exhaust system for the car with the Oldsmobile engine, we ended up with some very simple straight exhaust pipes poked up in the air.

Time was limited because we were off to Mosport in Canada for a sports-car race, with only a short trip to Goodwood beforehand to check things out.

There was also a problem getting some gear ratios ready in time to go with the freight. In the end, they had to be hand-carried. Fortunately, some good friends at Pan-Am got Wally and I a couple of the best seats in the front of the plane. The stewardess was a bit mystified when Wally and I insisted on putting our trench coats in the overhead locker. She obviously wanted to help hang them up, but since the pockets were filled with the late-arriving gear ratios, we thought maybe we should put them away ourselves.

By now, Teddy had reappeared on the scene, having arranged to transport the car and all the spares to the Mosport race track, near Toronto. The race was run in two heats and Bruce won both, but the poor old Zerex was fairly beaten up by rocks thrown at it when A. J. Foyt and other drivers would drop a wheel off the track as Bruce tried to overtake.

When the car returned to England, a fair amount of work was needed to repair the Mosport damage, along with fitting a proper set of exhaust pipes to replace the straight ones we'd used at the last minute.

It was at roughly this time that Teddy decided to be fully involved with Bruce McLaren in the world of motor racing. Bruce's charisma and engineering abilities, along with Teddy's lawyerly attributes, determination, and some financial input, were turned into a little company called Bruce McLaren Motor Racing, with a New Zealand kiwi as its logo. That particular name—and the company—still exists today, owned by Teddy's son and daughter, Timmy and Annie, and myself. It would be nice if we could do something with it.

Meanwhile, my learning process regarding England was continuing, thanks to various pieces of information I picked up in some unlikely places. One I found neatly carved on the inside of a wooden door on a loo at Norfolk's Snetterton circuit. I have never forgotten the priceless message, "Would the fellow with the asshole halfway up his back please sit well forward." How could you ever forget it?

We moved out of the small flat in New Malden to half of a beautiful old house called Warden that Eoin had found on Corcoran Road in Surbiton. This place was owned by a British army major who was away on duty. Eoin, Wally, Teddy, and myself (I'm not sure who else was there at the time; Gary Knutson and Roger Bailey appeared at some point) each paid £5 per week, which included the milk and rent, along with the young man and his wife who looked after various aspects of the place.

About three blocks away was the infamous house on Ditton Road where Mike Hailwood lived, along with Chris Amon, Peter Revson, and Bruce Abernathy, one of Chris's friends from New Zealand. Bruce, a flat-track motorbike champion, was a great character. He filled the front lawn with old Jaguars that were going to be sent back to New Zealand and make Bruce and Chris lots of money. Last I remember, they were still in the front yard waiting for the ship to come and collect them—how it would get to Surbiton in Surrey, I was never too sure!

Stories about the good Mr. Abernathy are legendary. He just happened to be at a race in Austria and came across the wedding party of some count or another. Bruce joined the procession and wasn't seen for several weeks, which he probably spent trapped in a castle in the Austrian mountains with an attractive female.

Needless to say, there were a lot of parties at Ditton Road. Among the most memorable (and disgusting) was one at which a guest threw up in several of the trophies in Mr. Hailwood's vast collection—and then carefully placed them back on the mantelpiece above the fireplace. Dear, oh dear.

The partying was forgotten briefly when the Guards Trophy at Brands Hatch came along on August 3, 1964. The sports-car race had an impressive entry—Graham Hill, Jackie Stewart, Chris Amon, Frank Gardner, A. J. Foyt—but, once again, Bruce won in the Zerex Special. The car had changed quite a bit since we'd gotten our hands on it, and while the result was damn hard to believe, it went to prove that it never hurts to keep trying. Our house on Corcoran Road was now known as The Castle, and after the race we hosted a victory party there! It was probably organized by Eoin Young and sponsored by Bruce, which really meant the drinks were on him. One and all were invited, from John Mecom Jr. to Jimmy Clark and Graham Hill. Pretty much everyone showed up at some point. Can you imagine doing that today? Of course there were a lot less people in racing then—but it still might be worth a try.

There was one particular night at The Castle when Peter Jackson of Specialized Moldings Ltd. brought down a bunch of fiberglass Roman helmets, shields, and swords to spruce up the party. Peter's company made the bodywork for most of the race cars, but on this occasion, he had made the Roman stuff for a movie. Since The Castle had some real weaponry hanging on the walls, it was easy enough to confuse the two, especially under the festive circumstances. In the throes of a mock battle with Jimmy Clark, Graham Hill nearly knocked Jimmy unconscious because he was wearing a fiberglass Roman helmet and Graham had hit him with one of the real swords taken from the wall!

Graham got it right a couple of weeks later when he won the Tourist Trophy at Goodwood

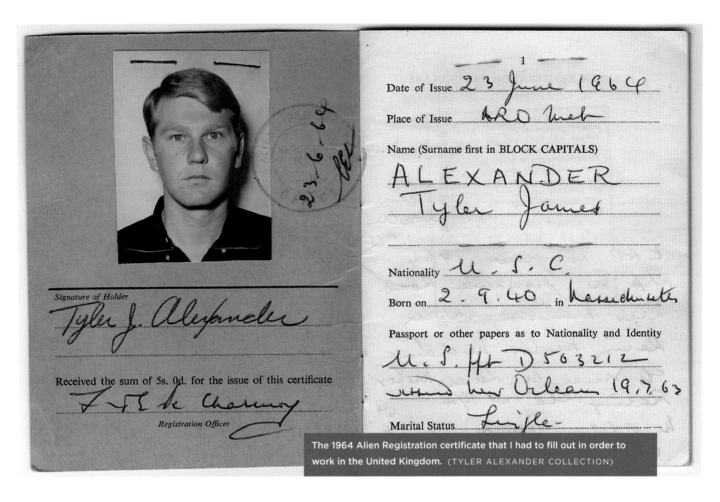

The 1964 Alien Registration certificate that I had to fill out in order to work in the United Kingdom. (TYLER ALEXANDER COLLECTION)

in a Ferrari 330 P. Bruce put the Zerex Special on pole and, having practiced refueling and a bunch of other stuff quite a few times, we felt we were in good shape. Bruce took the lead from Jimmy Clark's Lotus 30 halfway around the first lap, but was later forced to retire with a clutch problem. Bruce's fastest lap of the race didn't make up for the disappointment.

When we got back to Surbiton that night we went to eat in The Contented Plaice, a very good fish restaurant by the river at Kingston upon Thames. At this time, England had some serious fog, which made walking home—assuming you could walk, of course!—pretty difficult.

Meanwhile, things were starting to progress, and on July 27, 1964, we moved to the new factory at Belvedere Works in Feltham. The buildings were fairly basic, but still a vast improvement over the place in New Malden—except for the dirt road you took to get into the place. It was just big enough for us to be able to get on with things in a sensible manner.

In 1966 Gary Knutson took this shot of me at the Traco engine shop in Los Angeles. I'm studying the Ford Indy V8 engine that we used to little effect in the McLaren M2B Formula One car. (GARY KNUTSON)

# Gary L. Knutson

I first met Tyler at sports-car races in the United States when I was with Chaparral and he was with McLaren. We became acquainted, as well as people could, when our paths crossed on those race weekends. We were always inspecting each other's handiwork at those events.

In the early part of 1965, Teddy Mayer and Bill Smith Jr. descended on me during my vacation in Aspen and talked me into joining the McLaren effort in England. I was, of course, excited about the opportunity—not just to work with a team like McLaren, but also to work directly with Tyler, whose capabilities I'd seen over the previous years at various races.

When I moved to England and started to work with Tyler, I soon realized the extent of his talents. I also appreciated his work ethic, and we developed a good friendship. He was knowledgeable, intense, and competitive, but always able to have a good time. When I look back on that period, I realize how fortunate I was to work alongside Tyler. Our shared work was mostly on the technical end of things, and we didn't always agree at the beginning of a discussion, but in the end there was always a mutually agreed-upon solution to whatever problem had arisen.

I parted ways with McLaren in 1987, but I worked with Tyler again on another project in the late 1990s, when we were trying to get Pete Weismann's quick-shift gearbox to work. The respect I have toward him has never waned, whether it's as a mechanic, designer, team manager, or any other of the various hats he's worn. Most importantly I am glad to be able to call him a friend.

There was enough room to actually build racing cars, and it was a short walk to the pub for lunch. Once the place was cleaned and painted, a sign that read, DON'T KNOCK—WE DON'T HAVE THAT SORT OF TIME was put on the door to Bruce's office.

Late in 1964, we finished the McLaren M1A, which was Bruce's first car—the first of many racing cars to carry the McLaren name. We used the same Oldsmobile engine, which was now being rebuilt by Traco Engineering in Culver City, California. The M1A was called a Cooper Oldsmobile in some circles, because Bruce still worked for Cooper.

Our first race with the car was at Mosport in September, in the eighth round of the Canadian Sports Car Championship. Despite being reasonably quick, there was a problem with the throttle linkage during the race. Bruce had to make a pit stop, but still managed to finish third. Two races in October at California's Riverside and Laguna Seca circuits brought problems, with one of the water hoses coming loose. It seems strange now to think that we weren't able to fix what should have been a pretty straightforward problem. But we must have got it sorted out not long after, because in December Bruce finished second to Penske's Chaparral in the main Nassau Trophy race at the Bahamas Speed Week.

Accompanying us to the Bahamas were Wally Willmott, Larry Cronin Jr., and Gary Knutson, a friend of mine who worked for Jim Hall's Chaparral team and came from Boulder, Colorado. We stayed in a small rented house in Nassau for a week after the race, and spent the time snorkeling at a few places where the locals told us we shouldn't, as they were dangerous. There wasn't much point because we had already been there. There were some very large barracudas and small hammerhead sharks that went away when they saw us. One day while snorkeling, we even managed to catch quite a few langoustes (spiny lobsters) for dinner.

Meanwhile, at the end of 1964 Frank Nichols, the owner of Elva Cars, suggested an association between McLaren and Elva to build production versions of the M1A sports car. This meant there were going to be McLaren-Elva sports cars for people to buy. McLaren, via Elva Cars, was now in a position to provide "customer" racing sports cars. I think it was after the race at Riverside that Gary Knutson and I spent most of the night sitting in the rooftop garden of the historic Mission Inn. We were talking about Gary coming to work at McLaren, but the problem was, we kept falling asleep—first me, then Gary. I don't think either of us had slept much the night before the race. But this was to be the start of a productive association with Gary, who mainly worked on engines.

# 1965–66: Building the McLaren Team

**W**e had now been in the new factory at Feltham near Heathrow Airport for a while. It was the new home of Bruce McLaren Motor Racing, which now included quite a few new people: Harry Pearce and Ray Rowe from Cooper, and his wife, who became the secretary. Owen Maddox, also ex-Cooper, became the chief designer, and Alan Stait, the machinist. I was just one of the mechanics, and probably a bit more.

Harry Pearce was a very good motorbike rider. At Brands Hatch in 1950, he won his heat and the final race, beating a young chap named John Surtees. He later became chief mechanic for the Tommy Atkins racing team, and was hired by Bruce in 1962 to look after his 2.7-liter Cooper in the New Zealand and Australian races. A bit later Harry would become the general manager of the McLaren company, holding that post until he retired in 1980.

Ray Rowe (forever known as Tex) was another machinist. He made a lot of small parts and did sub-assembling, as well as rebuilding and maintaining various suspension and steering assemblies. To this day, he continues to work at McLaren Racing for a few days a week.

Owen Maddock designed the Cooper Formula 3, Formula 2, and Formula One cars

Waiting on the grid with Phil Hill during the 1965 Tasman Series. That year he and Bruce were no match for Jim Clark in the Lotus 32B. (TYLER ALEXANDER COLLECTION)

between 1954 and 1963. He parted with Cooper in 1963 and continued to act as a freelance design consultant to Bruce McLaren's new team until the late 1960s.

Alan Stait was in charge of the McLaren Racing machine shop early on. His brother, Eddie Stait, was a Cooper designer and mechanic before becoming a draftsman and designer at McLaren Racing for a short while.

Cooper built two new cars based on the 1964 T73 F1 car for Bruce and Phil Hill to drive in the 1965 Tasman Series. By the time the cars were finished, Bruce and Teddy had done a deal with the Firestone tire company. This may have been good for McLaren's future business prospects, but as it turned out, it was not very good for the Tasman cars, which had been designed for 13-inch front wheels and Dunlop tires. Firestone could only produce tires for 15-inch front wheels.

Needless to say, we struggled a lot, and Jimmy Clark won most of the races and the 1965 Tasman championship driving a Climax-powered Lotus 32B.

Phil Hill, Bruce's Cooper teammate, was a lot quicker than some people gave him credit for. He was also a great guy—a very interesting and personable chap with a wonderful sense of humor that produced several funny moments during the series.

Most places in New Zealand required a tie for dinner. Phil made every possible effort to wear the worst-looking tie he could find and encouraged the rest of us to do the same.

Another classic Phil moment came at a traditional prize-giving ceremony hosted by the local motor-racing club at a restaurant near the race track. Phil, who had finished third that day, said to us, "Pay attention to what is said at these do's. Listen to what I say when I give a little speech."

Phil's theory was that no one paid any attention to what was said; they just clapped and cheered. So, when he got up to say thanks for his trophy, "Thank you very much" became "Fuck you very much"—and everyone applauded as heartily as ever!

Phil had a passion for collecting piano rolls (a music storage medium used to operate a player piano) and beautiful old cars. There were lots of piano rolls in New Zealand, but the problem was getting people to accept £20 English bills in payment. While we were in Christchurch, Phil had gone to the local bank to change some of the £20 notes. Upon leaving, he was stopped by the police. When they asked him who he was, Phil said, "I'm Phil Hill, the race driver." When they clearly didn't believe him, he added, "Look, it says so on the back of this watch I got from winning the race at Le Mans"—only to discover that he was wearing a different watch. It was like one of those situations where, when asked "What's your name? Quick! Quick!," all you can answer is, "Ahh, I wouldn't tell you if I knew." After a few phone calls it was established that it was indeed the real Phil Hill, and not a person passing fake £20 UK notes.

The flight from New Zealand to Australia was fine until we were about to touch down on the runway. Suddenly, full power came back on and we pulled up to avoid another plane that was already there. I wish I could remember Phil's comment.

While in Sydney, we had a few days off and went to Bondi Beach a couple of times. Renting boogie boards to ride the waves was pretty good exercise and a lot of fun. Of course, only Phil could point out there were floats with flags on them in the water—the better to tell the sharks where people were swimming.

By the time we'd finished practice a few days later in Melbourne, I had come down with a nasty and strange flu or cold. On the night before the race, we had to take the cylinder head off the Climax engine and re-shim the Cooper sealing rings between the cylinder liners and the cylinder head. Fortunately, the engine did not have to come out. I was sitting on the rear wheel of the car and when I finished torqueing up the cylinder head, I was too weak to get up. Phil's bag of remedies for medical "needs" came to the rescue, and I was much better the following morning and for the rest of race day.

Firestone managed to fly a few sets of 13-inch tires from the United States in time for the final race at Longford, in Tasmania. The cars were much more competitive as a result: Bruce won, while Phil and Jimmy Clark waged a race-long fight that ended with Phil in third place and Jimmy in fifth. After the race Jimmy gave Phil a great compliment by saying, "I don't know how you passed me in places where there was only room for one car. But you did—several times!"

Onlookers were staggered when Phil passed Jimmy going over the Long Bridge. You have to remember that the Longford circuit used public roads, and sometimes during practice the cars had to stop and let the train go by.

The Tasman Series was always a lot of work, especially when the races in New Zealand and then Australia were only one week apart. But it didn't seem to be a problem, because you had a very keen group of people with you doing the series. When we did have time off, Bruce loved to go waterskiing; we would join him, along with Jimmy and a few others.

Soon after Bruce returned from the Tasman Series in early March 1965, he commissioned the M1B—the first proper McLaren Motor Racing sports car to be officially known as a McLaren.

The irreverent Phil Hill appears to be sharing a private joke with Jim Clark during the 1965 Tasman Series. Jim could afford to laugh—he won four out of seven races that year. (TYLER ALEXANDER)

The tubular frame came from Elva's production line, but based on directions from Bruce and some drawings, Colin Beanland (another mechanic from New Zealand) and I modified the chassis to stiffen it up.

Robin Herd came on board at this time, and although the artist Michael Turner sketched the shape of the M1B, Robin had a reasonable amount of influence on the car's aerodynamics. When Robin left Oxford, he'd worked for the Royal Aircraft Establishment (RAE) on the Concorde project, and was very much aware of the aerodynamic side of things.

The M1B's aluminum body was rolled from sheet metal, and the pieces were gas-welded together by Phil "Nobby" Sharp, who worked with the standard hand-rolled fag hanging off his lip. Talk about fucking skill!

Nobby worked for Maurice "Mo" Gomm at Gomm Metal Developments Ltd. in Old Woking, Surrey. Mo Gomm and his group of exceptional craftsmen built racing-car chassis, bodies, and parts for many teams, contributing to a great many victories around the world. It was also about this time that Gary Knutson came to work for us on a project that Bruce and Teddy had sorted out with Ford. This was to build a lightweight GT car to be known as the GTX. Gary was put in charge, with help from Howden Ganley..

A bit more background on Gary L. Knutson: Put simply, Gary was smart as hell. Having raced a Lotus sports car, he not only understood engines and racing cars but also electrical things and a lot of other engineering stuff as well. He'd worked for Jim Hall for several years, and basically he was a damn good all-around engineer. We got along very well; there were many times when Gary's profound sense of humor kept us going with "one-liners" while working on the race cars in the middle of the night.

Robin was also interested in using "mallite" material (balsa wood sandwiched between thin sheets of aluminum) on a single-seat chassis, with some intention of it being a Formula One car. It actually became first a Ford-powered car for tire testing, and then did a couple of races.

The M1B car was built in time to go off to Canada via my parents' house in Hingham, where the truck and trailer were kept. The plan was to run in several sports-car races in the States and Canada.

The first event at St. Jovite, north of Montreal, wasn't particularly successful, as there was a major problem during practice with the engine, which did some damage to the gearbox. It meant Bruce did not start the race.

We had a new engine (sent out from Traco in California) installed in time for the next

From left to right: Bruce, Gary Knutson, Howden Ganley, and Wally Willmott with the Ford-powered M2B Formula One car at Riverside in 1966. Later that year Bruce would finish fourth in the car at the United States Grand Prix at Watkins Glen. (TYLER ALEXANDER)

race at Mosport, where Bruce finished second to Jim Hall's Chaparral. The same race also saw the debut of the GTX Ford car, but overheating problems meant that Chris Amon, who was driving it, failed to finish.

Bruce had to go off and do some things for Ford, so Phil Hill stood in for him. With the next race scheduled for Kent, Washington, on the West Coast, Colin Beanland and I set off on the long journey across the top of North America. We made a short stop in Yellowstone National Park to have a look at the bears and the scenery. When we came across a group of bears resting comfortably beside the road, we stopped to have a look. When this provoked no movement, we tried blowing the horn several times. At which point, one of the larger bears stirred himself, came over to the trailer, and started to climb up on the race car.

We drove away before he got very far. I have to say, it was the last time we stopped in Yellowstone.

We were able to do some running on the Kent track to allow Phil to get familiar with the car. He said straightaway that we needed to play around with the Weber carburetors, as the engine had a dead spot when accelerating. With Phil driving up and down the straight and me leaning over the engine, putting my hands over the carburetor inlets—his idea, by the way—and changing the carburetor jets, acceleration pumps, and strokes, we made a considerable improvement!

We had a lot of assistance that weekend when Jim Travers and Frank Coon, the owners of Traco, flew up from Los Angeles to give the engine a good check-over and to generally help us out. They were two very clever guys, and great to work with. Then we had Bruce Harry come over from England with Teddy to give us a hand.

In the first of two heats, Phil finished third and gave the leading Chaparrals of Jim Hall and Hap Sharp a hard time. Phil actually led the second heat until bending the throttle pedal return stop, preventing the pedal from coming back all the way. But the cheers of the crowd when he came around in the lead of that second heat was something to remember.

Bruce was back for the next race at Riverside, where he finished third: a pretty impressive drive, considering he had been a lap behind at one stage after replacing a flat tire. The Ford GTX (now affectionately known as Big Ed) was also there, with Chris Amon finishing fifth.

There had been an interesting incident during the race at Riverside. There was a saying, probably from Indy or dirt-track ovals, that if you weren't quick enough, you had to stand up in the seat and drive the car harder.

Near the end of the long back straight, Bruce was passing Parnelli Jones, who then turned in toward Bruce. Bruce looked over at Parnelli—and turned back toward him. Bruce did not back off at all. It created the impression that maybe these blokes from across the pond were real racers after all. Certainly there were no further problems from "Rufus," as Parnelli was known.

Once again, the last races of the season were at the Nassau Speed Week, where Bruce won the Governor's Cup.

The Nassau Trophy was the main race at Nassau Speed Week, and it had a Le Mans start. We had practiced a lot and thought about the best way for Bruce to launch. Just as Bruce started to run across the track, I strolled over to the car and turned on the ignition and the fuel pumps so that Bruce only had to jump in, press the start button, and go. Unfortunately, the engine failed in the race while we were up front. Chris failed to finish after a gearbox problem with the Ford GTX.

Back in England new things were happening. Since Jim Hall was running a torque converter as part of the Chaparral's gearbox, Bruce thought that he should try one for himself. The first efforts with this project were pretty crude, and involved tying the car to a post outside the factory in Feltham to see what would happen when we shifted into gear with the engine running. There were no immediate problems. They would come a short time later.

We raced the Can-Am car with a torque converter at Oulton Park. I don't think Gary, who was overseeing the project—or anyone else involved, for that matter—got more than a couple of hours' sleep all weekend. At one point during the weekend, we had the gearbox off and the torque converter taken apart on the pit wall, which meant liberally spreading oil everywhere, as we weren't allowed to take the car around the back of the pits.

At one point in practice, when Bruce came in and said the engine was not running properly, we took the bodywork off for a quick look and discovered a hole in the side of the block. Since the conrod had broken just above the "big end," there was no loss in oil pressure. The problem was that the torque converter was keeping the engine in the wrong rpm range for too long. It seemed like a good idea at the time, or maybe it was just that we needed to try one ourselves.

By the middle of 1966 it was becoming obvious that although the Olds engine was light, it also lacked horsepower. After the Canadian Sports Car Championship race at Mosport on June 4, 1966, when Bruce managed to win both 100-mile heats in the M1B Oldsmobile, the car was taken back to Hingham and put in a workshop owned by Steve Marsh, a friend of mine. Colin Beanland and I had set about doing the normal rebuild when there was a phone call at my parents' house about a Chevrolet engine coming from Traco in California. Also, there was a ZF gearbox coming from England, along with a new gearbox mounting crossbeam and a bundle of welding rods—all for the M1B.

The instructions from Bruce were simple, "Just fit the Chevrolet engine and ZF gearbox, and I'll see you at St. Jovite in a couple of weeks." The only thing to do was to get stuck in and get on with it.

With a couple of weeks of hard work, everything was done, and we went off to St. Jovite for the race on the Fourth of July. Bruce won. Afterwards, Colin and I got into the car with Bruce for the victory lap. About two-thirds of the way along the main straight, Bruce yelled that this was where the Oldsmobile engine stopped accelerating. But with the Chevrolet engine now bellowing behind us, we just kept on gaining speed!

Although the 1966 Can-Am car was reasonably quick, we tried a number of different things on it, from a movable rear spoiler/wing to Hilborn fuel injection. Both Bruce and

Chris Amon during a Can-Am testing session in 1966. Just a few months earlier he and Bruce had won the 24 Hours of Le Mans driving a Ford GT40. (TYLER ALEXANDER)

Chris tried their hardest, but John Surtees became the 1966 Can-Am Champion, driving a Lola T70 that also used a Chevrolet engine.

The new McLaren company was already into a lot of projects, along with making modifications to the Ford Indy engine at Traco's place in Culver City, California.

I can't say very much about Formula One in 1966. I was in the States most of the time with the sports cars, as well as doing some work on that dreaded Ford engine. The McLaren Ford-powered car did actually race at Monaco in 1966, and thus became McLaren's first grand prix car.

Bruce or Teddy called me about going over to Monaco. So I went, flying over straight from the States. Bruce wanted me to look after the ZF gearbox, which I had previously worked on with the sports car. Bruce gave me a manual in English, a list of gear ratios he wanted, and then said, "See you later. I have to go to an important dinner."

The white McLaren M2B was going reasonably well at Monaco when a line to the oil cooler came loose. More than anything, you have to say that the noise the Ford V8 made was really something special, but at the end of the day the engine was just too big and too heavy, and didn't have enough horsepower.

Adapting the Ford Indy engine was pretty much Bruce's idea, pushed along by Teddy because it was less expensive than the other options available; there really wasn't much to choose from. The price was right, and Bruce was working and driving for Ford's GT40 effort at the time. We then used a Serenissima engine, built by Count Volpi's team in Venice, Italy, for a few races, but I don't know how that deal came about. I was in the States most of the time. It was no more than a stopgap until a promised V12 from BRM became available. Apparently, the Serenissima was blessed by a priest when it was first installed. I was not in Italy for the occasion, but was told about it by the boys who were there. Not that it did much good!

Since the modifications to the Ford Indy engine did not go very well, we were left in the lurch over a proper Formula One engine. The team's mood over the Ford problems and the delay of the BRM could be summed up this way, "Pissed-off, but never give up."

When it looked like McLaren would be unable to have a proper two-car F1 team in 1967, Chris Amon signed to drive for Ferrari after showing that he was quick in the McLaren Can-Am car. He could also offer all the things he'd learned while doing a great deal of testing for McLaren.

Meanwhile, back at Feltham, Texas, and GLK had converted one of the chassis-building jigs into a cannon. The plan was to use rutabagas from the local vegetable shop as ammunition. This caused some confusion and wonder at the shop, as people began using vernier calipers to measure the swedes and find the correct size. One of the firing tests inside the factory did a considerable amount of damage to several of the windows; at that point it was suggested that further testing ought to be done outside!

Holding the pit board at the Mosport Can-Am race in September 1967. Denny Hulme scored his third straight win of the season, with Bruce McLaren finishing second. (PETE BIRO)

# 1967: Daytona, Sebring, and the First Can-Am Championship

At the beginning of 1967, Bruce asked me to go with him to Daytona and Sebring to see how things were done there. Ford had two teams—one run by the Shelby American team, and another by Holman-Moody. Bruce was driving a Mk II Ford GT car for Shelby. Things got interesting when A. J. Foyt, who was driving the second Shelby car, started to complain to Ford about not being allowed to bring "his" own mechanic. It was a classic Foyt objection, but it didn't stop me from helping out with a few things that I was asked to do, as I knew several of the mechanics on the Shelby team. It turned out to be a useful trip for me, since I also learned lots of things not to do. This actually meant looking and listening, watching how other people work, and trying to learn from that, as well as taking some photos.

At Daytona I met a guy named Skip Scott who would later buy a couple of McLaren Can-Am cars to race. I remember asking Skip where he bought the shoes he was wearing, because they had gotten my attention. He told me they were Italian, made by Gucci. When I got back to London, I went to the Gucci shop on Bond Street and bought some. Believe it or not, I still have a couple of the pairs that I bought at the time. I guess it did seem odd to some people that I was wearing scuffed-up handmade Italian shoes and my old Rolex watch while working on a race car.

There were a lot of gearbox problems at Daytona, with several cars having to stop during the 24-hour race to actually change the gearbox. We eventually ran out of spare gearboxes, but the last one that went into Bruce's car seemed to keep running. On top of that, the engine was losing water. So each time we stopped to refuel, we put in as much water as we could. I remember Bruce waking up sometime in the morning, asking how the hell we had kept that thing running all night long. The Mk II Ford Bruce was sharing with Lucien Bianchi eventually finished seventh, some 73 laps behind the leader—which happened to be a 330 P4 driven by Chris Amon and Lorenzo Bandini, who led home a Ferrari clean sweep and humiliated Ford on their doorstep.

Ford made up for it when Bruce and Mario Andretti won the Sebring 12 Hours. This time I went there as Bruce's "observer," just to keep Foyt happy. There were several classic things that happened during the weekend. Some of the boys had been out, shall we say, very late. When the pizzas came for lunch, one of the mechanics—who shall remain nameless—opened his pizza box, threw up in it, and then put it back in the pile with the others. Dear, oh dear.

Then, as we were having sandwiches for lunch the following day, a little girl from behind the crowd barriers was overheard saying, "Look, Mommy—they're feeding them!" One final memory—and I don't wish to be cruel—concerned an Alfa Romeo team. It was very difficult to tell whether the Alfa cars were very untidy from the state of the crew, or the crew was very untidy from working on the cars.

There were a number of changes in 1967. Bruce McLaren Motor Racing had moved into a new factory at 5 David Road, Colnbrook, which was more like the size we needed in all areas. And I was starting to spend a lot more time in the United States.

I had moved out of The Castle, and Eoin Young got me a place to stay for a short time at one of Mike Hailwood's flats, near Heathrow Airport. Then I started to stay with Bruce and Pat at their flat in Kingston. This was when I came to learn more about driving at night in England, and the fact that the English didn't seem to want to use their headlights. Coming home at about 10:30 p.m. from one of the many late nights at the factory, I turned into the parking area for the flat and was hit by something coming the other way that I hadn't seen. My BMC Mini van and I ended up on the footpath, wondering what the hell had happened. Neither I nor the vehicle was hurt or damaged very much. But once Bruce

Bruce tests the new McLaren M6A Can-Am car at Goodwood in 1967. He liked to start by running the car without bodywork to get a basic sense of how it handled with no aerodynamic effects. (TYLER ALEXANDER)

had finished talking to the police and they had left the flat, Pat provided a couple of large glasses of brandy, for my shoulder!

Bruce and Pat then moved a couple of times—first, to the Grey House in Walton-on-Thames, where Colin Beanland came to stay with us part of the time. The next step was a much bigger house in Burwood Park, Walton-on-Thames, where I lived a great deal of the time, except when I was in the States working with the Can-Am and Indy teams. I became very good friends with Barry Newman, who lived next door. Barry worked for Peter Cameron-Webb, a friend of Pat's who had his own insurance company in London.

Living with Bruce and Pat at the new house in Walton-on-Thames in Surrey, Bruce and I usually had a bite to eat after getting back late from the factory. Quite often we would also dream up some new philosophy about motor racing. One question we addressed was: If there was a race with unknown drivers that paid the winner very well, or a less lucrative one with Jack Brabham, Jackie Stewart, Jochen Rindt, and Jimmy Clark, which one would we go to? We felt that we would go to the one with Brabham, Stewart, and the rest of them. Hell, don't misunderstand—we needed the funds, but these were the guys to beat. In the end winning is just a means of keeping score, and the better guys you beat, the better score you end up with.

The year 1967 turned out to be another one without a proper Formula One car. The plan was to have a BRM V12 engine, which did not show up until September. As a stopgap, we adapted an M4A-Cosworth Formula 2 car, which Bruce drove in some early-season F2 races. That car, now called an M4B, was modified to take a 2.0-liter BRM engine left over from the Tasman Series, and I worked on this engine quite a bit.

Joined by Mike Barney, an Englishman who had worked with Bruce at Cooper, I took the M4B to the Monaco GP, where Bruce was running near the front when the battery went flat. This turned out to be my fault. I had gotten two of the wires going to the alternator the wrong way around, which meant the battery did not charge. Even so, Bruce finished fourth after a pit stop for a new battery. Before the problem, Bruce had been right behind Ferrari's Lorenzo Bandini. Toward the end of the race, Bandini had a really bad accident at the chicane leading onto the sea front. His blazing car sat upside down on straw bales for a considerable time before the marshals eventually righted the Ferrari and pulled the driver out. Safety precautions were rubbish in those days. Poor Bandini died a few days later.

Bruce, relieved not to have been caught up in the accident at the time, said afterwards that it had taken him several laps to stop looking at the terrible scene and concentrate on what he was doing.

Bandini's accident increased the need to do something about improving the level of safety in racing. Jackie Stewart had crashed at Spa in 1966 and had spent far too long trapped in a race car full of petrol. After that experience he started to push and shout for more safety and medical attention at the races. He was not very popular as a result, even though he wasn't just looking after his own interests but the safety of all the competitors.

Some of the issues—including the cost of making the necessary improvements—were the responsibility of the circuits. And there were a few drivers who were not 100 percent in favor of doing something serious about safety issues. Fortunately, Louis Stanley of the BRM F1 team started pushing the safety and medical issues forward in a sensible manner, helping Jackie make progress. Lou organized the building of the Grand Prix Medical Unit that was taken to every grand prix in Europe during 1971. Regrettably, after a few seasons it was not used anymore.

You had to wonder who in hell wouldn't have wanted there to be more attention paid to safety measures. Because Jackie was winning races, he could make his voice heard, and he was gradually able to push that agenda forward. Jackie deserves a lot of credit for getting the ball rolling in the right direction.

When we got to Zandvoort with the M4B, we found we were working in the same local garage as Lotus. There were no private, individual team garages in those days. The Dutch Grand Prix was the first race for the Lotus 49, with the brand-new Ford-Cosworth DFV engine. Keith Duckworth of Cosworth was in the garage late at night with Colin Chapman when Duckworth was heard to say in a loud voice, "Who designed this fucking car?" We presumed the question was directed at Colin, as the two men were seen in close conversation at the time. It seemed there was a serious problem with the spacing of the rear upright bearings when the uprights got hot. I suspect that Keith must have played a role in that "fix."

A Formula One journalist happened to be sitting in a dark corner of the garage, taking notes about us, and, as it turned out, the better show that was happening right next to us! I wish that I could remember his name, because today there never seem to be journalists who are prepared to stay that late at night.

The V12 BRM 3.0-liter engine turned up just in time for the Canadian Grand Prix, where Bruce ran strongly until there was a problem with the alternator. I know very little about the whole V12 BRM project, other than the fact that the engine arrived very late, and Bruce poured oil all over his shoes the first time he tried to fill the oil tank, thanks to the bottom drain plug being missing.

Meanwhile, we had been building the M6A Can-Am car with the assistance of Alastair Caldwell, who had come to work at McLaren. Straightaway, Alastair was able to help me a great deal with putting the car together, particularly as he didn't seem too fussed about the late nights. He would later become the Formula One team manager, and would be involved in a couple of clever ideas on the F1 car.

Many years later Alastair described his first days at McLaren on his website (www.alastaircaldwell.com):

*I went to McLaren's and couldn't get a job as a mechanic, which is what I wanted, but I asked if they had any jobs at all. They said yeah, they had a job for a cleaner. "Okay, I'll be the cleaner then," I said. So I turned up at 8 o'clock the next day and I cleaned; I'm a very good cleaner. While I was there I talked to the race mechanics, and at the end of the day I went and gave them a hand working on a race car that they were building. At 3 o'clock in the morning we all went home. I asked what time they started in the morning and the chief mechanic, who was a director of the company at the time, said, "Oh well, I get here about 7:15." So I went home, and 7 o'clock I was sitting on the wall outside and watched him stroll in at 7:15. He let me in and gave me something to do. The works manager came to work at 9 o'clock and saw me working on a race car. The chief mechanic turned to him and said, "You'll need a new cleaner; this bloke's a mechanic." The chief mechanic and one of the directors at the time was someone named Tyler Alexander.*

Although the new M6A Can-Am car looked completely different from the previous one, Bruce's standard trick was to make sure it used quite a bit of stuff from several of the cars that we had already built and raced. The chassis itself was a proper monocoque for the first time, and used a Chevrolet engine and Hewland gearbox. This car was a big step forward, thanks in many ways to a new contract with the Goodyear Tire and Rubber Company.

We tried a rear wing used on the M6A at Goodwood. This wing was never raced, and that was down to Bruce and Robin Herd for some reason. I'm not sure why, but would guess it had something to do with the handling and balance of the car. We did take it off at one point and hide it in the tall grass because John Surtees—one of our competitors, and the defending Can-Am champion—had just shown up!

The really interesting part came when it was decided to fit the Lucas fuel injection system onto the M6A's Chevrolet engine, instead of standard Weber carburetors. It was Gary

Robin Herd takes notes on the performance of the rear wing we tested on the M6A at Goodwood. In the end we decided against using it. (TYLER ALEXANDER)

Knutson's project, with help from me and input from several other people.

We used a Weber carburetor cross-ram manifold (probably because we had some, and they suited what we were going to do—please read on) for the inlet system. We had noticed that Cosworth had done the trick of cooling the fuel by running the fuel-injection excess return fuel along the side of the inlet manifolds. To do this with the cross-ram manifold was not that easy because it was made of magnesium. We had to preheat this and keep it reasonably hot while welding some plates in the middle of the V to make a chamber capable of returning the fuel to the collector while cooling it in the process.

The next job was to sort out a fuel mixture cam for the Lucas metering unit. That meant running the engine on a dyno; I think Bruce sorted out a place to do this at Alan Mann's workshop.

It was all pretty basic stuff, with water spraying everywhere from the dyno while running the engine. In order to get the best power at different throttle openings and rpm, I was standing outside the building and using a long steel tube through a broken window to adjust the fuel mixture micrometer device on the back of the Lucas metering unit.

I think Wally Willmott was making a note of the micrometer positions. All of this enabled us to generate a fuel adjustment cam for the metering unit itself.

When all of this was done, the engine was fitted to the car, run up at the workshop, and taken down to Goodwood for a test. Bruce said the Lucas system didn't really feel any better than the Weber carburetors, which came as a low blow after all our hard work. With our tails between our legs, Gary and I drove back to the factory in Colnbrook. We took the engine out of the car and put it on its stand in the little engine room where we had been working on it. Later that night, as Gary and I were sitting on the workbench, somewhat tired and confused and just staring at the engine, I pointed to the inlet for one of the cylinders and asked Gary, "What cylinder is that?" He said, "Number one, of course." I pointed out that it actually went across the manifold to the number-five cylinder—it was a "cross"-ram manifold.

So when Gary had plumbed the injectors, the fuel timing was all wrong; hence, Bruce's comments about the way the engine ran. I think Gary said, "Ah shit! The steaks are on me," or something to that effect. I guess these things happen sometimes when you're working a lot of really late nights. But at least we had found the problem and were able to fix it without too much trouble, as was proved in a later test. The Lucas fuel injection was indeed the way to go on our Chevrolet engine, just as we thought it should be.

The first M6A was properly finished by the middle of June, a few months before the start of the Can-Am series. We then did over 1,500 miles of testing at Goodwood, with several 200-mile race distance runs. Some of the tests were done without running the bodywork, which was something Bruce always liked to do.

With the testing completed, the cars and spares were sent off to Massachusetts, where the trucks and trailers, delivered by Bill Smith Jr.'s people, were waiting at my parents' house in Hingham. After collecting everything from the airport, loading the trucks and putting the three cars on the trailers, my mother did a really great barbecue for everyone. We left the next day for the start of the championship and the first race at Elkhart Lake in Wisconsin.

I guess now is the time to say a few words about Denis Clive Hulme, OBE.

Denny Hulme was another New Zealand race driver who came over to England from a small town at the top of the South Island. Denny was basically a shy sort of guy who tended to hide behind a tough exterior. But he wasn't called "The Bear" for nothing—he was a fierce competitor on the track. Away from it, not many things bothered Denny, other than losing Bruce and, many years later, a terrible family tragedy. This was the death of his twenty-one-year-old son Martin on Christmas Day in 1988. Martin had dived off the pier at the lake where they lived. He struck his head on a large rock and died from the blow.

Denny's father was awarded the Victoria Cross for heroism in World War II, and I guess some of that got passed down. In 1974 Denny tried to save his friend Peter Revson from a testing accident at the Kyalami race track, located north of Johannesburg. After Revson's death Denny announced that he would retire from Formula One at the end of that season.

Denny got a drive with Brabham in Formula 2 and then Formula One, winning the World Championship in 1967. He moved to McLaren later in 1967 for the Can-Am program, followed by Formula One and Indianapolis. Denny was a special friend of Bruce's. A great, strong, talented, tough guy had just come to work with us.

At the first Can-Am race of 1967 at Elkhart Lake, Bruce qualified on pole but retired with an oil cooler leak. Denny, having qualified second, was perfectly placed to win the race. Denny was able to repeat that result at Bridgehampton and Mosport, with Bruce finishing second each time. But Bruce really had to work for that result in Canada.

Less than an hour before the start, Bruce's car developed a fuel leak. Trying to get rid of about 50 gallons of fuel, it got to the point where we were pumping it out faster than we could dump it into people's road cars and trucks. The ground was the last resort.

We replaced the fuel bag, filled the car with fuel from a new drum, started the engine, and sent Bruce on his way, just 40 seconds after the start of the race. He made an impressive drive to second place.

At Laguna Seca we had finished Friday's practice when it was discovered that Denny's chassis was somewhat bent in the middle—probably caused by Denny going straight through the famous downhill corkscrew corners.

The garage we used in town happened to be right beside the train tracks, and there were some loose railroad ties available. Sensing an opportunity were Don Beresford and Mike Underwood, a former aircraft technician known as Charlie Chins (his nickname was inspired by his jowls) who had worked at Lotus before coming to McLaren in the summer of 1967. We set about using some of the aircraft tie-downs that we had to strap the railroad ties to the bottom of Denny's chassis. Having removed the fuel tank, they then drilled out some of the rivets holding things together and got the chassis straight again. Stiffening panels were made, then glued and riveted in place. Mr. Hulme had his car returned with a request to please be a bit more careful at that one place on the race track.

We applied the same mods to Bruce's car—just in case. But at least it was still straight to start with. I'm not sure if we got any sleep that night or if we even got back to the hotel for a shower, because we showed up at the race track just before the second day's practice started.

Long working hours tend to cancel out the more-glamorous attractions of being a racing mechanic or engineer; unfortunately, this often comes with the job of going motor racing. I have been asked on several occasions if these long hours had an effect on the work that I had been doing to get the car ready. Well, it sure as hell can; when your hands get a bit fuzzy and your teeth feel furry, you just press on because you know the job has to be done by a certain time the next morning, as well as bearing in mind that there are people who are counting on you.

There was a lot going on at Laguna Seca because it was here that Denny bent the brake pedal in his car during practice.

When we got the spare brake pedal out of the spares, Denny managed to bend that in his bare hands! Needless to say, even allowing for Denny being as strong as hell, a stiffer pedal was made for the rest of the weekend.

When the weather on race day turned out even hotter than usual, Bruce decided he wanted some water poured onto him during the race. This was to be done at the hairpin just before the pits, the timing based on some sort of hand signal. Don Beresford and I went down to the corner. The plan was that Don was going to throw the bucket of water, but, at the last minute, he gave it to me! Chris Economaki of *National Speed Sport News*, wondering what was going on, had followed us to the corner. I don't believe Chris was alone in getting a photo of me throwing the water onto Bruce. Fortunately, the water went up the windscreen and onto Bruce as planned, and not into the inlet tray of the engine. When several other teams started to do the same thing, officials brought a stop to it because the exit of the corner was getting quite wet.

Bruce was leading at the time, and I'd like to think it helped him go on to win. But during the race, Bruce did have to pay a price. Having pulled down the Nomex scarf from his face because it was getting too hot, he managed to get quite badly sunburned—as you can see clearly in the photo.

Bruce went on to win at Riverside (one of his favorite race tracks), but Denny wasn't having much luck. After failing to finish at Laguna Seca because of engine trouble, he had some problems at Riverside, with an accident at the beginning of the race. This broke some of the right-front bodywork, and he was black-flagged as a result.

Engine trouble meant neither driver finished the final race at Las Vegas, but Bruce's two wins were enough to make him the 1967 Can-Am Champion. (Denny had won three of the races, but his retirement from the other three meant Bruce's pair of second places gave him 10 more points.)

At the end of the season, Colin Beanland and I took Bruce's car to Roger Penske's shop in Pennsylvania. Roger had bought the M6A for Mark Donohue to drive in the 1968 United States Road Racing Championship (USRRC) series, and then the Can-Am championship.

When we were leaving, Donohue said, "How can you guys sell the car that just won most of the races and the championship?" As we were going out the door, I turned and said to Mark, "Oh, I don't know—I guess we're just going home to build a better one." He made a note of this in his book, *The Unfair Advantage*, as he couldn't believe what he'd just heard!

I have been asked several times how I and the other people felt after winning the 1967

Don Beresford looks on as I aim my bucket of water at Bruce during the Laguna Seca Can-Am race in 1967. (TYLER ALEXANDER COLLECTION)

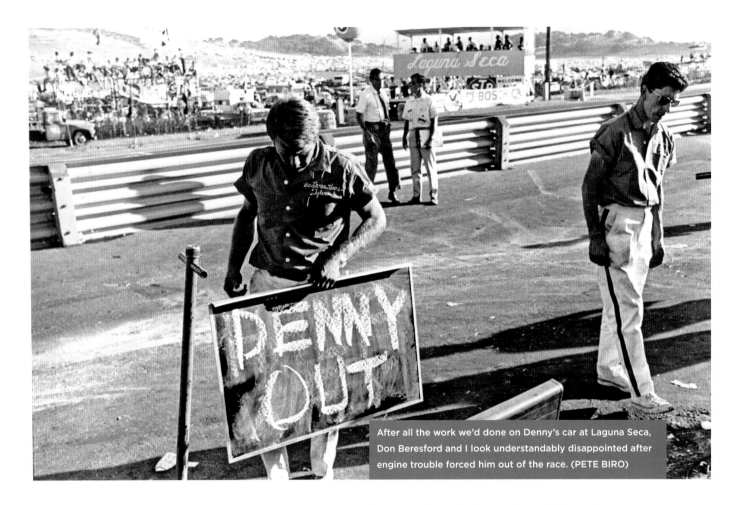

After all the work we'd done on Denny's car at Laguna Seca, Don Beresford and I look understandably disappointed after engine trouble forced him out of the race. (PETE BIRO)

Can-Am championship. I think in the 1960s and '70s we thought about things differently. I don't think we were preoccupied with a bunch of pondering about ourselves. We were a pretty close-knit group of people who certainly enjoyed winning, as anyone would. But I cannot recall even thinking, never mind talking among ourselves, about what sort of mental effect winning might have had.

Don't get me wrong here: The people at the factory and those of us at the race track were happy as hell we had won the championship. But we also accepted that this was only just the beginning of more hard work and late nights to come.

The fact that we were doing something we liked was the main thing. The objective was to try and do it better than the other people. I guess these days it's known as being focused. We didn't actually use the word *focused* then, but when you think about it, I guess we sure as hell were.

# 1968: Finding Success in Formula One, and Back to the Can-Am

**B**ecause we were still a small group, a few of us—Bruce, Teddy, the designers, and usually myself—would get together to discuss future plans. There was the usual back-and-forth about how to do something, but we always came to an agreement if everyone was convinced. Teddy did point out once that there was one guy who neither he nor Bruce could convince if he didn't want to be convinced. If this guy believed he was right, he would let you know right away—and possibly several times in the future. Of course, Teddy was referring to me!

Changes at the beginning of 1968 included Wally Willmott going to Australia to live, and a bit later, Robin Herd joining Cosworth to design their ill-fated four-wheel-drive car.

On the technical side, Cosworth decided to sell their Formula One engine to customers. In 1967, the V8 had been exclusive to Lotus, but this year the DFV would give McLaren its first real chance of having a decent F1 car.

For the Can-Am, the M6A chassis from 1967 was given a variety of modifications, some quite radical for the time. The monocoque pontoons beside the engine were cut off and replaced with a tubular tripod that ran from the chassis to the engine bell housing. This saved some weight and gave better access to the side of the new 7.0-liter aluminum-block Chevrolet engine; it also allowed a better exhaust system. The curved sides of the monocoque were replaced with flat side panels and a much smaller radius at the bottom that merged into the chassis. This became the test car, with the final version of it becoming the new M8A Can-Am car. Gordon Coppuck, who came from the National Gas Turbine Establishment, where he had worked with Robin Herd, designed the rear of the car, with Jo Marquart, a clever Swiss designer from Lotus, designing the front. It worked out very well.

While the various aspects of the Can-Am car were being dealt with, Robin Herd, before leaving for Cosworth, had been working on the design of the M7A Formula One car with its Cosworth engine.

I was working on the Can-Am car on Sunday, April 7, 1968, when news came on the radio that Jimmy Clark had been killed at Hockenheim in a Formula 2 race. Along with being an extremely talented race-car driver, Jimmy had also been a great friend to a lot of people.

During the Tasman Series we got together quite often to go waterskiing, which was usually organized by Bruce. Jimmy was an easy guy to chat with, which Bruce and I got to do several times. As for the effect of Jimmy's death on other people, all I can say is, despite the grief and sense of loss, they didn't stop motor racing. Some people said his death was unthinkable, but I think that is somewhat naive. To be sure, it was hard to believe, because Jimmy didn't make very many mistakes.

The best way I can express my real feelings about Jimmy is to say that if you were having a race from, say, London to Reading, on the back roads, and the drivers just went out to the parking lot and picked any car, Jimmy's smooth and careful ability would more than likely help him to win. Of course, I didn't know Ayrton Senna at the time, but let's say if he was there, he would have just made it more interesting!

Meanwhile, we were continuing with our preparations for the Can-Am season. There was an interesting occasion in the middle of the night when we were trying to start the new alloy Chevrolet engine for the first time in the M8A prototype chassis. There were some problems with the starter motor, so the car was put on the floor to allow us to give Bruce, who was in the driver's seat, a push start. With the middle of the factory clear, we pulled the car down to the end of the workshop, the grin on Bruce's face suggesting that we get out of the way. The two long black marks from the rear tires were there for quite a while! At least he got it stopped in time. It was a fun way to end the day. Or early morning, as it was by then.

Bruce looks thoughtful as he and a crewman work on a Can-Am car's chassis at Colnbrook in 1968. Denny Hulme is to the right with his back to the camera. (TYLER ALEXANDER)

The engine for the Can-Am car was built by Gary Knutson at Al Bartz's engine shop in California. Al had worked for Traco before setting up his own operation. During one of the long nights working on the engines, Gary had been bitching a lot about his watch not working very well. Al asked to have a look, and then put the watch in the bench vise and crushed it, saying, "Well, it won't give you any more problems now!" You got that fucking right, Al!

The development done at Bartz's shop led to the engine's very tall inlet trumpets, which smoothed out the power curve. There would be quite a few engine problems during the course of the season, mainly involving bearings, connecting rods, and piston ring issues. Nothing trivial, of course! But we did win four of the six Can-Am races, with Denny Hulme becoming champion this time.

I have good memories of Riverside, California—a great race track, where someone once said, "You know you are in Riverside if it's two in the morning, you walk outside or are just getting back to your hotel, and somebody across the street is watering their damn lawn because it is so damn hot."

It was very hot on race day that year. Dale von Trebra, a photographer, friend, and purveyor of cold gin martinis, kept the supply in a cooler in the trunk of his old Mercedes, which was discreetly parked in the paddock area. Having had only a few hours' sleep on Saturday night, a few samples of Dale's medicine was all that kept me and several of the other mechanics going after the race had finished. Then again, we had won the race!

Back in England in the early part of 1968, a few new people had arrived at McLaren. One was Charlie Scarano, a young guy from the United States who had showed up at the door of the factory with a small toolbox, asking for a job. Bruce always thought that if someone could find their way from another place in the world to Colnbrook, England, they deserved a job. Unfortunately, at the end of 1968, the people from the American army came to the factory looking for Charlie. In the end, he had to go back to the United States and be drafted, just in time to go to Vietnam.

Although I was working mainly on the Can-Am cars and racing in the States, I was also doing some things with the Formula One cars—mainly testing and a couple of early-season non-championship races.

Having never been directly involved with Cosworth before, it was interesting working with them now that we were going to use their F1 engine. We had some of our own views about the fuel system in the M7A, and there were some very lengthy and interesting discussions with Mike Costin, half of the Cosworth partnership with Keith Duckworth. Let's just say I don't remember having any problems with "our" version of the fuel system.

When the first M7A car was finished, there was an extensive testing plan, and I remember a lot of cold, wet days at Brands Hatch, but in the end, it was worth it. The first non-championship F1 event, the Race of Champions, was held on March 17, 1968, at Brands Hatch. Bruce was on pole and won the race, with Denny finishing third.

Moving to Silverstone a couple of weeks later for another non-championship race, the Daily Express International Trophy. Denny managed to win, even though half of his goggles had been broken by a stone. Bruce took second after a long fight with Chris Amon's Ferrari.

We had gone back to Colnbrook to work on the cars before the Silverstone race. I'm not really sure now what needed doing, but it must have been important, because it took us most of the night and into the next morning to fabricate and weld up some parts. You have to remember that there really wasn't much at Silverstone in 1968—hence, the epic trip back to the factory. Alan McCall and I slept in the two race cars while Allan Gordon drove the transporter to Silverstone. There were some questions afterwards about the route he took, as it seemed we were a long time getting there. I wouldn't be surprised if he was asleep part of the time, as well.

Winning the two non-championship races was down to a neat little car, a decent engine, and lot of testing. I'm not sure how to answer questions like "How did it go down at Colnbrook?," as each person has their own view. "Relieved" and "pleased as hell" would pretty much cover it all when you consider the time and work involved.

Goodyear ran a tire test at Jarama, where the Spanish Grand Prix was going to be held a few weeks later. Alastair Caldwell and I took the transporter, going from Southampton to Bilbao by boat. It was pretty rough crossing the Bay of Biscay, and almost everyone on the boat was sick. We were just about okay, but I do remember catching several plates of food just before they leapt from the dinner table onto the deck.

Bruce wanted to try wide chassis fuel tanks on the M7A because he thought they would make the car easier to drive. The only problem was the added weight, and although we didn't know it at the time, the changes probably affected the aerodynamics. In any case, the loss of Robin Herd by this stage didn't help. As a result, when we went back to Spain for the race, we were not as competitive as we should have been. Denny qualified third and finished second, while Bruce qualified fourth and finished sixth, with a mechanical problem.

The one amusing memory I have of that race was of an episode that occurred as the cars sat on the grid just before the start. Alan McCall was fighting off a Spanish policeman with

All our testing paid off when Bruce and the M7A won the Race of Champions at Brands Hatch in March 1968. Denny Hulme finished third. (TYLER ALEXANDER)

one hand while trying to adjust the metering unit mixture position in the middle of the vee on Denny's engine with the other one. The reason the police were involved in administering discipline on the grid was because it was Spain, and that was how it was done there.

Proof that things could change quite quickly in Formula One was to come a month later at the Belgian Grand Prix at Spa. Because we were based at the other end of the circuit, it meant Alan McCall and I had to drive the cars around the track to the garage once practice had finished. I remember doing the gear ratios and looking at the gear ratio chart, scaring myself even then when I saw how fast I had been going on the long back straight. And I think it might have been raining a little bit at the same time!

There was a lot going on before the race, but I do remember having coffee on Sunday morning with Sally Courage, Lady Sarah von Westenholz (known as Arabella, a friend of mine who happened to live with Sally and her husband Piers Courage, two really nice people), and some friends at Piers Courage's camper trailer. The trailer was considered a bit of a luxury in those days, but was in fact quite small, and mainly useful for getting out of the rain!

Piers Courage, eldest son of the Courage brewing dynasty, was educated at Eton, but decided a business career was not for him, and much to the disappointment of his parents, became a racing driver. He married Lady Sarah (known as Sally) Curzon, who was the daughter of Francis Curzon, the 5th Earl Howe. Curzon was an impressive, unique character with a huge appetite and love of life. He won the 24 Hours of Le Mans in 1931 and co-founded the British Racing Drivers' Club, serving as its president until his death in 1964.

Arabella von Westenholz was the granddaughter of the 6th Marquess of Anglesey, and the great-granddaughter of the 8th Duke of Rutland. In those days Formula One motor racing attracted the dashing and daring members of the British aristocracy.

Having said all that, they were just great people to be with now and again. One evening we were going to Annabel's, a members-only nightclub in London's Berkeley Square, for dinner and a few drinks. I was wearing a suede sport jacket and they didn't want to let me in. Sally, without saying a word, waved one finger, and we were immediately taken to our table!

Denny had been going well in the race at Spa when he had a halfshaft problem that the boys tried to fix in the pits. Bruce, meanwhile, was reasonably quick and outlasted most of the field to hold second place on the next-to-last lap.

At the beginning of the last lap, Jackie Stewart's leading Tyrrell had to stop in the pits for a bit more fuel. I was doing the signal board, and I didn't know if Bruce was going to be the next to come around the corner and into sight because Pedro Rodríguez had been right behind him on the previous lap.

When Bruce appeared—now in the lead—I didn't have time to put "P1" on the signal board, and could only point down the track. It was a futile gesture, but it was the only thing I could think of at the time. It explains why, when Bruce finished the last lap, he came into the pits not really aware that he had won his first World Championship Grand Prix in his own car.

Developments on the cars were moving pretty fast at the time. During practice for the French Grand Prix at Rouen, Jackie Oliver had a large shunt when the bell housing broke on his Lotus 49B, nicely taking with it the gearbox and rear suspension. It was not long after the crash that Colin Chapman came wandering down the pit lane and stopped to look at our car. The first thing he said to me was, "You had better have a good look at the bell housing on your car." It was a typical psychological ploy by Chapman. I told him, "Ours is okay, and yours is in the hedge back up the road." There was a bit of a huff and he wandered off. Sorry, Colin.

This proved to be a pretty bad weekend—there seemed to be quite a few of these at the time—when Jo Schlesser's development Honda crashed only two laps into the race and caught fire. The full fuel load and the car's magnesium body made for a terrible, fatal inferno. There didn't seem to be anything anyone could do for the poor guy, which highlighted the really bad safety arrangements, if you could even call them that. It was obvious that more and better safety equipment, and trained people who knew how to use it, were badly needed at all the race tracks.

Having finished fifth (Denny) and eighth (Bruce) at Rouen, we didn't figure particularly well in the next two races in Britain and Germany. But that was to change at Monza, even though we had a problem with Denny's car during practice. Denny had been reasonably quick but then he had an engine problem; the boys managed to change the engine in time for a few more laps of final practice.

Bruce had qualified on the front row and was feeling quite confident that he could do well, and perhaps win. Denny, meanwhile, was sitting quietly in the corner, saying he thought he had a pretty good chance of winning the race! What he didn't say was that the new engine pulled more revs on the straight (without a tow from another car) than the engine that failed had done with a tow. Bruce led the early part of the Italian Grand Prix, but eventually dropped out with an engine oil leak. Alastair Caldwell's feeling—which he shared with me some time later—was that we didn't have enough people to do a proper check on everything before the race, which was why a bolt had come loose on the engine and caused the oil leak. The positive part of the weekend was that Denny had indeed won!

For the last three races in the 1968 season, starting at the Canadian Grand Prix at St. Jovite, McLaren ran a third M7A for Dan Gurney, who helped out by bringing one of his own mechanics, Tim Wall. Dan finished fourth in the United States Grand Prix at Watkins Glen. Those points added to the team's first F1 one-two finish for Denny and Bruce. After that, Bruce's sixth-place finish at Watkins Glen and his second in Mexico put McLaren second in the Constructors championship, 11 points behind Lotus—a pretty good result.

In fact, Denny was in a three-way fight for the championship when we got to the final round in Mexico, but his outside chance (he needed to win the race, with eventual champion Graham Hill finishing fourth or lower) ended with a broken suspension.

Pointing Bruce toward victory on the last lap of the 1968 Belgian Grand Prix—his first championship grand prix win driving a McLaren car. (TYLER ALEXANDER COLLECTION)

After the race in St. Jovite, Paul "Batt" Wuori and another friend agreed to follow Bruce and Denny in their rented Thunderbird to the airport. The plan was for Batt and his mate to take over the Thunderbird and return it to the rental people in order to save Bruce and Denny some time. Paul was driving an ex-police car that was reasonably quick, but his efforts to keep up with Bruce ended with a punctured rear tire. Bruce stopped, backed up, jumped out, and ran over to have a look at the problem. His comment to Paul was, "Oh dear, all the air has gone to the top of the tire." Then he jumped back in the Thunderbird and disappeared down the road. So much for that plan!

At the end of 1968, Gary Knutson left McLaren and went back to work for Jim Hall at Chaparral. I was disappointed to see him go, but our paths would cross again just a few years later at McLaren Engines.

During discussions about building a four-wheel-drive F1 car in 1968 or 1969, BRM engineer Tony Rudd asked Bruce, "Have you ever put a twenty-kilogram sandbag on top of the gearbox, and have you had a throttle that only opens about three-quarters of the

Bruce lost the rear wing on the M7A when the mounting struts failed during a test at Goodwood. He managed to stay on the track, so the damage was minimal. (TYLER ALEXANDER)

way?" When Bruce asked, "Whatever for?" Tony replied, "You'll find it lots cheaper than four-wheel-drive!"

We did build a four-wheel-drive car, the McLaren M9. Jo Marquart was the designer in charge of the project. Bruce did several tests with the M9 at Goodwood, and then had some new front uprights machined to help with a basic problem: The steering load was quite heavy, which meant the car was not easy or smooth to drive. He tried these at Goodwood for a few laps, came in, got in his road car, and drove back to Colnbrook! He wasn't pleased with what he had made.

I didn't think a four-wheel-drive car was a good project, as it would probably be heavy and complicated. In the end, the M9 would do just one race. Derek Bell drove it in the 1969 British Grand Prix, where he started 15th and did five laps in the race before withdrawing with a suspension failure.

# 1969: A Perfect Can-Am Season for the M8B

It was around this time when Charlie Fox, an American journalist and friend who had followed us around during the Can-Am races, paid a visit to the McLaren factory at David Road Colnbrook, Berkshire. He must have been doing one of his stories for *Car and Driver* or whoever else he was writing for at the time, and it must have been a nice day, because Bruce and a few of us were outside, in a small field near the factory. Charlie wrote, "I remember how I came upon them sitting on a crate beneath a tree in some English sunshine at Colnbrook, one spring day late in the Sixties. There was that splendid sense of boys disguised as men involved in a pastime disguised as work."

Much later, sometime in the early 1990s, Charlie (now in a wheelchair due to multiple sclerosis) stopped in England on his way to France to talk with me for a couple of days. He wrote about our conversations in a piece for *Car and Driver* magazine called "The Ugly American." It's a story that I've kept.

Having known me for a long time, Charlie was aware that this American interloper to England didn't care if he slept on the floor, or if he was also regularly invited to dinner with the managing director. These things never bothered me, but being able to handle both can be an advantage at times.

It was not unusual for Teddy Mayer and I to have an argument on the shop floor as he was leaving to go home. Then, just before closing the door, he would turn around and say, "And don't be late for dinner at eight o'clock." It was hard for the others to understand this. After all, this was England, where it was unusual for a mechanic to argue with one of the company owners, especially with other people close by. But that was the kind of friendship/relationship Teddy and I had.

The 1969 Formula One car was an evolution of the M7A from 1968. There would be several iterations of the car during the year, particularly as changes were made to the wings.

We didn't have a particularly successful time in Formula One in 1969, a win for Denny in Mexico at the end of the season being the highlight in a year when McLaren finished fourth in the Constructors championship. But I do remember a couple of things that happened regarding the cars and team people.

A few days after a test at Kyalami, Alastair Caldwell, mechanic Vince Higgins, and I were somewhere in the suburbs of Johannesburg with a couple of trucks, one of which had an empty race-car trailer behind it and was being towed by the other truck. Vince was in the truck with a trailer. Going along a dual carriageway, I turned to Alastair and calmly said, "The trailer has come off the back of the other truck." "You must be joking," said Alastair. I said, "No. And it's gone across the center island, knocking over a couple of the guys mowing the grass—and now it's gone into the lane of oncoming traffic and damaged a tire on a small van."

We stopped, and a short time later, the police arrived, at which point there was a lot of yelling and finger-pointing from the local lawn-mowing crew. The police and a couple of the crew members gave us a hand getting the loose trailer out of the road and back onto the center island. One of the poor guys mowing the grass had quite a nasty cut on his leg. And there was the van, with a shredded tire.

The police had a look around and asked us if there were any problems with the trailer. When we pointed out that there didn't appear to be any problems, the police said, "You'd better get it connected up to the truck and get it out of here." They did give us some paperwork, and we were asked to show up the next day at the local police station near where we were staying, which we did. They looked at the paperwork and at our driver's licenses and passports. We said thank you and left. It was terrible that a couple of the black workers got hurt—something the police didn't seem to be too concerned about at the time. This was a long time ago, and thankfully, a lot of things have changed since then.

There was another collision of sorts, this time with the race car, at Watkins Glen. On race morning, the cars had to be driven from the large garage to the pits at the bottom of the hill. The road was packed with people. Vince Higgins was driving one of the cars down the hill when a group of fans moved out of the way. Suddenly, directly in front of Vince, was a wooden post—which he hit, damaging the left-front suspension. By the time I got down to the pits there was a fair bit of commotion going on, but the car was repaired in plenty of time for the race. Despite that, it proved to be a bad omen: Bruce didn't make it to the start because of an engine problem, and Denny, who had qualified second, went out with gearbox trouble.

The large-capacity garage that housed most of the teams at the Glen was known as the Kendall Technical Center. It had turnstiles at one end, and race fans were charged 10 cents to get in to have a look. Colin Chapman thought that the admission charge was a means of keeping the riffraff away from the "Bog," a notorious area in the middle of the circuit, where hard-partying fans stayed overnight in campers, buses, and other vehicles. Vandalism and some violence were standard, expected activities.

I thought Chapman was truly an interesting person who had a lot of experience with racing cars. He, and the very good people who worked for him, seemed to always be at least one step ahead of the rest of us. His cars were always lightweight and were usually driven by some of the quickest drivers. Quite often, he would come around and look at everyone's cars. In Mexico, while examining the back of our F1 car, Chapman asked who had done the Aeroquip braided stainless-steel oil and fuel lines, because he reckoned they were quite neat. When I said it was me and then asked why he wanted to know, he just looked at me, smiled, and walked off.

The 1969 Can-Am car, the M8B, was one of the best cars we ever built for that series. It would be great to build that car now, with the technology and materials that are available today. The high rear wing pushed down directly on the rear uprights. This kept the aero-dynamic download directly on the rear uprights and tires without upsetting the whole car. (Normally, the rear wing would have been mounted directly to the rear bodywork, hence making it harder to set up the handling of the car.) Part of the high wing's testing included attaching it to my Mini van and running up and down the long straight road leading from Colnbrook into Staines.

It was a peculiar-looking van, so one would probably have to ask what the hell we were doing! But it was interesting and fun measuring the small differences between two different wing constructions.

Two M8A Can-Am cars inside the Smith Ford dealership in Norwich, New York, in 1968. The dealership served as McLaren's home base for most Can-Am races. (TYLER ALEXANDER)

On my trips back and forth to England during the course of the season, I usually built several sets of rear wing vertical struts so that we had low-mileage ones for the next races coming up. The size of the rear wing depended on the circuit. Otherwise, I don't think that we changed very much of anything regarding the setup on the car during the course of the year—except the crown wheel and pinion, which was changed every Saturday night before the race. When and if problems arose, Mike Hewland, whose company made the gearbox and the internal parts—the crown wheel and pinion and gear ratios being the main ones—would always say, "Never seen one of those fail before. Put it in the box with the others." Since we were all good friends, his joking comment was a standard reply when a part failed.

We started a sponsor/partner relationship with Reynolds Aluminum in 1969. Other than the obvious reason for this—a lot of the car was made out of aluminum—there was also a very interesting development regarding the engine. For some time, Reynolds engineer Harold Macklin and his group had been working on an alloy engine block with no steel metal cylinder liners. This got Bruce's attention right away. There was quite a bit of work to be done once the special alloy blocks had been cast, but late in 1970, Denny would win the first Can-Am race with one of these special engines—which naturally made Mr. Macklin and his group very pleased, as well as the man whose family owned the company, William "Bill" Reynolds. At one point during the season, when there was a gap between the races, we brought a Can-Am M8D car to the Reynolds headquarters in Richmond, and Virginia and Denny gave Bill a ride around the parking lot.

For most of the 1969 season, we worked out of Bill Smith Jr.'s Ford dealership in Norwich, New York, and then at Steve McQueen's workshop in Van Nuys, California, between the races at Laguna Seca and Riverside.

Bruce spent time helping out some guys who were building a dune buggy for Steve, because it looked to most of us as if they weren't sure what they were doing. Steve was a neat and quite friendly guy. He used to come by with his kids, and we would let them sit in the cars, which they thought was fun.

After the Can-Am race at Watkins Glen, we did a commercial for Gulf Oil, our sponsor and partner. It turned out to be a great photo shoot, with the commercial featuring some fantastic scenes of the car coming out of the rising sun in the morning. Paul Wuori had come up to the Glen to give us a hand, and some of the footage was shot using Batt's car with the camera on it. It would be really nice to find a copy of that commercial.

We used three trucks with trailers to carry the three cars, with one on each trailer. Two of the trucks carried car parts and tools; one had engines and spare engine parts. There were two or three of us in each truck, and we rotated the driving spells, with one tank of fuel for each stint during the long trips across America.

One thing we did in 1969 was to have a large New Zealand flag flying in the pits by the trucks. We won all 11 races, but it was hard work. I don't think anyone got more than a couple of hours' sleep on the Saturday night before each race. It may have looked easy from the outside, but it took a lot out of everyone. At one point during the series, I fell asleep at dinner on the evening after a race. I landed pretty much facedown in my plate. Everyone else just continued their dinner and never woke me up.

The Chevrolet engines were built and rebuilt in England by George Bolthoff, who had come to McLaren from Traco, and several other blokes. This was done in the little engine shop in the factory at Colnbrook. The engines were then started up on a pretty basic test stand built out of old car parts. The run-up test stand allowed us to get the engine properly hot so the cylinder heads could be retorqued and the valve-to-rocker arm clearance set.

In case you missed something here, building the engines in England meant sending them back to the United States. We were taking the engines out of the cars after the race and Frank Zimmerman, who was the McLaren gofer at the time, would take them to the nearest international airport and get them sent back to England. When we got to the next race, Frank was off to another airport to complete the circle by collecting the engines that had come from England.

Frank went on to become a bank manager in San Francisco before sailing his boat down the west coast of California to the Panama Canal and on to Miami. I get e-mails from him quite often, and these days he's a private jet pilot, which is really great for him.

In July 2010, Frank said he had flown to Boston and then had gone down to Hingham to take a few photos of what had been my parents' house, which was where we usually started off for each Can-Am season. Frank then sent the photos to me, which was really nice of him.

We felt we had such an advantage at Bridgehampton on Long Island that the cars were actually spotted leaving the race track after just a few laps of qualifying. My friends Larry Cronin Jr. and Batt had come down to Bridgehampton with Larry's boat on a trailer. Bruce's love of waterskiing was such that when he was told about the boat, he gave Batt a couple of hundred dollars to go buy some water skis and a tow rope and then to find a suitable place nearby. Batt managed all of that without too much trouble—and today he still has the

Bruce at the wheel of the McLaren M8B Can-Am car during the perfect 1969 season. He and Denny won all 11 Can-Am events that year. (DUKE Q. MANOR COLLECTION / THE REVS INSTITUTE)

water skis up on his garage wall at home.

It was also at Bridgehampton where Charlie Scarano, now part of the US Army's Special Forces, got a chance to visit us before going off to Vietnam. I know he did come back to the United States, but not the way you wanted him to. Charlie was involved in night missions with a couple of other guys, and one of those outings went very wrong. It was a kick in the guts for all of us at the time.

A day or so before practice started at Mosport, Lee Muir (a very good engine man from America) and I drove down to Detroit with a couple of engines in the back of the truck. We were heading for the Chevrolet research and development facility, where we were going to run some new parts on their dyno during the night. Chevrolet general manager John DeLorean met us when we got there and told us how to get in the back entrance with the truck. Then he quietly said, "Please be gone by morning." We did just what we were told to do, and having found a bit more horsepower with a new camshaft, Lee and I were heading back to Mosport just as the sun was coming up.

The race at Michigan was, in many ways, something a bit different. Jack Brabham had been having problems with his Ford G7A race car in practice, so Bruce loaned him our third car to do some laps. It was interesting to hear Jack's comments about the car from Bruce, but for some reason he didn't race it. The car was then loaned to Dan Gurney, who had to start from the back of the field because he hadn't qualified. He was also under strict instructions not to beat either Bruce or Denny; Dan, being very quick, was quite capable of doing this. At the end of the race it was Bruce, Denny, and Mr. Gurney. We couldn't have asked for much more than finishing first, second, and third!

At Riverside, Bruce's car broke a bottom rear wishbone while leading, which spun him off into the desert sands, leaving Denny to win. After the race, Carroll Smith, a former Formula Junior Cooper driver, arranged for us to work in his boss Carroll Shelby's very large building in Torrance, California, before setting off for the last race just outside Dallas.

College Station, Texas, didn't have a lot of places to stay, so Rick Holt of Gulf Oil rented a house for some of us. It wasn't until after a couple of days that we noticed the condemned sign, which probably accounted for more than one cockroach. Rick was asked to find something better, or have someone come and really clean the place.

Having gone back to England straight after Riverside, Bruce brought some stronger wishbones with him to Texas. It was a good idea, because part of the race track was on a high banking very much like the track at Michigan. Bruce won, while Denny retired with an engine problem, but set the fastest lap.

That meant Bruce won the 1969 Can-Am championship, with Denny finishing second after we had won all 11 races. I thought at the time that this was quite a reasonable achievement! Okay, we did have a couple of DNFs, but one of our cars always won the race. All of this success was helped by having the correct design to start with, the generally good reliability of the M8B, and two very good drivers.

After the race in Texas we flew straight to Indianapolis, where our new mechanic, Hywel "Hughie" E. Absalom, was waiting with the prototype McLaren Indy car—basically a single-seat version of the Can-Am car. We also had on board the infamous Herbie Porter, a Goodyear engine development man who had a host of knowledge about the Speedway. Even so, we ran afoul of the rules there pretty much right away. We had an oil pressure problem and worked late—as you do—to fix it. Then we found we couldn't get out of the damn place; hard to believe, but that's how it was at the Indianapolis Motor Speedway.

Hughie Absalom was more than just a mechanic. He had worked for Jack Brabham before moving to Team Lotus and their Indianapolis program, followed by Formula One. When Hughie came to McLaren, it was to work on the four-wheel-drive F1 car project, then on the F1 and Indianapolis teams. He later went to California to work for Parnelli Jones on his Indianapolis program, doing the same for Al Unser when he won Indy, Pocono, and Ontario (all three 500-mile races) in 1978. Hughie ran his own race team for a few years, and he now owns Spot-On Control Cables. We keep in touch with the odd e-mail now and again.

With the Indy car program ramping up along with the Can-Am, it was decided at the end of 1969 to establish a proper facility in the United States, where we could build and maintain the cars and engines. Teddy, Bill Smith Jr., and Bruce set up McLaren Engines on Eight Mile Road in Livonia, Michigan, a suburb of Detroit. Colin Beanland was dispatched to set up the place and be the manager.

It was around this time that I went to Texas to see Gary Knutson. I wanted to persuade him to work at McLaren Engines because George Boltoff, who was in charge of building the Can-Am engines, wanted to leave. In the end Gary returned to the team, and ultimately remained with McLaren until 1987.

The relationship between Bruce and myself at this point was interesting and inspiring, partly because I was staying at his house, and because we both thought along somewhat similar lines. You could talk to him and, almost all of the time, understand what he was on about. He was very good at putting his finger on problems with the car and knowing what he wanted to do to fix them.

Bruce was also capable of doing things pretty much on his own. Everyone had faith in him. A good example was when he designed a hillclimb car for Patsy Burt, one of Britain's most successful female drivers. Bruce sketched what he wanted on scraps of paper, got John Thompson to make the tubular chassis in the fabrication department, and used the suspension from one of the other cars. The hillclimb car was built by Mike Barney. I think it took just a couple of weeks, and although offically known as an M3, we dubbed it the "Whoosh Bonk" car. The name came from Bruce's explanation of what he wanted, "You make this, you do that, put it all together, and *whoosh bonk*, there's your car."

I think McLaren also made a few cars for other hillclimb people. I know we also built a camera car and sometime race car for the John Frankenheimer film *Grand Prix* in 1966. Driven by Chris Amon, it used a couple of different engines during the course of the filming, which no one really noticed. The film was and still is a classic, with lots of real race-car noise.

Bruce would come out with classic comments such as, "If it looks right, it probably is right, and if it looks wrong, it probably is wrong." But even with all his talent and knowledge, Bruce was not an egotistical person, and gave credit when and where it was due.

I certainly learned a lot about motor racing by being around Bruce and working with him on his car. I don't think I have changed a lot, as I have always thought that passion, trust, focus, and dedication were important. But I also learned from Bruce and Teddy just how important it was to work with a first-class team of people who were not afraid of a bit of perseverance.

Checking in with Bruce before the fourth round of the 1969 Can-Am series at Edmonton. In the race Bruce would retire with a broken piston while Denny won ahead of Chris Amon's Ferrari 612P. (PETE LYONS)

# 1970: The First Year at Indy, and McLaren after Bruce

Chris Amon did some of the early testing of the new M15 Indy car. Chris was very good in a Formula One car, especially on high-speed circuits, but he didn't like Indianapolis at all. He thought if they painted trees on the wall, for F1 track scenery, he might feel a bit more at home. Bruce also did some testing, but neither he nor Chris actually raced the car at the Speedway.

The M15 had a few interesting features. Because it carried roughly 75 gallons of methanol fuel, the car had some hand-operated hydraulic pistons to raise and lower the front ride height as the fuel load changed during the race. And two refueling connectors on the left-hand side of the car meant you didn't need to go around to the far side of the car with a very long fuel hose. Much to everyone's amazement, we also had a rear wing. Amazement because we were the only ones game enough to try a wing and the only ones with the confidence that it would be a benefit. The Indianapolis rule requiring the rear wing to be attached to the bodywork had a few gray areas, because no one had done one before. The one exception was Honda, which had run one of their Formula One cars with a high rear wing at Indy during a test a few years earlier.

The United States Auto Club (USAC), which sanctioned the 500, didn't believe our design was legal and made us modify the bodywork pretty much every night for a week. Bill Eaton, our English fabricator extraordinaire, was kept busy doing something a little bit different each night. When the officials realized we were not going to give up and were serious about this Indy racing stuff, they finally gave us a proper scrutineering sticker to allow us to qualify—with a wing that turned out to be legal after all.

Why we had to be there for a whole damn month I'm not sure, and never really did understand. Being new at the place, we wanted to run every day, the end result being that pretty much everyone was knackered the whole time. It would take us a couple of years to understand what you really need to do at Indianapolis, and how to do it.

The car also had two refueling vent caps. Since these were open to the atmosphere, the possibility of spilling methanol when refueling was quite high. (Christ, when you think about it, it really was quite dangerous!) Our caps had a very neat little external safety latch keeping them closed. It was one of the standard snap caps that you can buy from most racing shops. But the USAC guys didn't like our nice little safety latch and made us change it to a spring. Now came the fuck-up.

The good old Offy engine shook like hell, causing this spring to vibrate and allow the breather cap to open on Denny's car while he was on the back straight. The car caught fire from the leaking methanol. Denny slowed down and jumped out of the car onto the grass in the infield.

The first safety trucks arrived straightaway—a pretty damn good bunch of guys. Unfortunately, they chased the car and didn't notice that Denny's hands were actually on fire from the methanol that had soaked into his gloves. Once the safety crew realized what had actually happened to him, he was immediately taken to the Indianapolis hospital with quite bad burns on his hands. Denny had a lot of friends visit him in the hospital while his hands recovered, which, in fact, took a long time.

Peter Revson, then driving for Brabham at Indy, was not doing very well. So Teddy asked Peter if he would be interested in having a go in our car. (We still didn't really know for sure what had caused the fire, but the spring was the only thing that had been changed.) Peter drove the car for a reasonable number of laps and came in to the pits. The first thing he said to Teddy was, "You're going to have a hard time getting me out of his car." I guess what he had been driving so far was not to his liking.

While this conversation was going on, Allan McCall, the number-one mechanic on the

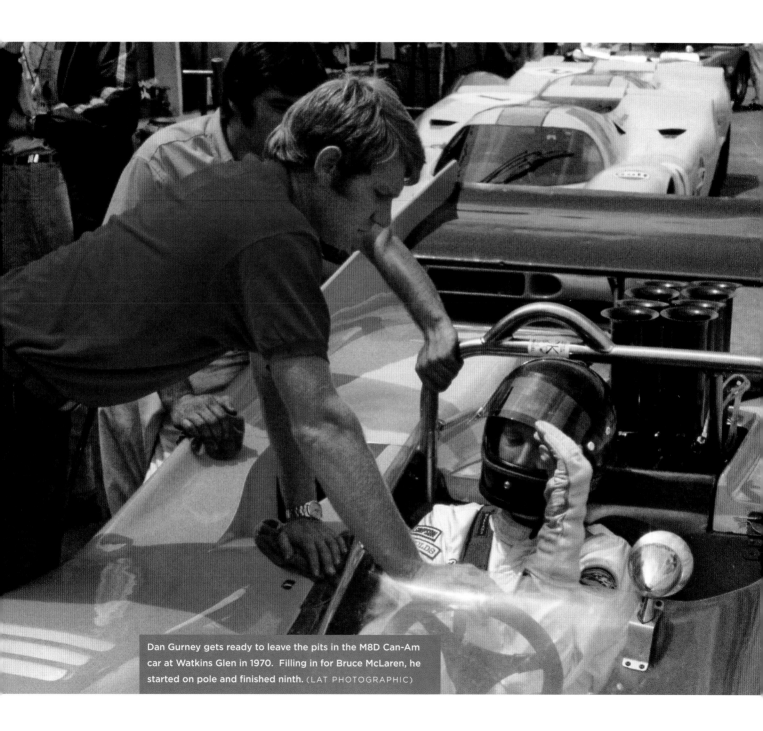

Dan Gurney gets ready to leave the pits in the M8D Can-Am car at Watkins Glen in 1970. Filling in for Bruce McLaren, he started on pole and finished ninth. (LAT PHOTOGRAPHIC)

I look slightly worried while Bruce projects his usual air of calm in a picture taken at the 1970 Indy 500. I was still in Indianapolis when I learned that Bruce had been killed at Goodwood on June 4, 1970. (BRUCE R. CRAIG COLLECTION / THE REVS INSTITUTE)

car, called me over. He had noticed that the refueling breather was nearly ready to pop open. To prove it, a thump with his hand on the side of the chassis did the trick. It had nearly happened again. We went straight off for a quiet chat with USAC, and after that we were allowed to make our own safety latch.

On one occasion, Ron Tauranac, the engineer who had co-founded Jack Brabham's team, was walking past our garage when he noticed Denny's chassis propped up against the wall. He started to ask about the fuel system in the car, and what followed was really quite priceless stuff. Our car had a neat standard fuel system designed by Bruce. This allowed something known as physics—and a few flap valves—to move the fuel around the car. It was very similar to the Can-Am car's fuel setup, which worked very well.

It seems that Ron had been having problems with the Brabham fuel system, and he wanted to know how ours worked. I'm not sure why the hell I told him, but when I did, he said it couldn't work like that, and we proceeded to have a bit of a heated discussion. It was just as well Ron didn't believe me. Which probably explains why he was seen dripping fuel from a Coke bottle into the inlet trumpets of the Brabham Formula One engine while trying to get it started at the French GP in Rouen.

Peter was one of the few drivers to run at an average of just over 169 mph on Saturday before qualifying. But qualifying turned out to be a lot hotter than it had been in the morning. Peter qualified 16th and dropped out of the race with a magneto problem. Teddy had hired Carl Williams, an Indianapolis regular, to drive Chris Amon's car, as Chris had been having trouble getting up to speed. Going back to England seemed a better plan. Williams qualified 19th and finished 9th.

Bruce and Teddy flew home right after the race, which was won by Al Unser. Bruce wanted to be available to test the new Can-Am car, as the series would be starting in a couple of weeks.

I was in the Howard Johnson's motel restaurant not far from the Speedway, having breakfast with Dan Gurney, when I was called to the telephone. It was Teddy. Bruce had been killed that afternoon at Goodwood when the rear wing and bodywork came off the new Can-Am car, causing it to lose all rear downforce.

The shock of what Teddy had just said—and the look on Dan's face when I told him—tended to take your breath away, at least for a moment or two. Of course, the next thing that pops to the surface of one's mind is, "What the hell do we do now?" The first thing was to tell the guys who were still packing up at the Indy garage what little I knew.

Next was sorting out a flight to return to England as soon as I could. My trip back, with my mind in a kind of kaleidoscope of confusion, sure as hell prevented me from getting any sleep.

Of course, the factory was in a terrible state, with the feeling of doom and gloom as the shock, sadness, and uncertainty all came to the surface. The reality of it all was that the guy you would follow anywhere—or, as Howden Ganley once said, "single file across the Sahara Desert"—was now gone. The world of motor racing can be tough. It's times like these when you have to get ahold of yourself and keep people together—in this case, the people who helped to make Bruce McLaren Motor Racing the team that it was. It was now time to use the things that we all had learned from Bruce, without showing personal sorrow.

Bruce apart, there was another person who was a very big part of Bruce McLaren Motor Racing (BMMR), and who contributed more to the company than anyone gave him credit for: Edward Everett (aka, Teddy, or just EEM) Mayer. There was also Phil Kerr, another

New Zealander friend of Bruce's who had been working for Jack Brabham before coming to BMMR. And there was Gordon Coppuck, the chief designer, who had already spoken to everyone in the factory, saying that if they felt the need to take the next day or two off, to please do so.

It was then that Teddy stood up in front of everyone at the factory and said, with no fuss or preamble, but in standard Mayer-speak, "We all realize that something not very pleasant has happened, but we have a company called Bruce McLaren Motor Racing, and it has a Can-Am race in two weeks—so best we get on with it!" And, by Christ, we did. I think just about everyone came in to work the following day. Those who had learned a great many things from Bruce were now the ones who knew it was up to them to get their shit together to keep BMMR going.

Phil Kerr had taken on the job of dealing with various concerns associated with Bruce's wife, Patty. Teddy had been on the phone, chasing and sorting out a deal with Dan Gurney to drive in the Can-Am alongside Denny, whose hands were still in bandages and not yet fully healed from the fire at Indianapolis.

Like many other racing people, Bruce McLaren was more than just talented; he was also versatile. His achievements, especially his contributions to the development of motorsport, will never die. Bruce's long-term plan was to win and expand his team carefully.

I'm not really sure how to say all of the next bit, but will give it a go anyway.

When we arrived in Mosport for the first Can-Am race, Denny's hands were still in bad shape, and Dan never had a chance to drive or test the new car. I had known Dan for a long time, but I had never actually worked with him. I guess it was qualifying that told you just how good he was and how much he liked to try new things.

Dan asked us to put most of the selection of springs and rollbars on the car for him to try during practice. With about 10 minutes left in qualifying, I said to Dan, "We need to do a proper lap time. What would you like on the car?" He said something about just needing a couple of laps. Then he jumped in and put it on pole with whatever the hell springs and rollbars were on it at the time.

Dan had a long battle with Jackie Oliver in the race, but in the end, Dan won, and Denny finished third. When it was over, Denny sat in the car in the pit lane for a very long time. He didn't really have the strength to get out, and, in any case, he couldn't get one of his hands off the steering wheel for quite a while because of the unhealed damage from the Indy fire.

Those two guys and that day brought BMMR back to life, along with the fortitude and

Dan Gurney listens from the cockpit of the McLaren M8D Can-Am car at Mosport in 1970. Dan ran several Can-Am races with the McLaren team after Bruce McLaren's death in June. (BOB HARMEYER)

Denny makes light of his bandaged hands as Dan Gurney looks on during practice for the 1970 Indianapolis 500. (LAT PHOTOGRAPHIC)

hard work of all the people in Colnbrook who had made it possible to be there in the first place. Denny really had the balls and the guts to do what he did, considering how bad his hands were. Later on, he told us that he just had to do it for his friend Bruce.

Dan was also signed to drive the Formula One car, but I'm not sure he really liked it, because he was not as quick as I thought he would be. I believe he was thinking about stopping racing. It was while we were at the Dutch GP, having dinner one night in one of the nice fish restaurants along the sand dunes outside Zandvoort, that Dan started talking about the number of his personal friends who had died in motor racing. It was a lot. That's when I felt sure he really did want to stop.

In the end all of this sorted itself out, because Dan's oil company contract clashed with McLaren's deal with Gulf Oil. Peter Gethin took Dan's place in both Formula One and Can-Am for the rest of the season.

Denny won the 1970 Can-Am series, and judging from a few of his quiet comments during the season, a lot of his effort and thoughts were related to Bruce. The rest of us obviously had thoughts of our own on the same subject, but we had to stay focused on our jobs and the business of winning races—which I know Bruce would have expected us to do.

# 1971: A Reunion with Revson and a Close Call at Indy

Peter Revson came to drive for us in Indy cars and the Can-Am in 1971. Having known Peter for a long time, it was nice to be working with him again.

To comply with the rules, Gordon Coppuck had designed a new Indy car with a rear wing integral with the engine cover, and it looked like we were going in the right direction. A. J. Foyt's integral rear wing was a thin strip of aluminum running from the wing to the gearbox. All USAC legal, of course!

The Indy series races were not much different from most other kinds of racing—except that most of them were on oval tracks, so you only turned left! And there were often track-elevation changes. As you might have expected, the rules were different, along with the people who ran the races and made those rules.

An obvious difference was that generally there were more pit stops, usually the result of the amount of methanol fuel the car was allowed to carry. Having raced at Indianapolis the year before for the first time and having learned things the hard way, we realized that the Indianapolis race track was not just an oval with four corners. It had taken us a while to appreciate and accept just how complex it really was to be quick around Indy. Hopefully, we had learned enough to do a better job in 1971. Of course, like any form of competition, you are happy when you win and sad and/or pissed-off when you lose.

Peter and Denny ran quite well in practice, although Denny was still a little spooked by the fuel problem of the year before. We had sold one of the new M16 Indy cars to Roger Penske to help pay the bills. His driver, Mark Donohue, was talking on TV about how great it was to be on pole position, as his car now had some oversteer and loose handling that it didn't have in the morning practice due to the hotter track. Donohue had been genuinely quick for most of the time leading up to qualifying. While he was chatting on TV, Teddy picked this up and changed the angle of the front wing on Peter's car. Then Peter went out and stole pole position! Donohue had played a reasonable part in developing the M16 car, which meant losing pole like that made it even more of a "piss off" for him!

Peter's father, Martin, had come to Indianapolis, along with his sister Jennifer, and his uncle Charles, the Revlon cosmetics founder who used to wear nail polish to see how durable it was. The visit to Indianapolis was significant because it was the first time in many years that the two brothers had actually spoken to one another.

Jennifer Revson recently sent me the following reminiscence; I thought it would be appropriate to include it here:

> The fact that nearly everyone thought Mark Donohue and Penske had pole position in the bag, especially after Mark's run just bested A. J. Foyt's new record, meant that when the green flag dropped for Peter's qualifying session, the fans were practically snoozing in their seats. But when his times kept getting faster and faster, and Tom Carnegie, the famous voice of the Indy 500, announced, "It's a new track record," the crowd went wild!

> They jumped up from their seats, clapping, whistling, and cheering Peter on. It was so exciting! Peter, considered the underdog, was going for the pole . . . and he got it! Wow! What a moment, and what an upset for the record books. I heard the Penske team was dumbstruck. Peter drove down pit road, grinning from ear to ear, holding his right index finger up, signifying No. 1. I can't tell you how proud I was of my brother, and the entire McLaren team. Fantastic!

Bobby Unser and Donohue screwed Peter around at the start by speeding up and slowing down, but the classic bit came at the end of the race. One of the USAC rules for a yellow-flag situation stated that the gap that existed between the car in front and the one behind during the previous green-flag period should be maintained under the yellow. Peter was running

I took this portrait of Peter Revson during the Nassau Speed Week in 1966, about four years before he joined the McLaren team in 1971. Peter and I had been friends ever since the days of Rev-Em Racing in the early 1960s. (TYLER ALEXANDER)

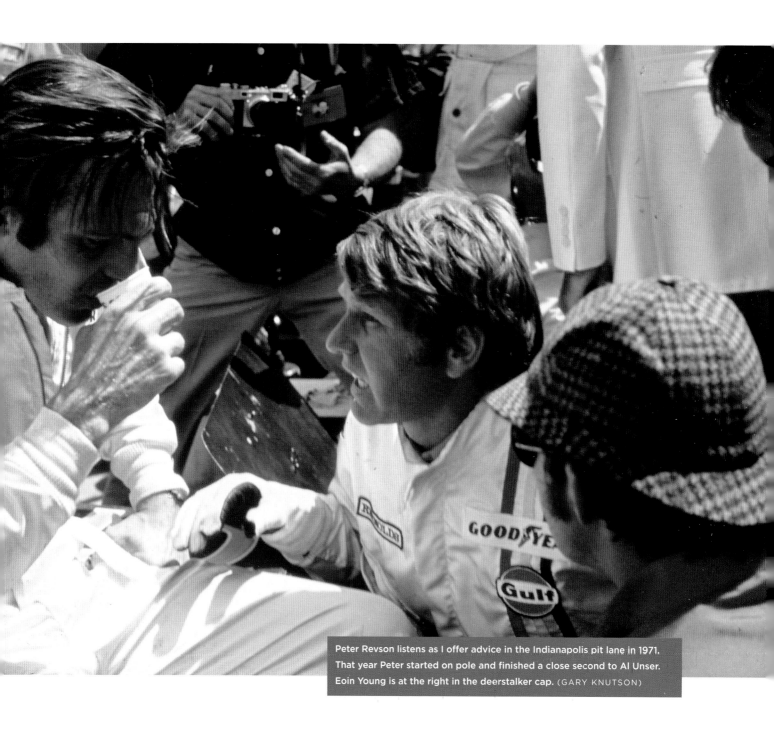

Peter Revson listens as I offer advice in the Indianapolis pit lane in 1971. That year Peter started on pole and finished a close second to Al Unser. Eoin Young is at the right in the deerstalker cap. (GARY KNUTSON)

second, some six to eight seconds behind Al Unser, and closing on him, when there was a yellow flag that came out near the end of the race. When Al pulled away from Peter under the yellow, Teddy—not really trusting the implementation of the rules—ran to see Harlan Fengler, the chief steward, to check and see if it was okay for Peter to close up. It was in the rules, but of course, no one had told Al to slow down. This "ability to manipulate" foreshadowed what lay ahead in the future.

We tried everything on the signal board. Even Denny, who had dropped out with a car problem, was on the pit wall doing his best to get Peter's attention by pointing at the board, telling Peter it was perfectly all right for him to close up on Al Sr. In the end, Peter finished second in our second attempt at Indy. Later, when we asked him why he hadn't closed up on Unser, Peter's reply was that he didn't trust "them"—presumably a reference to the rulemakers at Indy!

We were also competing in the Can-Am series, and when practice was over at the next Indy car race at Pocono, we needed to leave immediately for St. Jovite. Teddy had chartered an airplane to take himself, Peter, and me. We left Hugh Absalom in charge, with Charlie Chins (Mike Underwood), Chalky (Eamon Fullalove), and the Rabbit (Graham Bartells) preparing to do the things on the job list. In fact, they just put everything away in the garage and did nothing on the job list, as they had the next day to deal with that. Needless to say, they were back at the motel before us when we stopped off to get cleaned up before heading for the airport.

Flying to Quebec was fine, but coming back wasn't particularly good. At one point on the return trip, we needed to stop for fuel. The gray clouds went all the way to the ground, and finally, the third attempt at landing was successful—although scary. A lot of thought was given to driving the rest of the way, but the weather cleared up and we were able to fly on to Pocono.

At that time, 1971, we were only doing three 500-mile races—Indy, Pocono, and Ontario—with the Indy car program. At Ontario, Donohue ran out of fuel because the Captain, Mr. Penske, was so mesmerized by Mark leading the race that he didn't tell him to pit—or Mark didn't see the signal board because of traffic. After getting back to the pits and refueling, the engine soon failed due to running lean because of the low fuel level.

Around this time, we were in New York City quite a bit with the Goodyear people for discussions about tires for the future. They took us to what at the time was a very fashionable bar and hamburger place, where I remember having a chat with an old acquaintance,

Denise McCluggage, the journalist and sometime sports-car driver, and her friend Miles Davis, jazz trumpet legend and Ferrari 275 GTB owner. We had a short "nice to meet you both" kind of chat, and then they got in a taxi and disappeared.

We were also taken to the 21 Club for lunch, where we met up with Jackie Stewart, who I recall was standing at the bar, sipping a glass of water. We said hello and went to sit down for lunch with the Goodyear people.

It was about this time that Boyd Jefferies, a friend of Peter Revson's, became involved with McLaren as a sponsor/partner for both the Can-Am and the Indy car programs. Boyd was a great guy and an after-hours big-block stock trader. (A block trade is usually at least 10,000 shares of a stock, or $200,000 of bonds, but in practice is often significantly larger.) Boyd had his own company in Los Angeles, and would be in his office at 5:30 a.m. for a meeting with his people before the stock market opened in New York.

He also had a Learjet that was flown by Bill Lear's son, and there were several interesting episodes when he was helping us get from point A to point B. Having finished the Can-Am race at Road Atlanta, Boyd was giving us a lift to Miami to catch the TWA flight back to London. There were too many of us on board the Lear, so Gordon Coppuck had to lie on the floor between the seats to avoid being seen by the control tower at the small airport.

When we reached Miami, Bill Jr. neatly taxied the Lear just under the wingtip of the TWA plane. We got out, ran up some stairs by the loading ramp, and rapped on a glass door just beside the TWA boarding gate. The people there thought we were coming from the Eastern Airlines flight that had just landed, because those passengers were also coming up the stairs on their way to the immigration desks. There was a lot of arm waving and frustration as we tried to speak to the ground crew through the glass door. The first thing they wanted to know was where the hell we had come from. "We just came off the Learjet parked under the wing of your plane," we explained, "and we need to get back to London!"

There was Gordon Coppuck, Jackie Oliver, Teddy Mayer, and myself. The normal boarding had just finished, but they let us get on the plane, which fortunately had quite a few empty seats. The nice stewardess asked for my seat number and I pointed out that I didn't have a boarding pass or a ticket, and neither did the others that had just boarded with me! As we landed at Heathrow, an announcement came over the loudspeaker system, asking a certain Mr. Alexander to see the TWA person at the door of the plane with his credit card—to pay for the tickets we never had!

We had another memorable trip after a Can-Am race at Elkhart Lake. Peter Revson

and I needed to get to Los Angeles, as we had an Indy car test at Ontario a few days later. Boyd was going home. He gave us a lift, and we spent most of the trip sleeping on the floor. Coming over the mountains just before Los Angeles, the view of all the lights was quite something as we looked forward from the cockpit door. Then Bill Jr. asked Peter, "Want to see LA upside down?" He flipped the Learjet into a positive-G roll, and there was LA, upside down. I guess everyone was awake by then!

Not so enjoyable was a flight to New York following a very nice party thrown by Larry Truesdale, the boss of Goodyear's racing division, at his house in Akron, Ohio. We didn't stay particularly late, as we had a plane chartered for early the next morning to take us to Kennedy Airport in time to catch a flight back to London. Peter Revson, Eoin Young, Denny, and I were on board, with Teddy sitting up front with the pilot.

About halfway to New York we flew into a very nasty hailstorm, accompanied by some high winds. (Teddy had been looking at the radar, which showed that the front was just ahead of us; true to form, he said we should just keep going.) The plane was leaping around quite a bit, and I have to say that the pilot did a good job keeping things under control. By the time we had cleared the weather front, Denny, who had been trying to hold on to some full cups of coffee and a couple boxes of donuts, had the whole lot pretty much all over him and part of the cabin. When we reached Kennedy, Peter got out and kissed the ground, which was not surprising, given that the ride had been pretty damn scary. But we did make it in time to catch our flight to London.

This was a period of time during that summer when a few of us were competing in a Can-Am race in the States one weekend, a Formula One race in Europe the next, and then back to the States for the next Can-Am race, and so on. The flights back and forth were fine, as they gave you a chance to rest and sleep. The logistical part was sorted out at the factory, and we knew where and when the races were, so it wasn't at all stressful.

During 1971, Roger Penske had Mark Donohue drive the M19 Formula One car at the Canadian and United States GPs. It was what you might call an interesting design, with rising-rate suspension, front and rear. Mark came over to England to do some testing, and to cut a long story short, he was as confused as everyone else about setting up the car. Ultimately, he had the rear suspension changed to a normal configuration.

Sometime later, he told me that his thoughts might have been a bit wrong, as a lot of the problems may have been caused by the rear wing not working very well. He said the only time the car felt okay was during the wet race at Mosport, when a lot of rear wing was used.

If Mark was right, then the airflow over the rear wing was only correct at a high angle; if he was wrong, then it would have been the wet race track that had had more of an effect on the handling.

# 1972–73: Ramping Up in Indy Cars, and Farewell to the Can-Am

A short time before we arrived in Buenos Aires for the 1972 Argentine Grand Prix, a bomb inside the Sheraton Hotel had done a reasonable amount of damage. As a result, there were armed guards at the front door of the hotel and chauffeured cars with police escorts to take the drivers from the hotels to the race track.

Peter explained to us that the only safe place in the chauffeured car was down on the floor in the back, with your hands over your head. The police motorbike riders, standing on the pegs, would go straight up Avenue Fifth of May as fast as they could with sirens blaring, straight through the red lights and whatever else was in front of them. If you've ever been in Buenos Aires and traveled on Avenue Fifth of May, you'll understand why Peter was hiding on the floor of the chauffeured car. There are a lot of people and traffic all the time.

The year 1972 ended up being rather fraught, with a lot of reliability problems. This was a shame, because both the Indy and Can-Am cars were quite reasonably quick. Peter was now doing all three types of racing for us: Formula One, Can-Am, and Indy cars. Brian Redman had to take Peter's place in the Formula One car at Monaco, Clermont-Ferrand, and the Nürburgring, as these events coincided with Indy car races. The Formula One car

Peter Revson takes a break during an Indy car testing session held at California's Ontario Motor Speedway in 1973. (TYLER ALEXANDER)

was more reliable than the others, and Peter did reasonably well, with pole position and second place in Canada and three more podium finishes. Gordon Johncock had come to partner with Peter in the 500-mile events, which were the only Indy races we were doing that year. Engine reliability issues at Indianapolis were the most frustrating that we had seen for a while. We were damaging pistons as soon as the boost pressure from the turbo came up. The problem turned out to be incorrect piston-to-bore clearance, because someone had measured from the wrong place on the piston. This caused the piston to "scuff" the cylinder liner as soon as the temperature went up, increasing its diameter by a small amount. Ironically, Mark Donohue won the 1972 Indy 500 driving a McLaren M16B after suffering multiple engine problems of his own in the weeks before the race.

The M20 was quite different in layout to our previous Can-Am cars because it had the radiators positioned just in front of the engine on both sides of the car.

The writing was on the wall when Roger Penske appeared with a Porsche 917/10 turbo Can-Am car—a factory car with a lot of horsepower. We only won two races that season, and it was becoming obvious that we needed something quite different if we were to compete right at the front. George Follmer became the 1972 Can-Am Champion when he won five of the nine races for Penske.

Denny had a spectacular accident at Road Atlanta when he pulled out to pass Follmer's Porsche. Air got underneath the M20 and flipped it over, with Denny landing upside down. He received a thump on the head and was covered in the red dust and dirt associated with the Georgia race track. The accident did cause quite a bit of concern among those who were first to reach the car. The doctors spent a long time with Denny. He stayed the night at our motel with Eoin Young, who had instructions from the doctors to only allow Denny to sleep for short periods of time. According to Eoin, it led to some tense moments, because Denny didn't take kindly to being woken and Eoin didn't dare drop off in case he slept right through. It meant a couple of grumpy Kiwis in the morning. But at least Denny was okay.

For 1973 we decided not to do the Can-Am series after testing a twin-turbo Chevrolet engine that had about 1,200 foot-pounds of torque and somewhere in the region of 900 bhp.

Peter Revson tested an M20 with this twin turbo at Road Atlanta. Gary Knutson was the project manager for the Chevrolet engine, and at one point during the test Peter gave Gary a ride to point out how easy it was to spin the rear wheels in any gear, anywhere on the race track, and at about 150 mph. With this sort of engine the car needed a lot more downforce, a completely new gearbox, and a much stronger drivetrain. The real problem was, we didn't have the money to do that.

Mario Andretti also did a test with the M20 twin-turbo car, but this was much later, when the car was owned by the Agapiou brothers in California. Mario said that turbo lag made the car hard to drive, and he didn't finish either of the two races he did with it.

Another issue was that Goodyear wanted McLaren to do the whole USAC Indy car series. I moved to Bloomfield Hills, near Detroit, to run the Indy team, which would be based at the McLaren Engines facility that we had established in Livonia at the end of 1969. The only real difference was that I was now living a lot closer to McLaren Engines.

Teddy hired Johnny Rutherford to do the full Indy season; it was the start of a really great relationship. Peter Revson would only run the 500-mile races, since he was also racing the Formula One car with Denny.

Gordon Coppuck's 1973 Indy car, the M16C, showed that we had learned a few things, although, as always seems to be the case, it was never enough! We were pretty quick most of the time leading up to Indy qualifying, with the usual large amount of help from Herbie Porter.

We were in the qualifying line and getting close to our turn for four laps of qualifying with Johnny Rutherford, when Roger Bailey, one of the guys involved in building the engines, asked me how far he should turn in the wastegate bolt. When I replied, "Three or four turns, I guess," Roger said, "To hell with it! Let's wind it in all the way."

This meant the engine would have as much boost pressure as the turbocharger could generate. Which was a lot of power! Johnny Rutherford, with his knowledge of Indianapolis, his nerve, and the balls of a large gray elephant, went out and won pole position with a record four-lap average of 198.413 mph. There were people at turn two who said the Gulf McLaren was coming off the corner with all four wheels smoking on every one of the four laps. It took your breath away. Roger Bailey has been known as "Boost" ever since!

The race had to be held over three days due to rain and two major accidents. The rain returned on Wednesday, and finally stopped the race after 133 laps, or 332.5 miles. Pole position was going to be as good as it got, with Johnny Rutherford black-flagged for a fuel leak and then finishing ninth with boost problems. Peter Revson hit the wall at the race's final restart on Wednesday.

Johnny would win at Ontario and Michigan, but the best we could do at the 500-mile races was fourth for Rutherford at Pocono. Even though Johnny finished third in the championship, the rest of the season seemed to be dominated by engine-related problems.

On the grid with Johnny Rutherford at Ontario in March 1974. Johnny won the second qualifying heat for the California 500 USAC race held there one week later. (LAT PHOTOGRAPHIC)

Tyler,
Thanks for all those
years! Sincerely,
Johnny Rutherford

Johnny Rutherford signed this photo taken with me during his days with the McLaren Indy car team. The partnership was successful: Two of JR's three wins at the Indy 500 were for McLaren. (TYLER ALEXANDER COLLECTION)

# Johnny Rutherford

Team McLaren and Tyler Alexander must have been on the top of every list for every race-car driver who had aspirations of winning, especially at the Indianapolis 500. I was no exception. By 1973 I had been competing for 14 years in every racing car I could find—beginning with the first modified race car that I built myself. I went on to sprint cars, midget race cars, stock cars, and Indy cars, and I raced on both pavement and dirt tracks. My first Indy 500 was in 1963, but in 10 years at Indy I could not seem to finish any of my races.

Then, in 1972, I was given the opportunity of my life. Through my mentor and good friend Herb Porter, I was called in for an interview with Teddy Mayer, the managing director of McLaren. I was hired to drive the "works" Indy car for Team McLaren. We began testing at the Speedway in March 1973. This was a big first for me. I instantly recognized that this team was very serious about this racing business.

After I met the rest of the team and crew (with names such as TJA, Booster, GLK, EE, Tulip, Abo, Chicken Lips, Sid, Trellis, Hanger, Deadly, Wombat, and even a few more colorful handles), I knew this was a team with a passion for auto racing. This was a team that was willing to work together, and I knew that we were all in the business of auto racing to win—to be the best of the best! I had often told my wife Betty that if I could ever find a team that wanted to race as badly as I did, we would definitely be winners! How true that was.

Tyler is the best and most diligent, thorough, and conscientious team manager I have ever known. Our first race as a team was at Trenton, New Jersey.

During the race I spun the car and tagged the wall. I was devastated! I couldn't apologize enough to Tyler and the crew. Tyler then set the tone of our relationship for the next seven-plus years. With his hands on my shoulders, he said, "John, we [meaning the team] will not keep score—if you will not either!" And what a run it was! We set a new track record at Indy in 1973, followed by two wins at the 500 in 1974 and 1976, plus 13 other victories during the racing seasons from 1973 to 1979. The team really did want to win as badly as I did!

The Team McLaren crew was unbelievable: dedicated, trustworthy, persistent, loyal, responsible, compatible, knowledgeable, and fun to be around. They also proved to be the fastest crew on pit lane. Under Tyler's guidance we all came together in a way that had other crews in the garage area talking to themselves and trying to find what "black magic" we were using in our car. It can now be told—we were just damn good! Tyler had taught us to run our own race.

However, we also had our share of fun. I am so thankful to have been part of the effort for Team McLaren, with friendships that will last a lifetime for Betty and me. I still think about that final lap of qualifying for one Indy 500 when I surprised Tyler on his headset radio with a serenade as I took the checkered flag, "Oh, what a beautiful morning, oh, what a beautiful day. Everything's coming up roses. Everything is going our way!"

Success is so sweet, isn't it, Tyler? I hope all of the readers enjoy your book as much as we enjoyed living it!

One of the good things that happened in 1973 was having Jim Ellis (a friend of Johnny's and an ex-Marine aircraft carrier pilot) and Cliff Pleggenkuhle act as weekend warriors for the team. They were both captains with Continental Airlines (Cliff being the youngest in the company), and they would remain good friends for a long time.

Living in Detroit, I didn't see much of the new M23 Formula One car, but from what I was told, the F1 guys seemed to feel they may have had something good. Designed by Gordon Coppuck with input from John Barnard, it turned out they were right: The M23 became one of the great F1 cars of its time.

We got off to a good start when Denny took pole in South Africa; he was leading comfortably until he picked up a puncture. It took a while to regain that form, but when it came, Denny won in Sweden, and Peter scored his first GP win at Silverstone.

Just before that British Grand Prix, Peter told me he was going to bet £100 on himself to win at 14 to 1 odds. He did get a fair amount of help from Jody Scheckter, who was driving a third M23 and had come close to winning the previous race in France in only his third GP. Scheckter had taken Peter's place (he was racing at Pocono, where he qualified on pole) and led the first 41 laps at Paul Ricard, until there was collision with Emerson Fittipaldi's Lotus. At the end of the first lap at Silverstone, Jody put a wheel on the grass and spun across the track and into the pit wall. That caused a big shunt involving quite a few cars. Unfortunately, I was not there to see Peter win the race (and his bet!), and neither was I at Mosport when he won again. The three wins gave McLaren third place in the Constructors championship behind Lotus and Tyrrell.

# 1974: Victory at Indianapolis and in Formula One

There were a lot of big changes for the company in 1974. Marlboro and Texaco had sorted out a deal with Teddy. That included Emerson Fittipaldi coming to McLaren as part of the package, with Denny Hulme driving the other car. That seemed okay, but there were some other issues regarding having Peter Revson on board; there were already two very good drivers, which kind of implied that Peter might just be a bit too quick.

There was another problem in that the F1 team was sponsored by Yardley at the time, but McLaren could not really afford to pass up the Marlboro and Texaco program. The solution was for the team to run a third car for Yardley. That was not a problem, as Phil Kerr had sorted out Mike Hailwood to drive the Yardley car. There were also some issues about me working with Peter, as he and I had been working together for such a very long time. Despite spending most of a day trying to sort out something with Peter's management people at Mark McCormack's International Management Group office in New York, Bill Smith Jr. and I were unable to do that. So Peter was not able to drive for us.

Peter went off to drive for the Shadow Formula One team, but he was killed while testing at Kyalami in preparation for the 1974 South African Grand Prix. Denny and some other drivers had stopped at the accident scene to try and help, but they were too late.

Peter and I had been good friends, going back to the Rev-Em Racing team in 1962. We got along well, and I spent time fishing with him off the coast of Florida in a nice boat that he owned with Roger Penske. What can you say? Peter was a great guy, never making a fuss about the fact that his family owned the Revlon Company. He was quick in anything he drove. Having been such a good friend for a long period of time, this was a very sad loss.

Best that I get on with things.

We were testing at Indianapolis at the time. I flew to New York for Peter's funeral and sat in the church with the writer, Leon Mandel. At one point, Leon asked how I felt. I said, "If you're asking about a one to ten rating, I'd say about an eight." He thought that wasn't a very nice thing to say, but several weeks later, he wrote something about it once he understood what I meant. You need to be pretty strong to deal with the business of motor racing.

Many years later, Leon wrote in *Auto Week* that I was "the exemplar of the independent artisan crew chief. Nasty, clever, sarcastic, demanding, and obsessive." He did say a bit more . . . about being the best of his kind there ever was. Dear, oh dear—a bit over the top, but at least he spelled my name right. Always great to have Leon say such nice things about someone.

Unlike some people, I always thought that the other USAC races we did were just practice for Indianapolis. The rules there had changed a lot, especially after the carnage of the 1973 race, which had been plagued by bad weather, accidents, and spilled fuel that had killed All American Racers' Swede Savage and a crewman, and injured Salt Walther and 11 spectators. Following this race, the fuel cell size was reduced to 40 gallons, and it had to be placed in the left-hand side of the center section of the monocoque, away from the more-vulnerable right-hand side. In addition, the four weeks of running in the month of May were reduced to three.

The 1973 M16C/D was modified to suit the new rules and ended up being a good car. There were also some very good improvements with the engine, which was still the old Offy, but which now had a new inlet manifold for the Hilborn fuel injection system, which made it run a lot better. And, just as important, we had a better idea about building these engines.

We ran two cars at Indy: one for Johnny Rutherford, and a second sponsored by Carling Black Label beer for David Hobbs. David was an old friend and a good driver, and he fitted into the team with no problems. A very straightforward kind of bloke, David had a lot of

Johnny Rutherford waves to the crowd on Victory Lane after winning the 1974 Indianapolis 500. Meanwhile, I seem to be searching for something inside the cockpit of the M16C/D. (LAT PHOTOGRAPHIC)

Emerson Fittipaldi takes questions after his third-place finish at the 1974 United States Grand Prix gave him the Formula One championship. It was the second for him, and the first for a McLaren driver. (LAT PHOTOGRAPHIC)

racing experience, and he was a good choice for our second Indy car. It's difficult to forget his easy manner, great sense of humor, and endless jokes.

Johnny Rutherford was quick most days, and he was happy that we had learned when and when not to run the car. The new fuel injection system gave us good fuel mileage, thanks, yet again, to help provided by Herbie Porter. The other major thing we had going for us was a young Goodyear tire engineer by the name of John Taube, who many years later would become head of Goodyear's Formula One division in Europe. We all got along very well, and John's contribution toward protecting the sets of tires became a major factor.

A lot of time was spent scrubbing in and getting the stagger selection for the sets of race tires. *Scrubbing in* the tires meant running each new set for several laps to have their initial smoothness from the tire mold abraded and ready to race. *Tire stagger* refers to the tire's diameter, mainly that of the rear tires. Using a slightly larger diameter tire on the right rear helps to prevent understeer, or "push" on the left turns. It helps to make the car more evenly balanced. The objective is to keep the best set for the last pit stop, and the real shoot-out at the end of the race.

We were one of the few teams, if not the only one, able to run the softer tire that was available. The car itself was easy on the tires, and John's plan for preparing them to prevent blistering was the key thing.

Having been one of the quickest three or four cars throughout practice, we should have been okay for qualifying—but things didn't go to plan. A problem with part of the fuel injection system meant we had to pull out of the Saturday qualifying lineup and go back to the garage to fix it, which Gary Knutson did. This should have been okay, as we were back in the qualifying line well before our time to go out on the track. But I guess someone didn't like us doing this, or we just misread or were confused by the rules of the qualifying lineup. Gary said, "We attributed the cock-up to USAC (and probably A. J. Foyt). I don't think they were really very helpful to us in those times. I also remember that the qualifying line rules were very convoluted."

It meant Johnny Rutherford had to qualify on Sunday, the second day of qualifying. He may have been second- or third-quickest overall on the day, and singing "Oh, What a Beautiful Morning" for most of his four laps, but we were still 25th on the grid. The good Mr. Hobbs, meanwhile, was able to qualify in ninth position without any real problems on Saturday.

Danny Folsom, a local businessman and special friend to all of us, kept the garage refrigerator filled with food and drinks. He was also a good friend of Peter Revson's. Danny put on a great party—one of many—at his house for all the guys to finally get a chance to relax, and more than likely, a bit more than that. Another friend of Danny's and ours was Freddie Bartlett, who owned some fried chicken take-out restaurants; you can guess what he brought us at the track, as well as to a few parties at his house. It's sad to mention it, but Danny passed away in October 2009.

Carburetion Day. Why the hell it's still called that, I have no idea. The name sticks even though no one has run a carburetor since the early 1960s. I guess it comes from a time when teams could tune their carburetors in conditions similar to those likely to be encountered on race day. Now it's just another practice day before the race. Anyway, there were no problems with David's car, but when Johnny's gearbox jumped out of gear down the front straight, it over-revved the engine and bent some of the valves in our race engine, built with such tender loving care. Dennis Davis, the number-one mechanic on Johnny's car, later found a part of the gearbox that had not been machined correctly.

The spare engine was fitted, but very few people knew that this engine had a couple of chromed crankshaft journals from some previous damage. Hard chroming damaged crankshaft journals is a common thing. After this is done, they are then re-ground to the correct diameter. The worry when you do this sort of thing is that the thin coating of hard chrome might not stay on the crankshaft journals. It's not exactly what you want in your race-day engine.

I don't know about anyone else, but the first few laps of the Indianapolis 500 were always scary as hell to me. We had no problems at first, but then David made an early first pit stop because he thought he had a tire problem; fortunately, he didn't. Just before his first pit stop, Johnny moved into 2nd place—from 25th on the grid! Then he was into a race-long fight with Foyt, who was a bit quicker on the straights but nothing like as fast in the corners.

There was a classic head-on picture on the cover of *Sports Illustrated* magazine at the time showing Foyt going through turn two, with the Texas Lone Star painted on Rutherford's helmet just peeking over Foyt's rear wing. He was that close, at around 170 mph. An oil leak eventually put Foyt out of the race and helped to give Johnny Rutherford our first Indianapolis 500 win. David finished a very good fifth. It was a great relief for all of us, as we'd thought we had a chance to win here at Indy if we could finish without any problems.

At the end of the day, Rutherford had used one set of tires that hadn't had a chance to be scuffed, and which developed some small blisters from getting too hot. Gary Knutson fell asleep while standing up and holding the rear quick-lift jack; Don Bartells, the guy who

Emerson Fittipaldi leads John Watson's Brabham-Ford at the 1974 Canadian Grand Prix. Fittipaldi won the race after leader Niki Lauda spun out on the 67th lap. (LAT PHOTOGRAPHIC)

actually built most of the engine used in the race, was finally able to take a deep breath.

Milwaukee and Pocono gave us three wins in a row, but reliability issues meant the rest of the season was not so great.

I was flying back and forth to England, chasing up development parts and going over issues we had during the races with the engineers, but at one point, we had a break in the Indy car race schedule. Teddy invited me down for a week to a house he had rented in Sotogrande, Spain, not far from Gibraltar. While there we ran into an old friend, Hap Sharp, who also had a house there, and had brought along his Argentina polo team as well. At the end of the week, Teddy, his wife Sally, and I set off by road to Lake Como and the Villa d'Este Hotel, one of the great hotels, which has a magnificent view over the lake. This is where we would be staying with the Marlboro and Texaco people for the Italian Grand Prix at Monza.

On the first night, we had a fine dinner on the terrace overlooking the lake. It was an interesting group of people: Emerson Fittipaldi and his wife, Maria Helena; his manager, Domingos Piedade; John Goossens from Texaco; Paddy McNally and John Hogan from Marlboro; as well as Jochen Mass (who would drive the Yardley McLaren M23 in the United States and Canada) and a few others. The great part for me was listening to Domingos using several different languages while in a conversation with the people around us, and then turning to me and asking, in perfect English, "Tyler, would you like another glass of white wine?" "Yes, thank you."

The 1974 Formula One championship was pretty close. No one team or driver was dominating it. Ferrari had started to make a comeback, as we would find out the next year, but Monza summed up their 1974 season when both cars dropped out after leading. That left Emerson to have a big fight with Ronnie Peterson, Emerson eventually finishing second, less than a second behind the Lotus.

A win for Emerson in Canada—only his third of the season—set him up for the final race at Watkins Glen, where he finished fourth to become World Champion. McLaren and the M23 won the Constructors championship for the first time from Ferrari and Tyrrell. It was a great job by everyone involved: We ran good, steady races, which was great for the sponsors, as well as the race team and the hardworking guys at the Colnbrook factory. Just very pleased, to say the least.

Having expressed an interest in taking a look at Indianapolis, Emerson came along to a Goodyear tire test there. The car was set up as Johnny Rutherford had raced it in the 500, and he did a bunch of laps to make sure everything was okay. Then Herbie Porter and Johnny took Emerson around the track in a road car to give him some idea of the place.

After two days of running, Emerson's best four-lap average run would have put him on the second row of the grid. Some years later, he would do a lot better than that!

# 1975–76: From Fittipaldi to Hunt, and Rutherford Repeats

There were aero mods for the new 1975 Indy car—including reshaped radiator ducts, along with a few other small bits and pieces. But when we got to Indy, the M16E did not behave very well at all.

Johnny Rutherford, who was damn good around the Speedway, was not happy with the rear stability of the car when turning into the corner. We tried everything, including changing back to the 1974 radiator duct shape and asking Goodyear if the tires were the same construction as before. The reply was something along the lines of "Yes, they are the same—well, maybe just a couple of small changes." We ended up qualifying seventh. It was a brave run by Johnny—affectionately known as "JR"—because he didn't feel right about the car at all.

After asking various people a lot of questions in the days after qualifying, we tried something that we hadn't done before. Simple as it was, we put some more negative camber on the rear wheels and lowered the rear of the car a little. On the first timed lap down the front straight, JR came on the radio and said, "Thank you for giving me my car back." We tried a few more steps of negative rear camber until we were happy with the setup. I remember

V for victory: Johnny Rutherford celebrates his second Indy 500 win after the rain-shortened 1976 race. I'm at the left behind Johnny's wife Betty. (TYLER ALEXANDER COLLECTION)

sitting down with my back against the pit lane wall and taking 10 or more deep breaths before I could get up. Goodyear's "small changes" had included a sidewall that was a lot softer on the rear tire. A hint about that from Goodyear might have helped us a lot earlier.

Toward the end of the race, we were running second, getting better fuel mileage and catching Bobby Unser at quite a reasonable rate. Then it rained. JR kept the car on the track until the race was stopped, which meant we ended up second. JR did a great job, because for a couple of laps there were a lot of cars sliding all over the place until the officials finally decided it was best to stop the race.

We didn't score any wins in the other 500-mile races, although Rutherford would finish second in the 1975 USAC Championship after taking second in the qualifying race for the California 500 at Ontario, winning at the Fast Track Speedway in Arizona, and then scoring top-three finishes at Milwaukee, Michigan, and Trenton.

Lloyd Ruby, a really nice guy with a lot of Indy experience, also drove for us at Indy that year. He qualified sixth, but unfortunately his engine had a piston problem early in the race and he failed to finish. This may have been caused when we warmed up the engine on Sunday morning before the race.

The Formula One program got off to a good start when Emerson won in Argentina, finished second in Brazil, and then led the championship until just before the halfway point in the season. That's when Niki Lauda and Ferrari really started to get going. Not even a win for Emerson in a pretty chaotic wet race at Silverstone, plus a couple of second places in the final races, were enough to get him ahead of Lauda in the championship.

With Denny Hulme now retired, the other M23 was driven by Jochen Mass, who got half points for winning the Spanish Grand Prix after the race at Montjuich Park was stopped because of a car that flew off the road and killed four people. McLaren actually finished third in the Constructors championship, behind Ferrari and Brabham.

The year 1976 started off with a jolt. I had gone over to Teddy's house for dinner, and when I opened the door, Teddy was a strange gray color. (I mean his pallor, not his hair; that hadn't changed!) Emerson Fittipaldi had just called from Brazil to say he and his brother were starting up their own F1 team and he would therefore not be re-signing with McLaren. I said to Teddy, "Best you get John Hogan of Marlboro on the phone right now." John asked what we thought of James Hunt, the freewheeling English driver who had made a splash with the Hesketh team in 1973 and 1974. "Could be quite all right," we said. John asked us to leave it with him.

Sometime the next day, James Hunt was driving for Marlboro McLaren. I thought James fitted into the team just fine and drove very well. Any more specific comments will need to come from the people who were there all the time—I only went to three F1 races because of my United States racing responsibilities. Those races were, Paul Ricard, Mosport, and Watkins Glen, all of which he would win!

I went to Paul Ricard for the French Grand Prix during a break in the Indy car series. During practice, I was looking for something to drink and picked up a cup of water belonging to Ray Grant, one of the very good mechanics. First taste showed it was, in fact, a cup of straight gin; pretty damn strong water if I do say so. It didn't look to me that it had any effect on Ray, as James's McLaren M23 won the race.

The Italian Grand Prix at Monza didn't go very well for either James Hunt or Penske's John Watson. In what became affectionately known as "The Monza Scandal," both drivers were penalized. The trouble was all about the octane level of the fuel in the two cars before

Teddy Mayer and James Hunt in the garage at Zandvoort before the 1976 Dutch Grand Prix. Hunt would win the 1976 Formula One championship after a tough battle with Niki Lauda and Ferrari. (OVE NIELSEN PHOTOGRAPHIC ARCHIVE / THE REVS INSTITUTE)

Rutherford in the Offenhauser-powered McLaren M16E at the 1976 Indianapolis 500. JR started on pole and won the race with a little help from the weather. (LAT PHOTOGRAPHIC)

practice on Saturday. The usual suspects had put out rumors about special fuel being used. In the absence of a proper check by the officials, as well as a misunderstanding of the rules and the legal octane levels available in England, James and "Wattie" were sent to the back of the grid—just where "they" wanted us. One could say it might well have had the feeling of political manipulation that weekend.

The race didn't go much better for James. He had worked his way into 12th place when he got it all wrong at one of the chicanes and left the road. It was the end of a dramatic weekend in many ways because Niki Lauda had made a sensational comeback at Monza, still healing from a serious crash and fire at the Nürburgring that had nearly killed him two months before.

Mosport came next, and I had a chance to go to the Canadian GP. Bill Smith Jr. brought his motor home, and after the race Jochen Mass drove it from the track to our hotel with a

Here I am arguing with A. J. Foyt over pit lane tactics during the rain delay at the 1976 Indianapolis 500. In the end the weather would help Johnny Rutherford to his second win in three years at the Speedway. (TYLER ALEXANDER COLLECTION)

roaring party in the back, led, of course, by one Mr. Hunt, the winner of the race. This was followed by a lively dinner at the hotel. A rollicking good time was had by all, though one wonders how many were able to remember it afterward!

James then closed down on Lauda's lead in the championship even further by winning at Watkins Glen to set up that much-talked-about final race in Japan. It rained heavily as it can only at Mount Fuji, and Lauda pulled out, saying it was too dangerous.

I was not there, but Niki's comments to me later (when he was racing for McLaren), about driving the car with your head, explain to me, anyway, why he decided to stop in the rain at Mount Fuji. The driving conditions and terrible visibility made it too much of a calculated risk to continue. Being alive was the important part.

All James had to do was finish in the top three to clinch the championship, but, with the track starting to dry, and the left front tire shredded because of the drying, James was forced into the pits. It was considered a pretty good performance in those days when the guys changed all four tires in 27 seconds. James rejoined in fifth, and in the final five laps got himself back to third, enough to win the championship from Lauda by just one point.

The Indy program saw some further updates made to the 1975 car, now designated an M16E. When we started practice at Indianapolis, we were quickest almost every day. Qualifying morning practice saw a couple of front anti-rollbar changes, with JR helping to speed up the change by telling us on the radio what he wanted while coming down the pit lane. The car stayed well balanced for qualifying, and JR had another pole position.

The race in the early stages was another battle with Mr. Foyt. We had used up most of the high-stagger sets of tires in an effort to balance the car. As ever, this was meant to make the car more evenly balanced while trying to keep the best set for the last pit stop and the real shoot-out at the end. Just after halfway we were leading A. J. when he had a problem with his front anti-rollbar, which was either broken or had come loose. At this point, it started to rain and the race was stopped.

While we were standing around in the pit lane waiting for the track to dry, Foyt, in one of his usual belligerent attacks, told me we were cheating on the exit of the pit lane. (I think this involved a new rule that had to do with coming back onto the track either before or after turn two.) I pointed out to A. J. that Bill Smith Jr.—our spotter, who was up in the top of the turn one grandstand—had told me on the radio that we were not doing anything different than Foyt was! End of interesting and intimidating conversation.

It was late in the day when the cars were lined up in the pit lane in the order they had been in when the race was stopped. The jet engine hot-air blowers had helped to dry the track, so it seemed the race could be restarted. But at the moment Dennis Davis plugged in the starter motor and pressed the button, the blackest storm clouds seen in a long time rolled over the top of the front-straight grandstands and dumped very large amounts of rain on us. It looked like this would go on for quite a while. It wasn't long before USAC said the race was over because there would not be enough time to dry the track before it got dark—although it seemed like it was already dark in any case because of the storm.

Not really believing what we had heard, I told the guys to wait until they came to get us. A couple of us just sat in this river of water coming down the pit lane until an official came over and said, "Yes, you have won the race, so please take the car to Victory Circle." A. J. was quite pissed-off, as he had been able to fix his broken front anti-rollbar problem while we waited for the track to dry up. Not a bad three-year run at Indy: From 1974 through 1976 we'd finished P1-P2-P1.

After the race, we had a problem with Dennis Davis. It was all about a pickup truck that we had won at Indy, which Dennis believed was going to be given to him. (I didn't know what this was about; it could have been something he had arranged with Teddy. All I could do was tell Dennis to talk to Teddy about it.) Dennis didn't get his pickup truck and, like a Jack Russell terrier, he would not let up about it. It got to the point where I felt I needed to ask him to go back to England and work at the factory. It turned out to be a grave mistake on my part.

Having won the next-to-last race in Texas, we went straight over to Phoenix, where we were able to work in Mirage team owner Harley Cluxton III's facility to prepare the two cars for the final round on the one-mile oval to the west of the city of Phoenix. Harley was very kind to give us more than adequate space, which was much appreciated.

We were running okay in the race and were in a position to win the championship when a hose fitting to the turbo came loose and pissed out a great deal of oil. The hose had been off when the gearbox was removed the night before to check the clutch, and it had not been tightened correctly. I don't think that would've happened if Dennis had been there. It still pisses me off when I think about it. I'm really sorry, JR. We finished second in the USAC Championship again after Johnny added wins at Trenton and Texas World Speedway to the Indy 500 victory.

# 1977–78: McLaren Engines, a Cosworth Turbo, and BMW

During the latter part of 1976, we were starting to look at having a turbocharged version of the Cosworth DFV engine for Indianapolis. Others were already going down this road, among them, Parnelli Jones's guys in California, with the help of John Barnard, I believe. Gordon Coppuck and the guys back at Colnbrook were doing a prototype M24, which was an M23 Formula One car with a variety of modifications that we would use for track-testing the engine.

Gary Knutson and I, along with a few other guys at McLaren Engines in Livonia, set about finding ways to get more cooling for the engine—particularly the cylinder heads—with a focus on the valve-seat area. Teddy had sent us over a couple of old F1 DFVs to start with. One of the first things we did was to make a water-flow test rig with an engine block, a left-hand cylinder head, a water-flow meter, a sensor to measure the water pump rpms, and an electric motor to run the water pump.

The engine had a separate water system for each side of the V8, so it made things easier to do just one set of test bits. We were interested in increasing the flow of water. To do that, we bought several different water pump impellers from a large used-car parts place on

Teddy Mayer and I compare notes during practice for the 1977 Indianapolis 500. That year Johnny Rutherford started 17th and dropped out with gearbox problems on the 12th lap. (LAT PHOTOGRAPHIC)

Eight Mile Road, just down from the workshop. The guy behind the counter was somewhat bewildered when we showed up with a set of vernier calipers. When we said we wanted to buy some water-pump impellers, he naturally wanted to know what car they were for.

In the end, he let us go into the vast warehouse and choose some that we could modify. Several shapes and sizes later, we machined three standard water-pump housings to take a bigger-diameter impeller; a Studebaker impeller worked best, and gave us a place to start.

One of the things we learned early on was that by cleaning up all the sharp edges we could get at in the water-flow passages of both the cylinder head and the block, we were able to improve the water flow and get rid of air in the system. You could plainly see the difference through the clear pipes we had put on the test rig. There were people much later on who would ignorantly and emphatically dismiss this approach for both the water and fuel systems, but after all, it's just physics, really.

There were several problems we had to deal with, the main ones being the exhaust-valve seats and the pistons. It took us a while to sort out the exhaust-valve seats. We were getting part-machined cylinder heads from Cosworth through John Nicholson at Nicholson McLaren Engines in England, which had been established in 1972 to maintain Cosworth's engines for the F1 team. Graham Bartells (the Rabbit) was machining the finishing on the valve-seat bores and installing the valve seats, which were cooled down with methanol and dry ice to shrink them a bit for the installation. The problem was, the exhaust seats were sinking in the cylinder heads. I'm not sure why we didn't twig what was going on. It really shouldn't have taken us as long as it did.

At the same time, we were also doing a turbo engine program for BMW's 320 International Motor Sports Association (IMSA) car—and yet we had no problems with the exhaust seats in the BMW cylinder heads. Something we should have done straightaway was to compare the hardness of the material in the Cosworth and BMW cylinder heads. The BMW heads were 120 on the Brinell scale, but the fucking Cosworth heads were only 95 to 98. I guess the mistake we made was taking it for granted that the Cosworths would be as good as that company's reputation. We would learn something even more important on that subject much later on.

The second main problem was the piston. This turned out to be too heavy, causing the engine to vibrate too much. This also caused a third problem of cracked exhaust pipes, which occurred mainly at the 500-mile races, one of which was of course Indianapolis. I hate to think how many sets of exhaust pipes I welded up out of a variety of types of stainless steel, but we still had problems.

After much trouble and strife and a fair bit of dyno work and track-testing to get the oil system to work correctly, along with the Hilborn fuel system, we went to the first race at Ontario, the 2.5-mile oval just outside Los Angeles. We had also sold one of the cars and an engine to Roger Penske's team.

JR qualified on pole but missed a gear at the start of the race and over-revved the engine. That summed up the season. Rutherford qualified on pole five times and won three short-track events, but he didn't do well in the 500-mile races. This was due to engine trouble in the California 500 and time lost changing an exhaust manifold at Pocono. A. J. Foyt won his fourth Indy 500, but Tom Sneva took the championship in Penske's McLaren-Cosworth. It was a big disappointment to know that our own reliability issues had allowed our customer to beat us for the Championship. The result was a general feeling of being pissed-off.

There was an amusing incident at the race in Phoenix. Well, perhaps it wasn't that amusing at the time. JR won and had lapped pretty much everybody, and;after the race the good Mr. Foyt, who had finished second, came to pay us a visit. He grabbed my shirt and almost lifted me off the ground, yelling, "Why don't you damn Limeys go back to England!" I said something to the effect of, "Piss off! I'm from Boston!" With a somewhat-puzzled look, A. J. let go of me and stormed off in the opposite direction. Guess he didn't like being beaten very much.

Milwaukee was one of the races we won, and I remember that on the second or third lap, JR passed Bobby Unser around the outside between turns one and two, with the engine going *pop-pop-pop* while running on about seven and a half cylinders. It did this for most of the race because of a small water leak in the cylinder head beside one of the spark plugs. I remember Bobby telling me afterwards that he could hear this strange noise, and then he saw JR just driving around outside of him in turn one, which he didn't think was possible. I guess he underestimated JR once in a while, not to mention the car, which was pretty good, too.

It was a bit of a mixed year in Formula One. The new 1977 car, the M26, took a while to develop, and we relied—for a fifth season!—on the M23 for the first few races. James Hunt won at Silverstone in the M26 and again at Watkins Glen. But it all went wrong at the next race in Canada, when James, leading at the time, came up to lap Jochen Mass, running third in the other M26, and they managed to collide. James wasn't impressed—and neither was the marshal he thumped as the poor guy came to help him away from the wrecked car.

Waiting in the pits with Johnny Rutherford and the rest of the McLaren crew at Mosport in July 1977. (LAT PHOTOGRAPHIC)

Hunt and Mass finished fifth and sixth in the championship, with McLaren third—just two points behind Lotus and some distance behind Ferrari—in the Constructors championship.

As 1978 began, Phil Sharp, Steve Roby (Abo), Keith Devereaux (Wombat), and Neil Pennell were now the key guys on the Indy team, looking after the race car and the spare one. The M24 had some minor mods, and we had a better understanding of the engine, although the heavy pistons and resulting vibrations were still causing an exhaust-pipe problem some of the time.

The first race was at Phoenix, where JR qualified fifth but didn't finish due to an engine-related problem.

We spent quite a bit of time and effort preparing a special qualifying engine for Indianapolis. It had slightly different cams and bigger-diameter exhaust pipes. On the dyno it produced 840 to 850 hp at 80 inches of boost pressure—the maximum allowed under the rules, and a reasonable amount of horsepower over the regular engine.

What followed next were three major screw-ups. We were quickest most days of practice with a standard spec engine and only using 75 to 76 inches of boost, so we had a reasonable amount of performance in hand. We fitted the qualifying engine and ran a few laps at 75 to 76 inches of boost before planning to run at 80 inches to check everything. To hide our true speed (a practice known as sandbagging), we were only going to turn it up to the 80 inches maximum for half a lap. That was our first screw-up. Johnny was not keen on this, as it would upset his rhythm; he said he was not worried about the extra power for qualifying. You had to remember that JR was very good around Indy, so I agreed, along with the boys, who were always kept informed.

Our intended plan was to be the first to qualify at an average speed over 200 mph, which we felt was possible based on our practice times and 76 inches of boost with a normal race engine. When JR went out to qualify and got up to speed, he came on the radio and said he only had 76 inches of boost and yet was managing 198- to 199-mph laps. So (second screw-up), I waved him off and we aborted the run before completing the four laps of qualifying. Not understanding what the problem was, and with not much time to go out again, we used the spare car, which had a magneto wire problem. So much for the best-laid plans.

We spent a long time that Saturday night going through everything. We found (third screw-up) a tiny flap of Teflon in the fitting of the Aeroquip hose attached to the boost-pressure adjuster valve. It only seemed to move and then block off the air supply when more than 76 inches of pressure was demanded. At this point "Not Cleverest of the Year" Awards were duly handed out! Still, one mustn't forget that the Indianapolis is a 500-mile race, and just being in it is the first major thing to remember. This is something that would come up again some years later.

To make matters even worse, if we had completed the four-lap run, we would have been on the front row of the grid. Dear, oh dear. I still feel a sickening twinge as I remember and write this part of the story. As it was, JR qualified 4th and went on to finish 13th due to more problems with the engine. Wins at Michigan and Phoenix and a bunch of second places were not enough to help JR finish beyond 4th in the championship.

Late in 1977, we (Teddy, Bill Smith Jr., and I) had started McLaren North America to run and operate an IMSA program with BMW's motorsports group. This was run by Jochen Neerpasch, a really great guy to work with. The aim was to develop and race a 2.0-liter turbo engine in a saloon car. When we were sorting out the early details of the program, Teddy and I met up with Jochen in New York City and took him to the Palm Restaurant on 42nd Street. He wasn't sure what kind of a place we had brought him to, as there was sawdust on the floor and no menus. The nice old waiters just asked what you wanted to eat. When the delicious dinner came, it didn't take Jochen long to change his mind about first impressions.

David Hobbs was hired to drive in all the races and do most of the testing, with Ronnie Peterson joining for the long-distance events, and our engine builder from McLaren Engines, Tom Klauser, acting as test and sometimes race driver.

Roger Bailey was recruited back from England to be the team manager, and Wiley McCoy was brought in to be in charge of the engine program; not an easy task for either of them, to say the least. Years later, Wiley led the group of employees that would buy McLaren Engines.

The IMSA program involved First National City Travelers Checks, which was run by Citicorp's Fred Stecker and was already on board with our Indy team. When Bill Smith Jr. and I went to New York for meetings with Mr. Stecker, we would usually end up at the Palm Restaurant for lunch—liquid for some, and steaks for others. It was Fred Stecker who got them to paint a layout of the Indianapolis race track, along with our names, on the ceiling of the upstairs dining room; it stayed there for a long time.

The car and all parts were supplied by BMW, with the engine development and installation delegated to McLaren North America and a good bunch of guys we had found to work under Roger Bailey. The engine was a big part of the project; a lot of development work was required to convert the normally aspirated four-cylinder engine to a turbocharged one.

We built one race car and a spare. They were painted in white with blue and red trim—standard BMW colors that looked very smart. A notable exception was when Jochen had artist Frank Stella prepare a one-off modern art design as part of BMW's Art Car series. Stella's livery involved a design of French curve shapes on what looked like graph paper covering the car, which was great. Stella had come to several races with us to see what this racing thing was all about.

The completed IMSA car and engine were not bad, although there were some reliability problems, mostly with the engine or the turbo, and mainly in the long-distance races. Trying to compete with the fully developed turbo Porsches was very difficult indeed.

The Indy team and the IMSA team were in a separate part of McLaren Engines, with a fire door between the two. This was just as well, for reasons you'll quickly understand.

Earlier, the BMW motor home in Germany had had its windscreen broken. Since the motor home was from the United States, we purchased another windscreen, but it was broken in shipment. Another windscreen was bought and boxed up, this time with expandable foam. The wooden box was packed and pushed against the office wall in order to clear the entrance to the workshop for the BMW team, due back from a race very late that night.

That same night the guys at the workshop had gone across the street for something to eat. When they came out of the restaurant, there was a nice dull glow from part of the roof of the building where McLaren Engines was located. The fire had started because of a chemical reaction. The packing foam had not finished hardening when the box was sealed, and got hot enough to catch on fire. The fire had gone up the office wall and set alight a bunch of tires and other things that were stored there. The heat and fumes from the tires caused the most damage, right down to about four or five feet off the floor. The telephone on the wall in the workshop looked like it was from a Salvador Dalí painting, and the lower half of the Indy cars, which were on high stands, had turned a strange color that matched the height of the toxic sulfur cloud from the burning tires.

With a couple of weeks' break in the Indy car series, my friend and I had taken a week off to go to Bermuda, stopping in Hingham to say hello to my parents on the way back to Detroit. Soon after I got there came a phone call from the engine shop, which is when I first found out about the fire. Aarrgh!

It was fortunate that we were able to get some space for the Indy and IMSA cars in other units in the building. Even more fortunate was that fire door between the race team unit and the engine unit. There were ozone machines running for weeks after the repairs and painting were finished to reduce the odors from the fire. BMW did get their motor home windscreen on the third attempt, and the IMSA cars got back late enough to miss the fire. There were a lot of things damaged in the blaze, of course, but, fortunately, most of them were not current parts, and those that were damaged mostly required nothing more than repainting. The sulfur fumes caused the worst damage by corroding a lot of metal things in the building, along with some of the guys' tools.

Jochen also wanted Wiley and his guys to prepare a 1.5-liter turbocharged engine. In the short amount of time available, and using the parts that we actually had on hand, Wiley was able to do a 1.6-liter engine, which turned out very well under the circumstances. This was put into the spare car for Tom Klauser and run at the Mid-Ohio IMSA race, where it was not slow. The proper 1.5-liter version never ran as competitively, and in the end we ran out of development time. One related note: John Baldwin, one of the McLaren design engineers back at the factory, had done a Formula One car layout for the 1.5-liter turbo engine.

I believe that Wiley's work on the project was the start of BMW's own successful 1.5-liter turbo Formula One engine, which would be used by Brabham and other teams in the 1980s.

Things were much worse in Formula One when the M26, which was never on the pace, was completely blown away (along with everyone else) by Colin Chapman's ground-effects Lotus 79. Mario Andretti became the first American driver since Phil Hill in 1961 to win the World Championship. McLaren's relationship with James Hunt gradually went off the boil, and Mario's Lotus teammate, Ronnie Peterson, was signed for 1979. Unfortunately, he never got that far. Ronnie died in a hospital from injuries sustained during a multicar crash at the start of the Monza GP in September 1978.

Driving the McLaren BMW 320, David Hobbs won IMSA's 100-mile Camel GT Challenge race at Mid-Ohio in June 1977. (BOB HARMEYER)

Roger Penske and Dan Gurney may be discussing CART strategy in this photo from the Twin Dixie 250 at Atlanta Motor Speedway in April 1979. Johnny Rutherford won both races in the two-part event—his only wins of the season. (BOB HARMEYER)

# 1979–80: Launching CART, and a New Era at McLaren

**M**eanwhile, on the other side of the Atlantic, there was growing unhappiness about how Indy car racing was being run. Attendance at many races was low, prize money was often inadequate, and television coverage was limited, among other things. McLaren and other teams were getting frustrated with the United States Auto Club (USAC) and felt that we should try to do something ourselves.

Early in 1978, Dan Gurney wrote what came to be known as the "Gurney White Paper." This would become the blueprint for a new organization, Championship Auto Racing Teams (CART). Gurney took his inspiration from the improvements Bernie Ecclestone had forced upon Formula One with his creation of the Formula One Constructors' Association (FOCA). The White Paper called for the owners to form CART as an advocacy group to promote USAC's national championship, doing the job where the sanctioning body would not. The group would also work to negotiate television rights and race purses, and ideally hold seats on USAC's governing body.

The proposal was rejected by USAC's board in November 1978. USAC's rejection led to the formation of CART as an alternate sanctioning body under the principles laid out in the

Gurney White Paper. The newness of the organization, however, prevented it from being recognized by the Automobile Competition Committee for the United States (ACCUS), the American arm of the Fédération Internationale de l'Automobile (FIA), the international motor racing organization. An arrangement was reached whereby the Sports Car Club of America (SCCA) would act as the sanctioning body for the new series. This would allow the events to be listed on the International Motorsports Calendar.

I'm not sure that Dan Gurney was actually the leader of the group. He was perhaps more of an instigator, promoting the action that followed his initiative. Dan was probably not the only one who helped some of us to believe we could achieve something, but he certainly set things in motion with the stuff he had written during 1978. We had a good group of people who certainly knew it was going to be a tough struggle.

One of the major things going for us was that a number of people in our group had control over several of the race tracks that we raced on, which gave us a leveraged start in setting up the series. Jim Hall and I were delegated to sort out a rulebook, while the others did various aspects of setting up CART. The directors were Roger Penske, Pat Patrick, Dan Gurney, Jim Hall, Bob Fletcher, and I, with each of us representing the teams that were actually racing.

Roger Penske and Pat Patrick's people played a big part in establishing the organization, along with the help and enthusiasm of other teams that were going to join us. There were many meetings to attend in a variety of places, and it helped that I was often able to fly with Pat Patrick in one of his two Learjets. One of the planes had normal seats, but the other only had two seats; the rest of the floor was covered with plywood. The plane was on call 24/7 with a couple of Detroit car companies for the emergency delivery of small car parts that were about to run out on assembly lines in various parts of the United States.

We had been trying for several months to get A. J. Foyt to join us in CART. Predictably, it was a long, hard struggle. At one meeting in Phoenix, A. J. took a gun out of his briefcase and calmly put it on the table. We told him he could put his gun away, as we wanted him with us and we'd come to talk, not to shoot one another! Foyt did join us initially, but then with no warning, he suddenly went back to USAC, which of course welcomed him with open arms. A. J. subsequently won the 1979 USAC Championship, which wasn't much of a surprise because he had virtually no opposition.

The nasty bit came when the directors of CART submitted our entry forms for the 1979 Indianapolis 500. We were told by Indianapolis and USAC that our entries would not be accepted.

Roger Penske had a lawyer by the name of John Frasco working for him in Detroit. Frasco was summoned to have a look at what was going on and come up with a plan. He made contact with a very good law firm in Indianapolis who would help represent us when arguing our case in the federal court in Indianapolis.

It was a hard few days, especially for those of us who were used to talking and giving instructions rather than just sitting there, not saying anything at all and just passing notes between us. Each evening, some of us would go to St. Elmo Steak House for dinner and then to the law firm's office to go over what had happened during that day, and what we would consider doing the following day. We usually finished quite late. H. W. Smith Jr., who was a business partner and friend of Teddy Mayer's and mine, was there with me, and was as usual a great help.

The Indianapolis Speedway lawyers were going to argue that it didn't matter if we participated in the race, because our drivers could always drive someone else's car instead of one from a CART team. At this point, John Frasco realized that he needed to put a couple of our drivers on the witness stand. The drivers told the judge and the rest of the courtroom that they were not really interested in driving someone else's car—a car that they didn't know anything about. As drivers, they relied on the people and the cars from their own teams, pointing out in particular how dangerous racing could be, and how much they trusted the people they had been working with for some time. It was a good move on John's part, and the judge took this on board. The drivers who would be affected by the Indianapolis Motor Speedway not accepting our entries were Wally Dallenbach, Al Unser Sr., Johnny Rutherford, Rick Mears, Bobby Unser, Mike Mosley, and Steve Krisiloff. Johnny Rutherford and Al Unser Sr. were the only ones that Frasco put on the witness stand.

There were a few slanging matches on both sides, one in particular involving Pat Patrick, who was alleged to have said some inappropriate things about USAC on a tape brought into court by one of the teams that had not joined CART. Pat was put on the witness stand and questioned by the opposition's top lawyer for more than half an hour about this alleged indiscretion. Pat sat there throughout, calmly chewing on some hard candy and answering each question with pretty much the same answer, "Well, that sounds like something I would like to have said, but I'm sorry I can't recall ever saying it." In the end, the Speedway's lawyer threw up both hands, gave up, and sat down. That night at St. Elmo Steak House, Dan Gurney reckoned that if Pat Patrick had been H. R. Haldeman, Richard Nixon would still have been president.

On the final day, the federal judge found that the CART teams should be allowed to race in the 1979 Indianapolis 500, noting that the harm caused to us and our sponsors by not being allowed to race there was far greater than any harm that might be caused to the Speedway by letting us race.

With a deadpan face and cold stare, the judge told the six of us that we were not to cause any trouble while we were at the Indianapolis Motor Speedway, or he might reconsider things!

The Indy 500 turned out to be a triumph for CART, as our cars dominated, although it wasn't so great for McLaren, with JR spending 30 laps in the pits with gearbox trouble. The M24 was showing its age by now. Johnny won both parts of an early-season "twin race" at Atlanta, but nothing else. He finished fourth in the series, with half as many points as the 1979 champion, Rick Mears in a Penske. In the end, CART staged 10 of their own events, with USAC running just 7, down from 18 in 1978.

The McLaren Indy car program was closed down by Teddy at the end of 1979. We didn't have a suitable sponsor that would allow us to do a good job. Teddy and the company needed to concentrate on the Formula One effort, which was not going particularly well at the time. There was a lot of pressure to try and fix this problem.

The ground-effects era of Formula One had been started by Chapman's Lotus 79 in 1978, and I don't think there was a very good understanding of ground effects at the time in the Colnbrook factory. Mario Andretti, who had been actively involved in Lotus's development efforts, won the World Championship that year. At the end of 1978, McLaren's latest F1 car, the M28, was sent to Watkins Glen for a test. It seems that when the car was jacked up on the right front, the left front just stayed on the ground! Not an impressive display of chassis rigidity. Alastair Caldwell, now the McLaren F1 team manager, more or less told the crew to put the M28 back in the crate and send it back to England. It was a shame for all those who had worked very hard to build the car, but it just wasn't very good. In fact, Teddy would eventually call it, "Ghastly. . .a disaster. . . quite diabolical."

The car was too big, overweight, and aerodynamically poor. By the time the Monaco Grand Prix came around in May, McLaren was already on the "C" version of the M28, having modified just about everything from track, to wheelbase, to bodywork. It was no surprise that when the M29, a completely new car, was rushed through in time for the British Grand Prix in July, John Watson (who had replaced James Hunt) finished fourth. At the end of the season, Watson was ninth in the championship, but his teammate, Patrick Tambay, scored no points at all.

With mechanic Robin Day before the 1980 Austrian Grand Prix. Our worried expressions may have something to do with the underperforming McLaren M29. (LAT PHOTOGRAPHIC)

With John Watson and Teddy Mayer at Monaco in 1980, the last year for the original McLaren team. New management would be brought in to turn things around in Formula One. (LAT PHOTOGRAPHIC)

The 1979 Indy 500 was the first in which a pace car was used during caution periods. McLaren's last visit to the 500 was a disappointment, with Johnny Rutherford starting 8th and finishing 18th. (LAT PHOTOGRAPHIC)

There was an F1 test at Paul Ricard in the fall of 1979, which saw Alain Prost's first drive in the McLaren. Watson had done a few laps to make sure everything was okay, and then Prost was given the chance to drive. I'm not sure exactly how many laps he did, but he was a reasonable amount quicker than John. When he came into the pits, Teddy had his clipboard ready. Prost thought it was the timing sheets to look at; it was actually a contract that Teddy wanted him to sign!

So for 1980 Alain Prost replaced Patrick Tambay and immediately made his mark by taking sixth in his first grand prix in Argentina, followed by fifth in Brazil—both times ahead of his teammate John Watson. Having booked my trip before I knew I would be heading back to England, I went to Buenos Aires via Hawaii, Los Angeles, and Miami.

Now that I was moving back to England, I needed to sell my shares in Nicholson McLaren Engines to John Nicholson, in order to help buy my town house in Surrey.

Because there were two weeks between the races in South America, the team and quite a few other people after arriving in Sao Paulo went over to Guarujá, a very nice place on the ocean. Keith Botsford from the *Sunday Times* newspaper found this great restaurant in the jungle. The place was made of basic cinder blocks with a corrugated tin roof, along with naked lightbulbs hanging from bits of wire. The first night we went there with Keith, who spoke Portuguese; he had them bake a very large and freshly caught sea bass in their makeshift oven. It was very, very good.

Paddy McNally from Marlboro organized a dinner party for the team in this restaurant one night; I think it was Alain Prost's birthday, or near it. As we sat at our tables having snacks and a few glasses of good Portuguese wine, all the lights went out. Everyone thought, "So much for Paddy's dinner party." But it was actually done to add greater effect to the waiters bringing flaming platters of seafood to the tables. What really great food, and in such a simple place in the middle of the jungle.

Interlagos at Sao Paulo was quite a stunning and very fast circuit. But the worst feature of the place was a disgusting loo that team personnel were supposed to use. It was so bad that someone who shall remain nameless spray-painted in large letters on the wall "This is the worst shit house in the world." This was painted over the next day, only for the message to reappear that night.

This went on for several days until a fire truck came and hosed the place out—very handy! We tried to use the loo in the medical building whenever we could.

When a suspension failure on the M29C threw Alain Prost off the road at the next race at Kyalami he had to go to the medical building. He had sustained a broken wrist, which meant Alain had to miss this race and the next one at Long Beach, California. It wasn't a great season, and the introduction of the M30, which Prost raced for the first time at the Dutch Grand Prix in August, didn't help. Alain finished 6th at Zandvoort, and that would be the only point the M30 would ever score. John Watson didn't have much better luck struggling on with the M29C. In the end, Watson and Prost were 11th and 16th in the Drivers championship, and McLaren a joint 7th among the constructors.

It was pretty clear something had to be done, as we were just not getting anywhere with the design of the car. At the end of 1980, Marlboro's John Hogan set up the merger between Ron Dennis's Project Four Racing and McLaren to become McLaren International. Hogan had previously worked with Ron and Neil Trundle on their Rondel Formula 2 team. At the new McLaren, Ron Dennis, John Barnard, and Teddy Mayer would be the directors and I would be the team manager. This was Marlboro's way of doing it.

Teddy did tell me this was going to happen; he said it was one way to keep the McLaren name in business. It certainly didn't feel right, but on the other hand, the place needed some new people. John Barnard, the designer who had been at McLaren in the early 1970s, returned, along with engineers Steve Nichols and Alan Jenkins. John was in charge of design and a lot of other things. So, the first stages of work on a chassis built out of carbon fiber began, with help from Hercules Aerospace in the United States.

With this going on, it was time for our current chief designer Gordon Coppuck to depart and join Robin Herd at March Engineering.

The McLaren people were glad to still have jobs. In general terms, things were working out okay from my point of view, as long as I could deal with the three rather large egos of Ron Dennis, John Barnard, and Teddy Mayer. I just hoped that relations between the four new partners would not reach the point of causing damage to the business.

Ron Dennis (center) meets with Teddy Mayer before the Canadian Grand Prix in September 1980. By the end of the year Teddy and I would become partners with Ron and John Barnard in the new McLaren International team. (LAT PHOTOGRAPHIC)

# 1981: McLaren International

**W**ork had started on a brand-new car for the 1981 season, to be known as the MP4/1, which was the first use of the new MP4 designation. But in the meantime we had to persevere with the 1980 car, now known as the M29F after further modifications. January started off with an attempted test with John Watson in the car at Donington. There was rain, ice, and more rain. I always did wonder what the hell we were doing there at that time of year.

Andrea de Cesaris, who leveraged his Marlboro connections in Italy, now had the drive alongside Watson on the new McLaren International team. Prost, after being let down more than once with the unreliable M30, had left to go to Renault, taking with him the Elf fuel and oil company, which, according to Teddy, still owed McLaren Racing sponsorship funds.

The first race of 1981 was at Kyalami. This turned out to be a non-championship event because of a fight for power and control between most of the teams, who had organized as the Formula One Constructors' Association (FOCA) and the sport's governing body, Fédération Internationale du Sport Automobile (FISA), a subcommittee of the FIA. In South Africa the two groups were basically at a standoff, with FOCA hoping to show that they could go ahead and hold a race without FISA or the teams that still supported it—Ferrari,

Renault, Ligier, and Alfa Romeo.

When we got to Johannesburg, I had a chance first thing one morning to see a sports doctor who had been recommended to fix my "tennis elbow." When I arrived at the race track a bit later, George Langhorne, who was (and still is) in charge of the McLaren race-car painting department, asked why I was such a strange color of gray. I guess it was a side effect of the cortisone shots, but my left elbow has never bothered me since.

The race started in wet conditions but the track dried out quickly. Watson went well in the damp, but a stop to change to slicks lost us ground to the drivers who had gambled by running slicks from the start. Wattie eventually finished fifth, while de Cesaris spun off.

Agreement between FISA and FOCA was reached just 10 days before the opening round of the 1981 championship at Long Beach, California. Sliding skirts, which had been favored by the FOCA teams and were the catalyst for the trouble, were banned.

John Barnard's MP4/1 was taken to Long Beach for promotional duties only because it was not yet a proper running car. This was the first carbon-fiber chassis and a big step forward for F1 safety—although at the time, safety was probably not the main reason for using carbon fiber. From a competitive standpoint, greater stiffness and lighter weight were the major benefits. Nevertheless, I believe that John's contribution to safety proved to be a lot more significant than anyone realized at the time. Meanwhile, the struggle with the M29F continued, with de Cesaris colliding with Prost on the first lap of the United States Grand Prix West and Watson going out with engine failure.

By the time we got to Brazil for the second round at Rio de Janeiro, Brabham had fitted their cars with clever hydropneumatic ride-height lowering technology, which sidestepped the ban on skirts. The spirit of the all-new Concorde Agreement was soon forgotten—ironically by the same man, Bernie Ecclestone, who was then owner of Brabham. Ultimately he would stand to gain most from the agreement, and continues to benefit to this very day. But back then the other teams immediately followed Brabham's lead, adding similar technology that made just about every car on the grid during the entire 1981 season illegal.

Two weeks later, we had one MP4/1 ready for Watson to race in Buenos Aires. The exhaust pipes were oval-shaped, and I do remember Phil Sharp and I welding up the cracked tailpipes each night in a tiny little workshop with a dirt floor over at the airport. Some vibration or other really didn't like the oval shape. Trying to weld with a Heli arc machine that had no foot control was more than a small challenge for those of us dealing with the thin-wall tailpipes.

Marlboro
ritish Grand Prix

John Watson celebrates his first victory in five years at the 1981 British Grand Prix at Silverstone. It was the first victory for the new McLaren MP4/1, and a hint of better things to come. (LAT PHOTOGRAPHIC)

Ron Dennis and I look on from the left as photographers scrutinize the McLaren MP4/1 at its 1981 debut. The carbon-fiber monocoque designed by John Barnard would have a lasting impact on speed and safety. (LAT PHOTOGRAPHIC)

We lost a lot of time on the first day of practice chasing a handling problem that was eventually traced to a faulty shock absorber. Watson qualified 11th, with de Cesaris regularly bringing his M29F back to the pits stuffed with grass as he tried to qualify the thing higher than 18th. Watson ran 7th before retiring with a transmission problem. It was a reasonably encouraging start for MP4/1, the first in a long line of MP4 cars.

It seems there are many people today, including at McLaren, who think the M in MP4 was for Marlboro; where they got this idea is beyond me. The M was for McLaren, and still is. Marlboro was the sponsor and partner, and P4 was from Ron's previous Project Four company.

When we went into the European season at Imola, Watson qualified 7th for the San Marino Grand Prix. He was in 6th place early on and pushing Rene Arnoux when he went into the back of the Renault, braking for a chicane. By the time we got him back out with a new nose, he had to climb from the back of the field to finish 10th.

Zolder showed even more promise when Wattie qualified fifth and was running in fourth place until gearbox trouble near the end of the Belgian Grand Prix dropped him out of the points and into seventh.

We had a second MP4/1 ready for de Cesaris in time for Monaco, the pair of them qualifying in the middle of the grid. De Cesaris went out on the first lap after colliding with Prost once more, but Wattie was looking good in fifth place when gearbox trouble ended his race.

Now Watson was starting a bit of a roll as he qualified fourth at Jarama and finished the Spanish Grand in third place. Two weeks later in France, he started from the front row and finished second. The Dijon circuit suited our new car: de Cesaris put his MP4/1 on the third row and finished 11th after a pit stop to have a wheel nut tightened. Afterward Marlboro organized a great dinner for us in a barn that was part of an old château. I remember walking through a muddy field with Paddy McNally and Sarah Ferguson, his "friend" at the time, as we looked for our car. (Sarah, of course, would later marry Prince Andrew, Duke of York, and become the Duchess of York.)

The momentum continued into the British Grand Prix, as Wattie and Andrea were reasonably quick and qualified fifth and sixth, with de Cesaris being quicker than Watson during some of practice. This wasn't bad when you consider that the grid on this quick track was made up of both turbo and non-turbo cars, and that the MP4 was one of the latter.

I spent quite a lot of time talking to Andrea about staying away from Wattie for the first few laps to avoid having a mishap with him. By the time they got to Woodcote Corner at the end of the fourth lap, Andrea was very close to Wattie, who suddenly slowed to try and avoid an accident among the leaders at the chicane. Andrea didn't see the trouble up ahead. When de Cesaris moved left to avoid Wattie, he looked up and went straight into the barriers! So much for my chat before the start of the race.

Watson, meanwhile, had come to a standstill but had managed to avoid contact. Once he got clear of the shunt, Wattie drove a quick, sensible race and got up to third place. When there were problems with the two cars in front, Wattie outlasted them both to win the race—the first victory for the MP4/1, and the third good race finish in a row for Wattie. It was a great effort from everyone on the team and at the factory, along with a very pleased Mr. Barnard and Mr. Dennis.

I don't know why, but some people had thought Ron Dennis and his people would take away the feeling of being competitive again for some of us, but this wasn't the case for me and the other hardworking members of the whole team, that's for sure. I guess what they probably meant (or thought) was that Ron and John Barnard would take all the credit. Say whatever the hell you want, but with the MP4/1, a much better car was built and raced than what we'd had before. The world of motor racing is not always easy to deal with.

Moving on to Germany, Wattie qualified ninth and finished sixth, while Andrea crashed in the race. De Cesaris crashing was something we were becoming used to. When we got to Zandvoort for the Dutch Grand Prix, the drivers were warned about some nasty bumps in the braking area at the end of the long main straight. The car would jump about and could lose downforce due to the plastic skirts losing direct contact with the track. Andrea had several shunts in practice, and the one doing the most damage was set off by the bumps at the end of the straight. He had qualified 13th, but after the last shunt in practice he was withdrawn at Teddy's request because there was only one spare MP4/1 that could be used.

Because the season so far had seen a string of shunts, it was probably the right thing to do. I thought so as well, but stayed out of the way. Some people didn't think so, but that view was most likely attributable to political reasons.

It got even worse at Monza after Robin Day, the number-one mechanic on Andrea's car, and his guys (along with our McLaren factory people) had rebuilt the Zandvoort car. Unfortunately Andrea promptly took one whole side off the car early in practice for the Italian Grand Prix. The boys worked most of the night repairing the damage—only for de Cesaris to have another shunt the next day, at which point Robin sat on the floor in the corner of the garage, just about ready to cry. He and the guys then got stuck in to repair this latest damage.

Wattie qualified seventh but then had a big shunt at the second Lesmo corner during the race. The car broke in half, with the engine and gearbox bouncing across the track and down the road, Wattie doing the same thing in the chassis. John was not hurt in the shunt, demonstrating another big plus for the carbon chassis, and silencing the doubters who had said carbon fiber would collapse in a heap of black dust in the event of an accident. Hercules Aerospace, the company supplying the carbon material and a lot of the construction know-how, took the chassis, along with a video of the shunt, to show people just how strong and safe carbon fiber really was. Meanwhile, the good news was that Andrea brought his car home seventh, in one piece.

Watson made up for the Italian disappointment in Canada, where he did a great job coming from ninth on the grid to finish second, setting fastest lap, and avoiding the general chaos going on during a wet race. There were no points scored at the final round in Las Vegas, so I guess one of the highlights of the weekend for me was going to see Sammy Davis Jr. perform.

The other interesting thing that came out of that weekend was the rumor that Niki Lauda was coming to McLaren in 1982. I was sure as hell pleased when the story was confirmed after I got back to England. After a season fraught with shunts and learning about the new car, we were making good progress. Having Lauda back in Formula One and on board at McLaren could only be another positive development.

# 1982: With Lauda and Watson

Niki Lauda was the kind of no-bullshit guy you liked working with. His trainer, Willi Dungl, was the same sort of guy. Niki was to make his mark at McLaren even sooner than we expected, once we got to the first race of 1982.

At the races, Ron Dennis was looking after the sponsors, and when John Barnard let him, pretty much running the team. Ron and Teddy were generally okay, so long as you didn't look too closely. With John in overall charge of the race cars, I was doing the team manager job, as well as race-managing Niki's car. Teddy was continuing to look after John Watson's car, along with dealing with FIA issues and that sort of thing.

I spent a lot of time working with Steve Nichols on various things. We got along very well, and it probably helped that I knew Steve from Indy racing in the States when he was working for a shock absorber company. I had kind of hoped I would get to catch up with him again, somewhere, sometime later on.

We got to the first day of practice for the opening race of the season and Niki Lauda was waiting with a bus at the main gate of the Kyalami circuit. Niki and a number of other drivers were not happy about a clause in the latest FIA Super License agreement that required them to drive exclusively for the team they were currently contracted to. Without a Super

Alain Prost (left) makes a point as Niki Lauda and I listen during practice for the 1982 Brazilian Grand Prix. By that time Alain was winning for Renault, while Niki had come out of retirement to drive for McLaren. (LAT PHOTOGRAPHIC)

Niki Lauda, John Barnard, and John Watson at Long Beach in 1982. Niki would take the win there in the third race of his Formula One comeback with McLaren. (LAT PHOTOGRAPHIC)

License, drivers couldn't compete in Formula One. So Niki got all the drivers onto the bus and headed off to a hotel in Johannesburg where they locked themselves in a room and started negotiating with Jean-Marie Balestre, president of the FIA.

The team was not too pleased, and having Niki in charge made it a bit worse. This may have been the first race of his comeback, but Niki is not one to give up, so it was really a case of wait and see.

There was no running on the first day, Thursday, and the drivers bedded down for the night in the room while negotiations continued. There was an agreement of sorts on Friday, which meant we had one untimed practice session and then qualifying for Saturday's race. Luckily, most of the teams had been testing at Kyalami not long before, so we had a reasonable idea about setting up the cars.

Niki had a minor off which bent one of the lower-front wishbones during the practice session before qualifying. The boys got it changed just in time for Niki to qualify 13th, having missed a great deal of practice. For his F1 comeback Niki drove a typical race to gradually move through the field and finish fourth. After the race, Niki said something to me about not liking the plus and minus signs on the signal board. He also pointed out to me that he was driving as fast as the car would go. Okay, no problem. I learned later that if needed, he could drive the car a bit faster than it wanted to go.

Wattie, after qualifying ninth, had brake and handling problems and took the final point for sixth place. He was to do a lot better (on paper, at least) at the end of the next race in Brazil.

On the road in Rio John came home fourth, but the first two finishers—Nelson Piquet (Brabham) and Keke Rosberg (Williams) were later thrown out because officials ruled that the large water tanks in their cars were more like disposable ballast than a means of cooling the brakes, as the teams claimed. I think some of the water might have actually reached the brakes, but the debate was over whether the tanks could be refilled before final scrutineering. The rules may have permitted this, but they also said the cars should be at the 580kg minimum at all times during the race. When Piquet and Rosberg were excluded, Wattie moved up to second. It didn't help Niki, who had retired after being hit by Carlos Reutemann's Williams.

As soon as the cars took to the track for the next race at Long Beach, the drivers were complaining about the bumps on the street circuit. Normally we would keep the same engine in the car for both days of practice, but Niki wanted a fresh Ford-Cosworth DFV each night because he felt the bumps were making it bounce around on the rev-limiter. The extra work didn't please the boys very much, but the engine was changed each night.

Niki qualified second, but we were a bit concerned about Andrea de Cesaris after he had taken what would be his only F1 pole position in the Alfa Romeo. Before the race, Niki mentioned to me that he would wait for de Cesaris to shunt because trying to pass him could be a bit too risky!

In fact, Niki didn't make a good start and came around third behind de Cesaris and Rene Arnoux's Renault. In a classic piece of Lauda cool on the sixth lap, he saw the Alfa Romeo of Bruno Giacomelli coming much too fast in an attempt to take third under braking for the hairpin. Niki calmly moved to one side and watched the Alfa pile into the back of Arnoux! Niki then took the lead nine laps later when de Cesaris got caught in traffic. Andrea then lived up to Niki's prediction by having that shunt about halfway through the race.

So Niki managed to win the third race of his F1 comeback for McLaren International by driving a very controlled 75 laps and staying out of the way of the mistakes of others. Needless to say, everyone was really pleased, especially Ron Dennis and John Barnard. After qualifying 11th, Wattie finished 6th, having been up to 3rd by lap 9 before having to make a pit stop on lap 29 to change his tires after starting on the softer Michelins.

We had an unscheduled break three weeks later when the FOCA teams boycotted the San Marino Grand Prix at Imola. This was the result of an FIA appeals court confirming the decision to throw out the first two finishers in Brazil and the ensuing ban on topping up essential liquids and coolants prior to post-race scrutineering. FOCA claimed that the FIA had framed a new rule when they shouldn't have. Their boycott meant there were only 14 starters at Imola—and two of those would not have been there had Ken Tyrrell, a staunch FOCA member, not felt obliged to honor a commitment to a new sponsor, appliance manufacturer Candy, who happened to be Italian.

When we got to Zolder for the Belgian Grand Prix, the mood in the paddock was pretty tense. It was made much worse, unfortunately, when Formula One lost Ferrari's Gilles Villeneuve in a catastrophe with another car that was trying to get out of the way at the end of qualifying. Gilles did a lot of incredible things on the race track, but I will never forget him doing loops with his new helicopter over Imola during a test. We lost a character as well as a great driver.

The water-tank ploy had been FOCA's way of trying to counteract the power of the turbo engines by running lighter during the races. It was no surprise to see the turbos on

John Barnard and Niki Lauda may be debating the finer points of car setup as I look on thoughtfully at Monza. Niki failed to finish in the 1982 Italian Grand Prix, while John Watson came in fourth. (LAT PHOTOGRAPHIC)

John Watson in the No. 7 McLaren MP4/1B at Long Beach in 1982, with Bruno Giacomelli behind him in the Alfa Romeo 182. John finished in sixth place, while his new teammate Niki Lauda took the win. (LAT PHOTOGRAPHIC)

the front row at Zolder, Prost's Renault being 0.35 seconds quicker than Lauda, who was fourth on the grid.

As had been happening, the Renaults ran into trouble in the race, but tire problems meant Niki had to drop back. Wattie, who had qualified 10th, had the perfect setup and came through to win.

Niki should have finished fourth but he was disqualified for being 1.8kg under the weight limit. Wattie's car was okay. The loss of weight on Lauda's car was more than likely caused by starting with a few less kilos of fuel than Watson, as Niki usually got better fuel mileage. This time he didn't, and the car was just that little bit too light. There was a reasonable amount of chaos going on in the post-race scrutineering checks, with some teams weighing their car several times. Much of this was watched by the very bemused father of Elio de Angelis. Elio had been classified fourth in the Lotus, and was obviously looking to move further up the order if other cars were thrown out.

Wattie left Belgium one point behind Prost at the top of the Drivers championship. The situation would be exactly the same after the Monaco Grand Prix, when Prost crashed out and John had an engine oil problem, but there would be a big change a couple of weeks later following the United States Grand Prix.

After two decades in Watkins Glen, for 1982 the race was held for the first time on the streets of downtown Detroit. The course was as bumpy as hell, which meant the MP4B wasn't great, and we weren't helped by rain during final practice, which meant that grid positions were established by times set during a practice session earlier in the day. Wattie was 17th on the grid, Niki 10th.

On the seventh lap, the safety car went out and, soon after, the race was stopped. While this was going on, we changed the tires for a harder spec (probably based on some information from Michelin), and added some fuel to be safe.

When the race restarted, Wattie, now 13th, really took off on what could only be called a charge through the field. He passed Niki, had a brush with someone else, and then took the lead from Rosberg's Williams on lap 37. Niki woke up and tried the same thing, but in the attempt to pass the Williams, he made a mistake and hit the barrier. Wattie ended up winning the race!

Wattie could be quick a great deal of the time, and he looked after the car, but he had a hard time dealing with John Barnard's standard setup because it didn't really suit his driving style. As the season progressed, Teddy began to realize what Wattie wanted with the car, and he ended up being quicker and driving much better in general. Wattie and Teddy were a very good combination. I always got along with Wattie, and thought he was a lot quicker than people gave him credit for. Oh—and we are still sending Christmas cards to each other 30-plus years later.

At the next race in Montreal, Niki got a hint of what was going on regarding changes to Wattie's car that were different from the ones on the setup sheet. Wattie was over two seconds quicker than him on the first day, and there was a scene in the back of the pit area. I can't remember any blows being struck or blood being spilled. It was one of those things that should never really have happened from the team's point of view, particularly when we had two good drivers. In the end, Wattie qualified 6th and moved up to 3rd in the last few laps, when two cars ahead ran out of fuel. Niki qualified 11th and only lasted until lap 17, when a clutch problem put him out.

Wattie still led the championship after Canada, as well as after the next race in Holland, despite only finishing ninth at Zandvoort. He was helped by the fact that 1982 was a strange season, one when a different driver seemed to win each race. But the fact that Wattie had twice as many points as Niki didn't hurt! We did a test with Niki at Zandvoort before the race, John Barnard having designed a new "floor" for the car that was intended to allow it to run without the rear wing. Niki tried this version for several laps, but in the end the car was more stable with the rear wing. Either way, it switched Niki's confidence back on and he finished fourth, after qualifying fifth, six places ahead of Wattie.

The momentum continued for Lauda at Brands Hatch, even though both drivers were struggling a bit for grip with the Michelins. Watson qualified no better than 12th, two seconds slower than Keke Rosberg's pole position for Williams with Goodyear tires.

There was an interesting and classic episode with Niki before qualifying. He said to me, "I've got to be a few more places up the grid because of the turbo cars if I'm going to have a chance to win." When I asked him what he wanted to do, or to try out on the car, he said, "Give me ten minutes." After about five or six minutes sitting in the car he said, "Okay, let's go." With what he described to the media as an "over the limit" lap, Niki moved up two or three places to qualify fifth—the fastest Michelin runner. When I asked him later about that lap, he said that to go quickly at Brands Hatch, you had to drive the car more with your head than with the physical aspects of it.

Niki came out with another classic after the Sunday morning warm-up. Having stopped in the pits to check things over, he was asked by John Barnard if everything was okay. His response was, "Get away from the car. Just leave it alone!"

Niki was as good as his word, although he received some assistance at the start. Rosberg had a fuel pump problem and had to start from the back, and Riccardo Patrese stalled his front-row Brabham, which was then hit by Rene Arnoux's Renault. Fortunately, this happened to Niki's left (as he started on the right-hand side of the grid), and he found himself second behind Nelson Piquet's Brabham. Brabham had planned to try mid-race refueling for the first time at Brands Hatch, but Piquet never got that far. A mechanical problem on the BMW engine gave Niki the lead on lap 10.

In the end Niki had a comfortable win, moving into third in the championship, six points behind Wattie, who had spun and stalled while avoiding someone else's accident.

While eating an apple and walking off with Willi Dungl right after the race, Niki turned to me and, with a large Cheshire cat grin, said, "Make damn sure it weighs enough," a cheeky reference to the post-race incident at Zolder. There were no problems this time.

There were several more tests with Niki, but the one at Paul Ricard prior to the French Grand Prix didn't go quite as planned. The car had a rear suspension failure in the very quick corner at the end of the long back straight. Niki ended up in the barrier, wrapped up in the chain-link fence. This didn't go down very well; given his past experience, I'm sure the thought of fire was never very far away. But the main thing was that he was not hurt—just pissed-off. Niki would finish eighth, while Wattie went out quite early on with a broken battery lead.

Didier Pironi had finished third in that race to extend his lead in the championship over Wattie, but the Ferrari driver was destined never to score another F1 point. The warm-up for the German Grand Prix was held in pouring rain, and Pironi, lapping quickly, went into the back of Prost's Renault, which was hidden by the spray. Pironi broke his legs quite badly and would not race again.

Niki was also a non-starter after a shunt during practice, which tore a wrist ligament. Wattie qualified 10th and was going really well, moving up to 3rd place on lap 19, without the help of most of his instruments, as we'd had to disconnect them at the last minute because of an electrical problem. With nine laps to go, Wattie had a front suspension failure, which may have been triggered by an off in the morning warm-up. In hindsight, the parts should have been changed.

Wattie didn't score points in the next two races (the Austrian Grand Prix at the Osterreichring and the Swiss Grand Prix at Dijon), but Niki came away from those two races with a fifth and a third, to leave him tied for fourth in the championship with Wattie, the pair of them 12 points behind Rosberg, who scored his first GP win at Dijon.

The organizers there were pretty inefficient—they forgot to show the checkered flag on the correct lap, and Rosberg had to do an extra lap just to make sure. I guess that's what happens when you hold the Swiss Grand Prix in France.

After the Austrian race, Niki had flown Joan Villadelprat, one of the very good mechanics on the team, John Barnard, and me to Vienna and then on to Niki's house, as we were going on from there to a test in Monza. Niki took us out for dinner that night, which was very nice after the hot race day.

By then we had twigged that a ploy of Niki's on the last day of a test was to mention that the engine oil pressure looked low on the circuit in a few places, or that the engine seemed to be acting a bit strange. The first thing we'd do was look around to see if the two pilots for his plane were still there; if not, he had decided he'd had enough with the test for the day.

As I said earlier, Teddy was working very well with Wattie on his car. Barnard didn't know that Teddy was changing the setup he had issued. Softer front springs and higher front-right height gave Wattie much more confidence in the car and meant, of course, that he was quicker.

At Dijon, I had noticed the spring sitting on the front of Wattie's car waiting to be fitted was different from the spring on the setup sheet. I thought it was only a last-minute change

Dan Gurney inscribed this photo of us together at Long Beach in 1982. Dan played a key role in bringing Formula One racing to the streets of his hometown in Southern California. (TYLER ALEXANDER COLLECTION)

between practice sessions. Although Teddy could be awkward at times, his understanding of the car and driver was good, and it's a shame to think that the ego factor between Barnard and Teddy could very well have cost Wattie the championship that year. I'm sure that if Teddy had told Barnard what he was doing, and why, there would have been an "I'm in charge" scene, and Wattie and the team would have been the real losers.

Wattie kept his championship hopes alive by finishing fourth at Monza, where Rosberg, the points leader, scored none by finishing in eighth place. It meant the World Championship decider would be a straight fight between Rosberg and Watson, with nine points between them going into the last race in Las Vegas. Wattie's only hope was that he would win and Keke would fail to finish. This result would give him the title even though they would be equal on points, because Rosberg had won only one race at Dijon, whereas Wattie had won twice. Wattie did all he could by finishing second, but fifth place and two points for Rosberg were enough to give him the title. Ferrari won the Constructors championship, we were second, and Williams fourth, behind Renault. Like I said, 1982 was a strange year.

At some point during the after-race party at Caesars Palace (good food, drinks, and scenery), Niki told me about Ron Dennis and John Barnard using Marlboro money to buy (or throw) Teddy and I out of McLaren when we got back to England. It was the first I knew about this plan. Teddy had agreed to being bought—rather than thrown—out. I didn't have much choice. Well, maybe I did, by not actually selling my shares but just by leaving. Being concerned about the possibility of things changing around in the company and ending up owning some shares in something that no longer existed, I stupidly sold my shares.

I think at the time Teddy was pretty worn-out, unwell, and fed up with the fighting and bitching with Ron Dennis and John Barnard. Life moves on, as they say.

It was a shame, because John Barnard is a very clever guy, though sometimes hard to work with—he's not known as the Prince of Darkness for nothing! But I do have a lot of respect for him. He knows how to make things, and then make them work—an important ability. Despite some bad moments in the beginning, he and I have been friends for a long time.

Like it or not, the company needed a few people who were entrepreneurial and who had a better grasp of what was needed in developing the race car. There were people there who already knew how to get it done, provided they were pointed in the right direction.

# 1983: Life after McLaren

The new year meant no more McLaren—at least, not for me. I did get pissed-off and a bit upset about the whole thing. But you have to remember: It's not that life is too short; it's that death is too long. So best get on with things. There were some people who thought I might feel as though I had lost my identity after 20 years with the team. Hell, no! I don't believe I thought about that at all, and I wasn't going to sit in the corner and cry. If they thought I'd do that, they didn't know me very well.

Only a couple of people rang me up about a motor racing job: John MacDonald and Mick Ralph, who had their own Formula One team called RAM, and Ted Toleman. Ted actually made me a reasonable offer with a respectable salary to become the team manager (or something like that) for the Toleman F1 race team. I didn't know very much about Toleman at the time. I was pleased about getting the offer, but needed a rest, so instead I went to Mexico for a while.

In March, a good friend who worked for United Airlines invited me to Cozumel in Mexico for the first time. It was a great place for snorkeling and scuba diving. It still is, except there are a lot more people, and they kind of spoiled the place when they had to put up traffic lights. But it hasn't been enough to stop me from continuing to go there.

Niki Lauda in the MP4/1C at the 1983 Belgian Grand Prix, where he qualified 15th and failed to finish the race. Maybe I wasn't missing much at the new McLaren. (LAT PHOTOGRAPHIC)

In the end I went to McLaren Engines on Eight Mile Road in Livonia, Michigan, to work for Wiley McCoy and Gary Knutson on an Indy engine program that they were doing as a one-off for Buick.

They had purchased a March Indy car and we installed a modified Buick engine. On several occasions, Tom Klauser drove it around a high-banked 7.5-mile test track owned by Honda in Ohio, known as the Transportation Research Center, or TRC. At about 240 mph, Tom would run through a tank of methanol in quite a short period of time. It was kind of scary because the car would actually go quicker than that, but we kept putting bigger and bigger Gurney flaps on the front and rear wings until we got it slowed down to a reasonable pace. We thought 240 mph was plenty quick enough for the testing we were doing.

While I was in Detroit, the Formula One race was on. Wiley McCoy and I were invited to a *Car and Driver* magazine party and got to meet a few old friends, including former

# Nick Butler

My first contact with Tyler was in Italy in 1980, when I was working for the Williams Formula One team. I was preparing to leave our hotel to travel to the Imola circuit for the setup day prior to the GP, and there encountered a disgruntled Tyler in his McLaren team gear, somewhat aggrieved at being left behind at the hotel by his teammates. He accepted our lift to the circuit and entertained us on the journey with colorful conversation and a few of his stories and opinions on racing matters. Here, clearly, was a real character with many stories to tell and a wealth of knowledge and experience. As I later came to realize, these first impressions were indeed correct.

In late 1983 our paths crossed once again when Tyler and Teddy Mayer hired me for their new racing team to contest the 1984 Indy car championship. Tyler was managing the team and had assembled a group of experienced engineers and mechanics. As a young and enthusiastic truckie/mechanic, I found myself in a very fortunate position among this group and under Tyler's leadership. The experience gave me a great grounding and appreciation of car preparation and the subtleties of race tactics and management.

I well remember the day of qualifying at Indianapolis. Tyler was extremely waspy prior to the start. By the end of the afternoon we had secured first and second on the grid, a fantastic feat for a rookie team. Tyler was euphoric. I have never seen him quite so ecstatic before or since, as if he was drunk on adrenaline. Clearly it meant a great deal to him.

The Indy car project ended at the end of 1984, and Teddy and Tyler turned their attention back to grand prix racing by setting up a deal to enter Formula One under the FORCE / Lola / Carl Haas banner. Again, Teddy and Tyler had assembled a great team of people that included Neil Oatley and Ross Brawn, and later (albeit briefly), Adrian Newey. I found myself in at the start of a new F1 project. We all had to stretch ourselves in so many ways as we built the team from the ground up. This included the construction of the workshop, the construction and operation of the wind tunnel model, as well as the construction and building of the race cars, along with the track tests and races. All of this was directed by Tyler, who seemed to have a bottomless pit of enthusiasm, experience, and talent to draw on as he drove us through a pretty intense program. For me this period turned out to be the most formative of my career in motor racing.

After two years the F1 project sadly came to an end when the sponsorship dried up. Later, in 1987, I was fortunate to find a job at McLaren and once again found myself working with Tyler, who returned to the team in 1990.

During the late 1980s and '90s, the F1 world was embracing the latest computer technologies. Tyler immersed himself in this arena, trying to get the best out of these new opportunities. I think he was instrumental in steering the development and implementation of these technologies and in helping to marry them to the racing environment.

In those days the number of test days available was unrestricted, and consequently I found myself attending tests pretty much every other week throughout the season, as well as extensive pre-season testing. Tyler was always there, too, and also had the stamina to attend all of the races. I still wonder where he was able to find the energy and enthusiasm, proof if it were needed of Tyler's love of the sport.

During that time I spent many long days and nights working closely with Tyler, learning much from him, and also learning together with the rest of the team how to get the best results from the latest technologies at our disposal. There were many laughs, too. A sort of gallows humor is required to help you through the long hours after a day of testing, and Tyler is a well-practiced devotee of that particular art.

My career in motor racing started in 1979 and continues today, so for the greater part of this time I have worked closely with Tyler in one capacity or another. I can honestly say that I am better for the experience.

editor David E. Davis and Carroll Shelby. A day or so later, I had a chance to chat with Mr. Shelby, who was telling me about a new project and wondered if I might be interested. I remember his final comment was, "Come on, Tyler, let's go make some money." I didn't go, but his project with Chrysler and Lamborghini worked out more than all right for him. Whatever it was, I didn't ask.

Teddy and I were trying to put something together, and we went to see the Buick people about an Indy program. But they really didn't have—or weren't ready to spend—enough money to do a proper project at that time.

Nick Butler is a trusted friend of mine. He came from Williams to work for Mayer Motor Racing's Indy team as a mechanic, then to Formula One Race Car Engineering (FORCE), and then on to McLaren International. He was a mechanic there until he moved into the design department, where he still works today.

In the fall of 1983 we formed Mayer Motor Racing Ltd., with Teddy Mayer, Bill Smith Jr., Robin Herd, and myself as the directors.

# 1984: A Fast Start for Mayer Motor Racing

**W**e had been trying to chase up the finances to run our Indy team for several months. In the end Mayer Motor Racing (MMR) had drivers Tom Sneva, with sponsorship from Texaco, and Howdy Holmes, who was backed by Jiffy, his family's company in the baking goods business. We also had help from Goodyear and a great many other people. Robin Herd, who was still with March at the time, contributed two March Indy cars, and we bought the third one with cash provided by Teddy, Bill Smith Jr., and myself.

Teddy rented a unit in Woking Business Park from (guess who!) Ron Dennis. We were able to hire a bunch of really good engineers and mechanics, some of whom had worked for Teddy and I before—a group of people that Teddy and I were confident could do the required job. We had people like John Baldwin, Phil Sharp, Don Beresford, Graham Fuller, Ray Grant, Nick Butler, Mark Scott, Tony Wybrott, Trudy Wybrott, Graham Fuller, Tony Van Dongen, Steve Roby (Abo), Russell Edrington, Mike Sales, Ian Paton, Dave Stephens, Bobby Edgar, John Hornby (Double "O"), and Bill McKeon.

Don Beadle was doing the engine work at McLaren Engines. His wife, Cathy, acted as

In 1984 I was back on the Indy car trail with the new Mayer Motor Racing team. That's Dick Gail of Champion Spark Plugs with me in the pit lane before the Meadowlands Grand Prix. (LAT PHOTOGRAPHIC)

secretary and bookkeeper at the MMR workshop in Livonia, along with doing the timing at the race track and a variety of other things thrown in. There were also the weekend warriors who just came to the races: Buddy Urbanski, Mike Mills, Steve Sharp, Jeff Collins, Phil Weider, Bob Santoro, Christopher Smith, and a couple of others. And not forgetting genuine help from Rusty Brett of Texaco.

I had gone to Livonia to sort out things with Wiley and Gary and found a reasonable building to rent, which conveniently was just across the street from McLaren Engines. Bill Smith Jr. provided the trucks, vans, and cars we needed.

This was when I first met Paul Morgan, who was working for Cosworth as we sorted out our Indy DFX engine program. It was the beginning of a long-lasting friendship for me. I would meet Mario Illien, Paul's friend and co-worker at Cosworth, several years later after they had formed their own engine-building and development company, Ilmor Engineering.

I was busy in the States sorting out the workshop, finding a truck to carry the cars around, and locating places for the guys to stay.

I had excellent help from Cathy Beadle and Russell Edrington, who was on loan from McLaren Engines and great at setting up the workshop and doing all sorts of general things—anytime, anywhere.

Meanwhile, back in England, Teddy was sorting out the cars and all the bits and pieces at our rented factory.

We were also looking at some developmental aero bits. Robin Herd knew this young guy by the name of Adrian Newey. Adrian would spend quite a bit of time with Teddy at the Motor Industry Research Association (MIRA) wind tunnel. Needless to say, Adrian, even then, had a long list of "things" to try out. Teddy, of course, had his own list of what might be useful and required! This association would go on for a great many years in one form or another. It was fascinating when Adrian came up with some interesting aero bits that we ran on the car on the short ovals and the road courses, because they worked quite well.

With the first race of the 1984 season scheduled for Long Beach, the cars and freight were shipped to Los Angeles, where everything was picked up by the race transporter and a large rented truck and taken a few miles north to Willow Springs in Rosamond, California. A shakedown session at this track had been set up by the CART people, and several teams took part.

Paul Morgan talked us into running a new eight-cylinder inlet system. It was meant to help the engine response, instead of using a single large butterfly, the normal turbo configuration. This was for road courses and short ovals. We ran the new system at Long Beach, where Tom Sneva qualified 15th and finished 3rd; Howdy Holmes qualified 17th, but had a small misfortune in the race and didn't finish.

Everything, including temperatures of about 105 degrees Fahrenheit (40 degrees Celsius), worked out perfectly at Phoenix for the next race. At Adrian's suggestion, we were running some small winglets—just in front of the rear tires, something the other teams were not doing but which worked a treat on the one-mile short oval. Tom qualified on pole and won the race, with Howdy starting fourth and finishing second. One-two for Mayer Motor Racing at our second race! Naturally, we were very pleased and relieved, because everyone on the race team, as well as the people in the factory in Woking, had worked extremely hard. It was a great boost for us all, particularly as three weeks later we'd be at the Indianapolis Motor Speedway for the 500, a place where Tom had a lot of experience and was usually pretty quick.

As usual, Indianapolis was an up-and-down affair. Tom was in the small group of quickest cars almost every day in practice. Because he thought that our rear wing was too big, Phil Sharp and one of the other guys—Graham Fuller, I think—spent at least three nights before qualifying in a fabrication shop owned by a friend, taking material off the rear wing's trailing edge and then gluing and riveting it back together.

Phil Sharp was impressed by Tom's ability to remember all the tire sets, their numbers and pressures, and then ask us as he came down the pit lane to change some pressures. We also made clever use of the Weight Jacker. The WJ is used to change the weight diagonally across the car by raising or lowering the ride height, usually on the right-rear corner. This helps to change how the car handles through the high-speed corners.

The day before qualifying, Tom was happier with the last mod on the rear wing, but he wanted to do one more spring change on the rear. The weather had been very humid and quite nasty. Just before we could make the spring change, there was a large thunderstorm, which meant going back to the garage to wait for the rain to stop, and a chance to try the spring change. When the storm moved away, it was much cooler and less humid, which meant everyone was running quite quick. When I went back to see if Tom was ready to go out, I found him walking out of the garage in his jeans and shirt. He said the car would be fine.

The car was indeed fine in the pre-qualifying practice session. Even so, Graham Fuller was still filing a bit more off the trailing edge of the rear wing while we were in the lineup, waiting for our turn to qualify! But Tom was proved right about the car when he took pole

Reunited: In 1984 Teddy Mayer and I were working together again as principals with the new Mayer Motor Racing team. (LAT PHOTOGRAPHIC)

position with a new track record of 210.029 mph (2 minutes, 51.405 seconds for the four laps, or 10 miles' distance).

Howdy had run quite well in practice, but because the track was getting hotter before his qualifying run, Teddy had put a bit more front wing on his car.

When your car goes out to qualify at Indy, you jump on a golf cart that takes you down the pit lane to the exit of turn four. Standing by the pit wall, you can give the driver his speed for that lap by timing him just as he comes into the turn. You lay some signal board numbers along the top of the pit wall to have at hand and use in a hurry. Since the morning practice session gives you a pretty good idea of what the lap speed is going to be, you only put out a few numbers on top of the pit wall. Howdy had run about 206 mph average in the morning. When he came by on his first lap, I was holding an 06 in my hand, with a 7 ready, just in case he had gone quicker still. But when Teddy said it was 209 mph, there was something of a panic with the numbers, since there's not much time when the cars are coming by at those speeds. The 6 quickly became a 9, and Howdy Holmes became second quickest. Mayer Motor Racing was on the front row of the grid for the 1984 Indy 500!

That was the good news. Now comes the part that would end up costing us a great deal. In the course of rebuilding the uprights and replacing the bearings, the metal grease retainers were replaced by new ones, which seemed prudent. That part turned out to be very wrong, particularly as the old ones had been pitched by then. The grease retainers for the axle bearings were really quite basic and needed a long time to be properly run in, which was not possible because there was only a limited amount of practice before the race. We used a machine for spinning up the wheels in the garage in an attempt to run them in, but it was probably nothing like enough.

Having rebuilt the cars before the last practice for the race, we went to Indianapolis Raceway Park, just outside Indianapolis, to check everything and to do a few laps, along with some pit stop practice. I always thought this was worth the extra bit of work. We were now ready to race.

Tom fought for the lead with Rick Mears (in a Penske-run March) for a great deal of the race. With one pit stop to go, Tom was a bit quicker than Rick into and through turn three, and was getting ready to try to overtake.

Knowing Tom, he would have come out ahead and probably would have been able to pull away a little, but we never got the answer. There was an accident behind us, and while we were cruising around under the yellow flag, the left-rear wheel bearing failed, basically because of the seal. It was indeed a shame. It would have been interesting to see how the battle would have turned out, as Tom and Rick were the only two cars on the same lap. Several March cars had a similar problem, but they managed to just finish the race, Mears being one of them. Howdy was not so quick over the course of the race and finished 13th, a few laps down.

Texaco had a nice party for the team after the race. That was very kind of them, but it sure wasn't the kind of celebration we were looking for.

Tom and Rick were having another race-long duel a week later on the mile oval at Milwaukee. Tom got caught out when he and Rick were at the back of the pack on a very long yellow-flag period. Tom was ahead, and just as he eased past the pit entrance, Rick darted into the pits to make his last stop for fuel one lap before the green flag. Tom now had to make a green-flag pit stop, and once done, he set off chasing Rick. In the end Rick had an engine problem, and with a couple of laps to go, Tom, pushing like hell, caught and passed the Penske March 84C to win the race. Howdy did a good job staying out of trouble and finished seventh.

While the oval races were generally very good, the road-course ones proved quite a bit harder for Tom, so Phil Sharp and I spent a lot of time trying to help him adapt. Howdy was pretty much okay, having had a lot more experience on road courses, but Tom's results—fifth at Portland, sixth at Meadowlands—reflected his difficulties, even though he continued to lead the championship.

At Meadowlands, in New Jersey, we had a problem with the rear wing on Tom's car. He'd had a small shunt around the middle of the race and the rear wing was sitting at a funny angle. It wasn't moving around and appeared to stay in exactly the same place, lap after lap. I told Tom on the radio several times that it looked okay until he didn't want to hear about it anymore. At least he managed to finish sixth and earn a few points. The car had been using a new John Baldwin–designed rear wing that Phil Sharp had hand-carried from England. Unfortunately, Howdy Holmes in our other car had a misfortune and failed to finish.

Tom still led the championship despite not finishing at Cleveland, where he qualified 16th and went out with gearbox trouble. For the next race, we were back to an oval and back into contention.

The 500-mile race at Michigan International Speedway was on a two-mile, high-banked circuit. We were reasonably quick in practice, and the night before qualifying, I got a phone call from Tom saying he wanted to take the rear wing off the car and run it during the Saturday-morning practice before qualifying! "Are you sure?" was my reply. He was. So we took the wing off on Saturday morning, which meant we were changing springs and anything else we could think of to try and balance the car. The CART people, meanwhile, seemed to think this was not allowed. But there was nothing in the rules that really said we couldn't.

Tom ran quite a few laps at 209-plus mph, which was quick! With not much time left in the practice session, we grabbed a bit of reality and put the wing, and nearly everything else, back on the car in time to get in a few laps. We did another chassis setup check before qualifying, and Tom ended up second fastest doing another lap he said he didn't really remember doing. He probably hadn't fully recovered from those 209 mph laps with no rear wing.

During the race, Tom had a long fight with the Newman/Haas team's Mario Andretti, who kept trying to ease Tom near the outside wall on the front straight. Tom had sorted out a plan of attack. With a couple of laps to go, he started to try to pass on the high side again, but instantly dropped below Mario. He was alongside him and going by when Johnny Rutherford crashed and brought out a yellow flag, which effectively ended the race. It was a shame Johnny didn't wait another couple of seconds, as those few extra points could well have made a big difference at the end of the season. Mario won with a time of 3:44:45.000, with Tom second on 3:44:45.140!

Poor Howdy, who qualified sixth, had a rather large disaster by actually going over the top of another car, doing a fair amount of damage to both. The only good thing was that neither driver was hurt.

Another win for Andretti at Elkhart Lake (a road course where Tom went out with an engine problem) put Mario on top of the championship, but Tom was back in front again after finishing fourth on the Pocono oval. The championship positions switched yet again when Mario won at the Mid-Ohio road course, and Tom finished seventh, one place behind Howdy.

Neither of them did very well at Sanair, where Tom had gearbox trouble, but the race on the oval in Quebec will be remembered for Rick Mears having a bad accident and doing a lot of damage to his feet. I managed to injure Teddy as we stood behind the Armco barrier that Rick hit. When I saw this coming, I pushed Teddy to the ground, resulting in a few bruises and cuts. But no serious harm was done compared to poor Rick, who would be out of racing for quite some time.

When Tom finished second at Michigan in late September, the problem was that the 200-mile race was won by Andretti. A couple of weeks later Mario was one place ahead again when Tom took fourth at Phoenix.

Tom still had a chance of winning the championship after the race at Laguna Seca, where he finished tenth, but only if we could do something about Mario Andretti—which was one of the reasons why we decided to go to the pre-race test organized by CART at Las Vegas.

John Baldwin had done some different front suspension bits, which Tom liked quite a bit during the test. Between the test and the race, one of our guys had found a place in Long Beach to prepare the cars and practice for the Las Vegas pit stop contest.

He also had a friend who got us into the Lockheed Aircraft facility, which was very impressive—full of people creating and building things, including a full-size mock-up of the space shuttle.

The pit stop contest in the middle of the old downtown area was going to be aired live on TV as a buildup for the race. The contest was divided into two groups, which allowed us to use the spare car for both drivers, but with their respective pit crews. The fact that our team won in both groups meant that the final pit stop was between our own two cars. This meant we had to get Howdy's race car out of the truck for him to use. It also meant we had to wait for the oil to heat up before starting it. As you might imagine, this didn't go down very well with the TV people, but the CART guys were a great help in smoothing things out.

In the end, Tom won and Howdy was second—a really great achievement for everyone on the team. I guess our days of practicing in Long Beach paid off. It was pointed out to the guys on Howdy's car that they needed to be careful, as it was his race car, and the guys on Tom's car wanted to win, of course! (I just happened to be doing the right-rear on Tom's car!)

Tom, who had qualified fifth for the race, said, "Well, to win the championship I have to win the race, so let's just get on with it."

At one point during the race, Mario fell off in the sand but, unfortunately, got back onto the track again. Tom had a bit of a confrontation with Al Unser Sr., which put Al off in the sand and prompted a few hand signals that involved using his middle finger while standing beside the track as he watched Tom take the lead.

You should know that by this time there had been some discussions between Teddy and Newman/Haas owners Paul Newman and Carl Haas regarding a Formula One team that they wanted Teddy and I to run. When Tom went into the lead and Mario was fighting to gain some places in Carl Haas's car, Carl sent his engineer Bill Yeager down to our pit to tell Teddy that if we won the championship, the Formula One Team deal was off!

Tom won the race, but Mario got enough points to win the championship, all of which reminded us that the second place under the yellow flag at the Michigan 500 earlier in the year was a real bummer.

At the CART end-of-season party and prize-giving that night (which was very well done; I recall Gary Knutson and I consuming a large quantity of some rather nice shrimp), Tom was gracious enough to thank Al Unser Sr. for holding up his middle finger as Tom went by several times, indicating to him that he was in first place!

There had been a lot of hard work during the course of the year, and second place in the championship was not at all bad for Mayer Motor Racing, thanks mainly to the really good bunch of blokes that we had working with us.

The Formula One project was now on with Carl Haas. This meant that Mayer Motor Rac-

# Adrian Newey

I got to know Tyler in late 1983 through early 1984, when Robin Herd introduced me to Teddy Mayer, who had just started up Mayer Motor Racing with Tyler, Bill Smith Jr., and Robin.

Robin had asked me to go with Teddy to the MIRA wind tunnel and help with various aerodynamic ideas on the March Indy car that they were going to use. Some interesting parts were tried, and several were used at some of their first races, to positive effect.

In 1986 I came to work for Formula One Race Car Engineering (FORCE), where Teddy Mayer was the managing director and Tyler was the team manager, and, as I found out, working long hours getting the team organized. He and Neil Oatley were working very late most nights.

The relationship with Tyler grew at this point, as we now worked closely together, with a group of very good people. Tyler's stamina and focus while dealing with a great number of things always impressed me.

Unfortunately at the end of 1986, FORCE's sponsor, the Beatrice Company, was bought and the Formula One contract was canceled. Carl Haas, who was the owner of FORCE, also had the Indy car team, Newman/Haas Racing (NHR). Carl talked to both Tyler and me about coming to work at his Indy team in 1987.

Since Tyler and I knew each other well, the conversation went a bit like this, "If you go, I'll go." "Okay, if you go, I'll go."

So we both went to work for Carl Haas at his workshop and office just outside Chicago, with Mario Andretti as the driver.

Tyler was the team manager and I was the race engineer and aerodynamicist. I stayed in England, flying out to the races, while Tyler went to stay near the workshop and office in the United States. Tyler knew several of the mechanics who were there, and he also hired a couple of very good people who had worked with him before.

Tyler spent a few weeks getting familiar with the people and then started to point out his thoughts and how to get on with things. His "straight to the point" work ethic when dealing with my flow of job lists worked very well.

I left NHR at the end of 1987 to go back to Formula One. It was not until I went to McLaren in 1998 to become the technical director that Tyler and I got to work together again. Tyler had changed his focus and gotten much more involved in studying the data coming from the car while bringing himself up to speed with the latest information technology, techniques which reveal his impressive flexibility and ability to reinvent himself.

Looking back, I think Tyler was a great force in a small team, such as McLaren would have been in the 1970s and then in Indy car racing in the 1980s. Certainly I hugely enjoyed our partnership at NHR. McLaren in the late 1990s was not an easy environment for individuals to thrive in just because of the size that F1 teams had grown to by then. In that sense, I think the new McLaren team was less able to use Tyler's individual approach to problems.

It is unusual for motor racing people not to have an ego, but Tyler doesn't seem to have one, or need one, which probably keeps him focused on the job—and good for him.

Teddy Mayer and company study Howdy Holmes' March 84C before the 1984 Meadowlands Grand Prix. The end of Mayer Motor Racing would lead to a new start in Formula One. (LAT PHOTOGRAPHIC)

ing would be closing down. Our decision was helped by the facts that Texaco and Howdy's Jiffy company were not going to continue sponsoring our team. Some of the guys decided to stay in the United States, and they either got a job with another CART team or started up their own businesses, while others came back to England to be part of the new company that was going to be called Formula One Race Car Engineering (FORCE).

The Indy car workshop in Livonia and all the equipment was taken over by McLaren Engines and would be used to do another BMW prototype car project.

# 1985–86: Back to Formula One with FORCE and Haas

Starting a new Formula One team requires the following: first, a lot of money. Then there's trying to find a suitable factory in a convenient place, acquiring all the machinery and equipment needed (a somewhat relentless task in itself), and assembling a group of very good people who will have to work quite hard a lot of the time. And on it goes, as you will see as this story goes on.

Coming back to a Formula One project after a few years was going to be interesting and challenging. We knew that a huge amount of work was going to be needed from everyone involved.

Starting a Formula One team with some really good people is one thing; dealing with others who were unfamiliar with the business proved to be quite hard work, especially for Teddy, who spent a lot of his valuable time dealing with these issues. The intention was to design and build two race cars and a T-car (for testing, an important third car) in time to run in the last three grand prix of 1985. Meeting this limited schedule would not be a simple task, I might add.

The MMR unit at Woking Business Park was not really big enough; there were several Portacabins stacked inside the unit to make more office space. Having spent a considerable amount of time looking for a more suitable place, I finally found one in a new industrial park in Colnbrook, right next to the new M25 motorway and not far from Heathrow Airport, which suited our needs at the time. The fact that it was around the corner from the old McLaren factory was just another bit of history.

Neil Oatley had come from Williams to join us as chief designer. Neil was followed later by Ross Brawn, who would be involved in the aero side as well as suspension design. John Baldwin was already there, and he was joined by George Ryton, working on gearbox design. D. C. Patrick-Brown would make the model for the wind tunnel, with direction from Ross. He was known as "Dustpan and Brush," as he was always cleaning up the shavings from working on the model.

A lot of time had to be spent with the FIA, and Teddy used his long-standing friendship with Bernie Ecclestone to get a great deal of help to sort things out correctly. Patrick Tambay and Alan Jones were hired by Carl Haas. We had worked with Patrick before, but not Alan, who had driven Can-Am races for Carl in 1978. We sure as hell should have spoken to Williams's Patrick Head about his experience working with Mr. Jones. Alan may have won the 1980 World Championship with Williams, but I can't think his time there was all sweetness for the team.

The main sponsor/partner for the team (which would run under the Haas Lola name, due to Carl Haas's role as a Lola distributor) was Beatrice Foods, a worldwide conglomerate that found the promotional environment of Formula One ideal. Jim Dutt, a friend of Carl Haas's, was the CEO. Mr. Dutt was also a good friend of Donald Petersen's, president of the Ford Motor Company at the time. An engine deal was sorted out with Cosworth, who, we were told, were building a new turbo Formula One engine. Believing in Cosworth as we did, this seemed okay. The rather large stitch was that the turbo engine was not going to be ready until November! This would be just the beginning of a relationship that became very contentious.

In the meantime we could have had a Renault engine, but FORCE would have been the fourth team they were supplying, and there were also some cost issues. As things would turn out, our using the Renault would have been a much better arrangement than the Hart engine we agreed to use. Although the Hart had a reasonable amount of horsepower, it was not very reliable. More about this later.

Finding all the necessary equipment and getting it up and running was, as you can imagine, another huge task. Luckily, we had a group of really good people to help get this

Teddy and I caught up with James Hunt in the pits at Brands Hatch before the 1986 British Grand Prix. (JOHN TOWNSEND)

done: Phil Sharp, Don Beresford, Ray Grant, Nick Butler, Harry Mendel, Rupert Manwaring, John Hornby, Ian Barnard, Tony Wybrott, and many others. We also needed to use a lot of outside suppliers, one of which was a truck-building company in Portsmouth. John Turner, whom we had known from our time spent at McLaren, became a great help when I was designing the main transporter and working out the weight distribution and location of various items inside.

Once the Hart-powered cars were under way, work started on the Ford-Cosworth car. Cosworth said it had to be ready in November to allow for the running in of the engine in the car at the Ford test track in Arizona.

Being a new team, and not wishing to let our side down by being late, Phil Sharp and his group worked long and hard to have the car ready by the first of November. But then it stayed in the factory, covered up. There was no evidence of the running engine—or even a simple sign from Cosworth saying "Sorry about that."

We were all doing a variety of jobs, and Neil and I seemed to be vying for who would be the last to leave every night. Neil was in the design office and I was welding wishbones and other parts for Mr. Grant, who would tell me they would never be ready in the morning, only to find them, still warm, on his desk and ready to be sent off to the heat-treating people when he came into work. I was a lot better at welding than fabricating, and I got a lot of subtle stick about doing the easier part. Late nights didn't bother me very much; the place was a lot quieter, and the parts were always ready in the morning.

The Hart-powered cars were finished in time for the last three races of 1985. At Monza, there was a variety of mechanical and engine problems. South Africa was more than confusing, as there seemed to be difficulties for Beatrice with anti-apartheid activists back in Chicago. I'm not sure what the hell they had to do with a Formula One race in South Africa, but you can bet your ass it was political. The end result was, we weren't allowed to race there. Alan Jones flew home to Australia on Saturday night, ready for the final race in Adelaide, where there were more small mechanical and engine-related problems. Although the results were not good, it did give the team a chance to learn a lot of things and start working together.

As 1986 began, the huge effort of designing and building the Ford-Cosworth continued, and I made many visits to Cosworth in Northampton. It was late January when, having promised the engine on a variety of dates, Cosworth informed me that there would be no engine until Monaco, with the chance that there might be one for one car only in the earlier race at Imola. A response of "What the fuck?" immediately came to mind.

I asked questions of the Cosworth people and was told vaguely, "Well, we've had a problem with this and that." The word *mendacity* seemed more than appropriate, as these were the same people who said we at FORCE had to have a car ready in November in order to test *their* engine. If they were having problems with the development of the engine, it would have been prudent—not to mention honest—to say so, and not to give us a bunch of phony delivery dates. I have never forgotten or forgiven the people who were part of this.

Having left the Cosworth factory and found the nearest phone box, I called Teddy and Neil, suggested they sit down, and then informed them of the mess in Northampton.

Although there had been many exceptional efforts in the past—and would be more in the future—I'm not sure a group of people ever worked as hard as we did in that month of February. We were building three Ford-Cosworth cars, and at the same time, we had to rebuild the Hart-powered cars for the first few races. Of course, Brian Hart had changed a bunch of things on his engine, which meant a new exhaust system, water system, and intercoolers for the turbo. We made quite a few of the changes in the factory, while the very talented people at Steve Good's fabrication company helped us out with the rest. There was a big thank-you to everyone for getting everything done.

At some point while this extravagant mess was being sorted out, Adrian Newey joined us and began working alongside Neil Oatley.

We did get the Hart-powered cars ready in time to be shipped off to Brazil for the test before the race in Rio de Janeiro. We should have scored a few points there; Patrick Tambay was running in the top six when the alternator failed.

Back in England, we had finally gotten a Ford-Cosworth engine to put in a car and took it for a test at Donington. I remember it being cold, and once we got the engine started, we couldn't shut it off! Jim Coates, in charge of electronics, discovered there was nothing in the software to tell the engine that there was an ignition on/off switch.

There'd been a few issues between Teddy and Alan Jones, not least of which was Teddy's thought that his driver's weight was too high. We made an attempt to sort this out with Alan over several planned private dinners, but he never showed up. As I said earlier, I guess we should have spoken to Patrick Head about how to deal with him.

There was one Ford-Cosworth car for Alan Jones and one Hart for Patrick Tambay at Imola. I think Patrick had a new or fresh engine for each session (which explains how I spent most of my time there), while Alan had a fresh engine for the race only. Patrick was out after

Patrick Tambay joined the Haas Lola team for the 1986 season. Patrick had already driven for McLaren, Ferrari, and Renault in Formula One, and before that had worked with Carl Haas in the Can-Am and Formula 5000. (TYLER ALEXANDER)

five laps with another engine problem; Alan had qualified back in 21st place, but by lap 14, he was 9th. A loose gear linkage meant a pit stop, and then 10 laps later, a manufacturing fault on the water radiator brought another long stop while it was changed. Unfortunately, it was not bled properly, and he stopped for good with overheating.

At Monaco we finally had all three Ford-Cosworths available. The Lola THL2 (to give the red car its full title) was reasonably quick, and both Patrick and Alan enjoyed throwing the car around a circuit where our lack of horsepower didn't matter quite so much. Alan was sixth-fastest on Thursday, but it all went wrong on Saturday when he dropped to 18th on the grid after a front wishbone broke as he tried to find a clear lap. Patrick had been frustrated by problems with traffic on Thursday, but got himself onto the sixth row on Saturday.

The warm-up on Sunday morning went okay, but the fun really started as the cars got to the grid. We had the last pit before the exit to the race track, and I was finishing work with the spare car when there was a cry on the radio about a problem with Patrick's car.

Patrick ran back to the pit exit, where we had pushed the spare car onto the track just before the pit lane closed. We only had one seat for each driver at the time, and Patrick's first comment was, "There's no seat in it!" I replied, "Just get in and drive the bloody thing to the grid!" While this panic was going on, several people had noticed that we had a rather large amount of ballast under where the seat would normally be, indicating immediately that we had a nice, light car!

The chain tensioner in the engine in Patrick's race car had worn out and the chain driving the cams had worn a hole in the cam cover; this was discovered on the grid when the rear bodywork came off. The two turbos were changed when the car got to the grid; a bit hard to believe, really. Even harder to believe was that once we got the T-car to the grid for Patrick, the turbos were changed on that as well.

Alan's race only lasted until the third lap due to a stupid incident. He was having a go at Philippe Streiff's Tyrrell (the Frenchman was having brake trouble after a change of calipers on the grid) for 14th place going into Tabac when the two cars touched and Alan spun. The car was actually undamaged, but Alan was pointing the wrong way, with the leaders due to arrive pretty soon. Alan worked out that the sensible thing to do would be to go back toward the escape road at the chicane and turn the car around in safety—which he did. Unfortunately, the man controlling the exit of the escape road wouldn't let Alan back out! You can imagine what the Aussie had to say about that when he eventually got back to the pits.

About 10 laps from the end, Patrick was close to getting some points, and he needed to get by Martin Brundle in the second Tyrrell. Patrick had a go on the inside on the downhill run to Mirabeau, but this unfortunately resulted in a shunt, with Patrick riding over the top of the Tyrrell and leaving a mark on Brundle's crash helmet! That was the end of the race for both cars.

While the wreckage of Patrick's car was sent back to England, we went straight to a test at Paul Ricard.

It was here that Elio de Angelis died when the rear wing came off his Brabham on the long straight past the pits, the car then landing upside down on the other side of the crash barrier. The response by the safety personnel at the French circuit was less than adequate, as I noted at the time. Shown below is the letter I wrote and sent off to Bernie Ecclestone. In no way does the following depict the confusion and general disorder that existed after the accident that took the life of Elio de Angelis; it only touches on the main points.

Many years later, I was told that Elio had suffocated from the smoke and/or the powder from the fire extinguisher; his only physical damage was a broken collarbone. It was enough to make you fucking sick.

By now the Ford-Cosworth engine was a reasonable package, and there were some good people working on it—and then there were some others. Teddy had informed the people in Northampton that they were running the wrong fuel, along with several other problems, as only Teddy could. One of the main problems with the engine was that when you increased the boost pressure for qualifying, it raised the water and oil temperature but did little for the horsepower curve.

There was never an event where we did not have a problem of one sort or the other. During the race morning warm-up in Montreal, Patrick had a big accident in what was then the chicane after the pits. Something broke, and it took us a little while to sort out just what it was. It turned out to be the lower rear wishbone clevis that attaches the wishbone to the gearbox.

The shunt did a lot of damage to the car, as well as to Patrick's feet. He was still hobbling a week later in Detroit, and Teddy had to make a last-minute call to ask Eddie Cheever to fly in from Europe and drive the race. Eddie did a pretty good job, qualifying 10th and lying 8th, when there was trouble with the drive pegs in the axle, which transfer the torque from the engine through the gearbox and halfshaft to the wheel. Alan went out with a similar problem a few laps earlier.

There was a humiliating point in Hungary when Nelson Piquet came alongside Alan Jones on the pit straight, waved his hand, and then just drove away in the Williams-Honda. Mr. Jones came into the pits at the end of the next lap, threw his helmet into the seat, and walked off.

Despite all the problems, the car had quite a few good aero bits on it, thanks to Ross Brawn and Adrian Newey. At one point, Teddy had hired a young aerodynamicist named Mark Hanford who developed something called an "Aero Map" program long before anyone else knew what this was. In simple terms, it was software that helped you to set up the car after making some changes to the front or rear wing.

In Austria, there were some improvements with the engine, but the main problem remained: The increased boost pressure for qualifying only produced higher temperatures rather than power. Nonetheless, we finished the race with both cars in the points, even

In no way does the following depict the confusion and
general disorder that existed after the accident, it
only touches the main points.

**PAUL RICARD RACE CIRCUIT**
**14 MAY 1986**

The problems at Ricard today needs careful thought so as not to
over-react or jump to conclusions.

Irrespective of the possiblity that the injuries to the driver
were fatal before the fire started, i.e. solely due to the
accident itself; what happened after the prolonged crash
stopped, is what one has to look at.

a.  Bad communications to the pits, i.e. no one knew who
or what was involved as several cars were on the track at
the time.

b.  The fire equipment did not appear to be adequate to deal
quickly with the type of fire that existed, nor did I see
any properly suited firemen to deal with rescue.

c.  The 'Safety crew/corner workers' had no means to turn
the car over (as it was upside down).  A 'tow' strap from
one of the teams was finally used to turn the car right side
up.

d.  Some of the equipment on the ambulance was incorrect,
i.e. the fittings on the oxygen bottle did not fit the face
mask or anything else.

e.  I am not qualified to say whether the doctors present
were good or bad and the larger of the two did get after
doing what he could.  Not knowing who the doctors were and
not being able to speak with them (it was a race team crew
memeber who first checked to see if there was any pulse)
was very frustrating to say the lease and what made it worse
was that there were several people who speak various languages
standing well back watching.

f.  It took a long time for the helicopter to arrive but
at least the medical people with it seemed to know what they
were doing but again I am not qualified to judge.

What all this means.... is that a close look at what sort
of safety and fire fighting equipment is needed, who actually
deals with it, who pays for it, and where does it go;  as
someone said, "you can't have an ambulance follow you home
on the motorway every night".

In the end Motor Racing has probably lost one of the few
nice guys involved...at least Elio will never know that it
took a long long time to get to him.... **but we certainly
do...**

A draft copy of the letter I sent to Bernie Ecclestone after Elio de Angelis
died following an accident during a test at the Paul Ricard circuit in France.
Hopefully it made a difference. (TYLER ALEXANDER COLLECTION)

though one had a slipping clutch due to a gearbox oil leak. After a spate of problems in the earlier races, this really helped to improve morale. And it wasn't a bad result for a new team.

A new spec Cosworth engine appeared at Monza. I think there were only one or two of these engines, but we couldn't really be sure because no one would tell us. Teddy decided to put the engine in Patrick's car for Sunday, as he had been the faster of the two drivers.

During the race-morning practice session, Alan was sitting on the pit wall with the Longines monitor, watching lap times and speeds on the straight, when Patrick came by about 9 mph quicker than Alan had managed. Alan stormed across the pit lane, pushed the bodywork for his car off its stands, made some unprintable exclamations, and went to the motor home.

Until now, Patrick had never been able to keep up with the Lotus-Renault of Ayrton Senna. When he came back to the pits, Patrick said he had followed Senna for several laps, wondered whether or not to pass him, but had chosen to just follow him, as it was such a treat! Needless to say, the engine scuffed a piston, and there was not another engine available—or so I was told. Maybe there was; maybe there wasn't. But it was funny how the answers from Cosworth seemed like nothing more than a crock of shit.

We asked if this spec of engine would be available for the next races, as there was no doubt it had considerably more potential. The answer was, "Oh no, that's not possible." Cosworth didn't like the arrangement between Ford and Beatrice, and Benetton, or so the story went, was willing to pay a lot more for the engines. Despite that, we did get along really well with the two Cosworth engine mechanics/engineers who came to the races. Several years later I was told by people close to Cosworth that the Monza engine had something like 100 horsepower more than the standard engine we were running. No wonder it was considerably faster on the straight.

To sum things up, both our drivers were quick. Patrick was always willing to help out, but I guess it didn't really do much for our relationship with Alan Jones when Teddy pointed out he should lose some weight to fit in the car! I guess Alan just thought he was winding his watch after winning the World Championship and then taking a year off from Formula One. He was getting paid, of course, and was quite good if he wanted to be. What a waste.

Everything changed when Beatrice was taken over by Kohlberg Kravis Roberts (KKR) in one of the first leveraged buyouts. At the same time, Ford decided it wanted to pull out of Carl Haas's team and move to the new Benetton operation. Design work on our new car was seriously under way, and the crew had left for the last race in Adelaide. It was announced on race day that the plug was being pulled.

Later Berni Haas, Carl's wife, said, "It was a shame Beatrice was taken over by KKR. The timing of it was very bad for us. I think Jim Dutt had a great vision that was very good for his company and for us, too. We had a great group with Teddy and Tyler, Neil Oatley, Adrian Newey, Ross Brawn, and a lot of other very good people."

It really was a sad and sick scenario when it all fell apart. Pointing out to KKR that we had a five-year contract only got the reply, "So what!" Should it be classified under the heading of "criminal practices" or "just business"? I'm not really sure—probably both, in fact. Knowing Carl, in the end he probably received some funds from Beatrice.

Needless to say the demise of the FORCE/Lola team was a very unpleasant thing for a great many of us. So much hard work had gone into setting up the company and building good race cars. The people who made this happen deserved a great deal of credit.

Carl Haas had some options and suggestions, but Teddy was so frustrated with several major things that had happened that he was not really interested. Carl had spoken to me about his CART Indy car team. I had a chat with Adrian Newey, and as he's already explained, we each agreed to make the move if the other one came along.

I had gone to the British Virgin Islands for a bit of a rest and then flew to Miami, where Carl and his team were doing their last race of the 1986 season. Carl and Mario Andretti

# Mario Andretti

Tyler Alexander never knew this, but I admired him for 20 years before we finally worked together. He first caught my attention in Can-Am when McLaren dominated the series with the "Bruce and Denny Show."

In 1987, when Carl Haas told me he had hired Tyler to manage our Indy car operation, I was quite pleased because I really wanted to work with him. Tyler had a stellar reputation and enviable winning record, and I was sure he would bring the dynamic leadership we needed.

Tyler was everything I expected and more. He brought an incredible work ethic, vast experience, and real passion to the job. He was a great motivator and the team looked up to him. On the track, we'd have our share of success and heartbreak. In 1987, for example, I sat on pole eight times and dominated most of the races, most notably the Indy 500, but won just twice. Engine reliability proved to be our Achilles' heel that season. But that's the nature of the beast . . .

Off the track, I got to know Tyler well and we became good friends. He's interesting and worldly and we never run out of things to talk about. I'm still curious after all this time to hear how he interprets things, and to learn more about what makes him tick.

The Haas Lola team finally scored its first championship points in August 1986 at the Austrian Grand Prix. Seen here is Patrick Tambay, who finished fifth, one place behind his teammate, Alan Jones. (TYLER ALEXANDER COLLECTION)

asked me if I wanted to be the team manager of Newman/Haas Racing.

Carl and Berni took Mario and me and a couple of others to Joe's Stone Crab Restaurant near Miami Beach. It was amusing to watch Mario egg on Carl to bribe the maître d' with more and more money to move us up the queue for a table. The dinner was excellent, and the talk with Carl and Mario productive.

I spent some time chatting to Carl's guys, some of whom I knew already. I told Carl I would go to his place in Chicago and have a look. At the end of the day, both Adrian and I decided to work for Newman/Haas Racing with Mario Andretti in 1987.

# 1987: Newman/Haas Racing and the Two Marios

Carl had sorted out an engine deal with Ilmor Engineering, the company owned by Mario Illien, Paul Morgan, Roger Penske, and Chevrolet. With Penske already using the engine in his Indy cars, the contract with Newman/Haas Racing would help Ilmor move on.

After staying in a hotel for a couple of weeks, I got myself sorted out with a place to live, thanks to help from several people working for Carl. I then made several trips back and forth to England. This included going to Lola to check progress with the car, have discussions with Ilmor regarding the engine program, and to see Glen Monk, who was responsible for the fuel-system electronics for the engine. There were other stops in between, one being to see Phil Sharp, who had set up a company with Dave Price to build carbon-fiber race-car chassis and parts. They would help us to acquire a few things every now and again.

I had struck up a very good and long-lasting relationship with Paul Morgan during our Cosworth DFX days, and when he and Mario Illien joined to create Ilmor Engineering and develop their own engine program, I chose to go with him.

The rebuilds and dyno work would be done at Franz Weis's engine shop in Midland,

Texas. Franz had worked for Jim Hall as a mechanic for many years before starting his own engine company. Franz was a first-rate guy, and the relationship with Ilmor would prove successful, with hardly any problems.

Midland, Texas, is not the easiest place to get to, and shipping the engines back and forth to Chicago and various other places around the United States was a bit of a problem. We did some homework with the airline freight people and with Alex Greaves, who had worked with me during the Can-Am days. Alex had started his own fabrication company, and I talked him into giving us a hand at Newman/Haas. He was able to build some engine-shipping crates that were an efficient, "airline-friendly" size.

Since Penske had been having niggling problems with the fuel-control system, I made a point of discussing this with Glen Monk during one of my visits to the UK. Glen was an interesting guy, and we came up with new ideas for fixing the problems, which I related back to Mario and Paul.

There was a fair amount to be done at Lola because their Indy cars were generally built for Cosworth engines. Bruce Ashmore and the people there were doing a very good job, working with Ilmor on the engine installation and wiring. We also had a very good group of people at B, many of whom had worked there for a long time. I brought in Graham Fuller and Alex Greaves.

Adrian did not move out to Chicago, but operated from home in England and flew to the States for the races and tests, with me usually collecting him from the airport. As usual, he did a few mods to the car before it went off to the first test at Laguna Seca.

Despite having known Mario Andretti for a long time, I'd never been in his company that much. After the first day of the test, he invited Adrian and me to dinner on Cannery Row in Monterey. Both Adrian and I noticed that Mario was holding his menu a long way in front of him to read it. At which point Adrian asked, "Is that why you can't see the damn dashboard?" A predictably clever retort from Mario was forthcoming, although his exact words escape me now, followed by an enjoyable seafood dinner!

The next day did not turn out so well when the rear wing split apart and came off on the pit straight, causing a serious crash. The car was left in several bits, but Mario was okay. His only complaint as he walked back up the track was that his watch didn't seem to work anymore! A phone call to Mr. Haas came next, telling him that bits of his Lola race car were on both sides of the track—but that Mario was fine. I was able to tell him that even with the small amount of testing, the car and engine seemed quite reasonable. The rear wing was

# Mario Illien

Paul Morgan knew Tyler Alexander from the mid-1980s, when he and Teddy Mayer were buying some Cosworth Indy engines for their company, Mayer Motor Racing. But it wasn't until 1987 that I first met Tyler.

After showing some promising results in 1986, we had several teams on board to use our engines for the 1987 season. These were Penske Racing, Newman/Haas, and Patrick Racing.

The season started with an excellent result in Long Beach, when Mario Andretti took pole and won our first race in the Newman/Haas Lola-Chevrolet. The Newman/Haas team was run by Tyler Alexander, and the car was engineered by a gentleman called Adrian Newey.

This was a very strong and competitive combination, with Tyler working closely with Paul and I to sort out various problems.

At Indy in 1987, Newman/Haas had the dominant car-driver combination at the speedway. Mario got on pole position, won the pit stop competition, and dominated the race with a 1.5-lap lead until the engine failed close to the end of the race. He had led comfortably. It was easy. In fact, it was so easy that Andretti reduced his pace, and that cautious but understandable act cost him the race. At first we couldn't work out what was wrong, but later learned the engine had a broken valve spring. We didn't know why it had failed.

In 1988, Newman/Haas started to run our electronic fuel and ignition management system. At the Cleveland airport race, after some difficulties with the mapping during practice on Friday and Saturday, a new map was created for the race overnight in the hotel room, using the recorded data and the feedback from Mario Andretti. He was the only driver taking the electronic option, and his open mind and willingness to take a chance paid dividends, as he won the race with this new system. Carl Haas was very happy with this win, and decided to give the troops a flyover in his private jet on his way home after the race.

The next step was when Mercedes-Benz joined forces with the very successful McLaren team in 1995. This was also the time I began working with Tyler Alexander again.

The beginning with McLaren was difficult, and the results were not great until 1997, when we won our first F1 race with David Coulthard and Mika Hakkinen finishing first and third in Melbourne, Australia. Things improved even further when Adrian Newey joined the team in August 1997. Ten years after Long Beach, Tyler, Adrian, and I were together again, and we enjoyed lots of success and fun.

In 2005 the Formula One part of Ilmor was sold to Mercedes-Benz, and Adrian Newey left for Red Bull. Only Tyler stayed on at McLaren for several more years.

Tyler was a man of no nonsense. He was very competent, demanding, and successful in his job, and it was always a pleasure and an honor to work with him. We worked together at McLaren for 10 years, experiencing some lows, but also many highs.

sent back to Lola and found not to have been glued together correctly.

Mario, quickest through most of practice, was on pole position for the first race at Long Beach. On race day, as I walked to the grid with Paul Newman, we bumped into George Harrison and another chap. George came with us because he wanted to say hello to Mario. As we chatted by the car, George's friend, who was wearing a tacky old Goodyear jacket and hat, was leaning on the rear wing and nonchalantly looking around. I quietly asked George who this guy was. "Oh, don't worry about him," said George. "That's Tom Petty." And then he went back to joking with Mario. Sometimes you do feel a bit foolish, not recognizing a famous musician like Tom! Nevertheless, I asked them both to come by the motor home for a glass or two of wine after the race, which they did.

Mario won the race, chased most of the way by Bobby Rahal. It was a great start for the team and particularly for Mario Illien, who was overjoyed with the first win for his engine. I'm told that this broke an 87-race winning streak for Cosworth, so no wonder he and Paul Morgan were happy.

Mario was looking good after taking pole position for the next race at Phoenix and leading most of the way, until right near the end, when the turbo wastegate valve failed. We ended up finishing fifth.

Despite it still being cold in March at Indianapolis, we did a few days of testing, and Mario was pleased with the results. The next time we were at Indianapolis was for the real thing, the Indy 500, which brought with it the usual large amounts of work, along with the joy, the frustration, and the heartaches.

Back at the workshop, Adrian had the guys do quite a bit of work on the floor of the Lola to enable us to make it lower by a small amount. Adrian had a long list of things to try during practice, and we were quickest most days, with Bobby Rahal and the Penske cars close behind.

We had been running some small front brake ducts, but they must have upset someone, because we were later required to remove or modify them.

That changed things quite a bit after having spent several days getting the original aerodynamic balance of the car sorted out to Mario's liking. A couple of days later, Adrian had the balance back very close to where it had been, but he was pretty annoyed that we had spent all that time running the front brake ducts before someone decided they didn't like them.

Franz and his guys had built us an engine for qualifying, but when we ran it on the Friday before qualifying Mario didn't like it for some reason. As a result, the lowest-mileage practice

The Newman/Haas crew on their way to victory in the pit stop contest held before the 1987 Indianapolis 500. At the center of it all is 1987 pole-sitter Mario Andretti. (TYLER ALEXANDER COLLECTION)

engine was refitted, and Mario was much happier during the Saturday-morning practice. We were quite pleased as well, as it meant we didn't have to do another engine change.

The air and track temperatures kept rising throughout Saturday. By the time it was our turn to qualify, the track was quite slippery compared to the morning practice session. With a couple of small aero changes from Adrian, Mario kept it together, and despite sliding around a little bit, he did four very good laps to take pole position. This was a really good effort, particularly for all the guys on the team: Colin Duff, John Tzouanakis, Carl Dean, Donny Hoevel, Dave Evans, Graham Fuller, Alex Greaves, Joe Flynn (the gearbox guy), Warwick Aiken, and Johnny Capels.

There was a lot of work to be done the following week in preparation for the race. Adrian and Alex Greaves modified the oil tank several times to cover ourselves in case we ended up running a low volume of oil in the tank. It was a big task that kept poor Alex working late for quite a few nights. Adrian also made a small weight-jacking device for the right-rear suspension, which worked well.

After the final day of qualifying, there was a timed pit stop contest live on TV, with the cars from the first two or three rows running against each other and the clock. The pit lane had been laid out with two pit stop boxes side by side. Teams were timed from the entry to the exit of the box. You had to change all four tires and hold the empty fuel hose against the fuel valve on the side of the car. You could not jump over the wall until the car had come to a complete stop.

Our pit crew guys were very good but, just to be sure, we spent a lot of evenings practicing inside the garage with the doors closed.

With our turn coming up, we went to warm up the engine in the pit lane—and it just started to rev up and down by itself. Aaaghh!

After several tries at sorting out the problem, and moving ourselves back in the lineup (which somehow we managed to get away with), Mario Illien noticed that the fuel-metering control unit was moving around on its own. The unit's housing had a hole in the top to line up the rotating disc inside with a yellow dot for the standard setting position. Mr. Illien, having just finished his ice cream on a stick, cleaned off the stick and used it to move the disk around to line up the yellow dot, and then jammed the stick in the hole to stop the disc from moving.

It did the trick. With all that chaos going on, Mario Andretti and the guys did a great job and won the pit stop contest, which brought $25,000, along with a fully stocked Snap-on toolbox large enough to warrant a trailer hitch!

Mario led 170 out of the first 177 laps. Leading by a lap, with one pit stop left, and 15 to 20 minutes of the 500-mile race left to run, Mario was slowed down a little to save the car, engine, and gearbox. Not long after we did that, part of an inlet valve spring broke. Game over! The distinct sound of a flushing toilet came to mind.

I'm not sure if I was too pissed-off to cry; I guess it would have been impolite to throw up in the pit lane.

Several months later, the cause of the problem was found on Ilmor's cam-testing rig. Running a lower rpm had caused a resonance in the valve springs that led to the failure. If we had kept running the engine close to its maximum, we wouldn't have had the problem!

Things didn't really go very well for the next bunch of races. At Milwaukee, Mario qualified third, but the rear wing fell off in the race, resulting in quite a hard hit into the concrete wall. I had some issues with Kirk Russell of CART, who said that some of the boys had jumped over the track wall near the accident—and they themselves told me they hadn't. I did point out to them a bit later that I had no problem standing up for the crew—but as for being "stitched" by them? I sure as hell wasn't interested in that.

Mario dominated the Michigan 500 until a valve problem stopped the engine, and he led from pole at Pocono until he had a heavy shunt that separated a shoulder. Typical of Mario, however, he was back in action two weeks later at Road America, the fast four-mile circuit in Elkhart Lake, Wisconsin. Fuel consumption is often an issue there, so Adrian had decided to use the Indy bodywork with the road-course wing configuration, to create less drag and give better fuel mileage. Fortunately, the Ilmor engine was quite good in this respect. Mario won the race from pole, although the fuel warning light was flashing on and off for the last couple of laps. We had checked this with a low-fuel run during practice, and thus knew how much fuel we had left when the light started flashing at a particular place on the circuit. It meant there wasn't too much of a "hold your breath" situation at the end.

The last race of the season at Miami was looking good for us; the car was not bad at all, and Mario had qualified on pole for the eighth time in 1987. But come Sunday, it rained on and off before the race, and when we went to the grid, Adrian decided to change to softer springs. The car was a handful in the race, as it bottomed heavily in several places, and Mario finished fourth at the end of 103 laps. On the way to the airport after the race, Adrian said, "Damn—I should have raised the car with the softer

I saved this newspaper image of Adrian Newey and me at the first test of the Newman/Haas Lola T87/00 at Laguna Seca in 1987. (TYLER ALEXANDER COLLECTION)

springs after we fitted the rain tires, which had a softer sidewall." The race was won by Mario's son, Michael, who finished second to Bobby Rahal in the championship. Mario was sixth.

The 1987 Lola was a very good car, and the Ilmor Chevrolet engine had plenty of horsepower, but there were way too many reliability problems, which meant we didn't do as well as we should have. As you can imagine, it was quite disappointing for everyone.

# 1988–89: Andretti and Son

For 1988, Adrian Newey decided to stay in England and be involved with Formula One—which was what he really wanted to do. Needless to say, he has become one of the most brilliant designers in racing history, enjoying an amazing run of success with Williams, McLaren, and, most recently, Red Bull.

Tony Cicale, who had worked for Carl Haas before, returned as the race engineer. Tony is a very fine guy and he got along very well with the team. He was another race engineer who was not based at the Chicago race shop but lived at the end of Long Island. (At least that was a lot closer than England.) I did talk him into coming back to Chicago after several of the races in order to sort out various problems we'd had, and to give the guys a bit more time to work.

The 1988 Lola was not as good a car as the previous year's T87, particularly on the high-speed ovals. However, the year got off to a good start again when Mario qualified fourth and won at Phoenix. The next race at Long Beach didn't go so well; after qualifying 2nd, he finished 15th after a problem with the clutch.

With Indianapolis next on the calendar, we focused on a new rule regarding a safety device for the wheel nut. Colin Duff and I came up with a wheel nut safety "pin" that was actually a centrifugal device in the axle. We spent quite a bit of time spinning the axle on a lathe at about 20 mph in order to sort out the retaining spring and the weight of the pin necessary to allow it to pop out at slow speed, to help speed up the tire change somewhat during the pit stops. When we showed the people at Indianapolis what we had and how it worked, they said okay.

Tony spent a lot of time running the gearboxes from the 1987 and 1988 cars on a proper dyno test rig at Chevrolet. When the 1987 version looked to be 2 to 3 mph faster on the straight due to mechanical losses on the 1988 gearbox, it was decided to run the 1987 car with the 1988 T88 as a backup.

This created a lot of gossip in the press about which car we were running. We just said it was the one painted white—which they both were! It was a bit tricky for Carl because he was the Lola distributor in the States, and he had sold a few 1988 cars!

Most days, there was the usual battle going on during the last hour of practice, affectionately known as "happy hour" because the sun would have gone down low enough to cool things off. Everyone wanted to see who would be first to run a lap over 220 mph. We were pretty sure that Mario had done it, but there were some noises that Rick Mears had beaten him to it. Needless to say, we didn't think so—and neither did quite a few other people. From what I recall, the teams were doing their own timing of their own cars, and of several of the usual competitors. Of course, the gossip up and down the pit road was rife with the usual incorrect information. At the end of the day, the Speedway printed the actual times anyway. Rick Mears did 220.048 mph, which was just a tick faster than Mario's lap of 219.995 mph.

Standing on the main straight with our radar gun during most of these late-in-the-day runs, the '87 car with a new set of tires would go past us at a bit over 240 mph, still accelerating on its way into turn one. I have to say, we thought it was very impressive—along with being scary as hell! On one of those runs, the lower engine mounts broke when Mario was halfway through turn one; he was able to get the car slowed down and drive back to the pits. There was not too much damage, but it was to be another long night for Alex Greaves and the guys, this time fabricating and bonding in new bottom engine mounts.

Mario qualified fourth, not as quick as expected because it had become windy, and the track was very slippery. There was a bit of a scene because I didn't wave off his four-lap run as several people thought I should have done. If you remember, I had done this with Johnny Rutherford in 1978 because of the low boost pressure problems when, as things turned out, we would have been better off leaving things as they were. But as I've said before, just being in the race is one of the most important things you learn at Indianapolis.

Mario was competitive in the race until some electronic box problems ended his run. We chose to take the time to change the boxes, as there were no mechanical problems with the car. Even though Mario was out of contention, it was a good thing to keep the car running for the sponsors and the fans that had paid to see the race.

Mario finished 20th at Indy, but a week later at Milwaukee we were looking in good shape, until Mario, having qualified 2nd, broke a halfshaft when he spun the rear wheels by going wide on a white line while leaving a pit stop. It was a shame because we were running a new Ilmor fuel injection system and getting quite good mileage, which would have been very helpful toward the end of the race.

Apart from the opening race at Phoenix, the only other win in 1988 came at Cleveland. We were not that quick at the beginning of practice, but Mario Illien improved things quite a bit by adjusting the numbers in the new fuel system software. As for the race on Cleveland's airport circuit, the challenge posed by the last pit stop was one of those things that you get right once in a while.

Due to the unusual elongated track layout and the position of the pits, it was possible to make a quick pit stop and get out ahead of the people just ahead of you if they didn't stop. Mario, running third, was about to make his last pit stop when Colin Duff, our very good chief mechanic, yelled to me, "Let's just change the right-side tires and maybe we can get out in front of the others." I quickly told Mario on the radio what we were going to do and got a typically laid-back "Oh-kaaay" in reply. Our pit stop area was at the entrance to the pit lane, which helped a lot, and the pit stop itself was very good. I remember yelling to Mario on the radio, "Go! Go! Go!" There was no pit lane speed limit at that time, and we all wondered just how quick Mario was going when he left the end of the not very wide pit lane! Whatever the speed, he was now leading the race.

There were a few interesting moments during the last laps when Mario's left-rear wheel made contact with the cement wall a couple of times—just helping to keep the car on the track—with Bobby Rahal's March about a second behind him. And that's how the race finished. Nice drive, Mr. Andretti!

There was some physical damage to the left-rear wheel, and the bearing positions had moved a bit in the upright, meaning we couldn't be sure how much longer it would have lasted.

"Larry Learjet," as Carl's Lear pilot was affectionately known, thought it would be only

I'd known and respected Mario Andretti for many years before we finally got to work together on the Newman/Haas Indy car team in 1987. It turned out to be everything I could have hoped for. (LAT PHOTOGRAPHIC)

appropriate to do a very low pass over the Cleveland airfield as we departed. Which we did—along with enjoying some of Berni Haas's rather excellent white wine on the rest of the flight home.

Mario qualified second in Toronto and the Meadowlands. Ignition problems meant a retirement in Canada, and we were lucky to finish second at the Meadowlands, because the gearbox had some broken bits in it.

We didn't finish either of the 500-mile races at Michigan or Pocono, but some quick thinking at Mid-Ohio worked well for us. About halfway through the race, Joe Flynn, the gearbox guy who was always listening on his radio to the CART people, heard there was an accident and that the pace car would be going out. I knew from my stopwatch that Mario was coming up to the pit entrance, even though I couldn't actually see him. I pressed the radio button and said, "Pit stop! Pit stop!" Mario responded—and we went from fourth to first before finally finishing second; a satisfying result from another quick call that everyone in the team participated in.

Mario may have finished third at Elkhart Lake, but a less pleasant memory from the weekend was one of food poisoning. When Tony and I had dinner on Saturday night, the food seemed to be okay. By Sunday morning, I had changed my view, as I was leaking from both ends. Once at the race track, I went to see the CART doctors and asked what they could give me, as I needed to manage the car during the race. Their best advice was to drink Gatorade and throw up. They said they would then give me "something" to help just before the race.

The cars were on the grid when Mario came on the radio, saying he wanted to see me about something. I replied, "I'm in the third loo behind the control tower and will be with you shortly!" When the race was over, I felt like I had been run over by a truck, but at least the medical guys' "something" had got me through the race.

At Nazareth, where Mario again finished third, we had a fumble with a pit stop, which was unusual because the guys were generally very good. Both rear wheel nuts were not tightened completely, and a quick bit of arm waving from the guys had me pressing the radio button and shouting "Stop!" Mario had moved about three feet. After that, we had a rethink about how the team radio should work, changed a few things, and practiced the new game plan. It worked just fine.

The Newman in Newman/Haas Racing was, of course, actor Paul Newman, and he was a great guy to have around the race team. He always had interesting stories to tell. One I remember was how a major hassle with the director of *Butch Cassidy and the Sundance Kid*, which lasted for months, was sorted out over a six-pack of Coors as the two of them sat on the Hollywood Boulevard sidewalk. Paul was a great one for playing pool and drinking beer with the guys, usually at the parties Mario would throw at his house when we were racing at Nazareth. Paul's general help with the morale of the team was always greatly appreciated.

After taking third at Laguna Seca, we didn't have a great finish to the season at Miami. Mario qualified 2nd, but we had some difficulties with the fuel system, which prompted another one of those "How did this happen?" moments, since we had not had any problems of this sort before. Mario finished a lowly 17th. I spent a lot of time in Miami trying to persuade Tony Cicale to continue with NHR—but he wanted to leave and go to Porsche. As I said, it wasn't a great finish to the 1988 season.

There were quite a few changes at Newman/Haas Racing for 1989. Engineer Brian Lisles arrived from Ken Tyrrell's Formula One team, where he had worked for a very long time, and Ed Nathman joined us from McLaren Engines. This followed Mario's discussions with Carl about running a two-car team, with Michael Andretti as the other driver. Carl and Berni had agreed, and they wanted me to stay and help set up the new operation.

At the same tme, Ron Dennis had been talking with me about going back to McLaren, and I was thinking about the possibility. I just thought it would be interesting and different—and it sure as hell was! I spoke to Carl and said I would stay until after Indianapolis to help get things running with the two-car team and the new people. Carl was very good about it, even though he and several of his friends and business partners did not want me to leave. Although Carl had made me several quite satisfactory offers, I had made up my mind.

One afternoon, Paul Newman called and spent some time talking to me about staying with his team. At one point in the conversation I told Paul I would consider it—if he would get me a date with Holly Hunter. There was a long pause on the phone, followed by what sounded like "You bastard!" and a burst of laughter.

Although I was interested in what Ron had been speaking to me about, and I wanted to go back to McLaren, it was going to be sad leaving a bunch of good guys who I liked working with—as well as people such as chief financial officer Neal Richter and sponsorship expert Ralph Hansen. Once Carl realized he and I wanted the same thing for his team, we had become good friends and gotten along very well—as I did with his wife Berni, who was always there with moral support when necessary.

After Indianapolis and my last race with Newman/Haas, I went to the grand prix in

Talking with Carl Haas before the 1988 Long Beach CART race. I enjoyed my time with the Newman/Haas team, but I was thinking about returning to McLaren. (LAT PHOTOGRAPHIC)

Phoenix at Ron's request. I came back to Chicago and met John Szymanski at the airport. John worked for Carl in public relations and is a great guy—always helpful and full of fun. He gave me my other bags and I flew back to England.

I took the opportunity to travel down to the Algarve in Portugal a couple of times, and also to have dinner quite often with Teddy and Sally. We made a trip to Miami and then Belize before going to Detroit to do a few things at McLaren Engines, and then back to England.

Ron and I met up again several times and discussed what I was going to do. We agreed on a variety of things, including my going to the last two races of the 1989 Formula One season in Japan and Australia in order to get a feel for what was going on at that time. My actual position would be decided later.

Ron's drivers, Ayrton Senna and Alain Prost, were fighting for the championship, the two of them colliding while disputing the lead at Suzuka. This ended up being nothing more than a stitch-up for Senna by the FIA when they took the win away from him (Prost having retired as a result of the collision). *The Sun* newspaper summed it up well with its headline the next day: malice in hondaland.

After the race, I flew up to Tokyo with Ayrton in one of the Honda helicopters, along with two boxes of Ayrton's model radio-controlled airplanes. He was keen on flying them.

While we were there, Ron asked me to go down to Cairns and then up to Port Douglas in Australia, on the way to Adelaide, and stay in the new Sheraton Hotel on Four Mile Beach with Gordon Murray, McLaren's chief designer at the time, and Gerhard Berger, who Ron had just hired for 1990. Gerhard is one of those people who is very easy to get along with, and he certainly helped to make my stay very pleasant.

While I was there, I had a long chat with Ayrton Senna by the pool. At one point, he said to me, "You know, no one tells the truth in Formula One." It was interesting to hear him say that at the time—and it would be even more significant later on.

# 1990: Back To McLaren—and On to Japan

f you're a professional, you're supposed to do things, even when, in some cases, you don't want to. I started at what was then the new McLaren factory in the Woking Business Park on January 2, 1990. Since I already knew quite a few people there, it made my presence a bit easier. Having said that, I got the feeling that not many of them seemed to know what I was supposed to be doing. Ron had asked me to be the team manager, which seemed strange because he already had a team manager: Dave Ryan. There was some talk that Dave didn't want to travel anymore, but I'm not sure how true that really was.

Very early on Dave Ryan and I were in Ron's office, and Ron said to us, "I want Tyler to go to all the races and tests. If he doesn't like things, then he has to sort them out. Also, if he thinks anyone is not doing the correct job, he can chase them up as well." I didn't really ask for that situation, but that's what Ron wanted. I was to find that the very same people who had said "We really need someone like you to get some things done around here" were the first ones to complain when I tried to do just that.

Not long after, Neil Oatley, Bob Bell, and I were preparing to go to Honda in Japan via Los Angeles, where we would stop off to see Pete Weismann. Pete made gearboxes and

Ayrton Senna in the Honda-powered MP4/5B during a testing session in 1990. By the end of the season he'd captured his second F1 Drivers championship and a Constructors title for McLaren. (LAT PHOTOGRAPHIC)

gearbox parts for some of the race teams, and was a friend of Gordon Murray's. We wanted to discuss a new type of gearbox shift mechanism. During a meeting before we left England, I had expressed my views and concerns over getting things done with Pete, which were based on past problems getting parts that were needed for the Can-Am cars. I don't think it went down very well with a couple of people at the meeting, but experience is experience.

Once in Japan, we met with Osamu Goto, one of the top racing engineers at Honda's R&D facility, to discuss aspects of the new car. After the two-day meeting finished, Neil and Bob went back to England and I went to the Suzuka test for a day before returning home.

I guess I didn't realize what the outcome of this was going to be at the time, but I ended up doing pretty much all of the Suzuka tests from then on. It seemed that other people at McLaren didn't like going to Japan, but I got along well with the Honda people, and had no problem with traveling to Japan or working there.

Honda had set up a small workshop to service and maintain the McLaren test car at their R&D facility in Wako, which worked out very well.

There were also tests at Estoril and Imola, followed by the season-opening F1 race at Phoenix, which Ayrton won. The next day, after waiting in Phoenix for several hours due to some kind of drama at LAX, I eventually flew to Los Angeles and on to Tokyo. From there it was the bus to Tokyo station, a bullet train to Nagoya, another train to Shiroko, and finally, a taxi to Suzuka, ready for another test. That was a fairly typical schedule, made all the more interesting by very few English-language signs.

At the next test in Imola, when we were having problems, Ayrton said, "Tyler, you've got to sort out some of these things." I told Ayrton that it was hard to do that when you're the only one who knows you're meant to be the general.

I think it was at the same test when Martin Whitmarsh paid us a visit. Martin had come from British Aerospace to be McLaren's head of operations. While chatting, I asked if I could help him with various things that go on in the motor racing world, particularly within Formula One and the FIA. I got the impression he was not particularly interested, and preferred to find out for himself. It would turn out to be an expensive lesson. By this time, Dave Ryan had become the factory team manager and I was the race team manager. This did seem kind of strange, and I picked up the scent of a rat. But it was not my intention to go anywhere.

Not long after, I happened to be in Los Angeles chasing up the gearbox project with Weismann when Martin called and asked me to come back to England for a meeting. There he pointed out that McLaren already had a team manager. No shit, Dick Tracy! Either Dave Ryan had been helped to get over his reluctance to go racing, or other people didn't like me doing what they had asked me to do. I came out of the meeting as special projects manager—with no FOCA pass. To say that I was somewhat pissed-off would probably be an understatement for a variety of reasons. Years later Martin admitted that he had taken away my FOCA pass, adding that I'd won his respect when I just said, "Okay," and got on with whatever job he threw at me. I passed the test with flying colors, and he quickly realized the word *quit* wasn't part of my vocabulary.

Not wishing (or willing) to walk away, I was determined to carry on. I made several calls to Pete Weismann and Gary Knutson, who was preparing the electronic system for Pete's "Quick Shift" gearbox control. A week or so later, I flew out to Los Angeles and drove down to Pete's workshop at Costa Mesa. We wanted to work on putting the system into a McLaren gearbox. Pete thought it would take two or three weeks. My thoughts, based on the experience I'd mentioned at that meeting earlier in the year, were a bit different. Sure enough, the project didn't finish until November. When this sort of thing happens, you just have to get stuck in and get on with it.

I went back and forth quite a few times during the summer, chasing up gearbox parts with Neil Trundle at McLaren. There were a lot of general problems thanks to having to build an electronic system to run the electric control motor, as well as the internal gearbox parts. Most of July and August were spent having the various parts made—and remade, and remade. It was an interesting and yet a frustrating time. And just to make things even trickier, we had to work with some drawings that had no dimensions on them.

With the help of Gary and Pete, I built a test rig that held the McLaren gearbox with a hydraulic unit to drive it, and a clutch control and a road car wheel and tire to provide some inertia. It was late in August, and we started to run a real gearbox on the hydraulic-powered rig, which produced even more problems. I went back to England for a few days, returning on September 5. The next day, we were ready to run again.

After various modifications we ran the box up to about 500C at 5,000 rpm input for 10 to 15 minutes. Then we put it in first gear and ran up to 10,400 rpm, slowed down to about 2,000 rpm, then put it in sixth gear and ran up to about 10,200 rpm, which was as fast as it would run. Everything seemed okay.

So . . . Pete decided to run maximum rpm and change gear. I ran it up to 2,000 rpm, selected first gear, ran it up to maximum rpm, pressed the button for second gear, pushed

Ayrton Senna studies the data during practice for the 1990 Belgian Grand Prix at Spa. He scored his fifth victory of the season aboard the Honda-powered MP4/5B. (LAT PHOTOGRAPHIC)

# Nick "Hogger" Cross

My first encounter with Tyler was in 1990 when he rejoined McLaren.

I of course knew who he was, and had heard lots of tales from people who had worked with him in the past. Over the next 20-plus years I would be able to draw my own conclusions about the man.

The first major project I was involved in with Tyler was the Weismann Quick Shift Gearbox. (Click click *bang!*) I was working in the R&D department at the time. This was a "challenging" project, but it allowed me to witness for myself Tyler's strengths and skills as a mechanic, machinist, designer, engineer, coordinator, and humorist, as well as his never-give-up work ethic.

Tyler was away at Pete's workshop in Costa Mesa, California, just south of Los Angeles, for the initial assembly and testing of the gearbox, with the help of Gary Knutson, who was also helping with the project. It was clear from Tyler's faxes that things were not going smoothly.

He would generally ask for various spares and parts to be sent out, but at the end of one of his faxes, he also asked for some "patience pills." A week or so later we received a fax asking for "A large bottle of extra-strength patience pills!" This project involved a lot of different parties, and Tyler did a great job of getting people to gel. He also laid down some strong foundations and relationships for future projects.

During the 1990s I worked closely with Tyler, both racing and testing. The pace of development and technology was advancing at an ever-increasing rate. Tyler showed his skills not only through his understanding of the gearbox control system, but also by getting the best out of people. The gearbox control system was getting ever more complex and advanced. This involved a group of very clever electronics and computer guys, but they had no real understanding of what they were actually trying to control.

Tyler went into the spares truck and returned with some gearbox internals. He then proceeded to explain how the drum rotated, moving the shift fork and sliding the dog ring along the hub to engage with the mating gear. He also demonstrated that if the shift timing was wrong it went "dog to dog," not engaging the next gear. These guys knew what "dog to dog" looked like on their computer screens and from the shift statistics, but now they had a much better understanding of what we were trying to achieve.

Tyler did a similar thing when the race drivers were complaining about harsh downshifts upsetting the car. He knew how to fix the problem, but needed to explain to the computer guys what he wanted.

He got a few of the guys in his VW Golf and demonstrated that if you let the clutch out too fast during a downshift, it made the car jump around, whereas if you let it out in a more-controlled manner, the car was much smoother. This clearly demonstrated to the computer guys what he wanted from the system.

Other than his motor racing prowess, Tyler is also known for his one-liners, along with his ability to sum things up concisely. I once was helping Lee Coleman, our race team fabricator, modify the quick-lift pneumatic race jack very early on a race morning. We were working on top of one of our flyaway packing boxes, and I was trying to hold it steady so Lulu could cut off a piece so it would fit our new nose cone. It kept sliding around, and out of nowhere a voice with an American accent was heard to say, "It's like watching two monkeys trying to fuck a football on wet grass." I guess it probably was!

This brought the garage to a standstill. We were laughing so hard we had tears running down our cheeks. God only knows how he makes up these expressions.

I have learned a great deal about motor racing, people, and life from Tyler, for which I am eternally grateful. All of the above can probably be summed up in a few words: Just one of the good guys.

the clutch lever—and the whole box exploded. Part of one of the gears came through the gearbox case and just missed me! It looked like the gearbox went into several gears at once. Just about everything was destroyed, except second and fifth gears. Dear, oh dear!

One day after the gearbox blowup, I had a large scene with Pete, who continued to come by, make some comment, and then walk off. I had to tell him if he wanted me to work on getting "his" fucking gearbox finished, he had better pay attention or I was going home. It seemed I was slowly losing my sense of humor—not something I would normally do.

Pretty much the rest of September was used up fixing the carnage from the blowup, replacing parts and making new ones. On September 25, we had another go. Shortly thereafter, on September 27, we had packed up all the bits and sent them off to England.

Pete and Gary came over to England in early October. With the help of Neil Trundle, Rob Irwin, Nick Butler, Nick Cross, and several mechanics, we fitted the stuff to one of the test cars. With Honda being happy we could run the car without them being there, we went to the test track at Chobham, not far from the McLaren factory. But there were still a lot of problems with the computer and the gears.

By early November, Rob Irwin had sorted out the computer bits. The work prompted a classic comment from Gary Knutson, who noted, "The secret of electronics is keeping the smoke inside the tubes." Another test was run at Chobham, this time doing proper power shifts. It broke the gears again. The test was run in the morning and Pete was meant to be there, but by the time he and his wife Michelle showed up, we were putting the car back in the transporter. It should have been time to move on.

Pete returned in December to see Ron and to tell him, among other things, that the project would never have happened if it weren't for my help. Although I had been able to get stuck into something and get on with it, the project had pretty much come to an end. There was also the benefit of striking up a good relationship with the people in McLaren's R&D department.

There had been some keen interest from Honda regarding the patent rights for this type of shift. Several years later, the Weismann quick-shift principle was implemented in power-boat racing, where all the parts could be much bigger and stronger. I believe it worked okay.

So much for that. Now it was off to another test at Suzuka, with Allan McNish doing the driving.

Ayrton Senna on his way to victory in the McLaren MP4/6 at the Belgian Grand Prix in August 1991, where his teammate Gerhard Berger finished second. (LAT PHOTOGRAPHIC)

# 1991: Testing with Honda and Winning with Senna

And so the traveling continued into 1991, particularly as there was still work being done on the Weismann gear change—the devil knows why—and I needed to go to Costa Mesa for a few days in the middle of January. This was on the way to another Suzuka test.

It turned out to be a bit of a prolonged trip thanks to the Singapore Airlines flight from Los Angeles missing the runway at Narita on the first attempt to land in pouring rain. By the time we finally got down and I made it to the Tokyo train station, it was too late to get the last bullet train to Nagoya. I spent the night at the Ana Hotel in Tokyo, and early the next morning called project engineer Ian Dyer, who was already in Suzuka, to tell him that I was still in Tokyo but leaving shortly. My delay was not a problem, as the Honda engine guys were waiting for some parts.

This was the first test for the new V12 engine, and things went very well. Honda was holding a press conference on the Saturday before I was due to leave and they asked me to be present, along with the other Honda engine people, who were now slowly becoming friends. I was happy to help out by doing that.

Senna and Berger were still driving for the team, of course, but I had spoken to Ron Dennis about the possibility of Michael Andretti doing an F1 test with us. Arrangements were made for him to come to Estoril in early February. This didn't work out too well for Michael because he came over just after the Daytona 24 Hours, and he was a bit jet-lagged. And then it rained for most of the test.

I was back in Japan the following week, along with Ron Dennis and David North, our gearbox designer. David and I had two days of gearbox meetings at Honda's Wako R&D facility. There were lots of strange and interesting questions for David—things like: How do you know how thick to make the gearbox case? Why did you do this? Why did you do that? Along with: *How* did you do it? A lot of the answers were based on David's long experience designing gearboxes; this seemed to confuse several people, who appeared to need some sort of answer with a formula attached to it. At least the coffee was very good.

After our lengthy meeting, we met up with Ron and were taken by the Honda people to dinner in a lovely restaurant on top of the Hilton Hotel in the middle of Tokyo. The excellent food, which was cooked in front of us, and the views over Tokyo were really very special. It was also a perfect opportunity to have an informal chat with a couple of the key Honda people. It was agreed that McLaren would send a couple of gearboxes to run on the Honda gearbox dyno at Wako.

The tests continued at Suzuka and were not without incident. This was winter, of course, and it started to snow at one point when former Williams driver Jonathan Palmer was out on the track. Typically, the Honda guys didn't want to stop until the number of laps that were on the test schedule had been completed. Jonathan ran until the buildup of snow on the engine air filter inside the airbox had become so bad that the engine wouldn't run properly and we had to stop!

On another occasion, McNish had a shunt on the second lap of a test. There was a reasonable amount of damage, a lot of it to the bodywork. This produced quite a few *mundai-da*s (big problems!) from the Honda guys, who had a lot of engine work to get through.

The incident really brought home just what this was all about. There was serious work to be done by Honda, and it didn't allow for our car flying off the road. Some of the boys thought that we couldn't do much about it, but I had to point out that Honda was relying on us to maintain the car correctly so that they could test their engines.

The broken pieces of the bodywork were gathered up and brought back to the garage to allow Jonathan Ostrowski, Richard Moody, and several of the guys to start the long

Ron Dennis is doused by Williams drivers Nigel Mansell and Riccardo Patrese after the 1991 Hungarian Grand Prix, with winner Ayrton Senna joining in from a distance. (LAT PHOTOGRAPHIC)

process of gluing everything back together. Ian Dyer knew a fellow with a machine shop just down the road from the circuit, so Ian and I set off to machine front suspension parts that we didn't have spares for.

Just as the track was in the process of closing at the end of the day, Honda got permission for us to do a couple laps with the repaired car. It was mechanically together, and a quick setup had been done to check things. The car actually ran without bodywork, as this was still being glued back together, with the help of a variety of hot-air heaters to speed the process and help counteract the cold.

The car ran okay for the rest of the test, but it was hard on McNish. The long runs required by Honda made the cold a physical problem for Allan, and quite often we had to take a break between runs to allow him to recover.

Since there was so much work being done at Suzuka and Wako, and since McLaren had a workshop there, one of the senior Honda people recommended that I stay at the Metropolitan Holiday Inn in Ikebukuro, a suburb of Tokyo. The hotel was not far from a large train station and a short trip to Wako.

It was a good hotel in a nice town, with the added attraction of sushi places that were near the station and always seemed to be open when I got back from Wako late at night. There were also several medical colleges there, and it was not unusual to be in a restaurant and have students ask if I would speak with them in English. This was almost always worth a couple of bottles of Asahi Dry beer, perfect for washing down chicken yakitori grilled on a bamboo stick.

While staying at the hotel, it was fairly normal to experience small earthquakes. They would first wake you up, and then you would see the small lamp slowly moving across the table, and the tall one on the floor rocking back and forth.

The train station had two very large department stores, the Seibu and the Tobu. The Seibu was impressive, offering every kind of food you could think of. There were large fresh tuna and a variety of other fish being cut up on the floors below ground level, along with lacquered wooden rice bowls for sale on the top floors, and everything else in between.

This was a much better arrangement than previously, when I would go from Tokyo to Suzuka and back in the afternoon when the test finished. Then it was a walk up the road from the Ana Hotel to Roppongi and a cheeseburger at the Hard Rock Cafe. The bus to the airport the next morning would be a trip in itself before the flight back to London. A typical trip would be from Narita to a bus to Tokyo to a bullet train, then to the Nagoya-Kintetsu line, and then from Shiroko to taxi to the Suzuka Circuit Hotel.

Staying in Ikebukuro was easier for many reasons, not least because there was a bus link from Narita Airport to the hotel. I could spend time at Honda before going on to Suzuka, and then stay for a couple of days for meetings with the Honda engine people. I could also help to sort out any problems with the mechanics without the hassle of staying in Tokyo.

Being in Wako for a meeting was one thing; going to the McLaren workshop was quite another, because everyone had to wear the standard white Honda shirt and trousers. The nice old ladies who looked after the uniforms always laughed when we *Gaijin* came in for our uniforms. Ian Dyer and I, for example, would start off with trousers that finished about halfway between our knees and our shoes. It didn't take them long to find some that were the correct length, or have them made for us.

The boys stayed at a hotel much closer to Wako to make life easier, because they would be there several days earlier to build the car before sending it to Suzuka. Then they would stay for a similar time after the test to take the car apart and pack whatever needed to go back to England for servicing.

It took a while to master the right thing to say when trying to contact the guys by telephone at the Cygnus Hotel, where they usually stayed. I would say, "Mushi Mushi, this is Mr. Alexander. Could I speak with Mr. Dyer?" "Aaagh, so sorry, no Mr. Alexander staying here." After several goes you learned to say, "Could I speak to Mr. Dyer's room." "*Mundi-nai.*" (No problem.) The phone would ring and Ian would answer.

I spent some time with Phil McPherson, a young guy from New Zealand and a very good mechanic working in the gearbox department. Phil and I would meet in the morning at the Wako train station. We would then walk through the back gate and into the Honda R&D Center with a bow and a *Ohayo Gozaimasu* to the guard, who would bow back before we replied *Doumo arigato gozaimasu*. I was always intrigued by the fact that we could simply walk through the back gate, straight into Honda R&D.

Phil and I spent quite a bit of our time in the gearbox dyno rooms. We were pretty sure that the dyno testing of the McLaren gearbox was intended to check it against Honda's own gearbox project named FCZ. An MP4/5C with a modified wiring loom had been sent to Wako for the FCZ gearbox to be fitted and run at a Suzuka test during the last week in March. The gearbox had some basic problems, but it did run.

The FCZ gearbox had an interesting method of changing gear, but it was quite slow. Whoever was doing the testing, Jonathan Palmer or Stefan Johansson, said the slow gear changes, particularly when downshifting, made the car very hard to drive. Honda really didn't want us to see just what was inside the gearbox, but in the end we did, because we were starting to get along very well with the FCZ gearbox mechanics, and Phil was helping them to fix some problems. Phil noticed that they had changed some steel parts for ceramic ones; when he quietly asked why, he got some quiet answers and a few *mundai-nai*s from our newfound friends.

There was a funny scene at Wako when the gearbox people took Phil and me to look at some gearbox parts that were in the engine build shop. They had put up a bunch of banner-type sheets to close off the engine part of the workshop and prevent us from seeing anything. I had a look over the banners and was spotted by one of the engine guys, who recognized me and immediately came around, moved the banners, and invited me to come and see the new cylinder heads and camshaft arrangement.

Ayrton Senna on the podium at Spa after his victory in the 1991 Belgian Grand Prix. He would go on to take his third F1 Drivers championship after logging one more victory at the season's last race in Australia. (LAT PHOTOGRAPHIC)

The gearbox people were taken aback by all of this. They never realized I had been working with the engine guys for some time and that we were good friends—which was what the Suzuka testing was mainly about, because it was their engine program.

In April I went back to see Pete Weismann, do some more work with his gearbox project, and talk to him about what we could still try to achieve. With the materials and technology available at the time, it was somewhat hard to believe that the design didn't work better. It did work in powerboats, but that was because the parts could be much bigger than those in a Formula One gearbox.

At the beginning of May, Gary and Pete were meant to come to England together, but Pete either lost his passport or it was out-of-date, which meant he showed up a couple of days later.

We had run the gear change stuff on the test rig and then installed it into the race-car gearbox. We then had to wait for Jonathan Palmer to arrive and drive the car at Chobham. Some internal parts failed on both days.

This was, perhaps appropriately, the end of the project.

Meanwhile, back at Wako and Suzuka, more testing with the FCZ gearbox showed the gear changes were a bit quicker, but still seemed very slow to Stefan.

Martin Whitmarsh flew over to see the Honda people and then came down to Suzuka on the last day of the test before having more FCZ meetings in Wako.

Stefan and I flew to Chicago and then down to Indianapolis to watch the 500 while on our way back to England. Typically for a race-car driver, Stefan had to borrow some money from me to rent his car, as I was being picked up by someone working for Carl Haas who had also sorted out credentials for me at the race.

Michael Andretti came over to drive the F1 car again in a test at Magny-Cours in early June. Of course, it rained almost every day, so yet again it was not such a good time for Michael.

We then took two cars, one with Honda's FCZ gearbox and the other with semi-active suspension for Allan McNish and Jonathan Palmer to drive at Suzuka. After the test, the cars were put through some vibration tests at Wako before being sent back to England.

Honda always did a vibration test with a new car and engine, sometimes out in the back of the factory in Woking Business Park, where they would rev the engine quite high and probably scare the neighbors' cats. I never saw this happen with any of the other engine manufacturers we worked with; it was probably their mistake not to follow what Honda always did.

While all of this was going on, McLaren had quietly started our own gear-change project known as "6Y." David North was doing the gear-change stuff, and Robert Irwin was looking after pretty much all of the electrical control system, which became known as "Lobby's Logic Box." We had a good little group of people, including Nick Butler, Nick "Hogger" Cross, Paul Cann, Carl Hardy, and Trevor Lawes, along with Neil Trundle and myself, the special projects manager. Bob Bell was kind enough to design us a steering wheel with a couple of small paddles to be used for changing gear.

The good thing was that the kit of parts would fit straight into the current gearbox—nice touch, Mr. North. On July 16, 1991, we took a car with 6Y parts for Allan McNish to drive at Chobham—and it worked. There were a few small problems, but we made new parts that evening and went back the next day. After a few runs, a quick look showed that a trip back to the factory was needed to make the new parts out of even stronger material, which Ray "Tex" Rowe heat-treated for us in his small oven.

We ran long enough that afternoon to have the local residents call the Chobham military testing grounds to complain about the noise! They told them it was a new tank, but by then Martin Whitmarsh's phone was ringing with complaints and threats from the military. It was a pretty damn good effort, and the start of what would be a long and difficult winding road. But it would be interesting as hell, with some great people involved along the way.

A week later, Jonathan Palmer tried some more new parts on the Silverstone club circuit. A week after that, we returned to Silverstone, this time with Ayrton Senna on the grand prix circuit. On the next visit to Silverstone in August, we took two cars—one with an FCZ gearbox, and the other with 6Y parts in the standard McLaren gearbox. Ayrton thought the 6Y certainly had some merit, taking into account that it was pretty basic at this stage. Honda had been very helpful in connecting up the engine control box to Lobby's Logic Box in order to cut the engine for upshifts, while the driver had to blip the throttle for down-shifts. (This technique was one I'd learned many years before while riding my old friend Batt's Harley-Davidson motorcycle.)

When the test finished, Martin Whitmarsh suggested we take the 6Y stuff to the next race in Budapest and let Ayrton try it during practice on Friday. It was Wednesday after-noon. Bloody hell!

With the help of several people in the gearbox department, the 6Y parts were checked, cleaned, and packed in three Hugo Boss "sausage" travel bags. I told Martin that for us to do this, Rob Irwin and Paul Cann had to go with me, as I knew Trevor Lawes was already in Budapest. By Thursday morning, we were on Ron's plane along with the parts, heading for Hungary.

We spent Thursday afternoon and evening fitting the 6Y bits to the T-car. Robbie and Paul got on with doing the wiring while Trevor and I dealt with the gearbox parts. Since the parts had only been finished the previous day, reverse had never been tested before.

We started the engine and did a shift check. Everything was okay—including reverse, thankfully.

You have to realize that this was a very basic system using compressed air from an air bottle to power the gear-change mechanism and a digital display showing the gear num-ber as selected by the paddles on the steering wheel. Reverse was a little tricky to engage because of a sequence of things the driver had to do. I spent some time with Ayrton going

Senna takes the lead at the beginning of the 1991 United States Grand Prix. He started and finished first on the temporary street circuit in Phoenix, Arizona. (STUART SEEGER / WIKIPEDIA COMMONS)

over this and other aspects of the gearbox.

He did several laps during Friday-morning practice before spinning the car coming onto the pit straight and ending up with the nose of the MP4/6 almost touching the cement pit wall just in front of us. We all held our breath, hoping he remembered what I'd told him about getting it into reverse. He backed up slowly and made enough space to get going again. It wasn't long before Charlie Whiting of the FIA came along and said, "I was waiting to see if he could back up."

That was all we got to do in the limited time available. We didn't run the 6Y stuff any further because Ayrton needed the T-car in case something happened to his race car, which he would be using for the rest of Friday practice and the weekend.

We took all the 6Y bits off the T-car and returned it to a normal standard gearbox configuration as quickly as possible so that the car would be available if needed.

This was a key moment in the championship for McLaren and Senna. Ayrton had won the first four races but, by this stage (mid-August), he needed to maintain his lead after a couple of troubled races and three wins in a row for Williams's Nigel Mansell, Ayrton's main rival. Ayrton led every lap at the Hungaroring, and then another win a couple of weeks later at Spa helped to ensure his third World Championship and another constructors' title for McLaren.

A lot of people had been talking about what we had tried in Hungary. I remember Patrick Head saying to me, "It sure changes gear pretty damn quick." And we knew that Giorgio Piola, the Italian journalist who specialized in technical drawings, had been trying to get some overhead pictures of the car from part of the grandstand on top of the pit garage.

There were to be several more 6Y tests over the next few months, with smaller parts and a great many modifications, some instigated by David North and others by myself, Trevor Lawes, Phil McPherson, and a couple of the other blokes in the gearbox department.

Testing had also continued with the FCZ gearbox, resulting in several long meetings in October. I believe the meeting after the race at Suzuka concluded that the project should be put away, or at least, not run in a McLaren car.

Our group also agreed to change the operation of the 6Y to hydraulics. After a test at Silverstone, followed by another at Donnington in the week just before Christmas, I made the first small hydraulic rig to allow us to power up and bleed the system, as well as going up and down through the gears. The hydraulic rig made a strange squealing noise when it was running, and it didn't take long before it became known as the "Piglet."

# 1992: The 6Y Gearbox and the MP4/7

n 1991, Dr. Dieter Gundel had come from TAG Electronics to work at McLaren, specifically on the early gearbox software. He also wanted to learn about the mechanical aspects of the gearbox itself. What a great guy to have working with me. Dieter and I seemed to get along pretty much straightaway. It took a while for each of us to understand the other's perspective relative to how the gearbox actually worked. I knew how the shift mechanism functioned mechanically and what we wanted it to do; Dieter and Dave Bryers, another electronics guy, worked on the software.

I was off to Suzuka in the second week of January for yet more Honda engine test work and the usual cold weather. I don't think there was ever enough coffee to keep us warm in the garage at Suzuka.

By now there had been a reasonable amount of work done on a test rig with the new hydraulic system. A week or so after getting back to the UK from the Suzuka test, I was in Japan again with Dieter, Dave, and gearbox technician Barry Ultahan to run the 6YH gearbox stuff with the new GCU 121 electronics box on Honda's engine-gearbox dyno at Wako. It was set up to replicate driving the car with a steering wheel, throttle pedal, and so on.

Ayrton Senna in the MP4/7A at Monaco in 1992. That year he scored his fifth victory at Monte Carlo despite stiff competition from Williams' Nigel Mansell. (LAT PHOTOGRAPHIC)

We had some problems with the dyno halfshafts and output flanges on the gearbox, but Barry and I, with some of the Honda guys, were able to sort this out in a reasonable amount of time. When we got it all back together again, Barry and I stayed in the dyno cell to check that things looked okay after starting up the engine. It was then that we noticed raw petrol running out of the exhaust and onto the floor right next to us. This prompted lots of arm waving to get someone's attention and have the engine shut off, which they promptly did. How it never caught on fire, I don't really know—but both Barry and I were sure as hell glad it hadn't.

It seems that while we were working on fixing the problem with the halfshafts, Mr. Bryers was sitting in the driver's seat, playing with the throttle pedal. Since all the electrics were on, he was pumping fuel into the engine every time he pushed on the pedal. It was amazing that the engine was able to turn over with all that fuel in the combustion chamber; it must have had a lot of overlap on the valve timing.

There were no further problems with the gearbox from then on. That turned out to be the easy bit compared to what was about to follow as we attempted to get the gearbox parts back for a test in the UK. When we reached the hotel in Ikebukuro on the night before we were due to leave, it had started to snow a little. By the morning of February 1, there was a fair bit of snow, and the bus to the Narita airport was sitting outside the hotel going nowhere. We walked through the snow to the train station and then back again, as the trains were not running, either.

By now it had started to clear up a bit and the bus driver had decided it was okay to leave for the airport. Barry chose to stay and come home the next day, as no one was really sure what was going to happen at the airport. Because of all the delays, the traffic at the airport was hardly moving. When we got quite close, we left the bus, grabbed our personal bags and the 6YH bags, and walked to the terminal—getting there just in time to see our British Airways plane pulling away from the gate!

There was a fair amount of chaos going on, as you might imagine, with a lot of people missing their flights. Needing to get back with the gearbox parts (which were the only ones we'd produced at that time), I started going around the various airline counters, trying to get us a flight out to somewhere, but no one really had anything. After a while I realized that if we went in the "wrong" direction (i.e., east to the United States or Canada), we could effectively save a day.

I found the Canadian Pacific counter and asked if they had three business-class seats to England. It turned out they had a flight to Vancouver leaving shortly, with a connection to Gatwick. The only problem was that the flight to Vancouver had just one seat available. We decided Dieter should have it and take the gearbox parts. More begging with the nice CP man got us another seat. By now, the flight was boarding. Then the very nice and helpful CP man, who had been on the phone for a while, got us a third seat. He also arranged a guy with a trolley for all of our bags, called the gate, told them we were coming, printed the boarding passes for both legs of the trip, and then took us, running with the trolley and bags, through immigration to the gate. What a great effort on his part! Getting us straight through immigration at Narita with no fuss was a miracle.

The different time zones meant we left Japan on Saturday, February 1, and got to Vancouver for the Gatwick flight on the same day. At some point, while the chaos was going on, we managed to contact race engineer Steve Hallam at McLaren to let him know what we were up to. When we checked in for the Gatwick flight in Vancouver, the CP lady asked how we got the boarding passes, because we hadn't paid for them! I quickly took care of this oversight. We had quite a long wait (and a lot of coffee) in Vancouver, but we did get back to Gatwick on time on Sunday, February 2. We were picked up and taken to the factory, where Steve Hallam was waiting for the parts, ready to take them for a test at Silverstone. An interesting trip indeed, and one that Dieter is still amazed by.

There was a lot of testing going on. The original plan was to have the new MP4/7 ready for the fourth round of the championship in Spain on May 3, to take advantage of a four-week break following the "flyaway races" in South Africa, Mexico, and Brazil. But when we saw the speed of the new Williams, it was decided to bring the debut of MP4/7 forward to Brazil. This would slice a whole month off the planned development program. When the time came to go to Brazil, it was decided to take six cars: three MP4/6Bs and three new MP4/7s, with only the latter having the 6YH gear-change system. Very few teams other than McLaren could have managed that.

When we got to Brazil, Gerhard Berger was fourth in the championship after finishing fifth and fourth in South Africa and Mexico. Ayrton Senna was one point behind him, thanks to a third-place finish followed by a retirement caused by transmission trouble in Mexico. This was actually a pretty good effort by Ayrton, considering he'd overturned his car during Friday practice. An upper wishbone had punched its way through the chassis, hitting Ayrton's left leg in the calf. He was lucky to get away uninjured. Meanwhile, the guys had built up a race car from the spare chassis. All of this would be a warm-up for what could probably best be described as a weekend of maximum chaos in Brazil!

Nigel Mansell pursues Ayrton Senna during the later stages of the 1992 Monaco Grand Prix. Mansell had the better car, but Ayrton's skill was enough to give him the win that day. (LAT PHOTOGRAPHIC)

The McLaren crew services the MP4/7A at Hungary in 1992.
Senna won the Hungarian Grand Prix, but Nigel Mansell took the
championship for Williams that year. (LAT PHOTOGRAPHIC)

At one stage during qualifying there were only two cars of the six we'd brought that were actually running, with the wounded ones sidelined by fuel fires, engine failures, and other problems. Despite all of the difficulties and jumping in and out of various cars, Ayrton qualified third in his MP4/7. Gerhard, having been stranded out on the circuit twice, tried to use the spare MP4/7 for qualifying, but unsurprisingly, he couldn't quite get his long legs inside a chassis that had the pedals set up for Ayrton. After just one lap of final qualifying in this car, Gerhard got into his MP4/6 and joined Ayrton on the second row of the grid.

The drama continued when Berger had an engine failure during the warm-up on race morning. Since it was going to be a bit touch and go to have the fresh Honda V12 installed in time, Gerhard went out in the spare MP4/7, with the pedals now suitably adjusted. Just as he was about to go to the grid, we radioed him to come back to the pits as fast as he could and swap to his race car, which was now ready. We got him back onto the track three minutes before the pit lane closed.

But we weren't done with the drama yet.

There had been a few strange things going on with the 6YH gearbox software, since it was, of course, quite new to everyone. When we started Gerhard's car for the parade lap, the gearbox software crashed. Gerhard didn't get the recovery sequence quite right and there was a bit of chaos around the car until Mike Wroe from TAG Electronics could get close enough to the steering wheel to sort out the problem.

All of this meant Gerhard had to start the race from the pit lane exit in keeping with the rules. Due to the overheating on the grid, he was only able to run four laps, as the damage had already been done. Ayrton held third place for several laps until an electrical problem put him out after 17 laps.

As you might imagine, there was some pretty intensive testing in that four-week gap between Brazil and Spain. We were beginning to understand the gearbox a bit better, but it was becoming very clear that the V12 needed more fuel and was not as powerful as the Renault V10 in the Williams, or, it seemed, the Ford V8 that newcomer Michael Schumacher was using in the Benetton. He was running third in the championship behind the Williams drivers Nigel Mansell and Riccardo Patrese, and ahead of our guys. Then, to add to Ayrton's problems, he spun into the wall while lying third in the final laps of what had become a very wet Spanish Grand Prix.

At Imola, it was Gerhard's turn to have a shunt when he collided with a Ferrari as they fought for fourth. Ayrton's third place was only the second time he had scored points in five races, but he was about to put that right at Monaco, at the end of what you might call another interesting weekend for us.

Qualifying was the usual deal with an hour each afternoon, but of course the difference at Monaco was the first day of running was Thursday, with Friday left free. That first qualifying session had only been going for 20 minutes or so when Gerhard had a big accident at the top of the hill, where the road goes left toward Casino. A front suspension failure was thought to be the cause, and Gerhard was lucky to climb out unhurt, get back to the pits for the spare MP4/7, and set the provisional fourth-fastest time. The suspension wishbones were strengthened on Friday and he eventually qualified fifth, with a last-minute effort to improve on that resulting in a spin coming out of the last corner.

Ayrton also hadn't been without his dramas. On Thursday he had been in a great fight for fastest time with Williams's Nigel Mansell (who had won all five races so far), and that was set to continue on Saturday afternoon. You could see that Ayrton was driving the wheels off the car, but it got away from him going down the hill to Mirabeau, where he backed it into the barrier. He got the car back to the pits (but only after losing the damaged rear wing in the tunnel!) and then used the spare MP4/7 to go after both Williams drivers. In the end he had to be satisfied with third, behind Mansell and Patrese.

On Saturday night, there were some issues with the T-car engine and it had to be changed around midnight; I'm not sure why it was so damn late. The next morning I asked Rick Goodhand, the number-one mechanic on the T-car, if he got any sleep. The answer was, "No; I just went back to the hotel, had a shower, a couple of rum and Cokes, and came back here!"

There was constant work going on with the gear-change bits and software. I seem to remember that when the race cars were on the grid, I was finishing some mods on the hydraulic system on the T-car, as there had been a couple of Moog valve O-ring problems.

Gerhard retired with a gearbox problem while lying fifth about halfway through the race, but Ayrton had been pushing Mansell as hard as he could for the lead. As Ayrton admitted afterward, "I knew there was no way I could beat him. It's impossible with the superiority of his car, and we were in no position to win. But you never know what will happen at Monaco. So what I tried to do was go hard enough to be in a position to benefit if something happened to Mansell."

That "something" happened on lap 71 when Mansell, whose car was acting a bit strange, stopped because he suspected a loose wheel nut. He came out of the pits just five seconds behind Ayrton, and the last seven laps saw some pretty impressive driving by Ayrton on

Software engineer Dieter Gundel in a photo I took at the Italian Grand Prix in 2006. We're still good friends today, even though Dieter went on to join the Ferrari team. (TYLER ALEXANDER)

old tires as Nigel quickly caught him on new ones. The Honda engine was a big help going up the hill and out of the tunnel. But it was Ayrton's ability to make the car as wide as the Monaco race track that won him the race by 0.20 seconds.

After the race and all the usual "thank-you" stuff, Ayrton made a point of thanking the little group of us working on the gear-change project. He said that being able to keep both hands on the steering wheel at all times had helped him hold off Nigel for those last few laps.

I was reminded recently by Nick Cross that just after the race I told the McLaren management regarding Ayrton, "Whatever you pay this guy, it's not enough."

Both Honda and McLaren were making progress with the MP4/7, as shown by Ayrton taking pole and Gerhard qualifying fourth in Montreal. This would be the race where Nigel Mansell put on one of his better theatrical performances. He had been trying for several laps to pass Ayrton for the lead under braking for the tight corner just before the pits. This was at the end of the long straight, and on lap 15, Ayrton went quite deep into the corner, but crucially left just enough room for Mansell to have a go on the inside. Which Nigel did—and went straight off the track and into the gravel. Game over.

Since the shunt was close to the pits, Nigel walked back, arms waving and yelling. He had a big go at Ron on the pit wall, claiming Ayrton had pushed him off. It was great to watch. Mansell then went to see the stewards, but in the absence of any condemning report from the observer at the corner, they figured—along with the rest of us—that Ayrton had suckered Mansell into the corner and done nothing wrong.

The real pity was that Ayrton then dropped out about halfway through the race with a gearbox problem, probably caused by the very high temperatures, as everything on the car was running quite hot that day. The good news was that this put Gerhard in the lead.

The bad news followed near the end of the race when Gerhard came on the radio saying there was something odd with the gearbox. The gear numbers on the dash display were all over the place, yet it was still changing gear okay. The gear-position sensor had failed because of the high temperatures, which meant the software was doing a few strange things, but still changing gear correctly most of the time.

Gerhard was shifting by using the paddles and getting it wrong now and again, much to the horror of the Honda engine guys. Needless to say, we were all holding our breath for those last few laps, but Gerhard won in the end.

After the race, Gerhard told journalists about his problems, saying he had been changing gear "manually." One of the journalists came to the garage and actually asked to see the gear-change lever in the car. Yeah, right!

We had the Honda guys saying *mundai-da*s a few days later at a test at Silverstone. With little or no fuss, Gerhard managed to do something that he hadn't done before, and that we hadn't thought of. He had started doing full-throttle downshifts going through the Maggots/Becketts complex, trying not to scrub off too much speed. The Honda guys were jumping about a bit with a few *mundai-da*s, followed by very few *mundai-nai*s (no problem) as the rpms got quite high on a few of the down changes. New software was produced, and continued to be updated and modified over a long period of time to help protect the engine during this type of driver request.

On the weekends when I was at home that summer, I was helping out *Top Gear*'s Tiff Needell with commentary on the CART races for Sky TV. It was a good experience, which went very well; the people doing the show were always very helpful. It was something I would like to have done more of then—and I'd still love to do now.

Meanwhile, McLaren picked up points, but no wins, in France, Britain, and Germany. One of the more colorful moments came during a test session at Hockenheim when Senna thought that Schumacher had deliberately pushed him off the track at very high speed. Ayrton lost no time going down to the Benetton pit, where he tried to grab the German by the throat and scream at him. They were separated by our own Ian Dyer, who was telling Ayrton to back off, as there were a lot of photographers lurking about.

Senna had been fighting with Schumacher over third place in the championship and would get some satisfaction from the next grand prix in Hungary, one of those races that produced a classic bit of radio traffic.

For a great deal of the race Ayrton was running second with Nigel Mansell third, and doing everything he could to get by—not an easy task, as Ayrton was doing everything he could to help Nigel wear out his tires. Patrese had led from the start, then spun off after 38 laps, putting Ayrton in front. After a few laps Nigel appeared to ease off, prompting Ron to suddenly come on the radio, "Mansell has a problem! Mansell has a problem!" Ayrton replied, "I have a problem!" "What's the problem?" came the nervous response from Ron. Long pause, then, "I'm driving a shitbox!"

Nigel did make a pit stop for tires, which is what put all this in motion, but he was able to rejoin, finishing second behind Ayrton and winning the World Championship. This win briefly put Ayrton ahead of Schumacher in the championship, only for them to swap places again when Schumacher won at Spa and Senna finished fifth.

It was about this time that Honda tried to smooth out the gear changes by cutting 4 cylinders instead of 12. Dieter Gundel explained this to Ayrton by saying, "Sometimes twelve is eight and sometimes twelve is twelve." Ayrton replied, "My math teacher in school always said that twelve was twelve, but if you think it's eight sometimes, that's okay with me!"

Ayrton scored maximum points at Monza, but only after both Williams drivers had dropped out of the lead with hydraulic problems. He was on the podium again in Portugal, finishing third, one place behind Gerhard.

After the race, Marlboro held a dinner for the team in one of Estoril's very nice fish restaurants. When the meal had finished, some people who were well up the food chain stopped throwing whole fish about and went off to a well-known disco and club. It seems that our hospitality manager Bob McMurray had to help Mr. Senna into the car that was driving him home. Ayrton at least had some time to recover; he was going back to Brazil,

A 1992 test session with Mark Blundell in the McLaren MP4/7. The boxy laptop computers look quaint by today's standards, but were cutting-edge at the time. (LAT PHOTOGRAPHIC)

as he wasn't scheduled to do the Goodyear tire test starting the following Tuesday.

Gerhard was going to do the test, but after a few short runs, he felt quite ill and had to lie down on one of the ramps in the transporter. Someone called Ayrton and asked if he felt okay, and whether he could come and drive the car on Tuesday. He agreed, and said he would also do the other two days of the test before going back to Brazil. Ayrton, always helpful, was probably getting back at Gerhard, whose problems more than likely had something to do with the events of Sunday evening.

Honda had decided to stop their F1 racing program at the end of 1992, so the Japanese Grand Prix was obviously going to be significant for everyone after McLaren's many years with Honda.

Honda had built a very nice engine for Ayrton to use at Suzuka. During the Sunday-morning warm-up, this engine pulled more revs with the car full of fuel and carrying more rear wing than the V12 had used to qualify third. If we had known that it was going to be that good, we would have used a longer top gear. As a result, the rpms on the straight had been a bit too much for the engine during the warm-up, which meant it had to be changed.

The engine fitted for the race lost air from the valve system, thanks to a small set screw coming out of the block, and it failed after two laps. Falling on one's sword was a strong possibility for some. It was a sad end for Ayrton's last race in Japan with Honda, particularly for those who had worked so hard to give him something a bit special. At least Gerhard finished second, which was some consolation.

The Log Cabin, a bar located on the grounds of the Suzuka Circuit Hotel, was the favorite place to go on the night after the race. As I arrived, Ichida-san, one of the top guys at Honda R&D, grabbed me and said he wanted me to meet someone. We walked around the back of the building and there was one of the Honda PR guys, sitting with two other people on the steps, holding a bottle of cold beer. Ichida-san introduced me to Nobuhiko Kawamoto, the president of Honda; he was a very quiet person with a keen technical understanding and a lot of questions.

The PR guy got me a bottle of beer and we sat and talked for a long time. Kawamoto had many questions about racing at Indianapolis, and he told me, along with some of his other thoughts, exactly when he had informed McLaren that they were really going to stop the Formula One program. Quite a few people outside Honda had been given the impression that the decision to quit came quite late and was something of a surprise. Kawamoto told me that he had informed the team in the early part of 1992. From that, I gathered that certain people at McLaren, believing Honda could be persuaded to change their mind during the course of the season, had perhaps misunderstood Japanese business culture. In that environment, when a decision is made, it's usually final.

It was very interesting and a lot more than just a rare treat for me. When I left, I gave a low bow, along with *Doumo arigatou gozaimasu,* a very polite way of saying "Thank you."

Berger won our final race with Honda in Adelaide. Mansell and Senna collided while disputing the lead, each driver inevitably blaming the other. The result didn't do much for either Gerhard or Ayrton in the Drivers championship, but it did help lift McLaren into second in the Constructors championship, 8 points ahead of Benetton, but 65 behind Williams. At least it was a reasonable way to sign off with Honda.

There were a few people at McLaren who didn't like the Honda people: They were Japanese and liked to copy everything, and they made notes and sketches all the time. My view was: So what? Honda provided engines—and a fair bit more—that won races. I really enjoyed my time working with them and made many good friends, and I know others in the company who felt the same way. I also enjoyed the time I spent in Japan, learning to eat raw fish along with other odd things in such a new and different place.

Yes, there were plenty of cold days and late nights while testing at Suzuka. Wanting to run the car until we filled the airbox up with snow; drinking coffee; answering lots of questions, and making sketches of how things worked while we waited for the weather to clear up. In the summer, it was so hot and humid that on one occasion, when we thought there was a water leak from the car radiator, the puddle on the floor turned out to be from Richard Moody sweating.

On the way back to the Suzuka Circuit Hotel at the same test, the boys stopped at the water slide park. Still fully clothed, they had "Deadly" Ian Dyer on the railing above them as they were coming down the water slide.

Then there was the time that Barry Ultahan and I arrived in the main entrance and lobby at Honda R&D in Wako and Barry went off to the loo. It was a very complicated toilet, with instructions in Japanese. Barry pressed several of the buttons without much result, but finally, one of the buttons produced a jet of water that went straight up the middle of Barry's shirt and face and then over the door, hitting someone who was standing outside wearing a suit. Barry did get some odd looks when he came back to the lobby.

There were times at the McLaren workshop in Wako when it was necessary to thump the table rather loudly to stop the coffee drinking and get the engine started and the checks done, so that the car could be loaded into the transporter and leave for the Suzuka test on time. But it never caused any personal problems. The job was always done. *Mundai-nai*.

All in all, it was a very interesting time. I still treasure my memories of Japan and the great guys at Honda I got to meet and call friends. I would do it again tomorrow.

# 1993: From Honda to Cosworth, and Senna's Swan Song

We went into 1993 with a new car, lots of new tricks, a new engine, and two new drivers. The car had an active suspension system that differed from everyone else's, a Cosworth engine (not the latest spec, as that went to Benetton), and a lot more updates on the gear-change system software and hardware. Ayrton Senna and Michael Andretti were the two race drivers, and Mika Hakkinen joined us as the test driver.

We did have our own paddle gear-change program, which I had been involved with from the beginning and was still working on, along with several other things. A special projects manager does whatever is required, and that is what I did at the time. I also needed to learn about new things (computers, for example) as we moved along in the world of motor racing.

I spent quite a bit of time in February at the Cosworth factory in Northampton, running our hydraulic system with their engine, paying close attention to the hydraulic throttle operation. It was an interesting experience, and I got along well with the guys running the dyno tests. Although I spent a lot of time with the Honda engine people, I never got a chance to be involved when they were running their engine on the dyno in Wako.

Former teammates Alain Prost and Ayrton Senna following the 1993 Australian Grand Prix. Senna won the race, but Prost, who had joined the Williams team after a yearlong sabbatical, took his third F1 Drivers championship. (LAT PHOTOGRAPHIC)

Ayrton came from Brazil to test the new car at Silverstone. He did quite a few laps and then spent several hours in the motor home with Giorgio Ascanelli, his race engineer. Ayrton's general comment was, "I think you guys have something here."

At the start of one of the tests on a very cold day on the Silverstone South Circuit, someone asked, "What's a good time around here?" "Five p.m." came the quick reply from Indy Lall, the test team manager.

There were a variety of software issues, which was not surprising, seeing as the MP4/8 car was much more complex than the previous one. Apart from gear-change and throttle-control issues, we had a hydraulic problem that needed sorting out. I asked Ayrton if he would come up to Silverstone for a short test we had scheduled just before leaving for the first race in South Africa. We had several modified and different parts to try, but Ayrton was very patient with us, his feeling being that the car was well worth the effort.

We made reasonable progress in the short time we had, as the car had to be back at the factory late that afternoon for checking over before shipment to the race at Kyalami.

One of the many trick items on the MP4/8 was traction control, which was allowed at the time. This led to an amusing incident during practice at Kyalami, when Tom Walkinshaw from Benetton came marching down the pit lane and demanded to know why our engine was making a funny noise coming off the corners. We told him it had a misfire or something like that. But he knew it was traction control—which Benetton didn't have with their Cosworth engines—and he stormed back down the pit lane, knowing he could do nothing about it.

As I said, the 1993 active car was not a simple one, and it would get more complicated during the course of the season. But at the same time, the clever software people—Dieter Gundel, Mike Wroe, and Dave Bryers, along with TAG Electronics—were making it easier to deal with.

Ayrton had a reasonable amount of testing in the car, unlike Michael, who did not have much test mileage at all, and was having a bit of a hard time as a result. Steve Hallam, who had been Gerhard Berger's race engineer, was now assigned Michael's car, and later, Mika Hakkinen's.

Michael's F1 career did not get off to a good start when he stalled on the grid and then had a collision on the fifth lap while trying to come through from the back of the field. Meanwhile, at the front, Ayrton made the most of his front-row start and got the jump on Prost's Williams. Ayrton managed to hold Alain off for 23 pretty hectic laps. From as early as lap 7, Ayrton had been having trouble with the handling, which we later found was due to a faulty electronic control on the rear suspension. He did really well to finish second and score six points.

This result for Ayrton added to a lot of intrigue over his future. Although the guys on the team were not party to what was going on, there were rumors—according to the press, as usual—that Ayrton had not done a deal with Ron for the whole of the 1993 season. From what we could understand, he was working on a race-by-race basis. That was interesting, because the next race would be Ayrton's home grand prix in Brazil. As far as we were concerned, we carried on as normal and prepared the car on the basis that he would be there.

Sure enough, Ayrton turned up at Interlagos for what would be an eventful race. It probably didn't do his mood much good when Prost put the Williams-Renault on pole with Ayrton directly behind him on the second row, but with almost two seconds a lap between them. Michael was on the third row, right behind Ayrton, the difference between our two drivers being just under a second.

Poor Michael had a big misfortune with Gerhard Berger at the first corner, actually flying over the top of the Ferrari. Ayrton had made a good start and held second for some time before being overtaken by the Williams of Damon Hill. The arrival of rain after about 20 laps brought chaos, as several drivers, including Prost in the leading Williams, spun off. Senna was brought in to serve a stop-go penalty, apparently for overtaking under a yellow flag—something he would strongly disagree with after the race. But despite all the chaos going on around him, Ayrton managed to win his home grand prix in what was a memorable drive. And there was even better to come.

Donington got to host a World Championship Grand Prix for the first time when a race in Japan was canceled. But holding it in England in early April was always going to bring the risk of rain. And we were to get plenty of that.

Ayrton was fastest during a wet first qualifying but, when it was dry for second qualifying, Prost and Hill (Williams) were quickest, with Schumacher (Benetton) third, just ahead of Ayrton. Once again, Michael was on the third row and directly behind Ayrton.

In the midst of all the work going on in the garage on Sunday morning, Princess Diana was being shown around by Peter Stayner of McLaren Marketing. Peter was good enough to introduce me. She was a very attractive lady, who didn't seem to have a problem with staring you straight in the eye. No question about it—definitely a player, not a spectator.

In the background, we had the usual things to deal with getting ready for the race. Dave Brown, one of the mechanics, had all the Moog valves off the hydraulic system of the T-car in order to flush the whole system with the Piglet following concerns about contamination. He was finishing up just as we went to the grid. We had been there for only a short time when some of the blokes came running past with a radiator for Michael's car. The leaking radiator was replaced in time by Mike Negline, Chris "Squeaky" Schofield, Trevor Lawes, and Colin Morgan. The dramas never seem to end.

No surprise to find it was raining at the start. Ayrton was blocked by Schumacher and found himself fifth, with Michael sixth at the start of the first lap. Ayrton, applying a bit of his magic in the rain, was leading by the end of the lap! Michael, meanwhile, had a shunt while trying to get past Karl Wendlinger's Sauber, and both were out of the race.

There was a reasonable amount of chaos with the rain stopping, starting, stopping—and starting again. Ayrton was in the pits five times, but on one occasion when the rain looked like it was starting up again, we weren't ready for him. So Ayrton went straight out to do another lap and then stayed out on slicks after deciding that the rain was not that bad after all. Ayrton led virtually all of the 76 laps. It was one of his most outstanding drives.

The win in Britain maintained Ayrton's lead in the championship, which he held on to despite retiring from the next race at Imola, followed by a second place in Spain. We were hoping for a good result at Monaco—where Ayrton had won five times before—although we knew this race usually provided some special challenges and chaos of its own. Monaco 1993 was to be no exception.

Ayrton had a big shunt at the end of the pit straight during Thursday-morning practice. This was caused by a problem with the active suspension software and did a lot of damage to the car. It was taken back to the paddock area on the quayside and we set about fixing it for the first qualifying session in the afternoon.

By the time we got the three missing corners and the rest of the bits fitted, qualifying had started. With the paddock area at Monaco actually being outside the circuit, Dave Ryan had been talking to Charlie Whiting of the FIA about letting Ayrton out of the paddock gate, onto the circuit briefly, and into the pit lane. As soon as we had the car in a running state, Ayrton drove it to the pits, where the boys finished off the setup before he joined in qualifying and set fifth-fastest time.

While the car was being put together, Dieter, Giorgio, and Mike Wroe were flat-out trying to establish what had happened with the gear-change software. They came up with a fix just in time.

As for Ayrton, he was okay after the shunt, except for a bruised thumb, which was bandaged up. When we were ready to go out again and I asked Ayrton about his thumb, he replied, "It's not my thumb that's the problem."

There was an issue with the gear-change software in final qualifying, which probably cost Ayrton a front-row position. He had locked up a rear wheel on bumps right where he started braking for the chicane by the sea front. Until that point, he had been quickest. He would start from third on the grid, but more modifications were in order for the gear-change software.

Ayrton held third for the first 11 laps, moving into second when Prost, in the lead, was given a stop-go penalty. By lap 33, Ayrton was in front when Schumacher's Benetton had a hydraulics failure and caught fire. By that point Senna's record sixth win at Monaco was never in doubt.

As usual we were testing between almost every race. I was using the dyno at Cosworth to sort out, among other things, issues with the potentiometers that controlled the electronic hydraulic throttle.

The Cosworth engines had slide throttles, and we had been thinking that butterfly throttles might help the mid-throttle drivability. David North had drawn up the system and several were made. I spent quite a bit of time with a prototype system on our hydraulic test rig, sorting out the Moog valve-control numbers. The system was then run on the dyno at Cosworth. Not much was said about it, but from what I heard from someone close enough to know, I believe that it ran quite well. We also ran a test at Silverstone, and Mika Hakkinen thought it had better drivability in the slower corners.

Of course, we were not aware—nor told—that there was a new spec series 8 Cosworth engine about to happen, and our throttle system didn't fit on the new cylinder heads. Oh, well . . .

At about the same time, McLaren was looking at the V12 Lamborghini engine, the program being helped by Mike Royce and Kim Lyon, two very good guys from Chrysler, which had owned the Italian company since 1987. There was a test at Imola before the race at Monza. When the test was finished, Mike Wroe and I took a box of parts to the Lamborghini factory in Modena and ran our hydraulic system on their V12 engine. We were looked after really well by Daniele Audetto, the two Chrysler guys, and the people running the dyno. The test was very productive and allowed us to record the power difference between running with the hydraulic pump and without it. And the whole experience was helped along later by a really excellent dinner in Modena.

Meanwhile, back at Woking, a chassis—to be known as the MP4/8B—was being built for the Lamborghini engine. A couple of weeks after Monza (where Michael Andretti would score his only F1 podium by finishing third), we had a test on the Silverstone South circuit with Mika running the 8B, along with an 8A, which had some new and interesting bits on it.

After a couple of days, it stopped raining long enough for us to pack up and head for more testing at Pembrey in Wales. Ayrton flew in by helicopter to try the new bits on the 8A, and we asked him if he would do a few laps in the 8B. It turned out to be more than a few laps because he thought the Chrysler-Lamborghini engine was quite reasonable.

We worked on the cars in a building that was suitable, except for some issues with methane gas that lasted pretty much all day and into the evening. It was deemed to have been caused by the previous night's chicken rogan, but I thought large amounts of Double Dragon Ale from a local brewery called Felinfoel (more affectionately and appropriately known as "Feeling Foul") probably played a more significant role in the matter.

By the middle of September, Michael Andretti had left the team, fed up with his lack of success in Formula One, and seeking a new Indy car ride. Mika Hakkinen, the test driver, took his place for the next race at Estoril, where he out-qualified Ayrton. Having qualified fourth to Mika's third, Ayrton was talking about using a different spec engine because he felt the drivability would be better going through the very fast downhill corner at the end of the pit straight. At which point Mika proudly announced that he was flat through there.

We changed Ayrton's engine, which unfortunately failed in the race when he was running second on lap 19. Thirteen laps later, Mika got too close to the third-place Ferrari of Jean Alesi. As they came out of the corner leading onto the pit straight he went off the track. Oh—by the way, Mika didn't out-qualify Ayrton again!

We stayed on at Estoril for a test with both the 8A and 8B. One afternoon when there was a lot of work going on with the cars, Ayrton and I had a long quiet chat sitting by the fence behind the garage. He asked me a lot of questions about the Lamborghini engine and the cost of doing something with it. He also told me pretty much all the details about the sale of McLaren to Ron Dennis and John Barnard, and that he reckoned we had sold it way too cheap. Ayrton was usually quite quiet about things and didn't really say a lot, but this was a really good conversation. Ayrton seemed much more relaxed than normal; maybe he had already signed with Williams for next season.

With less than an hour to go on the last day of the Estoril test, the Lamborghini engine had some problems and needed to be changed. Giorgio Ascanelli bet the mechanics they couldn't change the engine and get back out before the end of running. He said if they did he would buy dinner. They made the change in time, and Mika's first timed lap with the new engine was only about a tenth of a second off the quickest time set that day. I think that Giorgio may have paid for what we referred to as a hydraulic meal, one based on Caribbean mineral water (or rum, for those who didn't know better).

In the end, all that work was for nothing because, by the time we arrived in Suzuka for the Japanese Grand Prix, McLaren had signed a deal to use Peugeot engines the following year. Lamborghini wasn't pleased about this, but McLaren didn't think there was much future in an engine with a history stretching back a couple of years.

Ayrton qualified second with Mika third for what would be another dry-wet-dry race, with the usual bits of chaos that come along with that. While leading the last part of the race and trying to hold off Prost, Ayrton was blatantly held up by Eddie Irvine. There was quite a scene after the race between Ayrton and Irvine in the Jordan office, with the two having an exciting "discussion." Finally Senna turned to go, then turned back and took a swipe at Irvine. Later in the year the incident was subjected to an FIA hearing. Senna was sure he would be acquitted, but to his surprise he got a two-race ban, suspended for six months. That episode aside, Suzuka was a success, with Ayrton winning and Mika taking third.

The trip from Nagoya to Australia took a bit longer than normal, as the Qantas flight never showed up, forcing everyone to spend the night in a hotel near the airport before leaving the following day.

There always seemed to be something a bit new and interesting in Australia, and Adelaide in 1993 was no exception. Near the end of qualifying, Ayrton was a couple of corners before the pit entry when he asked Giorgio on the radio if he wanted him to stop. Either Giorgio's radio didn't work, or he didn't hear. The result was that Ayrton didn't stop and kept yelling on the radio, "What the hell do you want me to do?" all the way through the lap—a lap that was good enough for pole position! It was the first time in 1993 that a Williams had not been on pole.

Mika qualified fifth, and I'm not sure if it was in practice or the race, but there is a fantastic photo of Mika missing the chicane just past the pits, with the car at least a meter in the air. In the race, Mika didn't finish because of brake issues, but Ayrton was to win his last race with McLaren in Australia. Although we didn't know it at the time, it would also prove to be his last victory ever.

That evening Ayrton went to the Tina Turner concert in the park nearby, where they got him to come onstage. Tina Turner looked at Ayrton, gave a wink and a slight nod, and then

New boy Mika Hakkinen meets the press before the Portuguese Grand Prix at Estoril, where he started third, one spot ahead of Senna. Neither of them finished the race, which was won by Michael Schumacher. (LAT PHOTOGRAPHIC)

belted out "Simply the Best." It was the kind of thing that just gave you goose bumps—one of those moments that was genuine magic.

My thoughts on Ayrton Senna? The first thing I would have to say, having worked with him for several years, was that he was just damn good! He had a lot of passion for what he did and an ability to stay focused on what he needed to do when there was chaos around him. He helped me on numerous occasions when I was having some issues getting something done, which I'd like to think meant the respect went both ways. His ability to get the most out of the car and himself was always more than amazing to us all.

Keith Barnard, one of the mechanics who worked on Ayrton's car, did up his driver's seat belts as tight as he could. In qualifying, when Ayrton would always tighten them up some more, Keith thought it meant he was either going to be on the front row, or walking back.

Once upon a time someone wrote, "In order to do anything in the world worth doing, we must not stand shivering on the bank, thinking of the cold and danger, but jump in and scramble through as well as we can." Ayrton did just that.

It was a great way to end our season. The MP4/8A was a good little car, particularly in the last few races with the mods from the Pembrey test. If we would have had a bit more horsepower I think Ayrton would have won a few more races in his last season with McLaren. For 1994 he would be moving on to Williams.

# 1994: Tragedy at Imola and a Short Ride with Peugeot

For the second year in succession, we were starting off a season with a new engine—and with it another new group of people to meet and learn to work with. Added to that, Martin Brundle was joining Mika Hakkinen as the second McLaren driver, while the retired Alain Prost (who I believe Ron had been trying to persuade to return to the race team) ended up doing some testing for us.

There was also the reintroduction of mandatory refueling to add some excitement to pit stops—sometimes, as it would turn out, a bit more than you really wanted. Steve Hallam and I, along with people from other teams, went over to France to see Intertechnique, the company making the refueling rig. It was quite a large, heavy, and fairly basic beast, despite some of it being based on aircraft-refueling equipment.

We were to have all the usual problems with throttle-control and oil-scavenge systems, but we managed to complete lots of work and a race distance test in early April with the engine and gearbox. On one occasion we had to wait for some parts to be made somewhere in Paris while we went for dinner. After a nice meal in a very casual place, there was a phone call telling us the parts had just arrived, and so we finally got going.

The new Peugeot-powered McLaren MP4/9 as seen at the 1994 Canadian Grand Prix, in the hands of Mika Hakkinen. (LAT PHOTOGRAPHIC)

For 1994 McLaren turned to Peugeot to power the MP4/9. It's seen here being driven by Martin Brundle at Monaco, where he finished second to Michael Schumacher's Benetton. (LAT PHOTOGRAPHIC)

It was four in the morning when the test was completed and the wine opened. The Peugeot people, a pretty damn good bunch of guys, were pleased we had been able to achieve the race distance. They called a taxi to take Barry Ultahan and me to the airport and the 7:40 a.m. British Airways flight back to London.

In the late spring of 1994, there was a murmur of discontent bubbling to the surface at the San Marino Grand Prix over electronic driver aids. Of course, these aids were meant to be banned, but some people believed they were still being used in one form or another.

But people will remember Imola that year as the race where the sport lost two people in shunts, and came close to losing a third. It began on Friday when Rubens Barrichello crashed heavily. Then Roland Ratzenberger had his fatal accident during qualifying on Saturday, when part of the front wing on his Simtek broke as he was reaching upward of 180 mph on the approach to Tosa corner. There was more to come on Sunday.

Problems began that day when one of the drivers didn't get away at the start and others either ran into him, or parts of other people's cars, sending debris across the track and over the spectator fence. After several laps behind the safety car, the race restarted.

Ayrton Senna in the Williams was leading Michael Schumacher's Benetton. After one complete lap, something caused Ayrton to go off the track and hit the concrete retaining wall at Tamburello, the very fast corner not far past the pits. Ayrton was struck in the head by part of the right front suspension. Despite a lot of effort by Professor Sid Watkins and the medical team, it was not really possible to do the impossible. And the world became a bit less bright.

The race was stopped. One of the worst parts was waiting on the grid and not knowing how Ayrton was and what was happening, which was pretty typical at that time, I have to say. I remember walking to the top of the pit lane and crying, then returning and saying, "Well, we just have to get on with it, don't we!" Even though Ayrton wasn't with McLaren anymore, he had many friends and much respect from the team, and he was a good friend of mine. I just did what I always did and got on with the job.

Sometimes people's thoughts or views seem surprising. After Gerhard Berger's near-fatal accident driving a Ferrari at Imola in 1989, he and his close friend Ayrton Senna walked the track at a test during Gerhard's comeback. Their purpose was to see if there could be any better safety measures implemented to reduce the risk of accidents. They stopped at the Tamburello corner and took a good look all around it. They both realized that it presented a danger to the drivers and should be made safer. Unfortunately, when they looked behind the wall and noticed a stream running there, they knew it would be pretty much impossible to modify the corner runoff area. Having thought about this for a few minutes, Senna then said, "You know, someone's going to get killed here one day." And so it came to pass. On May 1, 1994, Ayrton lost his life at the same corner where Gerhard had nearly lost his.

It became one of those days that everyone wanted finished as soon as possible once they had done their jobs. There were a number of other things going on during the race—such as mechanics being run into or hit with broken bits during pit stops—but Mika managed to finish third. No one was in the mood for any celebration.

Monaco a couple of weeks later seemed strangely quiet. Even though Mika was on the front row, his race was over at the first corner when Damon Hill ran into the back of Mika's car, shoving it into the barrier. Martin, with a solid drive and a well-timed pit stop, moved up the field and finished second.

Part of the weekend's activities included Max Mosley, the FIA president, telling everyone about sweeping safety-rule changes. It was a shame that some of them were made a bit late in the day, but sometimes it's better late than never.

Development continued with both the chassis and engine, but we had more retirements than results during the mid-season. In Montreal, for example, we had electrical and engine problems. Having said that, in the midst of the general chaos before the race, the engine guys stopped working to enjoy a lobster lunch. No coincidence, of course, that they were French, and the fact that the lobster in Montreal is not to be missed. Just to add to some of the mishaps, Mika was doing a few laps in the T-car on Friday when he hit a poor beaver (or maybe it was a groundhog), who was not very pleased.

There was a strange moment at the start of the British Grand Prix when Martin Brundle's engine belched out great clouds of smoke from one of the exhaust pipes. It looked a bit like the navy laying down a smokescreen. Everyone, including Martin, thought the engine had blown up, but in fact, it had only gotten itself into a strange state of piston-ring flutter. It was fine later on when the Peugeot guys started the V10 in the garage. In the race Mika managed to finish third after Michael Schumacher was disqualified for thinking he didn't need to stop for a black flag.

The 1994 German Grand Prix will be better remembered by most for the Benetton refueling fire in the pit next to ours. It seems that a part missing from the refueling nozzle may have contributed to this. I remember grabbing one of the Benetton mechanics and holding him down while one of our mechanics got some water to pour onto his hands. It was a race Mika needed to forget, because he was charged with having caused an accident at the start, one which also eliminated Martin. As result, Mika was banned from the next GP in Hungary.

Flames engulfed the Benetton pit at the 1994 German Grand Prix. New rules making refueling mandatory had been imposed that year, and incidents like this were one result. (LAT PHOTOGRAPHIC)

Mika's place at the Hungaroring was taken by Philippe Alliot, who didn't really impress anyone. What should have been a very good third place for Martin was wrecked when the alternator failed halfway around on the last lap. Ugghh!

Mika picked up a second and three third places in the final European races to help move him up to fourth in the championship, while a couple of top-six finishes and a third for Martin in the final race at Adelaide maintained McLaren's fourth in the Constructors championship. It wasn't good, but it was about all we could hope for in a season where we'd experienced lots of problems.

At one of the Estoril tests, for example, we had an engine failure on the main straight in front of the pits. A connecting rod which came out of the bottom of the engine went through the floor and proceeded to grind a deep groove in the race track. We'd also had a problem with the flywheel emerging from the bottom of Brundle's engine during the Brazilian Grand Prix, triggering a multicar shunt that left a tire mark on Martin's helmet. All a bit unusual.

Under the circumstances, it didn't surprise many when Peugeot announced before the last two races that they were going to Jordan for 1995. To replace Peugeot McLaren agreed to a tie-up with the Mercedes-Ilmor Engine Company.

Nigel Mansell aboard the MP4/10B at the 1995 San Marino Grand Prix, one of only two races he ran for McLaren that year. (LAT PHOTOGRAPHIC)

# 1995: The Ilmor Era Begins, Mansell Takes Off, and Mika Takes Charge

**H**aving yet another new engine and a bunch of new people for the third year running brought the usual problems adapting the TAG software, the throttle-control system, and all the other things that came with getting the V10 fitted into the car. All part of the price of admission, I suppose.

The engine program with Ilmor and Mercedes marked the start of a long-term relationship, with Mercedes eventually buying part of McLaren. Ilmor was owned by Mario Illien, Paul Morgan, and Roger Penske, three people I had known for a very long time. Roger and I went back to my earliest days in racing, while my relationship with Mario and Paul really got going when I was at Newman/Haas Racing in 1987.

There was a lot of component testing at Ilmor's place in Brixworth, Northamptonshire, and then the usual rush to get the first engines to McLaren and have MP4/10 ready for a launch at the Science Museum in London on February 17, 1995.

The car had just arrived back from the launch and was sitting in one of the workshop bays while Phill Asbury, Davy Ryan, Dieter Gundel, and I were having a look at it. I seem to remember this was Phill's first day at McLaren after previously working at TAG Electronics. He asked Dieter, "Does this car look like a winner?" Dieter answered, "Nope." When Phill asked why, Dieter's reply was probably not meant to be mean, but it was straight to the point, "The guy who designed it is the same guy who designed last year's car!"

With all due respect to the people who worked very hard to build the car, MP4/10 was not really competitive at all, and didn't take long to assume the nickname "Hee-Haw."

After a disappointing season with Williams, former World Champion Nigel Mansell had joined Mika Hakkinen on the race team, and had his first experience with MP4/10 at one of the Estoril pre-season tests. There was a conversation at the back of the garage between Nigel and Ron Dennis that began with the question, "How did you ever think this fucking car could win a race?"

Things weren't helped by Nigel not fitting in the car properly. He was too large. While another chassis was made to accommodate Mr. Mansell, Mark Blundell, our test driver for some time, took Nigel's place for a couple of races. Mark had been doing a great deal of the early gear-change project testing, and he fitted in well with everyone on the team.

Interlagos brought the usual first-race misadventures with reliability issues and shunts, but somehow both cars finished, with Mika taking fourth and Mark sixth, much to everybody's relief and amazement.

# Phill Asbury

Anybody in Formula One would tell you what a legend this man Tyler is; I don't need to say that. I can tell you that we've shared a great many good times and a few bad times too. I guess you might have expected that also. He cared so much more about every aspect of the job than anyone had a right to expect.

What I can add, though, is the following truth: Tyler taught me everything of value that I know about Formula One—technically and practically, the economics and the politics. He also taught me a lot about myself, and probably more about life than my own father did. Although he probably doesn't know it, I guess that's really how I think of him.

One of Tyler's great gifts is his ability to identify the real issue among the noise when something needs fixing, and in Formula One, there's always something that needs fixing! He has inspired, encouraged, and motivated me along with a couple of generations of mechanics, technicians, engineers, managers, and drivers too! I am deeply indebted to him, and honored to have worked with him for so long.

For a short time after the race, we thought we might actually have a podium finish due to problems with the first- and second-place cars, whose fuel didn't match the sample given to the FIA. But the stewards decided the Benetton and Willams teams received no advantage, and they got to keep their points. Ferrari's third-place finisher, Gerhard Berger, complained that a driver could therefore win a race in an illegal car. We'll get to an aspect of that same issue later on . . .

We had a reality check in Argentina when Mika spun off with a puncture and Mark retired with an oil leak from a cracked gearbox casing. Then we were into Europe, and the return of Nigel Mansell at Imola, and a car that fitted him.

After qualifying 10th during the race, more than a second slower than Mika, Nigel told Steve Hallam on the radio that the car understeered everywhere. He would say it a great many times. Steve's answer was something along the lines of, "Yes, Nigel, we hear you." Nigel finished 10th, but Mika got us two more points with 5th, albeit a lap behind Damon Hill's winning Williams.

Things were looking a little better for Nigel when he qualified within a tenth of a second behind Mika in Barcelona, but the race was a different matter. Nigel had dropped back quite a bit and was about to be lapped by Schumacher's leading Benetton when he slid off the road. He came into the pits and drove straight into the garage, saying that there was something wrong with the car.

Keith Barnard and I had a good look around the car. When Keith asked me what I thought was wrong, I said, "There's nothing broken on the car"—as opposed to something "wrong"—"and he won't be back." I was right. He just quietly disappeared from the team. Nigel really didn't like the handling of the car, which meant he was not quick. Mark Blundell returned for the next race at Monaco, where he did a solid job by finishing fifth.

Problems with the car continued, as they did with the new refueling rig for 1995. The team's morale was also suffering. Let me explain, while protecting identities by calling the guys involved Person A, Person B, and Person C. Person A takes it upon himself to write a report about the fuel-rig problems, only for Person B to tell him he's an ass for writing it. Then Person B gets Person C to do what Person A has already suggested in his report. Fantastic!

A more-sensible move came from Dave Ryan during practice for the French Grand Prix at Magny-Cours. We had problems most of Friday with electrical and hydraulic gear changes, and although we were reasonably sure that they were fixed near the end of the day, Dave suggested that we take the cars to Lurcy-Lévis, a local track and airfield used by several teams for aero testing. We ran all three cars without any problems, and in the race Mika finished 7th and Mark 11th.

Ilmor produced an improved engine in time for the British Grand Prix, but unfortunately, things didn't go particularly well at all at Silverstone. Mika went out early with a gearbox electronic control unit problem, and Mark, having had a shunt with Rubens Barrichello on the next-to-last lap while fighting over fourth place, was classified fifth after crossing the line more or less on three wheels, his left-rear tire completely gone.

Things got worse in Germany when both cars dropped out of the top six with engine problems; not a great result for Mercedes at their home grand prix.

Both cars failed to finish with engine problems again in Hungary, even though Mika managed to do a brave lap in the unloved MP4/10B to qualify fifth. Things began to improve with the engines in Belgium, where Mark scored two points for fifth place. This was some consolation after seeing Mika spin out of a handy fourth place at the start of the second lap.

Monza was always going to be a good test of the engines after Mika qualified seventh. There was a fair amount of attrition in the race (both Ferraris and both Williams cars retired, along with Schumacher's Benetton), but by staying out of trouble, Mika finished third and Mark fourth. Ilmor's work had paid off on this high-speed, hard-on-engines circuit.

The latest version of the car, the MP4/10C, was run at Silverstone and sent straight to Estoril for the Portuguese Grand Prix. It seemed to me at the time that this was a public relations move on McLaren's part, because the new car had seen very little testing.

Having two cars with different suspension and bodywork caused a great deal of confusion among a bunch of very worn-out mechanics. On Saturday night, my notes suggest that the mechanics—and anyone who would or could help—built one MP4/10B, an MP4/10C with a B-type floor, and a MP4/10C with a B-type gearbox and rear suspension. Or something like that. After all that, Mika qualified 13th and had an engine problem in the race; Mark qualified 12th and somehow finished 9th.

We stayed in Estoril for testing that we hoped would help us to understand the general muddle over the race weekend. During the course of the two days, there was every combination of parts from the two cars mixed and matched with an MP4/10C, but with a 10B floor and gearbox with different suspension. Then everything was changed to some other odd combination, all of which produced pretty much the same results. The car was still not very quick, with different forms of chaos created by all the experimenting. As Dave Redding said later, he didn't know how he could work two 24-hour days in a row and get

With power now provided by Mercedes-Ilmor, the German manufacturer's name figured prominently on the 1995 MP4/10. (LAT PHOTOGRAPHIC)

nothing out of it. It was like shoveling shit with a pitchfork against an incoming tide.

As if that was not bad enough, we went straight from Estoril to the Nürburgring, where it rained on Sunday morning and was very cold. Both cars were set up very stiff to keep control of the imaginary downforce, and for some reason, we started the race on dry tires when just about everybody else chose wets. Mika, who described the car as undrivable during the early laps before others changed to slicks, struggled on and managed to finish eighth, two laps down on the winner, Schumacher. Mark spun off at some point trying to keep it on the "island."

Mika didn't do the Pacific Grand Prix at Aida in Japan because of an appendix operation, so Jan Magnussen took his place. Jan had part of a day's testing at Silverstone, which included practicing pit stops, and he did okay in the race, following Mark by a couple of seconds to finish 10th.

Mika was back for Suzuka, a track he always liked, and where despite his recent operation, he qualified third. Mark had to start at the back of the grid after not being able to qualify because the mechanics were still fixing his car. Following a couple of shunts—one of which was quite bad—Mark managed to keep things together and finished seventh.

Mercedes-Ilmor had produced an updated engine for Mika to use, and for some reason the MP4/10B seemed to be a bit better at Suzuka. By staying out of trouble again and driving a steady race, Mika finished second.

With two weeks between Suzuka and the last race in Adelaide, I stopped off in Cairns in the northern part of Queensland. Mario Illien, his wife Catherine, our friend Karl-Heinz Zimmermann, and the two Sabrinas who worked for him at the race track and his restaurant in Austria, chartered a small plane and we went to Lizard Island for a few days. Karl-Heinz soon discovered that the head chef there was an Austrian, so things were looking quite good in the food department.

While having a drink at the bar before dinner one evening, in walked Gerhard Berger. Where the hell did he come from? Karl-Heinz fell over backwards and bounced on the floor, "dead" from the shock, which caused a bit of a scene until Mario offered him another drink and he got up. Gerhard had sailed up from Cairns with Pasquale Lattuneddu of Formula One Management and a *very* nice-looking boat crew. I'm sure it was Gerhard who chose the boat.

While we were there we went out with a group of people to the edge of the Barrier Reef and a place called Cod Hole, famous for the very large grouper that live there. In Australia they are called potato cod. It was quite fantastic to be on the bottom with these giant fish swimming around us, the dive master helping things along with a box of something suitable for feeding them.

I was just snorkeling but, since they were in about 20 to 25 feet of water, I was able to swim down and go in among the divers and the fish. Karl-Heinz was wondering why he went to all the trouble with the scuba equipment when I was swimming around with just my snorkeling gear. Of course, it was easier to follow the fish with the scuba gear when they decided to wander off.

One of the scuba divers with a small underwater video camera followed one of the groupers back to its cave in the side of the coral wall and got a couple of minutes' footage of the fish with his giant mouth open, being cleaned by smaller fish. We watched this at the bar that night; it was something quite special.

I left a few days before the others to be in Adelaide when the other McLaren people arrived. Among the many good things about Adelaide was a selection of very nice fish restaurants and some of Australia's best wineries close by. We became good friends with the owners of the McLaren Vale (no relation) winery. They also had a town house right near the race track. This was very handy, particularly when we were invited to come by and try some of their product.

During Friday qualifying, Mika had a big accident when a rear puncture caused by something on the track sent him straight into a one-layer tire barrier against a concrete wall. Mika was hardly able to breathe. Two volunteer doctors, Jereme Lockins and Steve Lewis, arrived at the scene in 15 seconds, followed by Sid Watkins, who restarted Hakkinen's heart twice and performed a cricothyroidotomy (a simpler form of a tracheotomy) at the side of the track. Watkins would later describe this as his most satisfying experience during his time working in the sport.

This tracheotomy more than likely saved Mika's life. Watkins and the medical people worked to their usual high standards and got him off to the hospital as soon as they could. Mika had received a serious blow when his head hit the steering wheel—you could tell how hard the impact had been by the amount that his seat belts had stretched—and he would remain in the hospital for quite a long time.

Mark qualified 10th and finished 4th, which helped everyone, although it was a sober pack-up that night, with Mika's shunt and his health on everyone's mind.

When Mika's stay in the hospital was over, he traveled back to England with the two doctors who had looked after him and his girlfriend, Ejra. Ron Dennis had come to an arrangement with Qantas that allowed them to have the front of the airplane to themselves for a bit of peace and quiet. Ron's dedication and commitment to Mika, which included spending a lot of time with him in the hospital and after his release, did a lot to cement the close relationship they had.

In some ways, disappointment and disillusionment summed up a season which saw McLaren finish fourth in the Constructors championship, but more than 100 points behind the winners, Benetton.

One unusual development at the 1996 Monaco Grand Prix was that David Coulthard ran the race wearing a helmet borrowed from defending World Champion Michael Schumacher. Perhaps it helped, as DC came in second, his best finish in a mediocre year for McLaren. (LAT PHOTOGRAPHIC)

# 1996: Hakkinen Returns, Joined by Coulthard

After a season like 1995, there was a lot of work to be done by both McLaren and Mercedes. Ilmor built a Phase 3 V10 on which everything was new except the oil pumps. The MP4/11 was produced under the direction of Neil Oatley, with a lot of input from Steve Nichols, who had returned to McLaren from Ferrari, and Henri Durand, who was taking care of the aerodynamics. There was also a lot of work involved with a new TAG 2000 electronics box, with much time spent at Estoril testing the engine and sorting out the software.

There was, however, one very important and interesting test at the Paul Ricard circuit on February 5. Steve Hallam and I went with enough mechanics to look after the car, under instructions to keep the test low-key. Alain Prost, who was doing some testing for us, was at Ricard to do a few laps and make sure everything was working okay.

This was to be the first time Mika had driven a race car since his accident in Adelaide.

Having driven on his own from Monaco, where he lived, he had a chat with the boys and Alain about the car, along with taking some time to talk to with Steve and me about what he would like to do. You can understand the reason for the low-key operation, because in a lot of ways, Mika was "our guy," and we were very concerned about him.

It was a very quiet time in the garage.

Mika said he would like to do just a few laps and see how he felt. After the first or second lap, he basically felt okay with things. He did several short runs of 6 or 8 laps, and then we took a break and had some lunch. At that point, he said he'd like to do one more run of at least 25 laps, which he did. Then he said that was enough, as he felt a little tired. He was about two-tenths of a second slower than Michael Schumacher in the Ferrari that day. Mika had done about 60 laps in total. He said thank you, got in his Mercedes, and drove back to Monaco.

Everyone was able to take a deep breath. We were overwhelmed and very pleased with what had just happened. I don't think Alain could really believe what he had just seen. It was pretty clear that Mika would be racing with us again, joined in 1996 by David Coulthard, who had moved from Williams.

After nearly a month at Estoril dealing with engine problems, the new software, and constantly learning things with the gear-change project, we managed some reasonable lap times. But there was an underlying feeling that the MP4/11 might not be that great.

One night while we were testing in Estoril, Henri Durand and I went out for dinner. We got talking about Indianapolis when he was there with Ligier, doing the aerodynamics. I didn't mean to sound callous, but as he was telling me how good it was, I couldn't resist pointing out that 1984 was the year he didn't qualify, while Mayer Motor Racing was on pole with Tom Sneva.

Just before leaving for the first race at Melbourne, Martin Whitmarsh came into my office and had an uncomfortable chat about a conversation I'd had with Michael Schumacher at the Estoril test. Apparently someone at Mercedes had complained about me talking to Michael and admitting, "Yes, our engine had blown up." How can anyone be upset about a conversation regarding an engine that *had* blown up on the pit straight? The failure was blatantly clear and common knowledge in the pit lane, and probably in a great deal of England, as well as parts of Italy, France, and Germany. To think I would have said anything about *why* the engine failed was just stupid. I guess Mercedes just didn't know me very well at that point!

The MP4/11 did not fare very well in the first bunch of races, even though Mika qualified fifth and finished fifth in the Australian Grand Prix in Melbourne.

It was about this time when Mika decided that he had to have the tire pressures measured in bar instead of psi to match what the Goodyear people used. Steve Hallam, Mika's race engineer, did himself a table to convert the pressures quickly and keep Mika informed.

David got our first podium of 1996 by finishing third in the European Grand Prix at the Nürburgring, and he followed that up by leading the first 20 laps at Imola and then losing a podium finish with hydraulics trouble. But probably his best drive of the season would come two weeks later at Monaco in the middle of May.

Performance had been improved by a new engine spec, demonstrated by David qualifying fifth and Mika eighth. With all the practice sessions having been run in the dry, very heavy rain on race morning meant an extra practice session. Mika was fastest by quite a margin, but in the last few minutes, he had a shunt at Tabac that literally broke the car in half. That meant the T-car was used by Mr. Hakkinen in what would be a pretty chaotic race because of changing weather conditions. On the last lap, Mika couldn't avoid a three-car collision but was classified fifth. David, meanwhile, would finish second behind the Ligier of Olivier Panis. It had been that sort of race.

We ran an aero test at the IDIADA proving ground near Barcelona, just before the next race at Barcelona. Martin Hines, who was testing the new car, managed to go down the side of a bank, finishing upside down. When Hines showed up at Barcelona and asked Richard Moody, one of the mechanics, to borrow a pen, Richard said, "You can have the pen, but not a car anymore!"

A couple more points finishes in Spain and Canada were followed by a test at Silverstone. This was where my VW Golf GTI was stolen from the car park at the nearby Buckingham Lodge Hotel on the night of June 19, 1996. When we came out of the hotel to go to the circuit the next morning, I remember saying to Mark Slade, "That's strange. I'm sure that's where I parked the car late last night, and it doesn't seem to be there!"

It wasn't until August 7 that I received a call and a fax regarding my car. Apparently it had been sitting in some corrupt holding place until July 21, and then taken to another corrupt place after that. I could now have it back—the day before the insurance was to be paid! And just as I was due to leave for the Hungarian GP the next morning.

I have a file with the letters regarding the inept police and the corrupt insurance people who pretended they didn't know who the car belonged to until the day before the insurance should have been paid—and then suddenly they knew just who to call. Really pathetic.

There were several incidents at the Buckingham Lodge Hotel regarding things going missing from rooms as well. When Nick "Hogger" Cross asked the front desk for a wake-up call, he noted that the answer might as well have been, "What time would you like your

# Mark Slade

I have known Tyler for the best part of 20 years now, since the time I joined the McLaren race team as a junior trackside engineer at the start of the 1994 season. However, as someone who has always taken a keen interest in the historical background of the sport, I was already well aware of his hugely significant role in the development of McLaren, from its earliest days to the position it holds now as one of the most successful teams in the history of the sport.

The chance to work with such a well-respected person was a great privilege, if initially somewhat daunting, given Tyler's well-known inability to tolerate anyone who doesn't fit his view of being a good guy! As it happened I needn't have worried: Despite being very green at that point in my career, Tyler was kind enough to take me under his wing and help me avoid making too many blunders and gaffes as I tried to establish myself as a worthwhile member of the team.

It has stayed that way ever since. Tyler has always been a rock of support for me, throughout the time we have worked together and beyond, as my career has progressed and I have moved on to roles outside the McLaren team.

One of the things that has always impressed me about Tyler is his lack of ego. For Tyler, it has always been about the success of the team, and particularly, the group of guys he was working with directly. He knows just about everyone who matters in the business right to the very top, but he never had any qualms about getting involved in the nitty-gritty of the race weekend. From helping prepare the cars for the event to helping tear down the garage after the race, he was completely involved. There were never any airs or graces when working with Tyler, but that's because it was a high-pressure environment where decisions had to be made and acted upon quickly.

Tyler's methodical dedication to his role was an example to all of us, and his opinions were always worth listening to because he has a great knack for cutting straight to the core of a problem.

Another of Tyler's unique characteristics was that despite having been involved in the sport for so many years, he didn't dwell on the past or stop moving forward. Achieving the next win was always the most important thing, and if he needed to get involved with a new technology in order to do that, then that was what he did. I don't believe many, if any, engineers in the sport have successfully traversed such a huge stretch of technological advancement, from the days of wing-less, tube-framed cars with skinny tires to the complex carbon-fiber aerodynamic platforms of the modern era.

Tyler always had good relationships with the drivers with whom he worked, particularly during his time with Ayrton Senna, Mika Hakkinen, and Kimi Raikkonen. They would seek him out for advice and encouragement as well as his technical expertise. I think they realized that with all the experience he brought to the track, Tyler understood the pressures that they faced better than most.

When it came to winding down after a hard day at the track, Tyler was an excellent dinner companion. We would inevitably spend hours addressing the state of the business, interspersed with his stories of times past.

I am very proud to have worked with Tyler and to have played a small part in achieving great things with him.

early morning break-in, sir?"

The continuing struggle to find downforce on MP4/11 brought only points finishes in France, but at least it was good to see Mika make it to the podium by finishing third at Silverstone. He was there again in Belgium, although the race at Spa seemed to be more eventful for us off the track than on it.

We had just had dinner at the Fox Holes Hotel; although owned by the Sultan of Qatar, we called it Freddie's Place, after the manager. Team coordinator Jo Ramirez was driving Phil Collins, John Mulcahy, and me back to the hunting lodge where we were staying. It had been raining a little and the road was quite twisty. Jo didn't make it around a tight right-hand corner—he was not going very quick, I might add—and he stuffed the left-front corner of our nice Mercedes into a low brick wall, albeit not hard enough to set off the airbags.

The impact had pushed some of the metalwork close enough to the front tire to make it difficult to steer the car properly. We used the bumper jack and whatever else we could find to try to move the metalwork far enough away from the wheel. We didn't make a lot of progress until John Mulcahy had the idea of jamming the bumper jack against the bent metal and the wheel, then starting the engine and using the power steering to push the metalwork away. It worked well enough.

Just as we were putting things away in the boot of the car, a small Volkswagen came around the corner, spun, hit the wall, and turned over. We ran down the road to the car and could smell that the airbags had gone off. I put my head halfway in the window and said, "Hello? Are you all right in there?" only to hear the reply, "Tyler! Where the hell did you come from?" It was Tim Collings, a British F1 journalist who happened to be staying just up the road.

We decided to try and get the car back onto its wheels. During one of the attempts, Phil Collins fell over the stone wall and into the bushes. When we got the car back on its wheels, I walked to the corner and discovered that the road was covered with diesel fuel. This, along with the small amount of rain, had made the surface very slippery.

It was pretty late when we dropped Tim off at his place. The next morning, on our way to the race track, we noticed that on the other side of the stone wall that Phil had fallen over, there was a drop of about 25 feet to a small stream! Thankfully, Phil had gotten caught up in the bushes.

When we got to the track Gavin Beresford, the race team's very good fabricator, was asked if he could do something about tidying up the metalwork on the left-front corner of

Damon Hill leads the 1996 Japanese Grand Prix trailed by Benetton's Gerhard Berger and our own Mika Hakkinen. Hill would go on to win the race and the championship for Williams. (LAT PHOTOGRAPHIC)

the nice Mercedes.

There was damage to both race cars at Monza, caused by the tire barrier used to define the first chicane. When Jacques Villeneuve clipped the pile of tires on the second lap, David couldn't avoid them and was eliminated. A lap later, Mika found the same obstacle (caused this time by Jean Alesi). Mika made it back to the pits for a new nose, taking on fresh tires at the same time. He rejoined dead last, but helped by retirements (such as Damon Hill crashing into Michael Schumacher), Mika put in a great drive and finished third once more.

Mika ended the season finishing third again in Japan. There was quite a party at Karl-Heinz's facility, as he was doing the catering for Williams, and Damon Hill had just won the World Championship. Even though we had little to celebrate, the one thing to remember about 1996 is the way Mika dealt with his recovery. He did tell us at the end of the season that it had been pretty damn hard at times.

I think the commitment to drive a race car again after an accident takes more than just big balls; thanks, Mika. There was no doubt that he was ready for 1997 and whatever the year might bring.

# 1997: The Start of Something Big: First Wins for Mika and DC

The new MP4/12 for the 1997 season was finished in early January and tested a week or so later at Jerez, followed by Estoril and Barcelona. We were able to do a full race distance with both cars.

Needless to say, MP4/12 was a lot better than the previous two cars. It also looked very different because the West tobacco brand had come on board as a sponsor, with their silver-and-black livery, replacing the very familiar Marlboro colors of the previous 22 years. Once you got used to the new color scheme on the car, it actually looked fine, along with the new race uniforms. It certainly was a big change from the years of red and white, and once again we were involved with some good people at West.

There was a bit of a domestic issue following the return of Dave Bryers to McLaren after a few years with TAG Electronics. Dave had been involved in the software for various bits of the 1993 active suspension car. He was a clever guy, and I thought it a good idea that he had come back. Nick Butler, Nick Cross, and I had written a straightforward, user-friendly, step-by-step document on how to start the race car and do various steps and checks, from turning on the laptop through checking the gearbox shift.

One afternoon, Mr. Bryers appeared and said, "Here is the new procedure document for starting the car and shift check, etc." It was written in what you might call a more pompous manner. I said we had already written something suitable and pointed out that I had helped him get the job—and I could probably help him lose it. I did suggest that a bit more communication between us would be a good idea. Dave reminded me of this discussion last year!

Due to pretty major changes in the technical regulations regarding crash structures and various suspension dimensions, MP4/12 looked very different and had undergone many hours of research at the National Physical Laboratory in Teddington. We were as confident as we could be that everything worked, but as usual, you never knew where you stood against competitors such as Williams and Ferrari. The first race in Melbourne would provide some of the answers.

And those answers were very encouraging when David "DC" Coulthard won the Australian Grand Prix and Mika finished third. It was the first win for McLaren since Senna in Adelaide in 1993, and it gave everyone on the team an injection of confidence.

Waiting at the airport for our flight out of Melbourne, Benetton boss Flavio Briatore told me what had happened to Jean Alesi in the race. Jean's Benetton had run out of fuel, not through a miscalculation by the engineers, but probably because of a radio problem—which is why everyone still uses pit signaling boards. According to Flavio, Jean never looked at the pit board, and after several laps signaling him to stop, Flavio suggested that Joan Villadelprat should get over the pit wall with the board and maybe throw the board at him. If you've ever heard Flavio talk, you can probably understand it was very amusing listening to him tell the story in his inimitable style, using his colorful English with an Italian accent!

Before heading for the races in South America, we had a visit to the factory by Prime Minister John Major. He didn't bring much luck because we didn't even come close to following up the Australian win, as Mika finished 4th and David 10th in Brazil. DC held joint lead of the championship with Jacques Villeneuve, but that would be the closest we'd get to the Williams-Renault driver, as he went on to set 10 pole positions and win 7 races.

We went down to Argentina on the Monday morning after the race at Interlagos; this was always a good move, given the social scene in Buenos Aires. One memory from that weekend is stopping by a bar frequented by our mechanics. They were enjoying themselves as usual, when someone from the motor home collapsed and fell backwards onto the floor. The cry went out for "Lifters, please!" and several of those who could still stand up rose to the occasion!

Clad in our new West Tobacco livery, David Coulthard and the McLaren MP4/12 head out of the pits at the 1997 San Marino Grand Prix. (LAT PHOTOGRAPHIC)

A one-stop strategy (and a couple of safety car periods) in the race at Argentina helped to rescue 17th on the grid for Mika, as he came through to finish 5th, DC having been eliminated in a multicar collision on the first lap.

After the race, Steve Hallam and I were due to fly straight to a Barcelona test via London. Fortunately, we went to the airport with Pat Fry and some of the marketing people. It was a good thing, because we had a vast array of cardboard boxes filled with everything from gear ratios to the motor-home barbecue, along with several suitcases full of stuff and, of course, our own bags.

I wish I had been able to take a picture of the faces of the British Airways check-in staff when they saw us coming. Steve Hallam spent quite some time speaking nicely to them, which he did very well, being a diplomatic Englishman. The BA people were very helpful, and our marketing guys rewarded them with a few hats and T-shirts!

When we reached Gatwick, Pat helped Steve and me with the traveling circus. When the nice BA lady asked where we and all this stuff had come from, we proudly said, "We've just arrived from Buenos Aires and we're on your flight to Barcelona!" Of course, there was an issue about all the stuff we were carrying. When Steve started to explain that we'd just brought it all from Buenos Aires, I kicked him in the leg, because we'd managed to come from Buenos Aires only by paying for the extra weight with free hats and T-shirts. not to mention the fact that there was a group of us on the flight.

I said if there was a problem and we needed to pay for the extra weight for the Barcelona flight, well, I guessed we'd just have to. "So, where do we weigh the large cardboard boxes?" I asked. I seem to remember that the box with the gear ratios at one end of it didn't fit very well on the scales, which probably affected the total weight in our favor. Steve and I eventually arrived in Barcelona at 9:30 on Monday night.

The test went okay, except the new spec engine didn't arrive until Friday morning. We left at 3:40 a.m. and were back at the track at 6:00 a.m. for the last day of the test. I do remember it was well worth the effort involved in fitting the new spec engine.

Fifth place in Argentina would turn out to be pretty good compared to what happened in the next few races, Monaco being a typical example. DC and Mika did a reasonable job by qualifying fifth and eighth, but everyone's plans literally went down the drain when rain came on race day.

Racing on a course of public streets means the track doesn't always have a lot of grip, and when it rains it has even less. Rain tires are usually the best choice. Or so you would think.

A team portrait taken after Mika Hakkinen's win at Jerez in October 1997. Daimler Benz CEO Jurgen Schrempp is at the center between Mika and David Coulthard. At the far right is Mercedes Sport chief Norbert Haug. (LAT PHOTOGRAPHIC)

My old friend Adrian Newey (left) with Ron Dennis. His arrival from Williams as McLaren's new Technical Director would help usher in a new era for the team. (LAT PHOTOGRAPHIC)

I'll never forget the priceless look on the face of Roger Higgins, the Ilmor engine guy, as we stood on the grid, rain running off our hats, and the word from on high came to fit dry tires. DC chose to start on intermediates while Mika went for slicks. And still the rain continued! They managed to get through the first lap, but going into the chicane on the second lap, DC spun and hit the barrier. Mika was among the cars that went off in the confusion as everyone tried to get around David's car.

A new Mercedes-Ilmor engine in Canada proved to be a big step forward, and we made the most of it in the race when a one-stop strategy got DC into the lead after he had been holding a good fourth place early on. When he made his pit stop, a problem with one of the clutch paddles caused the engine to stall. Confusion surrounded getting the engine started again. I believe the other clutch paddle worked, but no one thought of that at the time. What made it even worse was the race being red-flagged a few laps later when Olivier Panis had a big accident in his Prost. That meant David was classified out of the points in seventh place. Had the pit stop been three laps later, he would have won.

We picked up points here and there—third place for Mika at Hockenheim being a mid-season highlight—but worse was to come at Spa at the end of August.

Mika had a large shunt at Les Combes when the left-rear carbon wishbone failed during practice on Saturday morning. Fortunately he was okay. After a bit of a thrash, all three cars were fitted with steel lower-rear wishbones for qualifying and the race.

After all that, it was good to have Mika cross the line third . . . but it wasn't over yet.

On Saturday, the fuel sample taken from Mika's car did not match the sample given to the FIA before the start of the event. There was no performance advantage as such; it was just that the two samples didn't match.

There was a lot of jumping up and down and a fair amount of bewilderment for Tony Harlow, the Mobil man in charge of the fuel. The team appealed, and Mika was allowed to race, only to be thrown out later. We eventually discovered that the drum carrying the fuel had not been cleaned properly beforehand.

There were no problems with fuel-matching at Monza—which was just as well, because DC won the race. Having qualified sixth, he made a really good start and was later running second behind Jean Alesi, trying to work out the best way to get ahead of the Benetton. DC figured we would make a faster refueling stop, and when he saw Alesi coming into the pits (he'd stop for fuel this time!), DC followed him. The boys did a really good job getting him out first.

Mika Hakkinen after his first F1 victory at Jerez in October 1997. At the left are Mercedes-Benz executives Jurgen Huppert and Norbert Haug, while a damp Mario Illien is at the right. (LAT PHOTOGRAPHIC)

We pulled the same trick with Mika, which got him ahead of a couple of cars and into fourth place. But a few laps later, a large piece of rubber parted company with the rest of his Goodyear tire, and the slow lap and extra pit stop put him back to ninth. For DC, the victory in Italy was a timely result, as he'd only scored four points since that win in Melbourne.

We'd been having a few engine problems, and one of the most frustrating came in Austria on the second lap, just after Mika had taken the lead. DC made up for that by coming through from 10th to finish 2nd. Mika had been on the front of the grid for the first time, just 0.094 seconds behind Villeneuve. Whether it helped or not is difficult to say, but the MP4/12 had a revised front wing, courtesy of Adrian Newey, who had recently joined the team from Williams.

Mika finally got his first pole position at the next race, the Luxembourg Grand Prix, which was actually held at the Nürburgring in Germany. But the engine problems were

David Coulthard on the podium after winning the first Grand Prix of the 1997 season in Australia. DC's first championship win had come two years earlier while driving for Williams. (LAT PHOTOGRAPHIC)

to come back and haunt us. It started when DC had a problem in the Saturday-morning practice session, the boys doing a very quick engine change to give him some running time in the second 45-minute session.

We dominated the first half of the race and right through the pit stops, with Mika leading David. Then, on lap 42, DC's engine failed—followed, not long after, by Mika's. It was not a great birthday present for Mika, and neither was it a happy day for the top people from Mercedes, as both V10s blew up in full view of the company's grandstand.

At least both cars finished the Japanese Grand Prix, where DC took fourth, but we didn't really expect much from the European Grand Prix at Jerez at the end of October. The last race of the season in Spain decided the championship, but there were also a lot of other things going on.

With about a third of the race to go, Michael Schumacher was leading by a very small amount when Jacques Villeneuve decided to get serious about winning this championship. Schumacher left a bit of space, and Jacques went up the inside—at which point Michael turned into him. That was par for the course, except it didn't work for Schumacher this time, and he fell off. The FIA took all 78 of Michael's championship points away from him, so he lost what would have been second place in the World Championship. Later Eddie Irvine was briefly spotted wearing a Michael Schumacher: world champion cap, on which he'd inserted the word "nearly."

Following the incident with Schumacher, Jacques thought the car felt a bit strange and slowed his pace. After some discussion in the pits, he let Mika and DC go by him—which was a scary maneuver, because Jacques only needed to finish fifth to win the championship.

So Mika won his first race with the help of DC, and, of course, Jacques. DC, having been ahead, was not amused about being asked to let Mika through. Whatever the politics, I believe it was a turning point for Mika and set him up for what was to follow in 1998.

On the other hand, it was a sad day for quite a few of us on the team because Dieter Gundel was leaving McLaren to work for BMW. (He'd later move on to Ferrari, where he still is at the time of this writing.) Dieter was last seen in Spain on the Saturday night at La Bodeguilla del Bar Jamon tapas bar in Puerto de Santa Maria. He was starting on the second bottle of a nice Spanish red after Phill Asbury had given up and returned to the hotel. I was never sure if Dieter really wanted to leave McLaren, but being at Ferrari would work out very well for him. He was and remains a very good friend.

# 1998: Newey, Hakkinen, and the MP4/13 Deliver the Goods

**W**e went into 1998 with Adrian Newey as technical director. Obviously, I had known Adrian since our time together in CART and had gotten on well with him; I was hoping that would still be the case.

I did wonder, however, if there would be a stitch in there somewhere for the hardworking Neil Oatley—or would that come later? For contractual reasons, Adrian had not been allowed to come and work for us officially until August 1, 1997, by which time the design of MP4/13 was well advanced, but it was pretty clear he had used his thinking time (or "gardening leave," as it's known in the business) to come up with ways of dealing with new regulations, which included a narrower track and more-stringent side-impact tests. Formula One was also moving to grooved tires, and McLaren was making a switch from Goodyear to Bridgestone rubber.

The first chassis engine start-up for MP4/13 was on Friday, February 6, and then on to Paul Ricard for its first test. The car, at this stage, was painted in the classic McLaren orange. It looked good, but we knew it would be changed later to suit our sponsors or partners. We flew to the south of France on the Saturday, and I made a note that we got to the hotel at about 3:30 a.m. the next morning.

There had been quite a few mechanical mods to the gearbox, but a few things broke on the first day. Gearbox designer David North and I had a reasonable idea about what was actually wrong, having had a close look at the computer data. But as usual, there were other engineers to whom I had a hard time trying to explain what we thought the problem was and why it had happened.

David and I had a plan to do something about the problem there at the race track for the following day. A few overnight mods to the gearbox allowed us to keep running, but early in the afternoon, a top-rear wishbone broke, and as there were no spares at this early stage, it was "game over" for now.

Chassis No. 001 was sent directly from Paul Ricard to Barcelona to start testing at the end of the week. DC was driving when the rear wing came off, doing so much damage to the chassis that it had to be flown back to England. Chassis No. 002 was flown out to Barcelona on Sunday, February 15, with chassis No. 001 reappearing later in the week. It was a busy time for everyone, with Chris Robson, the exceptional parts coordinator, having to pull a rabbit out of the hat by both ears.

This continued into the last week of February and a test at Paul Ricard with chassis No. 001. Meanwhile, there was a shakedown and refueling practice going on at Silverstone just before the cars went to the airport and the flight to Melbourne. It was a pretty hectic week for team manager Dave Ryan and the rest of us.

Indications from testing that we might be on the pace were confirmed when Mika and David, split by a couple of hundredths of a second, filled the front row of the grid in Melbourne. Michael Schumacher, third-quickest in the Ferrari, was seven-tenths slower. Practice had not been without its incidents. On Friday, Mika fell off at the corner just before the pits but didn't hit anything. He walked back to the garage with a silly grin on his face, saying, "Sorry—I was just fooling around."

In the race, both our drivers pulled away from the rest of the field by between two and three seconds a lap. At some point around half distance, there was some confusion on the radio when Mark Slade, Mika's race engineer, said something and Mika thought it was an instruction to come into the pits; I believe it was actually a question about the brakes. When Mika suddenly appeared in the pit lane, he was told to get the hell back on the track. By then DC had gone into the lead.

There would be a big fuss after the race because in the closing laps, David slowed and

**boro**

O MINISTÉRIO DA SAÚDE ADVERTE:
FUMAR CAUSA DIVERSOS
MALES À SUA SAÚDE

Driving the new McLaren MP413, Mika Hakkinen and
David Coulthard scored their second straight 1-2 finish
at the 1998 Brazilian Grand Prix. (LAT PHOTOGRAPHIC)

Ferrari's Michael Schumacher (left) and McLaren's Mika Hakkinen meet before the last race of the 1998 season in Japan. Mika's win there gave him the championship, the first for a McLaren driver since 1991. (LAT PHOTOGRAPHIC)

Mika went back into the lead. Team orders or team game plan? There is a subtle difference. I believe it was down to a prearranged agreement between the two drivers. To avoid our guys racing each other unnecessarily when we appeared to have an advantage, Mika and DC had said that whoever led into the first corner should—all things being equal—win the race. Mika had gotten there first, and it was a shame there was all this controversy floating about because it detracted from our cars finishing a lap ahead of Heinz-Harald Frentzen's third-place Williams.

There was to be trouble of a different kind two weeks later in Brazil. For quite some time, thanks to work by Steve Nichols and a few mods by Pat Fry, we had been running a slightly different brake system to balance the car entering the corner. This system, involving two brake pedals (one of which was in place of the clutch, now operated by hand-control paddles), had been approved by the FIA technical delegate. The cat had been let out of the bag in Austria the previous year when a photographer stuck his camera inside the cockpit of one of our cars that had been abandoned out on the track.

When we got to Sao Paulo, Ferrari led the complaints to the FIA stewards, which is something Ferrari has been known to do when someone else is quicker than them. The protest was upheld by the race stewards, and we—along with a number of other teams who had suddenly thought of the same idea—removed the system.

One does wonder just who or what changed the FIA's mind. Adrian Newey did give Charlie Whiting a piece of paper with some words and lines on it as an explanation after the showdown in the garage. Probably not a good idea, because by then Charlie had been overruled by the stewards.

Not that this made any difference to us for the race. We qualified on the front row again and finished first and second, Mika just ahead of DC. Michael Schumacher, third, was one minute further behind. I guess it wasn't all to do with the brake system!

Buenos Aires, next on the calendar, is such a great place to relax for a few days and enjoy some wonderful meals. We organized various trips, including one on the ferry to Colonia del Sacramento in Uruguay, where there were lots of quite old cars and very strange tea. Some other people went farther south to the Fangio House and Museum, where they were invited to stay for lunch after enjoying a look around.

There was a large traffic junction with six or more lanes near our hotel. One afternoon, Jo Ramirez stopped at the traffic lights near the front of the queue, only to wake up unharmed an hour or so later. Those late nights at the tango dances will get you every time!

DC qualified on pole in Argentina and led early on, but Schumacher, who was running with less fuel, got by Mika and then forced DC off the road. DC would eventually finish sixth, but second for Mika was more than enough to keep his lead in the championship.

Schumacher's win was the boost Ferrari needed for the next race at Imola, pretty much Ferrari's home ground. But this was to be DC's weekend, as he took pole and won the race. Mika had qualified alongside on the front row but there seemed little he could do about David in the race—not that it mattered in the end, because a gearbox-bearing failure brought Mika's first retirement of the season.

This unexpected failure highlighted just how much checking is required on the parts going into a race car. The bearing in question had the same part number as the others we had been using, with no failures. But it turned out this one was a counterfeit bearing. It was made for a damn trailer axle, and not the quality we had requested from our supplier. An ugly scene was in order.

About 15 minutes before the end of a test at Barcelona, and before the next race there, Mark Slade, Mika's race engineer, said we could run some engine-software mods. Phil Collins (don't go anywhere without him), the Mercedes-Ilmor engine-software man, and I had been pestering Mark about letting us try it.

Phil typed in some new numbers and we explained to Mika that he could select these numbers with one of the steering-wheel switches. But we recommended to Mika that it might be best to do one lap first, as we were not entirely sure about the results. Classic Mika: He switched to the new numbers going down the pit lane. He did a couple of quick laps and came in to say, "That's neat," or something to that effect.

For the race itself, it was back to what was becoming the 1998 norm, as Mika and David qualified first and second and finished that way. On this occasion, David could not get near Mika, who had been quickest in every practice session, led all the way in the race, and set the fastest lap.

Then it was on to Monaco. Monaco usually comes with a few interesting things—some with wheels, and some with nice legs and the rest!

During qualifying, Mika could not get a clear lap, which was frustrating; there were always the two quickest segments on the track to indicate what was possible if he could avoid traffic in the third sector. He finally managed it on the last run of qualifying—and took pole position, with DC a couple of tenths behind after he had been held up on his best lap.

On Sunday morning after the warm-up, we found a hydraulic leak from the overflow

David and Mika look pleased at having the first two spots on the grid as they take questions before the Brazilian Grand Prix. (LAT PHOTOGRAPHIC)

pipe on Mika's car just after doing the gearshift checks. When asked, "What do we do?" there could only be one answer: I told the guys to change the hydraulic set.

Keith Barnard, Mark Lunnon, and several others got stuck in while Roger Duff went all the way back to the truck on the quayside to get another hydraulic set. You have to realize that this was late Sunday morning, race day, at Monaco, and the place was jammed with people. Panic was starting to build until Roger appeared on a motor scooter with a black plastic trash bag containing the "Golden Hydraulic Set." The boys had it changed in 20 minutes, which was pretty damn impressive, really, given that this had to be done in the cramped Monaco pit lane.

Once again, no one could get near the McLarens. DC was pushing Mika hard until his engine failed, leaving Mika to extend his championship lead even further. On the Monday after, we drove to Monza for a test, which ended up being wet most of the time. But it showed we were not going to let up, even though we had five wins in six races. This was just as well, because Schumacher would win the next three.

Montreal started off okay, as DC qualified on pole, with Mika second. The race was stopped after a multicar shunt at the first corner. On the restart, Mika had a large amount of wheel spin in first gear, which made the rev drop between first and second gear (about 6,500 rpm) rather large.

The clutch opening/closing position was not in the correct location for this sort of rev drop, and it damaged the dogs on second gear, producing no drive in that gear. Mika drove around to the pits, telling us that the gearbox was broken, when in fact the only damage was to second gear. Trying to decide what to do was a mess. With hindsight, we should have asked Mika, "How are you driving the car back to the pits if the gearbox is broken?" It was my fault, as I didn't have the clutch set to deal with this amount of rev drop and the delay that goes with it. But I guess you could also say that if the clutch had been set for the large rev drop, it would not have been correct for the normal rev drop.

By the time I got to check what was going on in the race, DC was in the lead, where he would stay for 18 laps. Then the throttle linkage came undone. So neither car finished. Genuine bummer!

I spent a lot of time with Dave Bryers, the people at TAG Electronics, Phill Asbury, and Anton Stipinovich, the embedded systems guy on DC's car, sorting out a fix for the very high rev drop problem. It seemed there was something new in the gear-change software every other weekend.

When we got to Magny-Cours for the pre-race test—and before the first glass of Vacheron Sancerre—I thought it would be a good idea to have a quiet chat with Mika, Mark Slade, Mark Arnall (Mika's trainer), and Phil Prew (Mark's assistant race engineer) about what went wrong in Montreal. The real point of the chat with Mika was to tell him to drive the car until it simply wouldn't go forward anymore with the throttle wide open. Oh, and by the way, Mika, we believe you can win the championship.

People outside the team began to doubt the chances of that when things didn't go well at Magny-Cours. At the start, Mika was pushed down to third by Irvine, who then defended Schumacher's lead. DC, meanwhile, had various fuel-rig pit stop problems and came close to running over the fuel hose man, Steve Morrow—commonly known as "Forklift"—fortunately with no harm to Steve. Having got by Irvine and into second place before this chaotic pit stop, David had to accept one point, for sixth.

The drama continued at Silverstone, thanks to rain arriving during the race and Mika leaving the road and damaging a front wing while holding a 40-second lead. This prompted the officials to bring out the safety car, long overdue in the wet conditions. Mika recovered to take second place, but then the officials got into a real mess over the way they'd handled a 10-second stop-go penalty for Schumacher, who had overtaken under a yellow flag.

By the time they handed Ferrari the penalty notice, it was late in the race. Ferrari brought Schumacher in at the end of his final lap, completed the stop-and-go, and then had him rejoin for the slowing-down lap. This farce was rubber-stamped when it was deemed okay by people who were meant to be the stewards of the race meeting. Apparently, the team with the red car had their own rulebook.

It was incomprehensible to me that a professional organization such as the FIA should wish to appear like incompetent amateurs. Their handling of the Schumacher scenario was totally unacceptable. Incompetence was the first thing that came to mind, followed by the possibility of misinterpretation. For the sake of the sport and all those involved, it is necessary to have competent, qualified people. We noted that the same stewards had overruled the FIA approval of our brake system in Brazil.

David had spun off in the wet at Silverstone, and it looked like his luck wasn't going to get much better in Austria when a first-lap collision meant a pit stop for repairs. Happily, this was helped by the safety car coming out and giving us time to get David back on track, but down in 19th place.

In a great drive, David clawed his way back to second behind Mika, who had led most of the race. After a run of poor results, this helped Mika's championship effort and just about kept DC's title hopes alive. Schumacher, meanwhile, had several offs during the race, but with the usual "help" from Eddie Irvine, he finished third.

We stayed on at the A1-Ring (now known as the Red Bull Ring) to prepare the cars for Hockenheim the next weekend. Late on Sunday evening, someone scrounged food from the Mercedes motor home. In the course of handing it out, the catering girl said, "Austria today, and Germany next." Fortunately, I don't think she heard Jerry Good's retort, "I thought it was Poland!"

We continued to put that mid-season low period behind us when Mika dominated the German Grand Prix from pole and DC finished right behind him. But we were lucky because a few laps from the end, Mika's car began to lose engine oil and power. Both he and DC were able to slow down, as there was no immediate threat from Villeneuve's Williams.

I guess A. J. Foyt was right when he said, "I'd rather be lucky than just quick any day."

We were not lucky in Hungary, despite filling the front row of the grid. Mika had a problem in the race and finished sixth, thanks to the front anti-rollbar coming loose. DC might well have done better than finish second if he had been allowed to pass the wounded Mika earlier. I was not sure if it was amateurs playing at being professionals or professionals playing at being amateurs, because it was pretty obvious that faith healing was not going to fix Mika's problem. Sometimes you just have to press the button on the radio and make the call.

Worse was to follow at Spa, due to a lot of rain at the start. Despite being on the front row, we were in trouble just after the first corner when Eddie Irvine hit DC and triggered a collision with a bunch of other cars. The high level of chaos and destruction that followed forced the race to be stopped. DC was physically okay, but I don't remember there being any corners or wheels left on his car—just the sight of David sitting in the chassis.

We had started the race on intermediate tires, which were fine. But someone who should have known better suggested for the restart, we put on something totally different that "they" (one of the other teams) had tested. Wrong! Mika made it to the first corner before coming together with Michael Schumacher and then being hit by someone else. Mika ended the race sitting on the side of one of his favorite tracks.

DC was also hit by someone at the restart and had to make a pit stop to fix the damage, but at least he was able to rejoin. Later in the race, Schumacher was leading when he came upon DC in a cloud of spray. Schumacher didn't get it quite right and crashed into the back of DC, taking off one of the Ferrari's front wheels and the front wing. DC came into the pits and straight into the garage, where the boys started to replace the rear wing. He'd barely had time to get out of the car when guess-who showed up, ranting and waving his arms, and screaming at DC. It was Schumacher, who had been chased down the pit lane by Stefano Domenicali of Ferrari, who was yelling at his press guy to do something.

The reply was, "I'm just here to record the first punch."

Anton Stipinovich, Forklift, and a couple of others stopped anything serious from happening. It was suggested at one point that we might ask Schumacher if he wouldn't mind helping to change DC's rear wing, but then we thought, perhaps not.

The dash to the Brussels airport after the race is one of the epic trips that come up during the F1 season. This time, with Jo Ramirez driving, the journey had a funny twist. The trip involved mostly an east/west cross-country road, which was good once you got away

It was hugs all around after the season's final race in Japan. Mika's eighth victory there gave him the 1998 Drivers championship, the first for McLaren since 1991. (LAT PHOTOGRAPHIC)

from the race track—assuming you were going in the right direction! I was asleep in the backseat and woke up, probably from some rally-driving maneuver, and said we were going in the wrong direction. When someone asked how I could be so sure having just woken up, I said that Brussels is to the west and the sun was shining in the rear window, so best we turn around. Fortunately, we hadn't gone too far east, and we made it to the airport in time, thanks to Jo's rather keen driving.

We knew Italy would be a fight, particularly as Ferrari had completed 18 days of testing at Monza. Rain on and off during practice didn't help, and it was perhaps no surprise to see Schumacher on pole, with Mika and David on the second row. Maybe the pressure of being at home—remember, Ferrari was looking for their first championship since 1979—proved too much for Schumacher, because he made a bad start. Mika led for a few laps and then so did DC, until his engine failed.

Then Mika began to drop back when he lost the front brakes for the last few laps because of a leaking caliper. But he was able to keep up enough pace to finish fourth, which must have been pretty damn scary. When you are doing about 217 mph along the front straight before hitting the brake pedal really hard for the chicane, knowing the brakes aren't working properly can't be too comforting. Those points were vital, because with two races to go, Mika and Schumacher (who won at Monza) were tied for the lead of the championship. The Luxembourg Grand Prix at the Nürburgring was next.

As if we didn't have enough to think about with the championship, there were still the issues with the gear-change and clutch-position numbers that we'd experienced at Montreal. Someone must have asked or told another person to write a paper about it, or maybe they took it upon themselves to do it. Either way, a paper was produced which was filled with blatant arrogance, a few contradictions, and the usual political padding, along with an ignorance of the system we were now running in the cars.

When the person who wrote the paper came into the garage at the Nürburgring, Keith Barnard and the other guys on the car hid around the corner, waiting for the fireworks. They knew something was not right with me at the time. They got that right. I explained to the probable author of the paper that all the necessary things had been done before the paper had come out. This would have been explained to the culprit if he had been polite enough to ask either before (or while) writing the paper.

It was time to reflect on the fact that good leaders lead from the front. Bad ones protect their careers by playing politics at the expense of the people who work with them—and lose a great deal of respect in the process.

Around this time I saw Ron Dennis walking through the garage and saying hello to the bolters. Afterward one of them asked, "Who is that guy?" revealing how unusual it was for Ron to speak to anyone on the team!

We were able to put all that aside during a classic race from Mika in Germany. Thanks to clever thinking by Mark Slade, Mika ran more fuel than Schumacher and did four very quick laps between Schumacher's first stop and his own. Mika came out of the pits just in front, and with the two inside wheels on the grass and dirt at the first corner, took the lead. A very brave move, but something Mika was quite good at. The boys then did a great job on the second stop to keep Mika in front until the end.

This win was very important for us, especially after such a heart-stopping, hold-your-breath race. It was a real "stand up in the seat" performance by Mika, while DC waged a long, hard struggle to take third from the constantly wandering Eddie Irvine in the other Ferrari. Schumacher looked stunned after receiving the sort of punishment he liked dishing out. That put Mika four points ahead going into the final race in Japan. And just to build up the pain and the anxiety, there was a five-week gap until Suzuka on November 1.

Looking back through my diary, I noticed that October 7 was the first Wednesday I had been home since July 7, and October 8 was the first Thursday that I had been home since March 19.

You've got to love—or be crazy—to go motor racing, doing both testing and the races. Maybe that's what is needed to help get the job done. It's certainly possible with the right people.

I am not sure anyone would realize at the time how important it was going to be that a young guy named Pete Schroder, a smart and clever person, had come to work at McLaren in the race team software department. I remember saying to him at the first test he had come to, "I might yell at you once in a while about something, but it's not personal." When Pete replied, "Don't worry—it won't bother me," I remember thinking, "Christ! A real person; someone you can really talk to about problems." Pete was to become a good friend, and still is.

Before leaving for Suzuka, Dave Ryan organized a four-car shakedown at Silverstone with complete spare gearboxes and suspensions all set up the same way. It meant both drivers would have a spare car, and while the shakedown was a lot of work, everyone knew exactly what was at stake.

The way the math worked out, to take the title Schumacher had to win in Japan, with Mika finishing third or lower. Schumacher did the first bit right when he took pole position. But Mika was alongside on the front row, with DC third-quickest.

There's an old saying, "Warning! This machine is subject to breakdowns during periods of critical need." A specific part of the machine may well be called a "critical detector," which can somehow detect the emotional state of the mechanics, engineers, and drivers in terms of how desperate they are to get the machine to work and stay working.

The "critical detector," so the logic goes, is then able to create a problem proportional to the desperation of the people involved, which would be quite high under the circumstances at Suzuka that weekend. Hopefully we avoided that by having done a thorough preparation, keeping calm and cool, and saying nice things about the machine.

After the warm-up on Sunday morning, I was out in the back of the garage with Mika,

Number One: Mika with the winner's trophy after his strong drive in the season-ending Japanese Grand Prix. There would be more to come in 1999. (LAT PHOTOGRAPHIC)

Keke Rosberg, and Didier Coton, who worked with Keke as Mika's manager, and became part of Lewis Hamilton's management in 2012. Mika was feeling a little bumpy, which was a bit strange for him. Then again, there was a lot at stake that particular Sunday. When Mika asked, "What am I going to do?" Keke, taking a long drag on his cigarette, paused, looked at him, and said, "Just go have fun and drive the car as fast as you want. That's what you do." After a short pause, Mika said, "Umm, okay."

The outcome of the race turned largely on Jarno Trulli stalling his Prost in the middle of the grid. That meant a restart. We were quick to get the cooling fans to Mika's car—certainly faster than the Ferrari guys. This was quite critical because it's a long, slow lap to the grid, and then the front row can be sitting there for at least 30 seconds. Anyway, whatever the cause, when Schumacher engaged first gear for the second time, the engine stalled. That not only meant another restart, but also being moved to the back of the grid for Michael.

Predictably, Schumacher charged through the field to third place and then picked up a puncture from debris caused by a shunt by two backmarkers. Not that any of this affected Mika, who led from the start, won the race, and became the 1998 World Champion. In the process, McLaren won the Constructors championship by 23 points from Ferrari.

At the end of the race the boys had run to the pit wall to cheer Mika when he came by. Remember, it had been seven years since we'd last won the Drivers title in 1991, with Ayrton Senna. However, team manager Dave Ryan got quite concerned and started to tell people to get back. In some ways he was right, because there was confusion regarding some aspects of a new FIA rule, and there was also some uncertainty about where DC was on the race track. (It turned out that he was actually on the same lap as Mika, and would finish third, about 28 seconds behind him.) In addition to this, a team member was spotted with a cigarette hanging from a smiling lip!

Dave did some very good things as team manager, and brought a lot to the team, but sometimes he could ruin morale in the most inappropriate moments—and this was one of them. We'd just won the World Championship, and within a few minutes everyone's morale and good feeling had disappeared, which was more than a real shame.

Something else that didn't go down very well was the offer of some tickets to an after-race party. The boys said, "Either we all go or not at all." A prime lesson in how not to manage people. Just brilliant! Almost the entire race team was pissed-off—and we'd won the championship!

The FIA wanted to look at just about everything on the car, from inside the gearbox to inside the fuel cell and what all the switches did. I think it was Dave Bryers who took on the task of helping the FIA look for supposed rules infractions when they should have been examining Mika's balls. All of this added a great deal of time to the packing-up process, but it needed to be done. It was as if the officials were saying, "Now that we have tried everyone's patience and used up their goodwill, are we happy?" Not really what you need after winning both championships after quite a few years, thanks to the very good drivers, a well-designed car and engine, hardworking mechanics doing their preparation, the factory people, and *magic!*

It's never easy, and even harder being in charge. But when you've won, the thrill should be allowed to last at least until Monday.

# 1999: Defending the Championship

t had been the usual mad rush to get the new car completed in time for a launch and test in Barcelona. Although at first glance the 1999 MP4/14 looked similar to the 1998 car, very few parts had been carried over. Ron Dennis told the media at Barcelona that MP4/14 had the biggest number of new steps in any McLaren.

Our immediate concern was that the car didn't arrive at the Circuit de Cataluña until midnight, passing into the hands of a somewhat impatient group. When the car finally showed up, Phil Collins said to Neil Oatley, "Couldn't you have started this project six hours earlier?"

Why is it that we seem to learn nothing from our past mistakes and misadventures when getting organized for this sort of thing? We should know how to do it by now.

We were to pay the price for the last-minute rush when the car completed its first lap on the end of a rope! There had been a minor glitch with the engine side of the electronics, which was fixed right away, but by then the press photos of the reigning champion's embarrassment had been flashed around the world.

As far as we were concerned, what mattered was the quick lap times that we eventually

DC and Mika before the 1999 season opener in Australia, where Mika took the pole and David started second on the grid. The race was another story—neither of them finished. (LAT PHOTOGRAPHIC)

saw. I remember Trevor Lawes, one of the main gearbox mechanics, fixing cracks in the gearbox case and gluing the bearings in place—just to be safe. With a fast but undeveloped car, we set off to Melbourne.

To the outside world, everything looked good for McLaren, as Mika Hakkinen and David Coulthard filled the front of the grid for the Australian Grand Prix, with Michael Schumacher third, more than a second slower than Mika.

But inside the garage, we were aware that the new seven-speed gearbox had various problems because of the lightweight cases cracking. This problem meant the gearbox mechanics and a few of the car mechanics got almost no sleep for several days, and they used a considerable amount of Devcon to fix the cracks. It meant stripping the boxes, doing the fix, letting the Devcon harden, and then rebuilding the gearbox in time for practice.

As if this weren't enough, Mika had his first shunt in two years when he crashed the car quite heavily during Friday's practice and added to the mechanics' overnight work load.

It was turning out to be one of those weekends where nothing seemed quite right. Going to the grid, we found there was something strange with the way Mika's engine was running. There was a fair amount of panic when he came back into the garage. First he got into the T-car while we considered changing the ECU (the main software control box); then he climbed back into his race car before finally electing to take the T-car.

With time running out before the pit lane closed, Mika left the garage rather rapidly. Unfortunately, the umbilical cable with all the electronic wires from the overhead module got caught in the left-rear wheel and pulled the module down, hitting Mark Lunnon, one of the gearbox guys, and momentarily knocking him out. Poor Mark thought he had just passed out from lack of sleep over the previous three days.

There was more to come.

With Mika now in the T-car, it meant that one of that car's mechanics, unfamiliar with the grid procedure and somewhat in awe of what was going on, did not have his radio turned on and didn't hear the order to start the car. Someone, hands waving, actually yelled loud enough for him to get the message, and Mika finally left the grid just in time.

After 12 laps, Mika and David were leading by 17 seconds. A lap later David was parked in the garage; a hydraulic problem had caused the car to become stuck in sixth gear. Not long after that, Mika was another retirement, this time with a throttle-shaft problem, most likely caused by new parts not having been tested long enough.

The cancellation of the Argentine Grand Prix meant there was a five-week gap before the next race in Brazil. Naturally, the teams were making the most of this, with tests in Spain, France, Italy, and Britain.

We did a pre-Brazil shakedown at Silverstone with three race cars, one test car, and a 901 prototype gearbox project car to test. The race cars had been flown back from a test in Jerez, but since the test team mechanics were working on the fourth MP4/14 and a MP4/13, and others were busy with the hydraulic set for the MP4/13, it meant there were no extra people to help turn these race cars around. The logistics were mind-boggling, but we somehow got the job done.

We were on the front row again at Interlagos, but on race morning there was a problem with one of the engine sensors. Roger Higgins asked Alastair Hawkeswood, the Ilmor engine electrical guy, to see if he could fix the problem, which happened to be in the 50-pin connector on the top-left corner of the engine.

With time running out before the pit lane opened and seeing the connector still apart, I asked Alastair how it was going. "No problem" was the quiet reply. I thought it best to get out of the way! It was finished in time, thanks to clever, calm Alastair.

DC stalled at the start, and because of the crazy layout of the track and pit lane, he had to be pushed a very long way to the garage. We got David started and he emerged onto the track just as Mika was losing the lead, thanks to not getting sixth gear on the pit straight.

Mika fell back to third, at which point the gear change started working correctly. By conserving fuel, Mika ran four laps longer before his scheduled pit stop and took the lead from Schumacher to give us our first win of 1999. But we knew our troubles weren't over because of that brief gear-change problem, and the fact that DC had finally retired when his gearbox failed.

The promise was definitely there, however, as the two cars were on the front row again at Imola, and as close as it's possible to be. On the last run of qualifying, Roger Higgins, who had been tweaking every last bit out of Mika's V10, said to me, "That's it. I can't do any more." Mika was 0.02 seconds ahead of DC.

Running a two-stop strategy, Mika had a lead of about 20 seconds and looked to be on course to stay in front if he came in for his first stop sooner than everyone else. But pushing too hard coming out of the last corner, he put a rear wheel on the curb, went into a spin, and hit the pit wall. That gave the win to Schumacher. DC was not happy with second, claiming backmarkers had cost him the win he needed to stay in touch with the championship leaders.

Schumacher was leading the championship, but Mika hit right back with what could

Michael Schumacher removes the steering wheel of his Ferrari F399 after crashing heavily at July's British Grand Prix. He sustained a broken leg that would keep him sidelined until October. (LAT PHOTOGRAPHIC)

be described as a pretty brave lap to take pole at Monaco. DC was third-quickest, with Schumacher splitting the two McLarens. Knowing he didn't have much chance if Mika got away at the start, Schumacher and Ferrari had been doing a shakedown at the Ferrari test track at Fiorano on Friday, the day off at Monaco.

If they had been practicing Schumacher's starts, it worked, because he took the lead going into the first corner. Running lighter than Mika, Schumacher began to pull away, Ferrari then bringing Irvine in early so that he could come back and push our guys hard. Mika added to his problems when he was caught out by oil on the track that didn't show in any warning flags, and he went into an escape road. For some reason the car wasn't so great that day. Mika recovered to finish third, but DC was out after 36 laps with more gearbox trouble.

Based on testing and our one-two at Barcelona in 1998, we were expecting to go well in Spain—provided there were no reliability problems. We got off to a bad start when DC had a high-speed shunt thanks to a broken suspension during practice. He put that behind him and qualified third, with Mika taking his fifth pole position in succession.

The trouble this time was that Irvine had been second-quickest, and we didn't really know what he might get up to at the start. It didn't matter in the end because Irvine not only made a bad start, but Schumacher also got caught behind his teammate, and Jacques Villeneuve did us a favor by jumping ahead in his BAR-Honda and holding up both Ferraris for a while.

It was while we were running first and second—and hoping nothing would break—that Pete Schroder and I were looking at Mika's telemetry data and noticed that the colored lines for the left and right clutch paddles were moving around some on the straight. Not what you really want to see when leading the race. After a couple of laps spent watching this happen at about the same place on the straight, I told Pete that I reckoned Mika was fiddling with the clutch paddles.

Through Mark Slade, we got Steve Hallam to tell Mika on the radio to stop what he was doing. The colored lines were just fine after that, and we took our first one-two since Germany the previous August, keeping Mika within striking distance of Schumacher and Irvine at the top of the championship.

The race weekend at Montreal started out on the Wednesday evening with a great dinner put on by Mercedes-Ilmor. There was a fair bit of work for the boys before the race, as Mika's engine had to be changed after the Sunday-morning warm-up.

At the start of the race, Schumacher gave Mika one of his standard "chop across in front of you" moves, as his start wasn't great. Then there was a multiple shunt at the first and second corners, which had become standard for a Montreal race start.

Mika kept some pressure on Schumacher until the Ferrari crashed at the corner coming onto the pit straight, putting Mika into a lead he would keep to the end.

I thought you could see Schumacher's shunt coming as he was getting closer and closer to the wall for several laps. Meanwhile, DC had a shunt with Irvine in the pit lane and came off worse, finishing seventh in the end.

You could sum up the French GP in Magny-Cours by saying that at least the excellent food and wine in the area made up for the pain of getting to the place. And on this occasion, you could also say that the whole race weekend had a bit more than the usual chaos—something along the lines of a "kaleidoscope of shit" comes to mind. Most of this was caused by intermittent rain.

Rubens Barrichello, usually quite good in the rain, took pole position in his Stewart-Ford, with DC 4th and Mika a bewildering 14th after encountering traffic at almost every corner.

Barrichello led the race until DC passed him and then had an electrical problem and stopped. Mika came through the field without getting into any serious trouble and put himself in a position to have a go at Barrichello. I thought it was pretty impressive of Mika to pass Barrichello at the end of the long straight, only to spin off and then overtake the Stewart again at the same place—not falling off this time!

Both Mika and Rubens had to stop for fuel right near the end of the race, but Heinz-Harald Frentzen had been filled up at his last pit stop and was able to coax his Jordan to the finish and win the race, ahead of Mika and Rubens.

We went to the British GP knowing that both Mika and DC usually went pretty well at Silverstone. Sure enough—thanks also to the setup arrived at with Mark Slade—Mika was on pole by a reasonable amount from Schumacher, who then blew his advantage with a bad start. Irvine, on the second row, got ahead of his Ferrari teammate, but Schumacher, trying to get the place back, went straight into the tire barriers at the end of Hangar Straight, breaking his leg.

Ferrari said the accident was caused by a brake problem; others were not so sure. Irvine had left his braking for Stowe corner really late, but he'd also left plenty of room on the inside for Schumacher to make the overtaking attempt Irvine knew was bound to come.

Whatever the cause, it ensured that Mika was comfortably in the lead. That lasted until his first pit stop, when the kaleidoscope of shit reared its ugly head again. A loose left-rear wheel meant Mika had to come straight back to the pit. He went back out, only to have the wheel actually come off. One more attempt was made before he stopped for good. A closer inspection revealed that a piece of material caught in the axle thread had not allowed the wheel nut to tighten correctly. This entire act put DC in the lead, and he went on to save the day for the team by winning his home grand prix.

Trouble started on Mika's out lap at the beginning of qualifying in Austria when the mechanical fuel-pump drive broke and stopped the car. Mika was not far from the pits and ran back for the T-car. His first timed lap was good enough for second on the grid. It looked like DC had him now, but Mika followed up with three more laps, each one good enough for pole, both cars starting from the front row after being very close in lap times.

Mika led as far as the second corner—where DC ran into the back of him. There had been some feeling on DC's side of the garage that he was quicker and should have had a go, or maybe it was just a mistake. But whatever the reason, it sure as hell was not very clever. Everyone makes mistakes once in a while, but they're to be avoided when you really need the points.

Having ended up last on the first lap, Mika made his way to third, about 23 seconds behind Irvine's leading Ferrari. When Mika then came on the radio and asked Steve Hallam how many laps were left to go, he simply said to Steve, "I can't do that—not enough laps left to catch up." Irvine had taken the lead when DC had a hard time with his car following his pit stop.

The car got better near the end, and DC finished 0.31 seconds behind Irvine, with Mika third. You had to wonder what might have happened had Mika not been rammed in the ass at the second corner by his teammate!

You might be forgiven for thinking the season was not going well, but there was still a long way to go, and giving up was never an option. Saying that, the dramas were to continue at Hockenheim, where Mika lost the lead thanks to a problem with his refueling nozzle at a pit stop. Then, not long after that, a tire came apart on the straight. There was some discussion later about the tire being cut by the rear-wing end-plate, but that theory had little or no merit—unless you wanted to count the bits flying off the tire! Bridgestone would later issue a statement saying there had been no failure on their part, the implication being that we were at fault. As you might imagine, this did not go down well with Ron Dennis, who said categorically there had not been a tire failure caused by the car.

Then, just to finish the day off for Mercedes on home territory, DC ran into the back of Mika Salo (standing in for Schumacher) and had to stop for a new nose and front wing, as well as receiving a 10-second stop-go penalty. DC finally finished fifth.

Having resolved the refueling nozzle problem during a short test at Silverstone, I guess it must have been another good omen when we watched the eclipse of the sun at 12:56 p.m. on August 11, 1999, just as we were leaving the Budapest airport for the circuit.

Mika took pole position and he was quick most of the time in practice. One of his best laps had him coming out onto the pit straight with the car sideways! He was to say some time later that it may seem funny now, but it sure as hell wasn't then!

There was a bit of a scene on Saturday night thanks to a problem with some aspects of the reverse gear on one of the cars not engaging when asked. It added quite a bit of time to the race preparation, which not only involved fixing the problem but also checking the other gearboxes.

Our two cars sandwiched Irvine's Ferrari on the grid, but DC's chances of doing anything about him were spoiled by a poor start. That meant he spent a lot of the race catching Irvine and finally putting enough pressure on him to make a small mistake, allowing DC through to give us a one-two finish, our second of the season. It was an interesting trip home for a few of us, as we flew back to the Luton airport with DC in a Learjet 31 at 43,050 feet. I had been in a Learjet quite a few times before, but never at that altitude. It was something quite special.

We were to score another one-two at Spa, but things could have been better had there been some team influence regarding championship points and the finishing order.

As had become the habit, Mika had taken pole position, but he was a bit slow at the start. DC, starting on the front row, drew alongside Mika going into the La Source hairpin, banged into him, and moved into the lead coming out of the corner. Needless to say, Mika was not too pleased about this for the rest of the afternoon, and at one point had to be told "Just get on with it."

They finished in that order, and the end result was that Mika was just one point ahead of Irvine, who had been "helped" to a win by Salo in Germany.

Mika would take his 11th, and what would be his last, pole position of the season at Monza, this time by 0.500 of a second from Frentzen. DC qualified third and Irvine, on Ferrari's home territory, was back in eighth.

Everything was looking good for Mika as he led from the start and held an eight-second advantage at around mid-distance. Going into the chicane at the end of the long pit straight, he changed down to first gear instead of second. This spun him off into the sand trap. Mika got out of the car and sat under the trees for quite a while, trying to get his emotions under control. First gear had not been used at the chicane during practice; otherwise, we might have been able to do something with the software that could have helped. I probably should have done something in any case, if only to cover our ass as a precaution. As it was, we were left with a big "ouch"!

I did ask Mika later if he thought the car would have gotten away from him if he had changed down into second gear. "No" was the simple answer. Meanwhile, DC had spun off on the first lap, the car never feeling right after that as he went on to finish fifth. The good news was that Irvine could only manage sixth; Salo, who finished third, proved unable to help on this occasion.

The nice hotel we used at the Nürburgring had a sign by the main entrance saying "welcome Jo Ramirez race team." I'm not sure how some of the more-senior McLaren people

Mika, Mario Illien, and Jurgen Huppert celebrate after another big win at Suzuka. For the second consecutive year the combination of McLaren, Mercedes, and Mika Hakkinen had paid big dividends. (LAT PHOTOGRAPHIC)

took this, but the rest of us found it amusing.

Of course, it did help when Jo came back from a dinner party one night to find he was locked out. He wound up sleeping in the barn on a pool-deck chair.

When we got to the track, Mika was still feeling pretty down from the problem at Monza. We tried a few things, such as lowering the second- to first-gear rpm point, but Mika told me on the grid to put it back where it had always been.

Apart from the disaster when he qualified 14th in France, this was the first time in 1999 that Mika had not been on the front row. He was third-fastest, with David just a couple of tenths ahead, in 2nd.

The race brought a lot of chaos from the start, with a big shunt on the first lap. Frentzen led from pole, but DC was well placed to take the lead when the Jordan suddenly cut out just after a pit stop.

A determined-looking Mika prepares for the French Grand Prix at Magny-Cours in June 1999. After two consecutive wins in Spain and Canada he finished second in the MP4/14. (LAT PHOTOGRAPHIC)

Rain, which had been threatening all afternoon—so much so that we brought Mika in for wets, only to have him come back a couple of laps later for slicks—finally became serious at around half distance.

DC was holding a handy lead, and we were trying to get him to ease off when he spun and crashed out. The race was won by Johnny Herbert in the Stewart-Ford. Mika somehow recovered to finish fifth and score two points. That put him two ahead of Irvine, who had an even worse time on his way to finishing seventh. I seem to remember seeing Irvine in his pit with only three wheels on his car, looking around to see where his guys had gone with the other one. No wonder this particular GP would be dubbed the race of "Puddles and Muddles."

Around this time there was a great story going around about a nice man from Ferrari, chairman Luca di Montezemolo, calling Michael Schumacher at home to ask how his broken leg was doing. Michael's daughter answered the phone, and when asked where Daddy was, she proudly said, "He's outside playing football!" The nice man from Ferrari spoke with Michael and said it would be best if he got his ass down to Maranello and prepared to go off to Malaysia. Sounded like a pretty good story to me, especially if you would prefer not to have Eddie Irvine win the championship. (By the way, I've known Luca since he was the Ferrari team manager in the 1970s. He's a really neat guy, and we always say hello when we meet at the races.)

Schumacher duly showed up at Sepang, and his Ferrari was fast enough to put him on pole, a full second faster than Irvine, in second place. Schumacher led from the start, but after a few laps he let Irvine by and then slowed down even more to hold the others up. Very sporting of him.

DC had expected something like this and was not pleased, but got by Schumacher and was quite close to Irvine when the mechanical fuel pump failed. David had a good race plan, but it got flushed away.

Now Schumacher was in the position to deliberately screw Mika around, which he did for the rest of the race, changing his line at different corners on each lap, and also slowing down to let Irvine back into the lead after pit stops. Mika, needing the points, knew he had to avoid having an accident with Schumacher while trying to pass him.

It is always interesting when one team in particular issues constant rhetoric about the "Sporting Code" and how they are always doing what's best for "the Sport"—and then uses tactics that make such pontification sound like the nonsense it is. With Mika finishing third, the win gave Irvine a six-point lead, with one race to go. Or that was the way it seemed as the flag fell.

The next part was priceless. The two Ferraris were disqualified for having incorrect bodywork. The measurements were taken in the *parc fermé* by the FIA; the Ferrari people agreed, and signed the stewards' letter stating that the bodywork on the cars did not comply with the rules.

Ferrari challenged the disqualification, and the matter went to the FIA Court of Appeal, which, as you might have guessed, ruled that the Ferraris were, in fact, legal. A technical person from the FIA explained a "new" interpretation of the flat-bottom rule. The FIA also said that the expensive measuring equipment, in use all year, was now not accurate enough. (Someone should be ashamed of themselves.)

So we had a situation where the parts on the cars did not comply with the rules on October 17, 1999, a finding confirmed by Ferrari personnel who had signed their names to that fact at the time. Then, a couple of days later, presto! Everything was okay and legal. The politics of motor racing—don't you just love it!

Judging by the expression on FIA president Max Mosley's face during a TV program on October 23, it looked like he was satisfied with the outcome of the FIA Court of Appeal in Paris. It reminded me of a great line, one of many, I'm sure, that came out of Hollywood, "The most important thing in acting is honesty. Once you learn to fake that, you're in."

And so, as had happened many times before, we went to Suzuka to decide the championship. With Mika being four points behind, he needed to win the race. That was the only way he would be sure of the title, no matter what Irvine did. Even if the Ferrari driver finished second, the pair would be equal on points, and Mika would take it, on five wins to Irvine's four.

Of course, Schumacher was also in the mix, and he was on pole, but nothing like as quick as he had been in Malaysia—funny, that. Mika, having been held up by Alesi on his last qualifying run, was second, with DC third, and Irvine—who had a rather nasty misfortune during practice—qualifying fifth.

Mika hardly spoke to me over the weekend until Sunday morning, after the warm-up session. It was the same sort of thing I'd seen from him the previous year, except Keke Rosberg was not there to offer advice. So I repeated pretty much what Keke had said in 1998, "Just go and drive the car as fast you want, which is what you like to do." To which Mika replied, "Okay—I think I'll go have a piss." The rest was to follow, i.e., the race itself.

Mika made a great start with almost no wheel spin at all, pulling away. DC was running third until he fell off and had to stop for a new nose and front wing, rejoining a lap behind.

After the race, Schumacher was bitching that DC had held him up during the latter part of the race. Can you believe Schumacher's gall in saying this, after what he had done to Mika for most of the race in Malaysia? Well, of course you can. Tough shit, "sport."

Mika's win made him only the seventh driver in the history of the Formula One championship to win back-to-back titles. Judging by the cheering grandstand, the Japanese were big fans of Mika's. If he'd had hats and T-shirts for sale, I don't think he could have made enough of them.

When we got home I thought it might be not a bad idea to make some notes for Adrian Newey, Neil Oatley, and Martin Whitmarsh about a few basic things that came to mind regarding the 1999 season. I've included them here:

*The reliability of the engine and its bits is reasonably straightforward, in that during testing you run the engine for the full 600 km (or whatever), and part of that should be a couple of 15- to 20-lap runs (re: temps, fuel, etc.). We and Ilmor should discipline ourselves to do this as much as possible, and not say, "We can't leave the engine in, as it will upset our test program." What the hell do we think testing the engine is? Seeing it run a whole race distance in the car is not quite the same as finishing off the mileage on the dyno.*

*The engine/chassis drivability issue: Is it ego or arrogance that prevents us from learning and/or remembering anything from our relationship with Honda? Maybe it's only those of us who froze in the winter and baked in the summer while at Suzuka, where we spent days testing only engine bits and engine reliability and drivability. We criticize Ilmor, but we do very little to help and encourage their engine-testing efforts. Shouldn't one car be doing most, if not all, of the engine-testing work (within reason)? And shouldn't we request and ensure that Ilmor have things to test? Of course it would be nice to have someone driving the car who can make rational comments about the changes and developments. The "drivability" is probably more than just the way the engine "runs" (maybe not), but it does have to transfer the torque to the road through very hard tires . . .*

*The gearbox sort of treads on thin ice most of the time, but, if you want it light, then okay. But we need more new parts to cover both testing and racing. They need to be made in time to be inspected properly and rejected if not correct. The early 1999 testing showed what can happen when some things are not correct.*

*It is still possible to "peg" the wheels or have them not mounted correctly. "Peg" is a word used to describe when the drive pegs in the wheel don't go into the holes in the axle (Suzuka race, Mika Hakkinen), which seems hard to believe, as well as hard to do.*

*The rear jack mounts are not strong enough, and the rear jack is awkward to use and costs us time, especially when looking at some others in operation.*

*Shouldn't we be marking the tires with reasonably large L/R, as it can't be a secret that the lefts go on the left and the rights go on the right (Suzuka race, David Coulthard)?*

*The mechanical fuel pump needs some TLC (tender loving care).*

*Of course, some of these things are just stating the obvious, and being looked into anyway; then again, it never hurts to have a think about them.*

Regrettably, a couple of tests at the end of the year at Barcelona and Jerez were held at the same time as the Ilmor Christmas party, which was always very good. The Ilmor engine boys at the tests sent an e-mail back to their office, "From the workers at the track: We'd dearly like to be there, but they wouldn't let us back!"

All of this goes to show that you don't sit back and relax after winning the championship. The year 1999 was done. On to the new millennium, and the year 2000.

# 2000: Fighting Ferrari and Returning to Indy

t may have been the new millennium, but there weren't many changes at McLaren: same drivers, same engine, same title partner/sponsor. And the MP4/15 was more an evolution of the 1999 car than anything else.

The only change was Mercedes exercising its right to buy 40 percent of the TAG McLaren Group. Otherwise, it was the usual routine as the MP4/15 was first started up at the factory on January 31, and then shipped off to Jerez for the new car launch and the start of testing.

Testing continued all through February; I was away for 22 days at the various tests. Race-distance tests were done at Barcelona, with DC having an engine problem on the first day, and Mika, a gearbox problem on the second day. An ominous start.

At the February 10 Barcelona test there was more new software. When Phil Collins of Ilmor asked if it was year 10,000 compliant—in other words, was it going to be reliable?— Paul Spence, who had something to do with making it, answered, "It's not twenty-four-hour compliant!"

Olivier Panis had joined as test driver, giving Mika Hakkinen and David Coulthard feedback they could rely on, mainly because Panis had raced right up to 1999. The three-

Mika takes a corner at the Hungarian Grand Prix, where he started third and finished first after getting the better of Michael Schumacher. (LAT PHOTOGRAPHIC)

car shakedown at Silverstone took all day on March 1, before shipping to Melbourne the following day. There were a lot of pizzas consumed at the factory that night.

There was another late night on the Friday at Melbourne, particularly for Nick Lee, one of the Ilmor engine mechanics, who was having problems with the exhaust PADI cable/ piston. At about 1:30 a.m. I asked, "Can I hold something for you?" And got the reply, "I know it's late, Tyler, but it's not that late."

Things were going okay until Mika had an engine problem with the air system on his out lap on Saturday morning. When he got back to the pits, the boys got stuck in and had the new engine fitted in 45 minutes, giving Mika just a few laps at the end of the session before qualifying.

Mika was quickest on his first timed lap; DC went a bit quicker, and then Mika went faster still, which gave him pole position. DC had another go but stuffed it in the wall in the closing minutes, which meant Schumacher didn't have time to stop us filling the front row. Mika and David led the first 10 laps until DC stopped with an air-system problem on his engine. Eight laps later, Mika lost the lead with the same problem, similar to the one he had experienced on Saturday morning. Perhaps some "new" parts hadn't been run with enough test miles on them. I'd already mentioned this in another memo, part of which read:

> *We really must discipline ourselves to run the correct mileages with the correct parts and try to never have "new" parts on the race weekend. Every designed part should be run a certain number of miles/km before being fitted to the "race" car, engine, or gearbox. Unless of course there are immediate safety reasons.*

At least the girls are always good-looking in Melbourne, not to mention the delicious food and wine.

The Brazilian Grand Prix may have been a fortnight later, but we went straight to Sao Paulo via Auckland and Buenos Aires, leaving Jo Ramirez just enough time to see some of his racing friends during the stopover in Argentina.

Driving around Sao Paulo in the late-afternoon traffic gives a hint of why so many good race drivers come from this part of the world. When we finally reached the circuit, it was still being finished, which is fairly normal for Interlagos, where it seems that bare hands and a rag are the preferred way to paint things. Checking the electricity is best done with a couple of fingers, remembering to spit on them first to make better contact.

Qualifying came with a new twist when the red flag was used more than once because overhead advertising banners were falling onto the track. And then there was a downpour right near the end—but not before Mika and DC ended up first and second on the grid, with the two Ferraris of Schumacher and Barrichello third and fourth once more.

There was a bit of a scene following the warm-up on Sunday morning, thanks to an outburst from Roger Higgins, the Ilmor engine engineer on Mika's car, who was upset because the system monitor laptop wasn't always able to shut the car off. Roger received a speech from Ron Dennis in reply. Usually in times of stress and confusion, Ron's calming influence is a great help. It would have been in this case had Ron told Roger to calm down and take it easy. We knew there were problems with that side of things, and we were trying to correct them.

With all due respect, Ron, the outburst you directed at Roger was not a great deal different from his own. And it didn't help to tell me that this was a "no emotions" team, and that if I didn't like it I could leave. What a bunch of nonsense!

All of this added to the impression that Ron lacked charisma and motivation at various times. To say one should not show emotion once in a while is not natural. How come, for instance, some people can have tears in their eyes after a race? It was all getting to be too much.

I went to the office in the back of the garage, closed my computer, and told Dave Bryers I was off. At which point, Mario Illien came in and asked me to sit down and please listen to him. Which I did! And I didn't walk away, either. Thanks, Mario.

The mood was not helped later in the day when the race didn't turn out as we hoped. Schumacher, running light at the start and on a two-stop strategy, led most of the way. There was a point following Schumacher's first stop, when Mika led and was slowly pulling away. Then the engine had an oil pressure problem and put Mika out of the race after 30 laps.

DC, meanwhile, was having an eventful race, considering he had lost third gear, followed by first and second quite early on. Because David had also lost the use of his radio, he couldn't tell his engineer, but we could see from the colored lines on the telemetry data that he wasn't using the lower gears. After a great drive and a second-place finish, DC was thrown out because of a front-wing end-plate that was too low. It had obviously not been designed that way, and was damaged during the race. A twitch of one's nose, the feeling of being stitched, and a sense of smell that picked up a rat.

On to Europe and a race at a place with some of the best food and wine, as well as the biggest pasta factory anywhere. Imola is just down the road from Bologna, but it doesn't

Michael Schumacher jumps for joy after winning his third F1 world championship at Suzuka in October 2000. Mika and David were right behind him in second and third place. (LAT PHOTOGRAPHIC)

feel like that with its nightmarish traffic, particularly when trying to get to the airport after the race. This time we were hoping to leave with plenty of points after coming away from Brazil with a big "none."

We got off to a good start when Mika managed to steal pole position from Schumacher in the last minutes of qualifying—right on Ferrari's doorstep. It was what you have to call a genuine ballsy lap, one complemented by DC taking third ahead of Barrichello. Mika led right up to the second pit stop, but Schumacher's in and out laps were that much quicker, putting the Ferrari in the lead. Mika did have a few problems—first, with some trash on the track, and then, with the car's electronics, which shut off before thankfully resetting.

Poor DC had been stuck behind Barrichello, who was about a second off the pace for most of the race. A good job by the guys at David's second stop got him out in front of Barrichello, and DC eventually finished a good half-minute ahead of him. Looking at the gearbox data afterward, I don't think we had seen as many as 3,444 gear changes in one race before.

For reasons which only the FIA can explain, the British Grand Prix was shifted from July to April, and not surprisingly attracted all the rain and fog England had to offer. I think there might have been more work done in the car parks than in the race team garages. The mud won the unequal struggle with the fans, who were as usual the losers in any political F1 fight.

Qualifying was a very mixed affair, with wet and dry conditions which helped Barrichello claim pole position, while Mika and DC struggled into third and fourth on the grid thanks to compromises with the setup of their cars.

Thick fog on Sunday morning meant a lot of people who had planned to travel by helicopter had to drive. DC was in his motor home at the track, which turned out to be a smart move. Stuck in traffic and not getting anywhere, Mika got out of the car, stopped a bloke on a motorbike, and asked if he would take him to the circuit. The guy couldn't believe he had Mika Hakkinen on the back of his motorbike. The two of them ended up in the McLaren garage, the passenger arriving just in time for the fog-delayed warm-up. The motorbike guy couldn't believe his good fortune: straight from road to track, no passes required!

Having made a good start, DC spent the first 30 laps shadowing Barrichello until Rubens made a slight mistake going through Becketts and David pulled off a great move around the outside at Stowe to take the lead. It was just what the British crowd wanted to see. And McLaren too! What made our day complete was having Mika finish second, a great result thanks to changes instigated by Mark Slade and Phil Prew during the pit stops to improve

Hakkinen makes a point to an attentive Michael Schumacher during their post-race conversation at the Belgian Grand Prix. I wish I knew what was said, but Mika still won't reveal it to this day. (LAT PHOTOGRAPHIC)

a car that had not been good in the early stages of the race.

There was drama of a totally unexpected kind when we got to Barcelona and heard that DC, his fiancée Heidi Wichlinski, and trainer Andy Matthews had been very fortunate to escape unhurt when their chartered Learjet 35 had crashed at the Lyon airport. They had managed to jump from the front of the fuselage where it had broken off. Andy went out first and DC next, so he could help Heidi get out. DC also handed Heidi's dog, Moody, to Andy, who threw the dog about 30 feet across the grass like a rugby ball. Apparently after that every time the dog saw Andy he'd run away and hide, obviously more traumatized by being chucked across the grass than the crash itself. The real tragedy was that the poor pilots were not so lucky and died in the crash.

In Spain Schumacher was on pole for the first time in 2000. Mika ended up 0.08 seconds away in second, with a plucky—to say the least—DC taking fourth, less than one-hundredth of a second behind Barrichello.

The race was a great fight between Mika and Schumacher, with Mika getting ahead during the last pit stop. DC moved in to challenge and was not impressed when Schumacher chopped him before David finally got ahead to give us a one-two finish. It was a very brave effort by DC. He had not said anything, but both sides of his rib cage were very sore as a result of the airplane crash.

Schumacher, who had a slow puncture, finished fifth in Barcelona, which meant we could be sure he would want to turn that around at his home race at the Nürburgring. You can imagine Schumacher wasn't very happy when DC produced a great lap to take his first pole position in Germany in almost two years.

Schumacher's mood wasn't helped when Mika made a very good start from the second row to come between the Ferrari and DC to take the lead! Schumacher complained afterward, but I don't think anyone paid any attention because this was something Michael had been known to do more than once. You had to wonder what the hell he was complaining about—it was as if he was suddenly saying, "Dear boy, that's not allowed." Schumacher got his revenge when the rain started and a slow pit stop put Mika second, where he stayed. After a race-long fight, DC beat Barrichello into third.

Monaco is a lot more than just a sunny place for shady people. For F1 people, the race weekend may be all about heavily overpriced hotel rooms, but this is one of those places where winning is very special. It also has one of the best pizza joints in the world, Pizzeria Monegasque, which is just up the hill from the track. One of the first things we always do on arriving in Monaco is book a table for every night we're there. Obviously, other people think the same way; I know George Lucas always arrives for dinner during the weekend.

When qualifying finished, it looked like the win was going to go to Ferrari after Schumacher took pole position. Trulli had put his Jordan on the front row. DC was a tenth of a second behind in third, a bit disappointed to be there because of traffic. We thought that was going to be a big problem for Mika, when with minutes to go, he was running 17th. But then he found a clear lap, and fighting understeer, hauled himself up to fifth.

It took three starts to finally get the race going thanks first to a stalled car, then the starting lights malfunctioning to show an aborted start, and then a multicar shunt, which had various drivers running back to get their spare cars. Being on the grid for a long time was not great, as the day was very hot and humid; it felt worse than Malaysia.

When Trulli dropped out of second place just after half distance, Schumacher was 36 seconds ahead of DC. David produced a succession of quick laps, but there wasn't much hope of getting close enough to the Ferrari. As DC said afterward, "You have to keep pushing because at Monaco, anything can happen." And it did, on the 56th of 78 laps, when Schumacher dropped out with failed suspension caused by a broken exhaust pipe damaging one of the carbon wishbones. With Schumacher retiring, DC's second win of the season jumped him ahead of Mika and into second place in the championship.

Mika had held fifth place, stuck behind Frentzen's Jordan until he was forced into the pits, saying something was wrong with the brakes. When we got to look through the inspection hatch, we found that part of the radio antenna had dropped down into the pedals, a development that was neither clever nor desirable. Mika rejoined at the back and tried to regain some places, but a gearbox bearing problem right near the end meant he crept home in sixth place.

It was a great job by DC and the team, with points from both drivers keeping us close to Ferrari in the Constructors championship. But no sooner was that done—never wishing to slow down—we drove over to Italy to start a test at Monza on the Tuesday.

After this flat-out work effort a relaxing change of pace was just what I needed. It was nice to be able to stop off in Boston on the way to Montreal and go out to Nantucket to do some fishing with good friends I grew up with, Larry Cronin, Jr. and Paul Wuori. We had been doing this for a few years, and it was always a lot of fun.

That rejuvenated momentum carried into Montreal, a great city where the people always enjoy the race weekend. There are a variety of good restaurants (one of my favorites is a steak house called L'Entrecote St-Jean), and clubs and bars which keep everyone entertained when they're not at the race track. The setting by the St. Lawrence River is great as well. However, I'm not sure the wildlife living on the island where the race is held enjoy it that much.

Boosted by that win in Monaco, DC was quickest right up until the last minute of qualifying, when Schumacher went just under a tenth faster. Nonetheless, DC was pretty confident about taking the fight to Ferrari in the race. Meanwhile, Barrichello had qualified third, with Mika fourth.

Unfortunately, DC stalled on the grid. By the time the boys restarted him, it was within 15 seconds of the parade lap starting, by which time the grid is supposed to be cleared. DC made a better start, but Schumacher did his usual trick and just came across in front of him.

David pushed Schumacher but then, after about 10 laps, came the expected punishment

# Larry Cronin Jr.

While the fishing was always great, the tradition of cooking dinner together, with striped bass caught earlier in the day, was the best part of our time on Nantucket, and still is to this day. With Tyler bringing his European cooking and wine selections to the dinner, it's almost enough to make this old fisherman refined! Even after all these years, when we get together we always pick up where we left off from the last time without missing a beat! It seems we are as adventuresome as ever, and the rollicking dinners will continue.

from the stewards: a 10-second stop-go penalty which effectively screwed DC. He had a go at catching up, but fell off when it started to rain, and then had further mishaps trying to gain places before finishing out of the points in seventh. The Ferraris finished first and second with Mika fourth, a few seconds behind Giancarlo Fisichella's Benetton. It sure didn't end like we'd planned. And just to finish things off, the 9:30 p.m. British Airways flight home didn't leave until 1:30 a.m.

After Montreal, we headed for France. Since we would test at Magny-Cours quite often, there was usually a chance to stop off at the small but very nice Vacheron Sancerre warehouse on the way to the circuit. The track itself actually had a couple of corners where you could have a go at passing someone, an element which the flash people designing new race tracks never seem to notice.

During the two days of practice for the French Grand Prix, DC and his mechanics had a hard time fighting various aspects of the reliability monster. The list seemed endless: fuel pump failure, a cracked oil tank (twice), an engine change, and then another fuel pump failure, the latter forcing a last-minute swap to the spare car, which had been set up for Mika. All things considered, DC did a really good job to qualify second, just over a tenth away from Schumacher and ahead of Barrichello and a slightly off-form Mika, who was fourth-fastest and not really happy with his car.

We had another of Schumacher's chops going into the first corner. DC was forced to back off, and rather than using the same intimidating tactic himself, he let Barrichello through to avoid the sort of collision Schumacher seemed intent on if you didn't give way.

It took DC quite a while to get ahead of Barrichello, but once in front and driving brilliantly, David quickly closed down the gap to Schumacher. Several times he tried to get by at the hairpin, trying both sides of the Ferrari, only to have Schumacher attempt to take him off the road. A somewhat pissed-off DC then went down the inside and stayed there, banging wheels but coming out ahead. You did wonder if Schumacher now had a tiny bit more respect for DC, having been at the receiving end of one of his own maneuvers—not to mention a cheeky middle-finger wave!

Not only did DC win the race with one of his best drives, but Mika finished second. Schumacher had been holding him up until his Ferrari dropped out with an engine problem, poor chap.

At least that helped ease the long drive down to the Clermont-Ferrand airport and the usual late charter flight back to Luton. And one of us was very lucky to reach Clermont at all after having four wheels off the ground on a back road near Lurcy-Levis and cracking the gearbox case on the nice CLK-class Mercedes. Damn good cars.

Austria, next on the schedule, was another track that was a long drive from anywhere unless you had your own plane to reach the nearby airport. Having been strangely out of sorts, Mika was now on much better form, no less than three of his four qualifying laps being good enough for pole at the A1-Ring. With DC joining Mika on the front row, it was so far, so good. Then, almost predictably, a proper kaleidoscope of shit happened after the warm-up on Sunday morning.

It went something like this: Mika's race-car chassis No. 6 develops an air leak in the pneumatic system. Use the engine in chassis No. 2T for chassis No. 6. The engine is fitted and started up okay. Put the first backup engine in chassis No. 2T and start it up: Oh, shit—it runs on nine cylinders, so change wires, coils, electronic boxes. Still runs on nine cylinders. Use second backup engine in chassis No. 2T. It's now 12:45 p.m., and the pit lane opens at 1:30. Thirty minutes later, the engine is changed and started, using people from all three cars. There are some pretty long extensions on speed handles to get close enough to the action. An unbelievably great job, from everyone on the whole team.

Mika thanked them by leading from the start in chassis No. 6, having a better position into the first corner. DC was second, ahead of another multicar shunt that eliminated Schumacher and others.

After 20 laps, we were able to think about showing Mika pit signals telling him to lower shift revs, such was the lead he and DC had over Barrichello.

About five laps from the end, Justine Bowen, Ron Dennis's personal assistant, came into the back of the garage where we kept the telemetry computers and asked me, "What's happening?" I just said, "Well, it's still going around making a noise." And so it was. Mika's second win and second place for DC drew them closer to Schumacher in the Drivers championship. And McLaren was just four points behind Ferrari in the Constructors championship.

There was an issue later on about a missing FIA sticker on one of the electronics boxes which had not been off the car. There was a long, drawn-out scene that went on for days. My view was that it was hard enough to get the damn things to work in the first place, so why in hell would you want to take the lid off one that *did* work? Of course, there were some people who thought we should be burned at the stake. But then they (our competitors, of course) *would* think that.

Dave Bryers spent a lot of time on this matter, and finally convinced the FIA that no one could have changed anything in the ECU software control box between the start and the finish of the race—or even before. He argued successfully that the absence of a sticker was the only problem. Ron Dennis later took Dave, Phill Asbury, and a couple of others to London for dinner.

Talking to Steve "Forklift" Morrow just after we got to Hockenheim, he asked me something like "What's the matter, Tyler?" When I said, "I'm missing something," his reply was, "What—Carl Hardy and Paul Cann?" Carl and Paul were my two trusted cohorts, who had been coming to the races and now were not.

Robin Page, one of the Mercedes-Ilmor test team engine guys, had had a rather big motorbike accident, doing a lot of damage to himself, but he survived. When I asked Nick Lee, one of the Mercedes-Ilmor race team engine guys, if he had brought Robin with him, he replied, "We didn't have a bag big enough to put the pieces in." It was a pretty bad shunt.

Hockenheim unfailingly brings an untold number of camper vans loaded with as much beer and food as they can hold. It would be interesting to know how many of these spectators actually get to see the race, because it would appear they are pissed the whole time. In 2000, it sure didn't help their cause when rain, sometimes very heavy, hit the place throughout the weekend.

There was a short period when it was sort of dry for the first part of qualifying, but then it rained and stopped again before the end. DC timed it just right with a brilliant lap—nearly 1.5 seconds faster than Schumacher—to take pole. Fisichella was third-fastest and Mika fourth. Fisichella's Jordan would have a big influence on the outcome of the race.

Mika made a great start from the second row to lead into the first corner, which was just as well, because it meant he avoided the chaos as Schumacher was punted off by Fisichella.

With the Finnish flag waving from the stands, Mika heads for his second win of the 2000 season at the Austrian Grand Prix. (LAT PHOTOGRAPHIC)

This meant we were running 1st and 2nd, Mika looking good with a healthy lead. Barrichello, who had started way down in 18th, had worked his way up to 3rd, about 30 seconds behind the two McLarens, when a disgruntled former Mercedes employee ran out onto the track. The safety car and hunting party were dispatched, and there went Mika's 30-second lead!

It was raining on one half of the track but not on the other. Mika stopped for wet tires but Barrichello stayed out. Mika was about 10 seconds behind Barrichello, with both cars doing roughly the same lap time, and that's what won Rubens his first grand prix. Now DC and Mika were equal, with 54 points, with Schumacher just 2 points ahead and six races to go.

The races where you stay in a city always seem to be better, probably because you get a chance to go out, walk around, and see a few things. Budapest is a very good example, with plenty to see. It's a pretty city, set on the banks of the River Danube, and there are lots of good restaurants like Menza on the Liszt Ferenc square.

We had arrived in Hungary with fresh concerns about a big shunt for DC during testing at the Valencia race track. A rear-suspension failure had caused a wheel to take off the rear wing at high speed. It seemed the shunt—from which DC happily emerged unhurt—had been caused by a fatigue failure on a welded joint which was a long way short of its life rating. All three cars came to the Hungaroring with strengthened steel suspensions.

DC seemed hardly affected by the crash as he set second-fastest time, three-tenths away from Schumacher after one of his very quick laps. Mika, on the other hand, was not happy with the balance of the car for most of the weekend. But Sunday afternoon would be something quite different.

Mika made another one of his good starts, this time from third on the grid, and after a pretty tense couple of wheel-to-wheel moments, came out of the first corner ahead of Schumacher. Then he just pulled away, and was about 26 seconds in the lead when he slowed down to save the car and engine. Schumacher took second, with DC stuck behind the Ferrari for most of the race.

After the race, Mika told Mark Slade, Phil Prew, and I that he had been having a problem with the downhill corners behind the pits during practice and qualifying. When he came out of the first corner in the lead, he didn't have much choice but to go for it in those corners as well. To his surprise, the car felt okay for the first time all weekend. He pushed even harder for the next couple of laps and it still felt okay. Then he was happy! And, I have to say, so were we.

Some people were suspicious because Mika had not been that quick in practice, and yet he walked away with the race. I remember there were some post-race FIA inspections. I think they forgot to inspect Mika. He'd had the balls to go for it, as the car felt much better in the race than it had in practice.

I have often wondered whether the Hungarian GP is scarier than the police escort to the airport after the race, which whistles down tram tracks, through red lights, and the rest. I don't drive the race car but I have been in quite a few police escorts—and I think I know the answer.

Mika was now leading the championship, but we had time to think about how fragile those two points were during yet another long drive from the Brussels airport to the race track at Spa. The difference was that Spa is a magic, scary place—a real race track. Added to which, the food is very good, with probably the best *pommes frites* you'll find anywhere.

There were some new aero parts and they seemed to be quite good, along with the usual

David Coulthard leads the 2000 Monaco Grand Prix, followed by Jarno Trulli's Jordan and Mika Hakkinen in the second McLaren MP4/15. DC's patience paid off with a win after Trulli and Michael Schumacher dropped out of the race. (LAT PHOTOGRAPHIC)

new software bits from Pete Schroder, Charles Hawkins, and his guys. Mika proved it by taking pole position, but DC finished a disappointing fifth, a couple of hundredths behind Schumacher.

After two days of sunny and very hot weather, it rained on Sunday, so much so that the race started behind the safety car, even though the rain had stopped not long before. No one was prepared to take risks at Spa. Once the safety car had disappeared after one lap, Mika led and pulled away. As the track started to dry and people began to stop for dry tires, DC got caught out and had to do another lap because Mika was already in the pit.

Mika rejoined still in the lead, but with Schumacher catching him. When Mika touched a curb on the still-damp track, the car got away from him just enough to let Schumacher get by. It wasn't until after the next pit stop that Mika closed right up on the Ferrari, having a go up the inside at the top of the hill. Schumacher moved over to block him, and then moved over again to touch wheels—not very clever at about 200 mph.

A couple of laps later at the same spot on the approach to Les Combes, the leaders came across Ricardo Zonta in the BAR-Honda in the middle of the race track. Schumacher went left and Mika went right, with just enough room between Zonta and the grass and on the inside line. This time Schumacher didn't pull his normal blocking stunt, and Mika was in the lead, where he remained to the finish. (The TV footage of this incident is quite spectacular.)

After the cars had pulled into the *parc fermé* at the end of the race, Mika walked over to have a word with Schumacher. Later I asked Mika about it, but he just smiled. One can only guess! More recently at a very nice McLaren Fellowship lunch for a few of us at the McLaren Technology Centre, I asked Mika again about Spa—and got the same smile!

The nose and the front wing on Mika's car had a small amount of damage from hitting the curb. When the car got back to the factory, some misguided cretin cut up the front wing because of the damage. I guess he didn't know, never asked, or wasn't told that this wing and nose had been worth about one second a lap at Spa. But the possibility of understanding why was now flushed down the loo. I did have a quiet word with Pat Fry about passing on an instruction to the effect of "Don't cut damaged things up until I have looked at them after a race or test."

Regardless of that, Mika now led Schumacher by six points. DC, who had finished fourth, was a further seven points behind, and McLaren, having moved ahead of Ferrari after Hungary, was still leading the Constructors championship. But that was about to change during the final four races.

We were still leading both championships after the Italian Grand Prix, but the gap had narrowed after Schumacher managed to stay out of Mika's reach to win at Monza. DC had been caught up in a multicar accident at the second chicane, during the course of which a poor marshal was killed by wreckage from one of the cars. It was a reminder that this is not only a dangerous sport for the drivers, but for others as well. The marshals and other track personnel give their services free, and without them, we wouldn't have any racing in the first place.

Formula One returned to the United States after nine years, this time to the Indianapolis Motor Speedway. I'm not sure many people realized at the time how many Ferraris and Ferrari fans there are in the States, and a great many of them came to Indiana in September.

Having been to Indianapolis a few times for the 500-mile race, it sure looked like the people there had done a lot of work to accommodate the F1 teams, with changes to the race track and proper garages along the pit lane. Of course, the rest was still Indianapolis, and always will be.

It became quite obvious that the layout of the F1 track, which ran clockwise and included a long straight passing the pit area, meant that getting a tow from another car would be quite helpful, especially if it came from your teammate.

In qualifying Barrichello helped Schumacher get pole by giving up one of his runs to tow Michael down the straight and then get out of the way before the first corner. McLaren did the same thing right at the end of qualifying with Mika, second-fastest at the time, giving DC a tow. It worked; DC came in 0.10 seconds behind Schumacher, but at Mika's expense, as he slipped to third, ahead of Barrichello.

After qualifying, Ferrari had an issue over the placement of the start/finish line on the row of bricks on the main straight. I guess they thought they could do something about the famous bricks, but failed to realize this was Indianapolis, and that those bricks are a sacred part of the place. But because it was Ferrari, the front-row position was moved back. We were betting that the "someone" from the FIA didn't need to call Paris to get approval. The issue was really about spinning the rear wheels on the bricks at the start.

Unfortunately, DC jumped the start when there was, dare one say it, a fumble with the start lights. This meant DC was leading Schumacher, with Mika catching up. It was just what DC was meant to be doing, and it was a bit rich to hear Schumacher complaining about being held up when he, of course, had screwed Mika around for most of the race in Malaysia in 1999. Talk about priceless bullshit!

DC tries to hold off Schumacher early on at Indianapolis. Mika would make a run at him later before engine failure put him out of the race. (LAT PHOTOGRAPHIC)

It had been raining a bit, and Schumacher got by DC just before he received his stop-go penalty for the start-light problem. When the rain finally stopped and Mika came out of the pits on dry tires, he was in traffic and lost a lot of time to Schumacher. But he caught up and was within four seconds of the Ferrari when the engine gave up after 25 of the 73 laps. It would have been interesting, as Mika had a bit more fuel than Schumacher.

I guess the Ferrari fans got what they came for, with a bit of help from us. It meant Schumacher was back on top, now 8 points ahead, and McLaren had dropped 10 points behind Ferrari, thanks to Barrichello finishing second.

It looked, once more, like the championship might be settled at Suzuka, even though in 2000 the Japanese Grand Prix was the only penultimate round of the championship. For a brief moment, however, it seemed there might be no race at all when there was a small earthquake during Friday practice. These were actually a common-enough event in Japan, and this one brought a classic comment from Drew Miller, one of the support crew guys, "Bad news about the earthquake—the hotel is still standing."

As often happens when the championship reaches a climax, the contenders seem to dig deep and find something special. Mika came to within 0.009 of a second of taking pole position from Schumacher at the end of the 3.64-mile lap. Absolutely nothing in it. Mika was first away at the start and had to dodge Schumacher, who was doing one of his usual chops across the track, a familiar move which still didn't seem to be part of the "sporting" rules for some people.

The fight for the lead went on until the second pit stops, when Schumacher got ahead and Mika lost time as he tried to get temperature into his tires. There were some harder Bridgestone tires for this race and, funnily enough, they seemed to suit the Ferrari when it came to tire wear. Having said that, Schumacher's in and out pit-stop laps were usually very quick, and that helped him a lot. He went on to win by two seconds from Mika, and became the 2000 Drivers World Champion, the first for Ferrari since 1979.

The Drivers title may have been sorted, but there was still a chance that we could take the Constructors championship at the final race in Malaysia. Schumacher took pole, and Mika and David were not far behind, separated by two-hundredths of a second—a good sign that the two drivers were pushing each other to do a better job.

At the start of the race, Mika moved a bit but stopped before the lights changed; it was enough to get a 10-second stop-go penalty later on. Mika did lead into the first corner, but knowing a penalty was likely, he let DC by. DC stayed in the lead until he had a bit of an off, when he came into the pits to check the car and have grass removed from the radiator ducts. After the stop, David pushed as hard as he could, but Schumacher stayed about one second ahead to win his ninth race of the season. Mika, having set the fastest lap of the race, finished fourth, about 35 seconds behind the leader, which was pretty much what the stop-go penalty had cost him. It was enough to piss you off, as the race would otherwise have been interesting. But it was nice to work with someone who never gives up.

I left just after the race, Jo Ramirez having sorted a car to take me, a friend of Bernie Ecclestone's, and the French car-radio guy, who was doing some work for us, to the airport. I caught a flight to Singapore, had a welcome shower in the Qantas lounge, and then went on to Australia for a bit of snorkeling and underwater photography. It was October 22, just over seven months since I had last been in Australia for the first round of the 2000 championship. It had been a tough season, but no different than most.

Mika and David honor retiring team coordinator Jo Ramirez after the 2001 Hungarian Grand Prix. Jo's career in motor racing started around the same time as my own, and he'd been with McLaren since 1984. (LAT PHOTOGRAPHIC)

# 2001: The Flying Finn's Finale

'm not sure what prompted the comment at the first test at Jerez in January 2001, but Phil Prew, David Coulthard's race engineer, suggested that his driver didn't need a race engineer—he needed an escort agency! In other words, it might be good if he just concentrated on the test.

Meanwhile, on the track, there was a serious amount of work to get through, thanks to changes to the technical regulations, the most significant being the raising of the front wing by 50mm. That might not sound like much, but according to Adrian Newey, it had a major knock-on effect on the layout of the rest of the car.

The last week in February was the usual chaos, with a shakedown and pit stop practice with two cars at a very cold Silverstone. This was followed by a test in Barcelona with chassis No. 003, the T-car, which was flown back from Gerona, Spain, on the Friday, turned around (i.e., subjected to a complete rebuild), and flown to Melbourne to arrive on the Wednesday before the race. A very busy week for everyone, but not a lot different from most teams.

Michael Schumacher took pole position for the first race in Australia, but there was a slight change to the old order when Rubens Barrichello made it an all-Ferrari front row and Heinz-Harald Frentzen and Ralf Schumacher put Jordan and Williams between Mika, third-fastest, and DC, in sixth place.

As they pulled away from the others, Mika looked like making a race of it with Schumacher. Mika, running with more fuel and stopping later, was four seconds behind the Ferrari when a front wishbone failed at the end of one of the straights, resulting in a heavy thump into the tire barrier. Thankfully, Mika was okay. That left DC to carry McLaren's hopes. After getting pushed around a bit at the start, DC later pulled a great move on Barrichello to take second. He tried his best to catch Schumacher and finished a couple of seconds behind the Ferrari to give McLaren 6 points. Unfortunately, with Barrichello finishing third, Ferrari came away from Melbourne with 14 points.

Meanwhile, a young kid by the name of Kimi Raikkonen finished sixth in his first F1 race, driving for the Sauber team.

The heat and humidity in Malaysia seemed to be worse than before. The Malaysian Queen, while doing a tour through the garages, was followed by a small boy holding a tray with a lovely gold inlaid plate carrying cold towels. The thought occurred that we could have used someone like that ourselves!

The discomfort wasn't helped by events on the race track, as the Ferraris filled the front row and eventually walked away with a race that was made pretty chaotic by rain not long after the start. The confusion led to both Ferraris being lined up, one behind the other in the pits, clocking up more than 30 seconds for a pit stop—but they still finished one-two due to the situation on the track. This became known as the Cappuccino Pit Stop. DC led for about 10 laps but had to accept third place once Schumacher and Barrichello got going. It wasn't much consolation for Mika to set fastest lap on his way to sixth place, nearly a minute behind the winner.

Mika's luck didn't get much better in Brazil when he stalled on the third spot on the grid. DC, directly behind Mika, managed to take avoiding action, but the locals cared even less about that when their hero, Barrichello, went into the back of Ralf Schumacher on the second lap. Barrichello's fans had been in the grandstand opposite the pits from an early hour, led by a rather rotund MC and chanting *Rubinho!* at an unprecedented volume, over and over again.

Such loud support has always been part of Interlagos, as has the Fogo de Chao *churrascaria*, a great place for the Mercedes-Ilmor team dinner where you eat what you want, when you want. You need to be careful with the Caipirinha, Brazil's potent national cocktail, made with cachaça, a 96-proof liquor made from fermented sugarcane juice, caster sugar,

Coulthard stops for tires and fuel during the 2001 Australian Grand Prix, where he finished second to Ferrari's Michael Schumacher. (LAT PHOTOGRAPHIC)

and lime. One can go from being completely normal to not being able to stand up if you consume too many of these. In my experience three is about the limit.

The very close times during qualifying suggested this could be a close race, particularly as the MP4/16 seemed to be better here in Brazil than in Malaysia.

Schumacher led the first two laps behind the safety car before former CART champion and F1 rookie Juan Pablo Montoya in a Williams eased the Ferrari onto the grass as the racing got under way. A ballsy move for an F1 newcomer, which got everyone's attention—especially after what Montoya had said about Schumacher, "He's good, but he ain't no Senna." Montoya led until he had a collision with Jos Verstappen's Arrows, which allowed DC to take the lead. We lost the lead when it started to rain, but once the pit stops had been done, David got ahead of Schumacher with a great move as they went either side of a backmarker. He stayed there to score a really good win, which put him six points behind Schumacher in the championship.

By the time we had finished the next race at Imola, DC held the joint lead of the championship with Schumacher after finishing second to Ralf Schumacher's Williams, with Michael parked after brake trouble on the Ferrari.

Qualifying had been a real shoot-out, with places changing all through the session. DC ended up on pole with Mika alongside. Neither of our guys made particularly good starts, which let Ralf Schumacher's Williams take a lead he wouldn't lose. But at least we were pretty competitive, hoping for a good result in Spain.

There may have been two weeks between Imola and Barcelona, but the work seemed never-ending. This was thanks to a lot of changes in the software as the FIA opened up the rules to allow several new things. Well, maybe not "new"; it was more a case of "reallowing" them. It meant a lot of work for Charles Hawkins and his guys in the race team software department, along with the rest of us.

Schumacher was on pole with Mika second and DC third, which set us up quite nicely for the race.

Actors Michael Douglas and Catherine Zeta-Jones were with us in the garage as guests of Mansour Ojjeh. Mansour, one of the McLaren owners, and his wife Cathy are very personable and friendly people, and it was the same with Michael Douglas and CZJ, who impressed us by being very casual with no pretentious nonsense as they mixed and chatted with everyone. I do seem to remember the boys talking CZJ into getting into one of the cars on Sunday morning.

Talking about distractions—particularly on the grid, when there are always a lot of things going on and you need to concentrate—Sunday was quite a bit cooler, and the grid girls were not wearing very much.

On the serious side, the various new switches and software had a glitch, which caused poor DC to stall the car when they set off on the parade lap, meaning he had to start from the back of the grid.

Schumacher led Mika through the first pit stops, but Mika got ahead after the second stop and pulled away, thanks to something amiss with the Ferrari. Going into the last lap Mika was leading by 26 seconds. Then the clutch exploded. It made quite a mess. I'm not sure if I cried, but I sure as hell wanted to. Even Schumacher felt sorry for Mika.

DC, meanwhile, had a race-long struggle working his way to an eventual fifth place. There was a bit of nonsense between DC and Ron Dennis about stalling on the grid, with neither of them knowing exactly what they were talking about! Charles Hawkins and his guys sorted out that alligator once they understood what had actually happened. (If you're wondering about the terminology, most software problems are called bugs, but ours always seemed to cause a bigger and nastier result; hence, they became known as alligators.)

But these issues were soon put in perspective by a tragic event just before the next race in Austria. Paul Morgan, Mario Illien's partner at Ilmor, died when the landing gear on his newly acquired Hawker Sea Fury (a World War II–era British fighter plane) dug into the grass runway and tipped the plane forward, landing upside down on the cockpit.

Paul was a very well-respected engineer and in charge of production at Ilmor. He was a great friend to me and a lot of other people as well. A no-nonsense kind of guy who had massive respect at Ilmor, Paul knew everyone by their first name. A very sad loss indeed.

As for the race, both drivers had all sorts of problems balancing their cars during qualifying. They finished seventh and eighth on the grid, 0.7 seconds slower than Schumacher on pole, and not what we expected at all. Then it got even worse for Mika when he stalled on the grid after inputting an incorrect button sequence on the steering wheel. We eventually got Mika going after about three laps but retired him after that.

When he came back to the garage, Mika quietly asked me to explain what had happened. I showed him the positions of the colored lines on my system monitor and what he did wrong; it was a good move on his part before going to see the people on the pit wall!

While all this was happening, DC was on the move, getting himself into second place after 23 laps. We had fueled him heavy to give a bit of flexibility, and DC used it well by driving some very good laps as he ran long for his one and only stop and jumped Barrichello's leading Ferrari in the process. The two Ferraris chased David hard for the remaining 21 laps, but he had everything under control to take another good win from Barrichello and Schumacher.

Uh, sorry: Schumacher actually finished second, as Barrichello was told several times to let him by, which he did just before the finish line on the final lap. It was another great sporting gesture which got Ferrari a lot of very negative ink. Nice one, Rubens. It also meant that Schumacher was able to keep a four-point lead over David in the championship.

Meanwhile, 45 seconds behind, that young kid from Finland, Kimi Raikkonen, finished fourth in his sixth F1 race.

People believe Monaco is all about the parties and the girls. The problem is, this is the one race where we always have a lot of work on. But then Friday, a day when we don't run, always seems to take a lot longer than normal—which surely can't have anything to do with whatever had been happening on Thursday night?

Everyone knows the importance of being on the front of the grid at Monaco, and with about a minute of qualifying remaining, it looked like DC would be the loser, as his best time, at one point good enough for pole, was beaten by Schumacher, Mika, and then Barrichello. This would have been bad news for DC, because as we saw in Hungary, Barrichello would be asked to protect Schumacher and let him pull away. Then David really got it together with a great lap to take pole position, pushing Schumacher to the outside of the front row and Mika back to third.

On the way to the grid Mika came on the radio and said there were some problems changing gear with the auto upshift. He could have pulled on the shift paddle, but then we might not have been able to sort out some wrong numbers in the software. Phill Asbury, with the help of others, understood the problem, and it was fixed on the grid. That was the good news.

The bad news was seeing DC stall on the grid because of some numbers that were changed in his software, which meant he would start from the back of the grid—just about the worst thing that could happen at Monaco.

David would finish fifth, which was not bad since he got held up for a great deal of the race by various people, particularly Enrique Bernoldi in the Arrows. There wasn't much DC could do about it, but that didn't prevent Ron Dennis from receiving bad write-ups in the press because of his rather over-the-top comments after the race. You could understand

The press studies Michael Schumacher as he studies Coulthard's MP4/16 before the Spanish Grand Prix at Barcelona's Cataluña circuit. (LAT PHOTOGRAPHIC)

the frustration, because a win for Schumacher allowed him to pull 12 points clear of DC in the championship at the end of a race that we felt David could have won.

Mika had chased Schumacher hard in the first 10 laps, swapping quickest segments with the Ferrari as they pulled away from the others. Then Mika came on the radio, saying there was something wrong with the car as it was pulling to the right. He stopped in the pits for the boys to have a good look, then went out again, only to come back in and stop for good. I don't remember finding anything really wrong with the car, but I wasn't driving it. The plane to London left at 11:00 p.m., the conclusion of a Monaco GP effort that had promised a lot but brought very little.

Ron had other things on his mind at the time when the news became public about Adrian Newey going to Jaguar Racing. Adrian was recruited by his friend from Indy car racing, Bobby Rahal, who was in charge of the team at the time. In the end Adrian changed his mind and decided to stay on at McLaren. I have known Adrian for a long time, and I think he had some help in changing his mind; perhaps he was able to resolve some outstanding issues. Whatever the reason, the good thing was that he was staying. But you did wonder for how long, which was another issue he and Ron were trying to work out.

With the Canadian Grand Prix next on the schedule, I took the usual opportunity to stop in Boston and go out to Nantucket for some fishing. That trip turned out to be a bit more exciting than planned when we attempted to land at Nantucket in a small twin-engine Cessna. We missed on the first try because of thick fog, but somehow found the runway—well, just off to the right side of it, really—on the second attempt. Thank you! The lady pilot was pretty calm, and said that once she saw the runway, she felt a lot better. So did we! I do remember keeping an eye on the altimeter, reading 500 feet, then 400 feet, etc., and looking out the window for the ground to appear! On Nantucket the fishing, catching, and eating side of things was fine as always, and the fog had cleared by the time I needed to fly back to Boston for my flight to Montreal.

Mika did his fair share of getting off the ground when he left the road a couple of times during practice and qualifying and finished eighth on the grid, in among the Saubers and BAR-Hondas. DC was looking good in third until just before the start, when he found a large nut from the front suspension inside the cockpit and threw it at us over the pit wall. It took a little while to sort out what might happen without the nut. The suspension was not going to fall off, but the car setup was going to change.

Despite not having a very good time, DC kept going, but it summed up his day when the engine failed as he held fourth place in the later stages of the race. That was the end of his record as the only driver to have scored points in every race so far. Second place for Michael Schumacher (behind his brother, Ralf) also meant that David was now 18 points behind. Mika's first podium of 2001, which summed up his season, now gave him a grand total of 8 points—32 behind DC!

The gap at the top of the championship opened even further at the Nürburgring, a race that was not really great for us. It was beginning to look like the Bridgestone tires were occasionally not working as well on the McLaren as they were on some of the other cars, particularly the Ferrari. DC had to work pretty hard to get third place (behind Michael Schumacher and Montoya), while Mika was never really in the hunt after switching to the T-car for the race. Keith Barnard, one of the mechanics on Mika's race car, summed up the situation when he said, "Glad we didn't get our car dirty for that."

Mika's season seemed to go from bad to worse in France when the engine would not turn over with the starter motor as he sat on the grid, where he'd qualified alongside DC on the second row behind the Schumacher brothers. It was not a problem with the engine itself. We later discovered a flat, hollow dowel jammed between a couple of things inside the gearbox, preventing the starter from turning the engine. One might ask why the hell a dowel was floating around inside. It could at least have been good enough to get itself chewed up on the way to the grid!

DC's race didn't go that well either, as he had a 10-second stop-go penalty about halfway through for speeding in the pit lane during what should have been the first of two stops. He finished fourth, setting the fastest lap in a race won by Michael Schumacher. They were now 31 points apart.

A test at Monza followed the French Grand Prix. I had a call in the middle of the night from Indy Lall, the test team manager. There had been a call from Reno, Nevada, where my father lived, to say my dad had fallen off a ladder in the front yard of the house. He had hit his head and was worse than not well. After trying to get more information from Reno, made difficult by a nine-hour time difference, I went back to England, then off to Los Angeles and up to Reno. My father passed away just before I got to the hospital. He was on his way into the operating theater when he said to the nurse, "I'm going to try and move my toes." When he couldn't, he said, "To hell with it." The two doctors who were going to operate very quietly told me it was better for it to happen this way because of his age and the damage that had been done to his spine.

I was somewhere else in the world when both of my parents passed away: my mother (in Boston, Massachusetts, 1974), and my father (in Reno, Nevada, 2001). Motor racing doesn't allow for very much family time, but as I was their only child, it made it harder for my parents. Nonetheless, they always supported my racing life, even when it ultimately took me away from them. I was lucky to have such great people as parents.

During the following week, with the help of some friends, I managed to sort out the various things one needs to do: flying my dad from Reno back to Hingham and laying him to rest with my mother. Paul Wuori had sorted out things before I got there. Then I caught the British Airways flight from Boston back to Heathrow that Thursday night.

Having gotten some rest at home on Friday afternoon, I drove up to Silverstone on Friday evening in a car left for me at the factory by Charles Hawkins. Being in charge of the race team electronics department, it was not a problem for Charles to fill in for me on the Friday.

Schumacher and Barrichello lead the pack in Hungary on their way to a 1-2 Ferrari finish. The win gave Schumacher his fourth F1 Drivers championship. (LAT PHOTOGRAPHIC)

It was good to see the boys again. Mark Slade said, "I'm really glad you're here," which was very nice of him and helped me a lot. I had a few words with Mika, who quietly asked if I was all right, as did Ron Dennis. I assured them I was okay, and then got on with the numbers and colored lines. Like all of us, Ron can be awkward once in a while, but there are times when he can be very helpful and caring, as he was in his conversation with me that morning in Silverstone. It's moments like this when you realize how important it is to be part of a team.

Mika's season had received another blow in every sense when a rear-suspension failure had caused a high-speed shunt during the Monza test. But he came to Silverstone very determined to put things right at a circuit he liked, qualifying second, just ahead of DC and 0.08 seconds away from Schumacher's Ferrari.

Schumacher led into the first corner with Mika second, but DC and Jarno Trulli ran into each other and spun off. DC tried to keep going but the suspension had broken in the shunt, which meant it was game over for him.

Mika got in front a few laps later, pulling out a lead big enough to stay ahead after his first pit stop. Our two-stop strategy was paying off, as Schumacher, stopping once, didn't have the pace. Mika made his second pit stop with no problems and went on to win by about 30 seconds from Schumacher. Mika held his breath a bit on the last lap, thanks to dark memories of the clutch in Barcelona.

Mika said to me afterward, "You know, Silverstone is one of those places and races that you just have to win." Having come so close several times, I think he came to Silverstone with only one thing on his mind, "I'm going to win on Sunday." He did that with style, along with the kind of performance he was quite capable of producing.

Things were back to what you might call normal for 2001 at Hockenheim, when we qualified on the second and third rows. Only briefly did DC run in the top three, and that was during the pit stop period. Then we watched helplessly as both cars quit with engine failures due to some parts that missed out on a couple of processes in manufacturing. What can you do—except to keep trying harder to stop this type of thing from happening?

DC might still have been second in the points table, but by now it was a matter of *when* Michael Schumacher was going to win the championship rather than *if*. That moment came a couple of weeks later when Michael won in Hungary to retain his title. DC finished third, while Mika ended up in fifth place. At least they both finished, which summed up the way our season had been going.

With Ferrari leading us by almost twice as many points in the Constructors championship as we went to the Belgian Grand Prix at Spa, you might have been forgiven for thinking the guys in red were on top of us in every way. This was brought home during pit stop practice on race morning when Steve Hallam, carrying out the team radio checks, asked, "Can everyone hear me?" and Nigel Stepney, Ferrari's chief mechanic, put up his hand!

We started the race from the second and third rows and finished the opening lap fifth and sixth, Mika ahead of DC. But we were to get a bit of help when the race was stopped after a few laps because of a rather large accident.

This gave Keith Barnard time to fix a couple of bolts that were loose in Mika's exhaust system. When the cars set off on the parade lap for the "new" race, the Williams of Ralf Schumacher, a few places in front of us, was still sitting on low stands because his guys had just finished changing the rear wing when it was time to go. With the Williams now starting from the back, this helped give Michael Schumacher a very clear run. Unfortunately, it also helped Giancarlo Fisichella get into second place and hold up DC. But David never stopped and it paid off, as he finished second, with Mika ending up fourth.

The world was turned upside down on the day before we left for the Monza Grand Prix when terrorists flew hijacked planes into the World Trade Center in New York City on the 11th of September. This led to a very sober mood in the paddock at Monza. While we were trying to come to terms with all of that, McLaren put out a press release saying that Mika Hakkinen was going to take some time off. Oh, and by the way, the young kid from Finland, Kimi Raikkonen, had been signed up to drive alongside DC for 2002.

You could say that was the only good news in a weekend when DC had an engine problem in the race and Mika's gearbox decided to not change gear. Another low day for McLaren, but nothing compared to events in the United States, which, as it happened, would be our next stop in the championship.

Because of the problems created by heightened security after September 11, the freight bound for Indianapolis had to go through Amsterdam, as this was the only place that had X-ray machines big enough to cope with the aircraft containers.

At Monza, there were a lot of questions being asked as to whether F1 should go to Indianapolis. Chat, questions, and views were floating about all through the Monza weekend. I was asking myself, "Why wouldn't we go to Indianapolis? It's the next Formula One race in the series." My view, and the view of others, was that you cannot let these sorts of people, terrorists of any kind, stop you from doing what you do. You just have to have the determination to get on with things and show them that you won't be deterred!

The people in Indianapolis and at the race track were pleased that the race was going to happen, summed up by a banner in the grandstands saying "thank you for coming." I guess that said who had the determination.

On Thursday evening, Martin Whitmarsh organized a party for Jo Ramirez at the very impressive Eiteljorg Museum of American Indians and Western Art. It was a grand affair to mark Jo's departure from McLaren at the end of the year.

Mika had a shunt during the warm-up on race morning, giving us quite a job to repair the damage before the pit lane opened. Keen to get going and try the car, Mika passed some stopped cars at the end of the pit lane and went onto the track moments before the light changed from red to green. I don't think he saw the light because it was obscured by the waiting cars. The stewards took away Mika's fastest lap time from Saturday qualifying.

There was a reasonable amount of discussion about what happened, and Dave Ryan did the best he could with the stewards. But they wouldn't budge on the penalty, which moved Mika from second to fourth on the grid.

The race looked like Barrichello was going to be the guy to beat after Schumacher let him by, but when the various strategies played out and Mika made a single, very late stop, he had taken a well-deserved lead and won the race. DC finished third and was happy that it was over, as his car had not handled very well all day.

Mika was understandably happy. When he told me, "It's very special to win at Indianapolis," I replied, "Yes, it really is. I know; I've been here before when we won." This would be Mika's last of 20 F1 wins.

Mika did a nice thing at the last race in Japan when, without saying anything to DC, he let David through to finish third with one lap to go. DC held on to his second place in the Drivers championship. He'd done a really good job all year, also helping McLaren to finish second in the Constructors championship.

Given the technical problems we'd been having throughout the season, it was good to have both cars finish, particularly for Mika's last race.

Yes, there had been some ups and downs during his 9 seasons and 20 wins with McLaren, but the reality was, it had been fantastic for everyone, particularly Steve Hallam, Mark Slade, Barney Hassell, Phil Prew, Mark Arnall, myself, and all the mechanics who had worked closely with "The Flying Finn."

Perhaps the revered motor-racing journalist Nigel Roebuck summed it up best at the end of an article about Mika when he wrote, "On a warm Sunday afternoon, with the Championship up for grabs, I'd put my money on Mr. Hakkinen."

Retired champion Mika Hakkinen returned to visit with David Coulthard and Kimi Raikkonen before the 2002 Monaco Grand Prix. Raikkonen would prove a more-than-adequate replacement for his fellow Finn. (LAT PHOTOGRAPHIC)

# 2002: A Tough First Season for Kimi Raikkonen

As Mika's replacement, Kimi Raikkonen would be driving the 2002 car, the MP4/17A, which had its launch and first test at Barcelona on the 19th of January. It didn't take long to realize that Kimi didn't say very much, except to Mark Arnall (Mika's ex-trainer and mentor) and Mark Slade, his race engineer.

After the Barcelona test came the usual drill: tests at Valencia, Barcelona, and back to Valencia, always trying new stuff before a cold-as-hell shakedown at Silverstone on February 21, before shipping the cars to Australia the next day.

We tried a different airline and flight schedule for the trip to Melbourne and arrived there at 4:30 in the morning; perhaps it was not such a good plan after all. At least there was an opportunity to have dinner with Dieter Gundel that evening at the Fish Market restaurant, a chance to gather one's thoughts while enjoying some very good food.

For some reason there was a shortage of hydraulic fluid. Someone had forgotten it or just couldn't find it in the freight. This caused some concern in the garage at the time. But other than that, qualifying seemed to be pretty much where we left off in 2001, with Ferrari, led by Barrichello, filling the front row, Ralf Schumacher next in the Williams, and DC fourth and Kimi fifth. The only difference this time was that McLaren, along with Williams, was now on Michelin tires, while Ferrari was sticking with Bridgestone.

At the start of the race there was a bit more than the normal first-corner chaos when Ralf, just avoiding his brother, almost went over the top of Barrichello. The resulting eight-car shunt brought out the safety car.

All of this helped DC to take the lead at the restart, only to have another safety car several laps later. Just before the second restart, DC fell off thanks to the gearbox acting up, a problem that would bring retirement after 33 laps.

Kimi, meanwhile, was up to third place—a really great job, considering he had taken the first restart from the back of the field. Forced to avoid the carnage created by Schumacher's flying act and taking to the gravel trap, Kimi had to stop for a new nose and tires, as well as a general cleaning out of rocks and grass.

Kimi set fastest race lap on lap 37, held second at one point during the pit stop phase, and finished on the podium behind Schumacher and Montoya (Williams). Not a bad result in view of where he had been 57 laps before.

Trevor Lawes from the gearbox department found DC's problem when examining the gearbox after the race. At the same time, we heard from the factory that a gearbox from the Valencia test was about to have the same problem. It was a bit late in the day to discover this, and only thanks to the fact that we'd taken DC's gearbox apart after the Melbourne race. A better after-test plan was clearly needed.

If we thought our showing in Australia was a disappointment, it was to be much worse in Malaysia, where both cars retired with engine failure.

DC did get to score his first points in Brazil by finishing third, four days after his 31st birthday, which we celebrated—any excuse!—in the Fogo de Chao. I suspect that the partaking of Caipirinha could well have been more enthusiastic than usual, and it would probably be best not to ask where some of the guys went after dinner.

We would need the sustenance, because there was a lot going on leading up to the race, particularly building the spare chassis into a usable beast. It took between three and six people four days to build chassis No. 004. This had been our spare chassis in Malaysia; one wonders what we would have done if we had needed it there. Some of the problems may have been caused by updates or parts that were the wrong spec, but I'm not sure of that. All I know is that there were people grinding on carbon parts from Tuesday through Sunday morning. Why the hell were we doing all this in Brazil? I don't know. My view was that we shouldn't have been sent parts unless they were finished and inspected—like it or not.

If some people in the team wanted this arrogant indifference to be all-consuming, then I could see us sliding further down the row of pit garages in 2003. And there I was, thinking we were a "team."

On top of all that, we had a chassis change for Kimi between Friday and Saturday, along with another engine and then a mechanical fuel pump that had to be changed before qualifying, just to keep the boys focused.

The race started with pole-sitter Montoya and Schumacher coming together at the first corner. There was no penalty for Schumacher, but Montoya thought there sure as hell should have been. You could hear the ranting for a long time after the race had finished.

His mood wasn't helped by Schumacher winning the race, with Ralf (in the other Williams) taking second, while Montoya was fifth. He was lucky to get that, because Kimi had been lying fourth, about a second behind DC, when the right-rear-wheel drive pegs failed four laps from the end. That was very disappointing for everyone.

When we reached Imola for the first race in Europe, Doug Harvey, one of Kimi's mechanics, pointed out that the carbon grinder was still hot from Brazil! Heat would also be a factor in the race: Kimi was running fifth in the San Marino Grand Prix when one of the exhaust tailpipes broke and fell off. He stopped a few laps later because the carbon wishbones were getting too hot, which was the safe thing to do. We came away from Imola with sixth place for DC, who, just to rub it in, was a lap behind the Ferrari one-two. So much for the 2002 race at Imola.

The next day Pete Schroder, the race team's electronics control systems engineer, and I drove down to Mugello for the test that was just starting. I set up a meeting between Pete and Phil Collins, the trackside electronics control systems engineer from Mercedes-Ilmor, in the quiet office of the engine transporter. This was to discuss some engine issues and possibilities that were evident in some of our competitors' engines. It went well, with Phil commenting to me afterward, "Not so many minus signs." This was a relief to me, as I'd thought there would be a good feeling between these two very clever guys.

The catalog of things breaking continued in Spain, but was much worse this time, when Kimi's rear wing fell off on the long pit straight. This was after four laps while he held fourth place. It sure as hell was not very clever. DC managed to stay out of trouble and had the rear wing stay on his car as he finished third. Oh, and Michael Schumacher won.

Which Schumacher did again in Austria—only this time it was very different. Barrichello led right up to the last lap, when he let Schumacher overtake as they approached the checkered flag. They were booed by almost everyone in the place. It was nothing but blatant team orders and caused quite a moral stink. A great part of the controversy concerned the difference between what is meant to be a sport and what is actually just a business with a few sporting gestures thrown in every once in a while. There was nothing really illegal about letting Schumacher win, even though Barrichello had been quicker all weekend, and it probably wouldn't have caused such an outrage if the people at Ferrari weren't always preaching so much about how "sporting" they always were. As Roger Penske once said, "Business is business and love is bullshit."

We came away with sixth for DC and an engine failure for Kimi after five laps. After flying home from Graz to Luton on the Sunday night, it was on to Paul Ricard on the Tuesday for a pre-Monaco test. We would be using the short part of the circuit in hopes that the weather in France would be about the same as Monaco.

The real highlight, if you could call it that, was waiting for the Friday-night trip home from the Marseille airport, on Buzz flight number 2601. This was supposed to leave at 9:00 p.m., but because the aircraft was somewhere else in the world, we didn't get away until 1:30 Saturday morning, arriving back in Stansted (of all places) at 3:00 a.m. I remember Dave Redding buying a sandwich and coffee from the stewardess just as I fell asleep; it was difficult to know whether this was dinner or early-morning breakfast. Believe it or not, our bus was actually still waiting to take the wounded bodies home when we finally arrived.

The pace did not slacken off at Monaco, but then that's never a surprise for this race. This year, it was Kimi who had quite a fraught time. On Thursday he had a shunt while following DC a bit too closely early in the session. Then another shunt on Saturday morning meant going out to qualify in the second T-car, but it had an oil problem. So he jumped into the first T-car, but came straight back to the pits with a throttle-pedal sensor problem. Now time was running out, and there was a bit of a panic with Roger Higgins and me as we got the information from the colored lines on the computer. Then we shut off the faulty one of the two tracks on the sensor and sent Kimi out to do his last run. He qualified sixth, while DC put his car alongside Montoya's pole-position Williams. What an act! It felt like it was time to find a place to hide and take a couple of deep breaths.

Kimi's troubles did not stop during the race. He was running sixth when he got hit from behind by Barrichello, who must have forgotten that you need to slow for the chicane as it's a bit bumpy in the braking area.

David Coulthard is followed by Michael Schumacher at the 2002 Monaco Grand Prix. They remained in that order until the end of the race, giving McLaren its sole victory of the season. (LAT PHOTOGRAPHIC)

DC had taken the lead before the first corner and he stayed there for the whole race. At one point, there was smoke from his car, probably from some oil, which prompted breath-holding moments for a few laps. But then it stopped, and thankfully there were no signs of any oil pressure problems.

It was a great drive from DC as he managed to look after his tires while keeping Schumacher behind. The two of them were split by just over a second as they crossed the line after 1 hour and 45 minutes of hard racing.

Little did we know it, but this was to be our only win in what was obviously a disappointing season, even more so than 2001. DC would finish second in Canada, with Kimi getting on the podium with third at the Nürburgring. DC had been taken out of the European Grand Prix by a collision with Montoya.

These things happen in motor racing, but the British Grand Prix was to prove that McLaren, as a team, was sometimes our own worst enemy.

The race brought the usual Silverstone rain, and it didn't help that the Michelin wet tires were not that great. Saying that, the McLaren scenario was something else. Kimi was up to 3rd when it started to rain quite hard. He moved into 2nd for a short distance before coming into the pits at the last moment for wet tires. If he'd said something coming down the pit lane, no one understood it. Even so, there was every likelihood that he would be

David Coulthard talks with his new teammate Kimi Raikkonen before the 2002 German Grand Prix. Kimi joined McLaren from the Sauber team, and would soon prove an able replacement for Mika Hakkinen. (LAT PHOTOGRAPHIC)

stopping at some point for wet tires. However, it took a while to get them from the back of the garage, which moved Kimi down to 7th. But with the changing conditions, he was in and out of the pits and down to 10th at one point before the engine finally failed.

DC was even worse off due to issues with the radio that kept him out on the wrong tires when he was asking to come in. He finished 10th, two laps down on a Ferrari demonstration at the front. It really was a kaleidoscope of confusion.

Our ability to manage as a team was questioned when the travel plan for getting to Magny-Cours was changed. It meant getting on a bus that left Woking at 5:30 a.m. and arrived at the circuit at 4:30 p.m. It was a good thing we were traveling on the Wednesday. The engineers' travel plans were changed for the following day. Probably best not to say any more about that exercise!

Come the race and we'd forgotten all about that, as Kimi, who hadn't been lower than fourth, got himself in the lead after 43 laps. DC then took over for a few laps before making the second of his two scheduled stops, leaving Kimi to come under pressure from Schumacher. Kimi was doing a good job holding off the Ferrari until the engine in Allan McNish's Toyota blew up and dropped oil at the end of the back straight. The leaders arrived immediately afterward, and in the absence of oil flags, Kimi slid off line, just enough for Schumacher to pounce. He made sure Kimi wouldn't get back on the racing line by keeping him on the curb going around the corner. Schumacher won the race, and with it his fifth World Championship.

When I spoke with Ferrari guys that I knew after the race, even they felt Kimi should have won. In the season we were having, second and third places were a reasonable result. In France DC also made the fastest lap as he recovered from a drive-through penalty for being one of several drivers who crossed the white line at the pit exit.

With Hockenheim following just a week later, Steve Hallam, Phil Alexander, Mike Negline, and I drove to Germany from Magny-Cours, stopping in Dijon on Monday night, plus a lunch stop in Chablis the next day. It made a welcome change from that terrible journey to Magny-Cours.

Hockenheim had undergone a major rebuild which took away the very old straights, but the one thing that hadn't changed, and had come to be expected in Germany, was Michael Schumacher on pole.

It was quite a bit hotter on race day, and there were thoughts that the Michelin tires would be better. Schumacher won. DC, having started ninth, finished fifth. Kimi's day was going fine until a tire failed while he was lying fifth. He stopped for a new one, but a lot of the floor had been damaged by the failed tire, and he fell off a few laps later.

Hungary, Belgium, and Italy weren't much better, particularly when Kimi's engine failed while he was lying third at Monza, just as it had done two weeks before at Spa.

The trip to the last two races of 2002 was a bit different, as several teams flew in a Boeing 747. It belonged to Australian Paul Stoddart, who was also on board, and who owned European Aviation and the Minardi Formula One Racing Team. Paul is a great guy, and it was an enjoyable experience leaving from the Bournemouth airport for Indianapolis.

The United States Grand Prix turned out to be another rout by Ferrari, their eighth one-two of the season. The difference this time was that Barrichello finished first, but it wasn't supposed to be that way. The two Ferraris tried to stage a dead heat after Schumacher had led every lap except for the two pit stops and the last lap when, supposedly, he made a "mistake" and Barrichello got by. They actually crossed the line 0.011 seconds apart, with DC a good third, some seven seconds behind. Kimi should have been right with him, but a bad spark plug caused him to run on nine cylinders before he finally stopped.

Continuing our journey with Paul Stoddart, we stopped off in Hawaii for a few days on the way to Osaka. My girlfriend Jane and I had a very enjoyable few days with Steve Hallam and his Australian wife, Ada. I remember us all getting stuck into the great Mai Tai cocktails! I wasn't so sure about the 4:30 a.m. check-in at Honolulu, but at least the Hawaiian coffee was good, even at that time in the morning.

It really is a long ride in a minibus from Osaka to Suzuka, especially after a long and very bumpy flight across the Pacific Ocean.

Having filled the front row, the two Ferraris led from the start. DC was third until the throttle-control system on one side of the engine acted up and then failed. Ralf Schumacher held third until his engine failed, which allowed Kimi to finish on the podium—thanks to a fair amount of luck! A bolt had come loose inside the engine airbox, got stuck in one of the throttle barrels, then freed itself, only to become stuck in the movable trumpets, before jumping out of them as well! Given the season he'd had, with 10 retirements, Kimi deserved a bit of luck for once as he got himself onto the podium for the fourth time. At least it was something to be reasonably cheerful about at the end of a very poor season by McLaren's standards.

Toward the end of 2002, Richard Ford, another smart, clever guy, came to work at McLaren in the race team electronics/software department. He would prove to be a very good asset for the team.

# 2003: One Step Forward, Two Steps Back

The 2003 car, the MP4/18, was intended to be a great leap forward. It did have some different and unusual aspects, but in the end, the only leap forward was the amount of work required to keep it running.

It broke some rear-suspension bits the first time it appeared on a race track. At some point someone asked, "Why do we need a GPS on the 18 when we all know it's in the garage being worked on? (Many teams ran GPS to follow their cars on the track.) When there was a problem with the brakes at another test, the comment was, "Why do we want to stop it? We've only just got it going!"

And when someone asked if the MP4/18 had passed the crash tests, our test drivers, Pedro de la Rosa and Alex Wurz, said they had already done them!

The MP4/18 was destined never to race and was labeled by some as "design arrogance." It probably would have put a few other teams out of business. It took a long, long time to recover from the effort that went into it—physically, financially, and mentally.

Someone once said, "If you don't have problems, you won't have the opportunity to fix them." I guess that's one way to put it!

The upshot was a revised version of the 2002 car, now known as MP4/17D. When we got to Melbourne for the first race of the season, things were starting to look the same, as the Ferraris of Schumacher and Barrichello filled the front row, followed by Montoya, 3rd in a Williams-BMW. DC was back in 11th, with Kimi 15th. One of the FIA's more-significant changes for 2003 affected qualifying; now each driver would have a single lap to do his time. Kimi fell off on his lap, which explains his place on the eighth row, and DC made a mistake at the first corner of his flying lap.

With the track being damp at the start, the cars were fitted with intermediate tires. On the parade lap, Kimi came on the radio and said it was dry on the back side of the track, and since he was pretty far back on the grid it was worth coming in straightaway for dry tires and starting from the pit lane. The other advantage of being so far back was that the others were well past the pit lane entry when he came in, and therefore couldn't counter his move by doing the same thing.

DC came in at the end of lap two, and it was a while before the leaders started to think about doing the same thing. By this time, Kimi had worked his way into the lead until what should have been his one and only scheduled stop. Then he had a problem speeding in the pit lane. It was not his mistake like everyone thought, but a problem with a glitch in the software when he locked up one of the front wheels in the tight pit lane entry. This meant the pit lane speed limiter (PLSL) did not come on until that wheel moved. It was not much time, but enough to put him just over the limit for an instant and earn a penalty. DC, meanwhile, had got himself up to fifth before his stop, and he gradually climbed back to second, not far behind Montoya.

Then, with 10 laps to go, the Williams spun and handed DC the lead. It was another of DC's good, steady races and gave him his 13th win. Kimi, despite his drive-through penalty, still managed to finish third, just ahead of Schumacher.

Two days in Melbourne before heading for Kuala Lumpur and the Sunway Lagoon—a great place to stay, where you can also eat with the locals in the parking lot nearby! Malaysia is all about getting used to the heat and humidity, if one ever can. We had a bit of time at the swimming pool, and the "internal sun tan lotion"—sometimes referred to as Caribbean Mineral Water, provided by Steve Cook, one of the support guys—was always helpful.

There was a different look to the front of the grid when Fernando Alonso became the youngest-ever pole-position winner with his Renault teammate, Jarno Trulli, alongside. DC was fourth alongside Schumacher, with Kimi seventh after running wide at the final

The team waves as Kimi Raikkonen heads for his first-ever F1 victory at the Malaysian Grand Prix in March 2003. The win gave Kimi and McLaren a short-lived lead in both the Drivers and Constructors championships. (LAT PHOTOGRAPHIC)

corner during his single qualifying lap.

It all kicked off at the first corner when Schumacher ran into Trulli, causing other people to move around to get out of the way.

Having stayed out of trouble, DC was second behind Alonso when one of his car's large electrical connectors on the main software control box, the ECU, came undone, losing most of the software controls for the car.

The way things panned out, this should have been DC's race. But on this occasion it was Kimi who ended up in the right place at the right time to win his first F1 race, about 35 seconds ahead of Barrichello. What can you say but "A young boy's dream"?

It was interesting that several people said Kimi should have won in Melbourne and DC in Kuala Lumpur. We'll take it either way! Of course, it would have been better to have both cars finish. The result of all this was that Kimi led the championship from DC, and McLaren was clear of Ferrari at the top of the Constructors championship. That would last for a couple of races, but the truth was, we wouldn't see the top of the podium again for more than a year.

We should have known Brazil was going to be one of those weekends when there was no food for some of us on the Varig flight to Sao Paulo. The request "Could I have some dinner please?" was answered by a bag of peanuts and the steward walking away, never to return until morning. Barney Hassell (Mark Slade's assistant engineer) actually had broken glass in his pasta. I guess I was better off with the peanuts.

Friday was wet, and although the track was dry on Saturday, this being Interlagos, we should have known that might not have been the last of the rain. But so far, so good, particularly for the locals, as Barrichello put his Ferrari on pole, with DC alongside and Kimi directly behind, sharing the second row with Mark Webber's Jaguar.

Then on race day came the rain. I don't remember how many times the safety car was deployed, but it was a lot, thanks to some high-speed shunts caused by water running across the track. Because of the safety car, the timing of when drivers stopped for tires and fuel mixed things up. Kimi didn't stop at the time of the first safety car, and came in for fuel but no tires on the second safety car.

Mark Slade and Barney Hassell worked like mad on Kimi's strategy, trying to get it right after Kimi had led from laps 11 to 26. DC, meanwhile, had been right with Kimi and was in a good position to take over the lead when Kimi made that first stop, much later than everyone else. DC was looking good for a win when the rain returned. He stopped for tires at the end of lap 52, which was to prove critical. Had he stayed out for another lap, he might have won, because a big shunt at the beginning of the start-finish straight brought out the red flag, ending the race, since three-quarters of the total distance had been passed.

Initially it looked like Kimi had won from Giancarlo Fisichella's Jordan. When a race is red-flagged, the result is determined by the order of the field as it finished two laps before the flag. The officials got it wrong, having counted back one lap too many, and a couple of days later they gave the win to Fisichella. It meant Kimi had to give the trophy back—damn! DC was classified fourth, but if we felt bad, then poor Barrichello felt even worse, as his Ferrari had fuel-pickup problems just after he took the lead from DC on lap 45. This was a bad day for Ferrari, Schumacher having spun off on a river of water.

There was no broken glass in the pasta during the flight home, although it was hard to tell what it tasted like anyway. We knew we would have no worries about food at the next race at Imola.

A mistake by DC during his qualifying lap knocked him back to 12th on the grid, but a slow start by Schumacher's pole-position Ferrari created enough chaos to allow DC to move up several places on the first lap. Both drivers made further ground thanks to a good pit stop strategy, although Kimi wasn't helped by a slight gearbox problem on his second of two stops. He ended the race just under two seconds away from Schumacher, with DC fifth, trying to get by Ralf Schumacher's Williams. It was a sober podium because the Schumachers' mother had passed away that morning.

We came away from Imola still at the top of the Constructors championship, but that lead was to dwindle quite a bit at Barcelona, where the Spanish Grand Prix was something of a non-event for McLaren.

Kimi went into the gravel during qualifying, which meant a back-of-the-grid start. He was to pay an even bigger price by going into the back of Pizzonia's stalled Jaguar at the start. DC, having started eighth, got pushed off twice, the second time for good. There were some sad, pissed-off faces on the flight back to London that night.

The mood coming back from the next race in Austria was better, even though it was 2:30 a.m. by the time I got home! We came away from the A1-Ring with second and fifth for Kimi and DC—and we were pretty fortunate to get that podium. It seemed there were engine-related problems of some sort all weekend. Kimi's V10 was found to have a cracked exhaust valve in the No. 2 cylinder after qualifying. The Mercedes engine boys were allowed to remove the cylinder head and change it, which meant Kimi could keep his front-row grid

Trading places: On the podium in Brazil, Kimi holds the winner's trophy he would eventually surrender to Jordan's Giancarlo Fisichella (left). (LAT PHOTOGRAPHIC)

position alongside Schumacher's pole Ferrari.

The race took three attempts to get started, which meant that the water temperature got quite high and Kimi's engine never ran like it should have after the first pit stop. A fair amount of holding one's breath was required, as Schumacher led until a fire in one of his pit stops dropped him back to third behind Montoya and Kimi.

Schumacher got by Kimi due to the engine not running at 100 percent. Montoya's BMW engine failed, but Kimi's second place came under pressure from Barrichello, Kimi making it clear to Rubens that he was not going to get by. Second place ensured that Kimi stayed on top of the Drivers championship, but another win meant Schumacher was closing in as we headed for Monaco, with a testing interlude first at Paul Ricard for the 17D and a run for MP4/18, which had not yet been written off as a possible race car for 2003.

There was less than half a second separating Ralf Schumacher's pole-position Williams from Kimi, but we were in trouble once more with the V10. The engine people flew two of their best guys out from England, along with the required parts to change another cracked exhaust valve—cylinder No. 1 this time—on Sunday morning! The McLaren boys had the engine out of the car and ready for them to start on soon after they got there. This was another really good job, watched over by the FIA, in the tent alongside the transporter parked in the quayside paddock.

Because there was a lot of work done on Kimi's car, the weight needed to be checked on the FIA scales, which were at one end of the pit area and a reasonable distance from our pit box, making a slow task at the best of times even more difficult.

Kimi didn't make a very good start, which was difficult to understand because our data showed he had made several quite good starts on the track at the end of the practice sessions.

It was Mark Slade, Kimi's race engineer, who said, "The tires, perhaps . . ." He was right, thanks to the car having gone down to the scales with the set of tires used for the start, which meant they were not very warm! It was a harsh lesson for us.

It also explained why Montoya got the jump on Kimi to push him down to third behind the pair of Williams BMWs. During the pit stops, Ralf Schumacher dropped to third, and Kimi began to push Juan Pablo Montoya (JPM) real hard when the latter had to back off a little to save his engine. In the end the first three (Michael having pulled ahead of his brother) were covered by 1.7 seconds.

There was another close finish in Canada, with just over a second covering the first three cars. The problem for McLaren was that neither of our drivers was among them. Kimi had messed up qualifying by going off at the first corner, and DC, still struggling with his one-lap qualifying, couldn't do any better than 11th. With Kimi slotted on the back of the grid, we decided we might as well start him from the pit lane.

The plan, as soon as the start lights went out, was to immediately change the tires and add enough fuel for one stop. That worked, and Kimi drove hard until he had a tire puncture, which fortunately happened near the pit lane entrance and allowed him to come straight into the pits. DC, meanwhile, had gone well in the early part of the race and was running fifth, only to have a gearbox failure. A win for Schumacher and Ferrari moved Kimi and McLaren off the top of the respective championships.

Testing continued with the MP4/18 at Jerez. We arrived there to find a collection box by the back door of the garage. Courtesy of Peter Hodgman, who was in charge of part of the R&D department, it was labeled change appeal for the 18.

Alex Wurz, the test driver for McLaren, had a shunt on the first day with the 18. He could not understand what had actually caused him to fall off, as he had done several laps with no problem in that particular corner. Perhaps it was loss of downforce, but no one was sure. Kind of scary, you might say.

The MP4/18 was becoming the center of a lot of speculation, with a few articles in the "comics" saying that if the 18 was something like a second quicker than MP4/17D, then we would start racing it. There's nothing wrong with being positive, but there are times when it's a good idea to take a closer look and not dismiss reality.

The following day, an engine change on 18 took nine hours—something to do with oil pipes. I know I spent a lot of time with Barry Ultahan, helping out with the gearbox, again. Best to move on to the next race.

At the Nürburgring Nigel Stepney, Ferrari's crew chief, made the classic comment about testing, "The damn test team break everything. And when they don't break the stuff anymore, they give it to us!" Apart from perhaps explaining why a couple of red cars seemed to finish a lot of races, it was slightly ironic, given what was about to happen to McLaren in the 2003 European Grand Prix.

Kimi was quickest most of the time with a suitable amount of fuel, and DC was right there as well. And this time, when it mattered during qualifying, Kimi got his lap together and put MP4/17D on pole, our first in more than two years. Kimi led from the start and was pulling away when the engine went *bang* after 16 laps. It was believed to be a piston failure. Kimi, who does not really say very much, came out with something in Finnish—probably just as well it wasn't English. It had been a long time since I had seen that kind of performance with one of our cars.

Both cars did finish in France, although to be honest, Kimi and David should have been higher than fourth and fifth. Kimi was running third until he got caught up in traffic after a pit stop and Michael Schumacher got ahead. DC probably could have been just ahead of Kimi, but a problem with the fuel rig on his last pit stop meant a switch to the second rig and DC being waved away too soon. He knocked over the fuel-hose man, Steve Morrow. DC stopped; Steve waved his hand for him to go, but by then, DC had lost a fair amount of time. With Williams, led by Ralf Schumacher, finishing first and second, we had slipped to third in the Constructors championship.

Things were not helped at the factory by other forms of confusion. Here's an example: One of our best carbon-stress guys interviewed someone who he didn't think was correct for the job, and so didn't hire him. Sometime later, a new person interviewed the same guy—and not only hired him, but also put him above the guy who'd interviewed him earlier. And then they were surprised that the first carbon-stress guy decided to leave. Priceless stuff.

On the Wednesday before the British GP at Silverstone, we set off from the factory in Woking at 5:00 a.m. to go to Elvington for a shakedown. It was intended to help restore the confidence of the pit stop crew after the Magny-Cours fuel-nozzle problem, although no one seemed to know whose confidence needed to be restored.

There was a hint that it was really for the benefit of DC, who on Tuesday decided not to go anyway. As it turned out, there was an electronic box problem in the T-car and one of the refueling nozzles didn't work correctly, so the trip was worthwhile for good reasons.

But when it came to getting down to business during qualifying at Silverstone, DC was not happy with the balance, never got a clean lap, and finished 12th on the grid. Kimi did better with a place on the second row, directly behind Barrichello's pole-position Ferrari.

DC's problems were to continue into the race when he caused the first safety car after his cockpit padding flew onto the track. A stop to replace it dropped him to next to last, but then a few laps later another safety car would do DC a favor. This one was due to the appearance of a "not wrapped too tight" person in a kilt who ran onto the track. This caused a lot of chaos, not just on the track, but also in the pits, as the first 10 cars came in at once and put Cristiano da Matta, who didn't stop, into the lead. When the Toyota finally came in after 17 laps, Kimi moved to the front until his scheduled stop six laps later. The last set of tires were not right for some reason—perhaps the pressure—and Kimi finished third behind Barrichello and Montoya, DC taking fifth after a great drive fighting his way through the field following his second stop.

The podium finish had helped to keep Kimi in second place in the championship, but a first-corner collision at Hockenheim and an easy win for Montoya would later put the Williams driver ahead. Meanwhile, DC started 10th but was able to make up a lot of ground. Aggressively driving and running a longer middle segment helped to put him into second place at the end of a very hot day.

With four races left, the championship was to swing back in our favor in Hungary, the weekend ending better than it had started. The power-assisted steering (PAS) on Kimi's car had a huge hydraulic leak on Friday morning and had to be changed—a fair bit of work before practice had even started. And just to keep Chris Thompson, the number-one mechanic, and his guys on their toes, Saturday brought an engine change for Kimi before qualifying.

Fernando Alonso was on pole for the second time, and he used the clean side of the track to good advantage when Webber, starting third in the Jaguar, held everyone up on a circuit where overtaking is difficult.

Kimi took second at the first pit stop, with DC moving from ninth to fifth, thanks to his pit stop plan. With Kimi and Montoya finishing second and third and Schumacher struggling with his Ferrari and Bridgestones to finish a lap down in eighth, the championship was suddenly wide open: Schumacher, Montoya, and Kimi were all covered by just two points.

With Michelin cars filling the first seven places in Hungary, we shouldn't have been surprised when Bridgestone, just before Ferrari's home grand prix at Monza, raised a query with the FIA about how much of the Michelin tread was actually on the track. When the FIA suddenly said they would be measuring the tires after the race (something which had never been done before), Michelin had no option but to play it safe and make new tires. No surprise, maybe, that Schumacher and Bridgestone-shod Ferrari were back on top at Monza.

Apart from easing Schumacher ahead in the championship (Montoya finished second; Kimi, fourth), this meant Schumacher now had 37 races without a mechanical failure. You might realize from this fact that whatever their faults, Ferrari has very good reliability. Tires—or, at least, the choice of tire—played an interesting role for McLaren during qualifying at Indianapolis. Kimi had done quite a good lap, but there were some quick cars still to run.

While I was walking down to the *parc fermé* with the jump battery (needed for ignition during FIA checks), I kept looking at the big leaderboard tower beside the track as other cars ran. Just as I was thinking "We can't be worse than fourth," I'll be damn if Kimi wasn't on pole. This was due largely to Kimi and Mark Slade getting the tire choice absolutely right.

Being in the United States, it was good to have my friend Paul Wuori at the race. He was clearly having a good time, particularly when he was spotted chatting to supermodel Heidi Klum, no less.

The weather on race day turned bad soon after the start, with intermittent rain becoming quite heavy at times and causing dramas over which tires to use, and when to use them. Kimi led for a while, but the Bridgestone wet tire was quite good. At some point in the chaos, guess who got in the lead and stayed there? Schumacher won, with Kimi taking second after fighting for places during most of the race. DC had a good run before being caught out with dry tires in the wet; then a gearbox problem finally put him out.

Going into the final round at Suzuka, Kimi was nine points behind Schumacher. The

Kimi and Michael Schumacher shake hands at a press conference before the 2003 Japanese Grand Prix. Kimi still had a shot at the Drivers championship, but it wouldn't be easy. (LAT PHOTOGRAPHIC)

mathematics meant that Kimi had to win with Schumacher outside the points. Or, put another way, the Ferrari only had to finish eighth or higher. Apart from our interest in the championship, we were looking forward to the annual team dinner put on by Kenwood, a really good group of people who supplied the team radio system. It was held at a restaurant where you cooked your own food. (This was as much fun as usual.) Another thing I noted that had not changed in Japan was the coffee stains and cigarette burns which were still on the carpet in the elevator at the Hotel in Suzuka-Shi.

Kimi finished second to Barrichello, but Schumacher made a complete mess of his race, hitting a couple of other cars, misjudging his braking, stopping for a new nose, dropping back to 20th, and eventually finding his way into the 8th place he needed for his fourth straight Drivers championship. While there was no doubt that Schumacher was very good, he also had a very reliable race car.

In September 2004 the first-ever Chinese Grand Prix was held at the new Shanghai International Circuit. It was a long way from the tracks I'd started out on in the early 1960s. (LAT PHOTOGRAPHIC)

# 2004: Making the Best of the MP4/19

After all the problems we'd had with the need to build two different cars in 2003, there was more than the normal amount of politics regarding the new one for 2004, the MP4/19A. It was a bad sign that some people referred to this as a "debugged" MP4/18. There were also some misgivings about serious modifications to the engine. These were considered necessary because engines now had to last the full weekend, from the start of practice on Friday to the end of the race on Sunday.

Whatever anyone thought, MP4/19A had to be built. There was consideration given to some big modifications that were needed for the chassis, but if these were made, it was going to take more than just hard work to make the first race. Not doing this didn't go down very well in some areas.

A thought came to mind at the time, "We're way behind, so we have to do twice as much. Maybe we're way behind *because* we are trying to do twice as much—and the end result is a mess."

The first test for 19A was in Valencia on January 20, followed by Barcelona, and then back to Valencia. On the next-to-last day of the second Valencia test there were some problems that stopped the race-distance run. Kimi Raikkonen must have asked about why the car was stopping, to which Steve Hallam simply replied, "We are in the closing stages of preparations," which I don't think answered Kimi's question at all. There are always a reasonable amount of problems in the first test of the year, but with each year it seemed like there were even more.

Although Kimi never really said a lot, those who thought he didn't know a lot about the race car were very wrong. If there was something that didn't feel right with the car, he knew it straightaway. At the early tests in 2003, for example, we had been running some new software. Kimi hadn't driven in the early tests with this software but the other drivers had. Yet when he came in after the installation lap, Kimi told Mark Slade that the traction control was not working like it had been before, and that something was wrong. It took the software people quite a long time to find and fix the problem.

On balance, the pace with 19A at the tests had been pretty good, so, ready or not, we headed for Melbourne. After a good flight with Singapore Airlines, we had an excellent breakfast at the Sheraton after arriving on Tuesday morning. And that was pretty much the end of the good bit when it came to the 2004 Australian Grand Prix.

Qualifying had been changed. The Friday run was moved to Saturday, with a couple of minutes between the two one-hour sessions. What hadn't changed was that each driver would still get a single lap to do his time. The look of the grid hadn't changed that much either, as the Ferraris of Schumacher and Barrichello sat on the front row, followed by Montoya's Williams. The fact that MP4/19A was proving difficult didn't help, as Kimi took 10th place, and DC, still struggling with this one-lap format, ran wide coming out of the final corner and ended up 12th.

In the race, the two Ferraris walked away in the order they had left the grid. Alonso finished third for Renault, with the Williams of Ralf Schumacher and Montoya next, followed by Jenson Button in the BAR-Honda. Kimi had an "anti-stall" incident at the start, and 10 laps later the right-hand radiator failed. He lost all the water, and, of course, the engine. DC did what he could and finished eighth, one lap behind. Not a good start to the season.

With two weeks between the races in Australia and Malaysia, there was time for some new bits for the car to be sent from the factory. On Friday there were some issues that kept the mechanics there until 3:00 on Saturday morning. Then there was an "engine reset," which prompted a couple of electronic boxes to be changed. And to add to the fun, there was a hydraulic problem just before first qualifying. But everything was sorted out in time,

Kimi Raikkonen in conference with Mark Priestley (left) and Chris Thompson (right) at Monza in 2004. Kimi was usually quiet, but he knew how to communicate with his crew. (TYLER ALEXANDER)

Kimi and DC doing a little better than Melbourne, qualifying fifth and ninth on the grid.

It almost goes without saying that Schumacher was on pole, and apart from the three pit stops, his Ferrari led every lap. Kimi, having got up to third at one point, was fourth when the right-hand inner CV joint failed with 16 laps remaining. That's the way it goes sometimes—but that sure as hell doesn't make it okay.

For Formula One's first race in Bahrain, Mike Negline had sorted out the Gulf Hotel, which was nice, with friendly and helpful people. The new track was out in the desert, a reasonable distance from town, but what they didn't tell us about was the traffic!

Because of the serious terrorist problems going on in the world, Dave Ryan, the team manager, had organized a very good security service to look after us. They gave us a long chat when we first got there about "do's and don'ts," driving, and being careful. We never actually saw them again until Sunday night, going to the airport for the flight home. Being proper security people they managed to blend in with the surroundings very well.

The track was very nicely done, with a suitable amount of room in the garages and paddock area. But once the action started, we didn't get time to notice all that after the engine failed on Kimi's car on Friday afternoon. That, along with a few other things, kept us in the garage until about 2:00 Saturday morning.

It had been very hot on Friday and Saturday, as one expects in the desert, but thanks to clouds on Sunday, the temperature dropped a lot, which probably helped the Bridgestone tires and Schumacher to just drive away from everyone else.

Because of the engine change, Kimi had to start from the back of the grid. The new one disgraced itself by failing after seven laps. It was noted by several people that Kimi, rather than switching off, had marked his third retirement in a row by driving the thing until it caught fire. DC's engine failed about seven laps before the end of the race while running eighth.

After the race, Lisa Dennis, Ron's wife, was chatting with Kimi and commented, "With all those flames, the car could have melted." To which Kimi replied, "It's a shame it didn't."

On April 8, 2004, a few days after returning home, we moved from Woking Business Park to the new McLaren Technology Centre (MTC), a rather large and grand place, with a big pond full of fish viewed from the tall glass windows in the restaurant. The new headquarters was a project that Ron Dennis had wanted to do for many years. It was a very fitting place for the McLaren Group.

With three weeks between races, we had time to get sorted out at MTC and find our way around, especially the long walk to find the coffee.

The bus for the run to the airport continued to leave from the old factory at Woking Business Park. That worked okay as long as you could still get in the old building to use the loo. And get a coffee from the machine!

I have to say that the bus journeys—particularly coming back from the airport—would be pretty quiet for the next few races; a lot of work was going on for very little reward.

At Imola, Kimi had to start at the back of the grid again due to an engine compression leakage problem. He finished 8th, with DC 12th after stopping soon after the start for a new front wing.

At Barcelona, we thought there had been enough problems on Kimi's car on Friday, but Saturday and Sunday went a few steps higher. There was a problem with the pneumatic pump-bottle pressure going down and the water pressure going up after free practice on Saturday morning. The Mercedes V10 came out of the car, the engine guys removed all the pumps off the right-hand side, and replaced the pneumatic pump; we finished 30 seconds before going out to qualify! It was a damn impressive effort from the engine guys, Nick Lee, Mark Grey, and Justin Howard, with the rest of us looking at our watches.

On Sunday morning, the chassis boys had to change the mechanical fuel pump. This meant getting the engine (complete with gearbox) off the back of the chassis and then getting into the fuel tank. There is a final time for adding fluids to the car before the race, and the boys finished 20 minutes before the bell—another good effort from Stephen Giles, the chief mechanic, along with Chris Thompson and his guys, Phil Taplin, Jon Rashbrook, and Mark Priestley. I'm sure Warwick Pugh was in there somewhere, too. For that Kimi got 11th, one place behind DC and a lap behind. Well, you don't need me to tell you who had won all five races of the 2004 season so far.

While we were packing up, someone said the Queen was coming to MTC on the 12th of May. It was fantastic to have recognition from the monarch. Unfortunately, by failing to use her electronic security pass while at MTC, she inadvertently locked herself in the loo for a short time. Everyone stood around until someone thought it a good idea to go and see what had happened. She was then released to continue with a very successful tour.

This year Monaco really was different: someone other than Michael Schumacher actually won. Jarno Trulli, with his Renault on pole, led from the start, while our race began to fall apart on the third lap. Due to a large cloud of smoke from one of the Hondas, DC slowed down and got attacked by Fisichella, who couldn't see him. Kimi had a pneumatic problem and stopped before the engine actually failed. It was little consolation to see Schumacher three-wheeling his Ferrari back to the pits after a shunt with Montoya in the tunnel.

A week later at the Nürburgring we had a repeat; this time both drivers went out with engine failures. You could feel what was left of morale, motivation, and goodwill being slowly flushed away. When you're trying to do a good job, it always makes it harder to have the cars keep stopping.

Meanwhile, there had been a lot of work at the factory, building a 19B chassis and aero package, along with the Mercedes-Ilmor people doing some serious work on one particular area of the engine. On June 1, the day after the European Grand Prix in Germany, Kimi did a short test with the 19B at Silverstone. About halfway around on the install lap, he came on the radio and said to Mark Slade, "This is much better."

Meanwhile, we had to persist with the 19A, which we took, with some more modifications, to Montreal. On Sunday morning there was a problem with the clutch-pressure sensor on Kimi's car—there always seems to be something! With no time to change it, the electric connector was just unplugged because the sensor was causing some other problems.

After several pit stops, a drive-through penalty, and a change of steering wheel—I don't think there was anything else—Kimi finished seventh on the road with DC, whose car had been hit at the first corner, finishing two places behind him. Glad of any help we could get, both drivers moved up a couple of places when the Williams and Toyotas were disqualified for incorrect size or positioning of their brake ducts. Having both our cars finish was also helpful.

We were still stuck with the 19A at Indianapolis a week later. Kimi took sixth; he might have finished a bit better had the engine run properly. DC was seventh after taking an extra pit stop to get some junk from a couple of shunts removed from under the car. Both cars were a lap down on the pair of Ferraris at the front, led by Schumacher. Ferrari was leading the Constructors championship with 142 points. We were fifth, with 17 points. The 19B could not come quick enough.

The fact that everyone knew this was demonstrated by a huge effort from the people in the McLaren factory and at Ilmor's Brixworth facility. A pair of 19Bs were already on their way to a test at Jerez as soon as we got back from the United States. I went down to Spain a day or so later and chatted with Kimi about how he thought the revised engine was running. He said it was much smoother and felt freer—which was exactly what we wanted to hear, because we thought that might be the case.

With the French Grand Prix approaching fast, the two 19Bs were flown back from Jerez, which bought the guys a lot more time to prepare the cars for Magny-Cours. Dave Ryan and the travel department had sorted out a charter for the team from Farnborough to Nevers, which is a lot closer to the Magny-Cours race track than any other airport, and saved a lot of travel time. The race result, sixth and seventh for DC and Kimi, was not great. But third on the grid for DC (Kimi would have been better than ninth had he not gone off the road) showed us that the 19B was a much better place to progress from, particularly with the British Grand Prix just a week later.

There were several good things at Silverstone: the Beach Boys doing a concert, the 19B, of course, and Kimi, who always liked Silverstone. Plus our hotel had some of the best scrambled eggs around, which probably had something to do with the price they charged to stay for the race weekend.

After a bit of a panic on Kimi's car after changing the ECU just before qualifying, he went out and put it on pole! Kimi led the race for 11 laps before a different strategy for Schumacher put the Ferrari into the lead, where he stayed. Still, by finishing second, Kimi gave us our first podium of the season. Progress at last! DC, meanwhile, was seventh after having a hard time all weekend. He was never really happy with the car's handling.

One person looking nervous was Bob McKenzie of the *Daily Express,* who said he would run naked around Silverstone if McLaren won a race in 2004. Betting against a Finn and a Scotsman suddenly didn't seem to be too clever.

On the day before we left for Germany, I went back to Silverstone with the test team guys to do a shakedown of the 19B/003, which had just been completed. Everything went okay, except for the usual wheel-speed sensor glitches, which we had occasionally, and no telemetry for the install lap. The car was set up for Hockenheim, including the right gear ratios, which allowed us to send it straight from Silverstone.

A scary thing happened to Peter Hodgman and Paul "Shaky" Harding around this point in 2004. They were involved with the brake-test rig (which was not at the McLaren factory at the time) when the rig, running at max speed and load, suddenly failed. Parts flew everywhere around the room. Some went up though the ceiling, never to be found again, and others cut a large electrical cable that was on the floor by their feet. They still have vivid memories of the event.

Hockenheim really should have turned out better than it did. Schumacher led the whole race and won, but there was a lot going on behind the Ferrari. Jenson Button, having started

13th, drove one of his better races to finish second—his BAR-Honda helped when Kimi, running second and catching Schumacher, had the rear wing fall off on the pit straight. Kimi was not amused, to say the least, after his high-speed attack on the tire barrier.

DC eventually finished fourth. He may well have done better had he not been hit at the start and then picked up some trash from Kimi's shunt, which did the front wing some harm. There are always a lot of ifs and buts in motor racing; nevertheless, it sure would have been nice to see how the Schumacher/Raikkonen fight would have turned out.

Budapest didn't offer us very much either, other than the usual business of counting how many Trabants—a long-discontinued, plastic-bodied, two-cylinder, two-stroke road car built in East Germany—were still about. Kimi didn't finish due to a voltage problem with the engine fuel injectors that occurred above a certain rpm. DC was out of the points, in ninth place.

Spa had a bit of everything to offer—from rain in practice, an "oops" from Kimi at the Bus Stop Chicane in qualifying, and DC getting onto the second row.

A multicar collision at the first corner brought out the safety car for the first of what would be three appearances during an eventful race. Having started from 10th on the grid, Kimi was on the move, picking off Michael Schumacher and DC when the safety car went in. By lap 12 he was leading as others ran into trouble, but his 13-second lead was lost when the safety car returned on lap 29. Kimi would teach Schumacher a great lesson in how to restart as he slowed down, thereby slowing the Ferrari behind him, and then went for it, leaving Schumacher struggling on his cooled-down Bridgestones. Then came the third safety car after DC had hit the back of Christian Klien's Jaguar. Kimi had to do it all over again, which he did brilliantly—and Schumacher had no answer.

It was a great drive, with all of us holding our breath on the restarts, and the winning result helped by really good pit stops from the guys. It's fair to say that Kimi's drive and result partly detracted from Schumacher winning yet another Drivers championship at that race. And Bob McKenzie was going to be running naked around Silverstone!

There was a two-day test at Monza the first week in September, which was the 36th test of the year. But it was not going to help us earn any more wins in 2004. DC finished sixth in the Italian Grand Prix following a retirement for Kimi, as he held fifth place. This time the right-hand radiator decided to leak, losing all the water and melting part of the cylinder head.

The first-ever race in China saw Barrichello leading the whole way, the Ferrari holding Kimi off for a great deal of the time. Kimi's strategy was changed, which turned out to be a mistake, as he ended up behind Jenson Button, stuck there for the rest of the race. It was

Kimi qualified second and finished third at the inaugural Chinese Grand Prix, held in September 2004 at the new Shanghai International Circuit. (LAT PHOTOGRAPHIC)

a bummer because it would have been a good fight between Raikkonen and Barrichello. Nonetheless, having both cars finish (DC was ninth after an extra pit stop following a shunt with Ralf Schumacher) was good for everyone, particularly with one car fighting near the front for a change.

Quite a bit of work was done on the cars on the Monday when we started the race backup engines; we finished packing up by midday on Tuesday. The race team guys and some of us stayed in Shanghai until the following Sunday, which was nice, as it gave us a chance to see a bit of the city.

Barney Hassell and I went to the zoo, where there were a lot of strange things to see, including a large hippopotamus with his own deep pond. We watched as he rose slowly out of the water and made a rather rude noise, spraying a group of people standing quite close to the stone wall before slowly going back under the water!

On the Sunday, we all set off by bus for the long run to the airport. The traffic there can only be described as horrendous. About 23 kilometers from the airport, the fuel pump on the bus failed. While Mike Negline got on the phone and sorted out another bus, the team sat on the grass as the locals slowed down, waving and shouting. Probably just as well that we couldn't understand them. As if we hadn't had enough of buses, there was to be another epic and even longer journey from Osaka to Suzuka.

The 2004 Suzuka race weekend had some different things to offer. On Friday, it rained quite hard and we didn't do much running. Then practice/qualifying was canceled on Saturday because of a typhoon passing along the coast. Which meant that on Sunday, we had qualifying and then the race. Of course, as often happens, you get the usual names in the usual places; in other words, Michael Schumacher on pole.

In the race, Michael did his usual thing and walked away with it. Kimi, who had not made a very good start from 12th, then had a shunt, which caused some problems with the steering as well as a small loss of hydraulic fluid. It can be a bit stressful watching the colored lines on the telemetry screen as they show the hydraulic level slowly going down while you check just how many laps remain. Kimi hung on to 6th place. DC was looking okay in 4th place until he had a coming together with Barrichello and did not finish. That left the Brazilian Grand Prix as our last hope to salvage something from such a disappointing season.

Interlagos usually brings something different, and it didn't disappoint this time. Almost on cue, it began to rain a couple of minutes before the start of the race. The rain caused some chaos while we tried to keep the laptop dry and make some wet-weather changes to the software. The race came down to a strong fight between Kimi and Montoya's leading Williams. (DC had started on the dry tires, along with several others, and it didn't really work out for him.) It was good to see Kimi finish on the podium, but it was a close thing, as there was some hydraulic fluid in the cockpit from the power-assisted-steering. Another race watching the hydraulic level slowly going down while counting the laps!

It was a shame DC's race didn't go very well, as this was his last for McLaren after nine seasons. In 2005 he would end up driving for the Red Bull team. David is a great guy and always did a good job—except when Ron Dennis would speak to him just before qualifying, which had some strange effect on DC.

The 2004 season had not started off very well, but it got a lot better when the 19B came along. Reliability was a big issue, and I have always thought that the philosophy of discipline, control, and patience plays a big part in that.

There seemed to be what one would call a "misunderstanding" about what happens when trying to keep the ECU temperature under control in the garage. We had been having this problem for some time, and regrettably had made very little progress, with the new ECU actually getting hotter than the previous one. Fortunately Phil Alexander was able to set up and test several different means for cooling the ECU on the bench and in a chassis. After a lot of tedious work he came up with a reasonable solution.

# 2005: Raikkonen and Montoya vs. Reliability and Ferrari

**W**hat was to be a promising but ultimately frustrating 2005 season started off on an unacceptable note on February 19, when it took us until 3:00 a.m. the next morning to get the first MP4/20A started because of some problems with the crank-trigger software and engine-starting rpm. Electrical systems engineer Jamie Lewis had a collection of batteries and wounded starter motors spread around, but he never gave up. It wouldn't have been so bad had we not found out there were people who knew about the problems all along but were callous enough not to say anything until the next day. So much for a cohesive team.

To finish pissing us off, there was new software to fix the problem and a hint from someone that it had been available the evening before. The usual tests followed at Barcelona and Valencia, then Jerez, where at one point we could only run one car, as there were not enough parts.

In the final stage of work before the freight had to be ready, some people were flat-out building the timing stand and some pit equipment. I thought, "How, after all these years, can we allow ourselves to still be building this stuff on the night before everything has to

Raikkonen and Montoya wave to the fans at Monza after scoring the fastest times during Friday practice for the Italian Grand Prix. (LAT PHOTOGRAPHIC)

leave? It should be finished by the first week in February—so why can't it be? There will always be some last-minute things, so get the obvious ones done and out of the way! What the hell have we been doing to the timing stand since the end of October of the previous year?"

There were quite a few changes to take into consideration for 2005. The biggest shake-up concerned tires, with one set now required to last for the entire race. And engines now had to stretch to two races instead of one. At McLaren, DC had been replaced by Juan Pablo Montoya (JPM), the driver who had beaten us at the last race of 2004.

Apart from all of that, we arrived in Melbourne to find a legal battle between the FIA and Minardi owner Paul Stoddart over whether or not he could run his 2004 car in 2005, even though it did not comply with the latest rules regarding raising and repositioning of wings to reduce downforce. There was also more work for all the teams now that you could run a third car on Friday, which would help the team to better understand important data on tires, etc. Added to this was off-and-on rain for qualifying, which set the stage for the race.

Having qualified ninth, Kimi made an uncharacteristic mistake and stalled on the grid (it's not handy letting the clutch paddle go with the engine idling). But he did manage to finish eighth, two places behind JPM, both on the same lap as the surprise winner, Giancarlo Fisichella, who had made the most of the dry period in qualifying and led from pole in the Renault. When things didn't go that well in qualifying in Malaysia, JPM was heard to say, "The problem with this team is they look too much at the statistics and not at reality. The Renault team is first and third, but we're sixth and eleventh." Maybe it was the 105-plus degrees Fahrenheit (40-plus degrees Celsius) air temperature and the 127-degree Fahrenheit (52-degree Celsius) track temperature that brought about his words of wisdom.

Having burned my knee kneeling down on the track while on the grid, the race took my mind off the pain when JPM finished fourth. In fact, it could have been even better, because Kimi had led for a couple of laps halfway through the race. He might have won if a new system for changing tire pressure in a pit stop hadn't stuck open. Kimi spun, and by the time he got to the pits for a new tire he was at the back of the field. He did well to get back up to ninth at the end, setting fastest lap along the way. This time it was Fernando Alonso's turn to win from pole for Renault.

There was a shuffling of driver seats in Bahrain when JPM hurt his shoulder. This seems to have happened when he was playing tennis with the help of an off-road motorbike. (Everyone just has to do their own thing, I guess.) Our test driver Pedro de la Rosa took over for Montoya, and even though he hadn't raced in quite a while, he dusted off the cobwebs and drove with great determination to finish fifth. Kimi rounded off a good weekend for us by finishing on the podium behind Alonso and Toyota's Jarno Trulli. On a weekend when we celebrated two cars finishing, it was interesting to note that Michael Schumacher retired with hydraulic failure. It was his first retirement for mechanical reasons in no less than 58 races.

Ferrari was also doing much better at Imola, which wasn't surprising, as they had refused to join the other teams in observing the agreed-upon rule requiring less testing between races. (As usual, it was a case of "My bat, my ball, my friends in high places.") After making a mistake and qualifying 13th, Schumacher came through and was held off by Alonso as Renault took another win.

As far as we were concerned at Imola, there were a few dramas before the race, with an oil tank leak on Kimi's car. The replacement also leaked the next day and had to be changed again—a lot of extra work that was rewarded with pole.

Kimi was three or four seconds ahead in the race when the right-rear CV joint failed. It seems that it got a high torque load leaving the grid for the parade lap. The software and/or the systems people were deemed to be at fault, but I thought it either wasn't strong enough or there was too much angle on the halfshaft. Our second test driver, Alex Wurz, took his turn racing JPM's car; he drove well and stayed out of trouble to finish a very good third.

Barcelona really did have some different things going for it, other than JPM being back in the cockpit. We had a lot of flaky Hall-Effect (HE) gearbox sensors over the weekend, probably due to a bad batch from the manufacturer. They would cause a few twitches in the race, particularly with Kimi starting from pole again. (A Hall Effect sensor is a transducer that varies its output voltage in response to a magnetic field. Hall Effect sensors are used for proximity switching, positioning, speed detection, and current sensing applications. In this case an actual "position.")

Kimi led the whole race, although he had a bit of a problem getting away from the first pit stop. The HE gearbox drum sensors failed on the first lap, which was not good, as they were the backups. This, along with a few glitches with the main gearbox drum sensors on the last lap, raised the heartbeat a fair bit.

JPM would have finished much better than seventh if there hadn't been a problem with the fuel rig that prevented fuel from going into his car on the last pit stop. When he came back in, the fuel rig worked correctly.

The 5:50 a.m. bus from the factory to the airport was probably not the greatest way to start the Monaco weekend, even though it turned out as good as anyone could hope for.

There was a bit of panic on the grid—Kimi's lap trigger was doing strange things as the lap trigger signal box was lined up nicely with car's grid position. Basically every time someone walked between the lap trigger and the car receiver it thought it was another lap. Usually the lap trigger box is not near enough to the start line or front row of the grid to cause these strange readings.

Kimi led from the start, and by lap 24, he'd opened a 5.4-second advantage when, typically for Monaco, one car spun and a couple of others ran into it. The safety car was sent out, but Kimi's position on the track as he came to the end of a lap left very little time to make a choice about stopping, which the four cars behind him managed to do. It looked like it would turn out to be a mistake, but on the restart Kimi was told he needed to pull out a gap to allow him to get in and out of the pits for fuel without losing the lead. In about 10 laps he had a 30-second lead, enough to make his stop and keep the lead. Pretty damn impressive, a few of us thought. Watching the TV footage of him coming out of the swimming pool complex about a centimeter from the guardrail every lap seemed pretty impressive as well! My admiration of Kimi is no secret.

Meanwhile, after fighting his way from 15th on the grid, JPM finished 5th.

Finishing at Monaco with both cars, all four wheels still attached, is always welcome. As for winning as well—we all know what that means!

It was straight from Monaco to the Nürburgring, where there were some very good aspects to the European Grand Prix. And one really crap one. Kimi, having qualified on the outside of the front row alongside Nick Heidfeld's pole position Williams-BMW, led from the start. Unfortunately, a bit later, he locked up the right-front at the first corner and flat-spotted the tire while trying to lap Jacques Villeneuve. Everything seemed okay at that point.

The rules for 2005, of course, did not allow for a change of tires, and the vibration from the flat spot became so bad that Kimi could not read his pit signal board. Not trusting the powers that be on the safety issue, and still leading the race, he stayed out. Kimi was still leading at the start of the last lap when the right-front bottom wishbone failed under braking for the first corner.

After the race, a lot of people said we were either crazy or stupid not to have stopped him. But when asked what they would have done if their driver had been leading the race, "Stayed out" was the usual answer. It was a shame all around, as Kimi drove an outstanding race to stay in the lead, given everything that was going on with the car.

Kimi was actually classified 11th, not that it made any difference at the end of a race won by Alonso, with JPM 7th. We packed up and went home, tail between our legs. Pete Schroder and Richard Ford went to work on the software to help us deal with this sort of issue. Hopefully by looking at some new colored lines we'd be better prepared to make a decision whether or not to stop in the future.

After a couple of days spent fishing with my friends on Nantucket, I arrived in Canada. I found the kaleidoscope of chaos much more intense than normal, starting with qualifying. Kimi had a tire issue and could do no better than seventh, a couple of places behind JPM.

It was a pretty eventful race, and just after half distance, JPM was leading Kimi, the pair of them quite a long way ahead of Jenson Button, who had started from pole. Under pressure from Michael Schumacher, Button then put his BAR-Honda into the famous wall at the exit of the last corner, which brought out the safety car. When JPM's guys finally told him to stop, he had just passed the pit entry. Damn! Kimi stopped okay, and took the opportunity to point out that his steering wheel was not straight. JPM came in next time around, got his fuel, and then drove out straight through the red light at the end of the pit road, his vision blocked by the red mist that had come down over his eyes after having to do the extra lap. All of which resulted in a black flag.

By now the track was not in good shape, and with his steering wheel askew, Kimi had a moment which allowed Schumacher to close right up for the last couple of laps. Kimi held off the Ferrari to take his third win and close the gap on championship leader Alonso, who had crashed out. It was a shame about JPM, because a one-two finish was looking likely.

At the end of the day, we were glad to get what we did, because when we checked Kimi's car and steering wheel, we found there was a loose nut on the right-hand track rod, giving him 11mm of toe-out. Eleven millimeters is a long way from what the setup sheet said, and the difference couldn't have helped the tire wear, never mind the problem of the incorrect steering wheel position!

The following Tuesday we flew to Indianapolis, where there is usually not much chaos, thanks to the place being very well run. But this time there was—and it wasn't the fault of Indianapolis Motor Speedway. There were some safety issues with the Michelin tires in the long fast corner before the pits, where Ralf Schumacher had a nasty shunt in the Toyota.

There were several ways to fix the problem, including slowing down the cars through that corner, which the Speedway was prepared to do. This was probably the only practical and sensible solution. Motor racing is still a dangerous sport today, and safety should be high on the list of priorities, closely followed by putting on The Show.

There were the usual issues regarding approval of any changes to the circuit. In the end the FIA people in charge of the sport would fail to provide The Show for their own political reasons—probably to appease 10 percent of the teams, including one team in particular. They decided that adding the proposed chicane would be unfair to the teams that were using Bridgestone tires—Ferrari, Jordan, and Minard—which hadn't had the same problems as the teams who were using Michelins. There was also the claim that reconfiguring the track might create its own set of safety issues.

The problem could have been fixed and approved, but the people running the sport failed to do so, instead finding a bunch of weak reasons for not doing anything. It is possible that the press could have helped to clarify the mess regarding the Michelin tire issues, although it has to be said that sometimes when there is a lot going on, it's hard for the press to get the correct information.

Of course, all this would happen on a weekend when Kimi in particular was quick in practice and qualifying. That may not have seemed to be the case when he was "only" second-fastest, but rumor had it that Jarno Trulli's Toyota only had about three laps of fuel on board when he took pole. (The rule was that cars had to start the race with the amount of fuel carried on board during qualifying.) JPM was 11th.

All of the field formed on the grid, but at the end of the parade lap, the Michelin runners, including JPM and Kimi, came into the pits, leaving the race with just the six cars running on Bridgestone tires. The fans thought this was a joke, and expressed their views in a variety of basic ways—booing, obscenities, and the rest. This is what pissed-off people do. This fiasco cost a lot of people a great deal of money and trashed the reputation of Formula One in the USA, potentially one of its most important commercial markets. Really well done, don't you think? What a shame.

We got to pack up early and go for a good steak dinner in one of Indianapolis's better restaurants, which sort of helped to get the bad political taste out of our mouths for a short time at least. Oh, and by the way—the race was "won" by Michael Schumacher, which had the unfortunate effect of allowing him to close in on Kimi's second place in the championship.

The only consolation (if you could call it that) was that Fernando Alonso's Renault, being a Michelin runner like McLaren, had not started the US Grand Prix either. But Alonso was to put that right with a win at Magny-Cours in France, with Kimi hanging in there, thanks to a strong second place after an eventful race for us.

There had been an engine problem on Friday for Kimi and a bit of bouncing around, deciding which spec engine to put in the car—which meant a late call on Friday evening. Of course, the engine change meant that he got put back 10 places from his qualifying position, which was third, but with about eight laps' more fuel than the others.

JPM, having qualified ninth, was running third when a hydraulic leak put him out of the race. A pretty impressive drive on Kimi's part got him into second place before his first pit stop.

There were several times near the end of a race when Kimi would slow somewhat, but these were not the result of a car issue. He then turned the fastest lap of the race, pointing out that he was actually okay. I would have to guess that starting third would have helped the intended outcome a lot more. The result, at the halfway point in the season, put Alonso on 69 points, with Kimi on 45. JPM was 11th on 16 points, but about to change that in the British Grand Prix.

On paper, things looked good after Kimi qualified 2nd to Alonso at Silverstone. In reality, he wound up 12th on the grid because of another engine failure and the same 10-place penalty for the second race in succession. There were some issues with the clutch on the new engine, but we left it alone, as there was not much time to do anything if something went wrong changing it.

JPM, having qualified third, just beat Alonso into Becketts Corner; Juan Pablo didn't have much to lose, whereas Alonso did. These two went at it really hard for 60 laps and finished a couple of seconds apart to give JPM his first (and very well-earned) win for McLaren. Kimi finished third, about 15 seconds behind, and might have been able to join in the fight for the lead had he not been held up quite a bit behind Michael Schumacher until his first pit stop. So both cars finished; it was good to have JPM take championship points off Alonso—but it sure as hell doesn't help starting 10 places back, thanks to reliability problems. Alonso, 77 points; Kimi, 51.

It was about this time that stories started to circulate concerning the departure of Adrian Newey from McLaren to Red Bull.

In the meantime, with Germany next on the calendar, we hadn't given up hope of winning another title in 2005. We got off to a good start when Kimi took pole position with a reasonable amount of fuel in the car. JPM should have made it an all-McLaren front row, but he forgot about the nasty bump in the middle of the last corner before the pits, and emerged onto the straight facing the wrong way before hitting the barrier. That meant a

Pole-winner Kimi Raikkonen leading the field at the 2005 San Marino Grand Prix at Imola. (LAT PHOTOGRAPHIC)

start from 20th and last place on the grid.

Kimi was pulling away from Alonso when, at about half distance, one of the hydraulic system bleed nipples started leaking fluid. It does tend to make you ill, watching the colored lines of the low pressure accumulator and hydraulic pressure slowly moving to the bottom of the computer screen; more so, of course, when you are nicely in the lead and quite quick. Yet another reliability issue, caused by a slightly loose hydraulic fitting. Alonso's win meant the championship table looked like this: Alonso, 87 points; Kimi, 51.

JPM did an impressive job, somehow getting up to ninth after a couple of laps, and then to third before his first pit stop on lap 27. Finishing second was a pretty damn good effort, along with the guys fixing the car after the qualifying off.

There is always a lot of work going on at the race track, but every now and again you tend to think, "Every night we seem to be *building* the car, not just putting it back together." Best go and get another cup of coffee, and look forward to the next race in Hungary.

Qualifying was a bit of a pain in the ass for Kimi. Failing to finish at Hockenheim meant he had to go out first on a track that is always dirty and provides very little grip to start with. A lower fuel load helped him to qualify fourth, directly behind JPM on the front row. Oh, and Michael Schumacher was on pole. Where did he come from? Perhaps he had some new tires? Schumacher led our two guys—JPM on a two-stop strategy, while Kimi was scheduled to stop three times. As the pit stops panned out, Schumacher was leading when he came in for his second stop; Kimi arrived in the next lap and, thanks to a light load of fuel and a very good pit stop by the guys, he got out ahead of the Ferrari.

Kimi, doing something he was quite good at, pulled out a 25-second lead in 11 laps, which gave him the opportunity to make his third stop without losing the lead. Schumacher probably backed off some, knowing the game was up (or at least Ferrari's technical director Ross Brawn did), finishing second. JPM lost third place with a broken CV joint.

Alonso came home 11th after a first-corner misunderstanding about available space for him. Alonso, 87; Kimi, 61.

A two-week break helped the trucks to deal with the extra long trip via a ferry from Italy to Istanbul and the first Turkish GP. A fascinating place, which is split by the Bosporus Strait. No one, of course, told us about the traffic. Our very nice hotel was a long way from the race track, and we had to use the large bridge over the Bosporus. At least the slow pace allowed us time to enjoy an excellent view. I'm sure there are people in Istanbul who set off for work in the morning and arrive at just about the time they should turn around to go home. There are also lots of shunts, mainly involving trucks, some of which come to rest quietly on their sides. We reached the circuit to find heavy security, but also buildings with lots of space. They'd done a really good job at Istanbul Park.

Having taken pole position, Kimi's start was not great, and he dropped to third behind the Renaults. But underbraking at the end of the long back straight, he went between Alonso and Fisichella!

JPM, fourth at this stage, was very fast, and by lap 14, he was second. With just a few laps to go, he passed one of the Jordans going into a slowish corner and then pulled across in front before locking the brakes; he must have forgotten the corner was there. The Jordan did its best to get stopped but hit the back of JPM, causing some damage to the floor. He was still second, but right at the end, he fell off on one of the high-speed corners, possibly because of the floor damage causing a loss of downforce. This was enough for Alonso to have a smile on his face as he grabbed second place. It was a bit of a strange act for someone with JPM's experience—and even worse, it gave Alonso a few more points. Alonso, 95; Kimi, 71.

The Tifosi were quieter than usual at Monza, especially after qualifying when Ferrari was sixth and seventh. At the previous race in Turkey, Schumacher had been at the back of the grid because of an engine change. We couldn't comment much because another failure on Kimi's car during practice dropped him 10 places from pole—a critical setback on such a high-speed place as this. Having gone quickest in qualifying with the car as full of fuel as you can get it, he had to start 11th, but at least JPM had inherited pole.

Kimi had to be careful with the tires, and it didn't help that he got stuck behind one of the slower cars until it stopped early. Able to push, and with the others either stopping or getting out of the way, Kimi was second before his pit stop.

Not long after that, however, he had a problem with his left-rear tire, probably caused by the extra load of fuel and his pace. It meant another stop costing 26 seconds and a climb back through the field.

JPM had led from the start, then began to have a similar problem with his left-rear, allowing Alonso to close in. JPM kept going, despite sliding about somewhat, and hung on just enough to win by three seconds from Alonso. Kimi finished fourth in the end, 20 seconds behind Alonso. It made you wonder what might have been but for that 26-second stop.

Sometime later, I had a chat with Italian journalist and artist Giorgio Piola, who told me about the heated conversation in the press room at Monza regarding Kimi's pole lap with the car full of fuel. He was amazed at how many people had no idea how impressive that lap actually was. One month on and he was still very frustrated about the lack of knowledge in the press room. That lap was one of those occasions when you could genuinely say that a driver had gone beyond his own self-imposed limits.

On Friday, September 2, at Monza, Lyndy Redding and her people at Absolute Taste, the catering company she founded, and which is part of the McLaren Group, did a 65th birthday dinner for me in the McLaren motor home. The engineers gave me a rather nice present of some great Italian wine, along with a very special Leica camera from Ron Dennis. Oh, and a kiss from all the girls; very special indeed!

Many thanks, guys: Ron Dennis, Steve Hallam, Dave Ryan, Pat Fry, Dave Redding, Dave Robson, Mark Slade, Phil Prew, Andy Latham, Sebastien Alberto, Phill Asbury, Phil Alexander, Richard Ford, Mike Elliott, Mike Negline, Tim Goss, Ed Gibson, Cian Shaffrey, Neil Martin, and Julian Hodgson.

It was straight to Spa, and being mid-September, the weather wasn't too kind in the Ardennes. There seemed to be a storm of a different kind brewing just as we were leaving the circuit on Thursday evening.

As I walked past Karl-Heinz Zimmermann's motor home, Bernie Ecclestone appeared and asked me to come in and sort out a dispute. Several journalists were arguing about Prost and Senna and wanted to know who I thought was the best. I mentioned Prost first, and a bunch of them quickly said, "See, we told you so." I had to stop the shouting and point out that I thought Prost was very good, but that Senna was quicker and more determined.

After rain throughout practice, it was wet again on Sunday morning, but not for the race. Saying that, the track was still damp, and the middle section remained wet for all but the last three laps. Most cars started on intermediates, including JPM and Kimi on the front row.

Early on, Fisichella had a large shunt at Eau Rouge, bringing out the safety car. Not wanting to have both cars in the pit at the same time, Kimi slowed down the whole field, while JPM kept going, which worked very well and gave us just enough time with the separate pit stops. Kimi had more fuel than JPM, ran a bit longer for the second stop, and came out in the lead.

Things were going well until about four laps from the end when JPM had a coming to-gether with a Williams on dry tires; it put them both out of the race and threw away some more very valuable points. Maybe JPM's guys should have told him to get out of the way, as the Williams was only trying to un-lap itself. Meanwhile, Kimi was untroubled at the front and nearly half a minute ahead of Alonso. Alonso, 111; Kimi, 86.

There may have been three races left but the championship was heading Alonso's way, particularly if he could finish at least third in Brazil. He made a good start by taking pole, with JPM on the outside and Kimi back in fourth due to a mistake at the first corner.

Alonso led the first two laps. Then JPM moved in front and stayed there for the rest of the race. Kimi moved into second to give McLaren our 40th one-two finish. But third was enough to see Alonso become the youngest-ever World Champion.

There was a feeling in the paddock that the championship belonged to both Kimi and Alonso, since they had won six races each at the time. But the fact was that Alonso had finished more races and hadn't been forced to start 10 places back several times.

There was no nonsense in Alonso's comments or feelings after the race. His compliments about Kimi were fine, as he added that now he could really have a race with McLaren. It was one way to make a subtle point about how to win a World Championship. Clever chap, Alonso. But wait a while, as we'll see that even he could make the odd mistake at times.

The Drivers championship may have been sorted, but the Constructors still had all to play for in in Japan and China. Everything was turned on its head at Suzuka, where changeable weather mixed up the grid, as the first half of the qualifying session was dry, and second half, wet. This put Kimi and JPM in 17th and 18th, with Alonso 16th.

It didn't rain for the race, but that did not prevent a fair amount of chaos on the opening lap, particularly when JPM hit the wall when trying to pass Villeneuve on the outside where there was only grass. JPM's crash was a high price to pay for trying to stay ahead of his teammate. His failure to finish meant the Constructors championship was pretty much flushed down the sewer.

There were more interesting bits yet to come, with Alonso passing Klien and then having to let the Red Bull back in front (as ordered by the stewards), only to pass him again, of course. Alonso then overtook Michael Schumacher around the outside of the very fast 130R corner—a ballsy move that gave the impression Michael Schumacher didn't think anyone would dare to do something like that.

Meanwhile, Kimi was stuck behind Schumacher until he passed the Ferrari in turn one and pulled away. By lap 38, Fisichella was leading Kimi by 19 seconds. But Kimi was not hanging around; Fisichella's lead was down to five seconds ahead, with about eight laps to go.

"You are five and a half seconds behind!" yelled Ron Dennis to Kimi, before turning to Dave Ryan and Phil Prew, who were just sitting there, and saying, "I want you guys to be calm!" Kimi's pace picked up a bit more until the two cars were a couple of tenths of a second apart. Kimi came on the radio to Steve Hallam and asked, "How many laps to go?" Steve said "One"; "Okay" was the quiet reply!

At the start of the last lap, Kimi went around the outside of the Renault at the first corner to take the lead and win the race—pretty damn good, from 17th on the grid. Even Kimi had some color in his face when he said he had to fight the whole race. What a treat for him and the whole team . . .

Traffic is something we hear about a lot on the race track, but in Shanghai traffic on the public roads brings you to a new level of awareness. Between the cars, trucks, motorbikes, bicycles, and carts all wanting the same space, and just missing each other most of the time, there is a lot of horn-blowing as well. After a while, you understand that using the horn isn't about saying, "Get out of the way," since there is usually no place to go anyway. It's actually meant to say, "I'm here—and I'm more than likely going to do something unexpected!"

Alonso took pole position in China thanks to Renault giving him a new spec engine, or one that was fresh for this race. Whatever its origin, it allowed Alonso to run it harder, whereas the McLaren drivers were on their second race with the same engines.

While Alonso took off in the lead, Fisichella in the other Renault was holding up Kimi.

It wasn't long before a drainage grate in the track came loose and JPM hit it, causing damage to one of his front tires. The appearance of the safety car changed the shape of the race regarding the fuel loads people were running. That became academic for JPM when his engine failed and put Kimi into second place. Kimi said his car felt much better after the second stop, and he set off after Alonso; it's always worth watching a driver not known to ever give up. In the end, we had to settle for second, but it might have been different without the first safety car.

And so ended an interesting year that really came to life for us by the time we reached Imola.

There were a few mistakes all around, but unreliability prevented Kimi from winning a bit more than seven races. The race summary (at right) points out the mistakes and reliability problems. It makes sad reading, not just for Kimi but also for the team.

At the end of the year, Mario Illien left the Mercedes-Ilmor Engine Company. Mario had originally established the company with Paul Morgan, but Ilmor had gradually been taken over by Mercedes-Benz. There was one part of the business that did not concern Mercedes-Benz. Ilmor, Inc. continued to be owned by Mario Illien, Roger Penske, DaimlerChrysler, and the estate of Paul Morgan. Ilmor, Inc. would be involved in preparing and, it was believed, developing the Honda engines for the Indy Racing League Series in the United States.

At the 2005 race team Christmas dinner, I was talking with Andy Latham, Mark Slade's right-hand man, when Andy's girlfriend asked me what I did on the team. Andy's reply was brief and memorable, "He keeps us honest." Thanks, Andy.

**Kimi Raikkonen
2005 Race Results Summary**

| GRAND PRIX | START | FINISH | REASON/COMMENTS |
|---|---|---|---|
| Australia | 10th | 8th | Stalled on grid |
| Malaysia | 6th | 9th | Tire valve failure |
| Bahrain | 9th | 3rd | |
| San Marino | 1st | DNF | CV joint failure while leading |
| Spain | 1st | 1st | |
| Monaco | 1st | 1st | |
| European | 2nd | 11th | Wishbone failure while leading |
| Canada | 7th | 1st | |
| United States | 2nd | DNS | |
| France | 13th | 2nd | Qualfied 3rd; started 13th after engine replacement penalty |
| Great Britain | 12th | 3rd | Qualfied 2nd; started 12th after engine replacement penalty |
| Germany | 1st | DNF | Hydraulic failure while leading |
| Hungary | 4th | 1st | |
| Turkey | 1st | 1st | |
| Italy | 11th | 4th | Qualfied 1st; started 11th after engine replacement penalty |
| Belgium | 2nd | 1st | |
| Brazil | 5th | 2nd | |
| Japan | 17th | 1st | |
| China | 3rd | 2nd | |

# 2006: From V10 to V8, and Montoya Moves On

For 2006 the FIA changed the engine specification, bringing in 2.4-liter V8s to replace the 3.0-liter V10 we'd been using. Due to development work, some of the new V8s were able to rev to 20,000 rpm, but it was also necessary to consider drivability and fuel consumption—not to mention our not-so-pleasant friend, reliability.

The first MP4/21A was started up on January 18 and sent off to Barcelona a couple of days later for Pedro de la Rosa to start testing, followed by Kimi Raikkonen a few days later. At that time Kimi was not too impressed with the engine; the word *turkey* was heard in the dark corners of the garage. Maybe it was the big difference between the V10 and the V8 that got his attention. Anyway, the next day it rained and then snowed.

Barcelona was followed by the usual round of testing at Valencia and Jerez, and then back to Valencia and Barcelona. At the second Valencia test there was an epic seven-hour effort to fit an Mk II front suspension to one of the cars, basically because no one knew where all the parts were. When it was asked why this had happened, the answer was the sound of silence.

I'm not sure we did a shakedown at Silverstone, as there were a lot of late things going on. All I do know is that Raikkonen, JPM, and Pedro de la Rosa covered about 8,500 kilometers in the MP4/21A, which is the equivalent of about 28 grand prix. You'd think after such impressive mileage, we'd be ready for the first race in Bahrain. Well, there was so much going on that on the Thursday in Bahrain, Richard Ford, one of the very good McLaren electronics gurus, made a comment about "struggling to be positive." At about 6:00 p.m. someone came into the garage and proudly announced that the engines needed to be changed in all three cars! It was starting to look a bit like a Third World civil service project.

The Bahrain weather was changing around a lot, mostly the direction of the wind, but I don't think that caused Kimi's wishbone to fail in qualifying. This meant he had to start 22nd, and last. The only good thing you could say was that not many people want to walk that far, and it was nice and quiet down on the back row. Certainly Schumacher and Massa in the Ferraris on the front row seemed a long way away.

Michael Schumacher and Fernando Alonso battled for the lead. Kimi was clawing his way through the field; with the extra fuel load running longer, it got him up to third, where he finished. The result was more than welcome for Mark Slade, Andy Laytham, Chris Thompson, and the guys on Kimi's car, as well as the whole team. JPM took fifth place. Having both cars finish was also well received by the Mercedes engine people on a day when Alonso won for Renault and Michael Schumacher took second for Ferrari.

The Renaults went even better in Malaysia when Fisichella led Alonso home for a one-two. JPM finished fourth behind Button's BAR-Honda, which was probably the best part of a pretty poor weekend for McLaren. Kimi had a shunt at the start so didn't finish.

Things had started badly with a bit of discontent and nonsense on Friday evening while waiting for gearbox parts, requested while we were in Bahrain, to arrive from England. At 8:15 p.m. two second-gear dog rings arrived, which allowed the race gearboxes to be finished. There must have been an international shortage if it was only possible to send two of the damn things. There was drama in the battle stations (our name for the home of the telemetry computers and software) regarding the logging set and sensors for the car data. All of this added to the fun and the need for another cup of coffee. Then, to round everything off, during the race Kimi was hit by Klien's Red Bull on the first lap and retired with a broken suspension.

On Monday, we moved from the Airport Hotel to the Sunway Lagoon, as we were staying in Kuala Lumpur for the week before going down to Melbourne. The Sunway Lagoon was becoming a home away from home, with some very good and helpful people working there. They were all friends with Mike Negline, our very efficient Mr. Fix-it, who knows

Raikkonen and his new teammate, test driver Pedro de la Rosa, before the 2006 French Grand Prix. (LAT PHOTOGRAPHIC)

everyone and always goes the extra mile in organizing the impossible.

It's a good thing we had been there for a while, because the 104-degree Fahrenheit (40-degree Celsius) heat of the past couple of days was enough for everyone.

The temperature and the mad pace had dropped when we reached Melbourne, where there was a fair bit more time for the boys to set up the garage. Qualifying was an improvement, too, as Kimi and JPM took fourth and fifth behind the two Renaults, but with Button getting a surprise pole position.

Button's advantage didn't last long. A safety car on the first lap saw Alonso get the jump on the BAR-Honda at the restart, and Kimi did the same thing to Button after another safety car a few laps later. The original start had been aborted thanks to Fisichella stalling his Renault, all of which helped JPM, who had managed to spin off while weaving about, warming up his tires. JPM was allowed to take his grid position as Fisichella was pushed away to start from the pit lane. That was not to be the only drama for JPM, as he spun off at the corner before the pits, hitting a bump hard enough to nicely shut off the ECU electronics—and his race.

The safety car would come out for a total of four times. Mark Slade used one of these periods to have Kimi's nose and front wing replaced after some bits had come off, all of which got Kimi back up to enough speed to keep second place.

Following the four-week period away from home McLaren was second in the Constructors championship, 19 points behind Renault, with Kimi third in the drivers' stakes behind the two Renault drivers.

The first race in Europe saw what looked like a bunch of new Bridgestone tires for the San Marino Grand Prix. That seemed to be the way of it, as Schumacher put his Ferrari on pole at Imola; we were back on the fourth row.

This general state of play probably caused Steve Hallam to tell the boys to "cover the blankets with the tires" when we were on the grid just before the start of the race. Everyone knew what Steve meant, but there would be a more-confusing message near the end of the race, when Ron Dennis instructed Steve to tell Kimi to "press the yellow button and pass Massa." I'm not sure what the hell Ron thought was going to happen, as Kimi was using everything he could get from the engine already, while doing his damnedest to make up for a bad start and get by the fourth-place Ferrari. Meanwhile, JPM was ahead of them both, finishing third behind Michael Schumacher's winning Ferrari and Alonso's Renault.

Clearly we had a lot of work to do if we wanted to return to being properly competitive and organized. With regard to the car, there were some feelings that this year's model "didn't come with a rabbit in a hat—just turkey feathers." It was not a question of giving up; that doesn't happen. But these thoughts were floating about as the Renaults looked very strong at this point.

The Nürburgring updates did bring some improvements for McLaren's 600th grand prix start, but we were still not players at the front, as Alonso took pole position ahead of Michael Schumacher. These two had a good fight in a race that Schumacher won, with Kimi finishing a close fourth. JPM had an engine failure seven laps before the end, but Kimi did think the car had made some progress, which made people feel a little bit better and more positive.

Steve Hallam, Mike Negline, systems engineer Ed Gibson, and I flew to Barcelona with the boys on the Monday afternoon. We arrived at about 7:30 p.m., the boys picking up their vans and heading off to their hotel. The rest of us went looking for our cars, having been given sets of keys before leaving the Nürburgring. Yes, there were several new Mercedes in the airport car park, but none that liked our two sets of keys. After several calls, Mike found someone who assured us that the cars were there. No, they were not! We knew that, having now spent almost an hour and a half scouring the Barcelona airport parking lot.

"Oh, dear. We must have brought the wrong cars to the airport." No shit, Dick Tracy! A person from Mercedes came and took us to where they kept cars that suited the keys we had. Fortunately, it was near the airport, and it was just as fortunate that they eat late in Spain. Dinner at the hotel was more than welcome, along with a drop of red. The problem locating our cars was a bad start to a weekend that didn't get much better, Kimi doing about four laps on Friday and qualifying 9th, with JPM 12th. Kimi got himself up to 5th in the race, but no further; JPM spun off and beached himself on a curb.

Monaco always has its standard problems: steering lock, brake cooling, engine cooling, and what Flavio Briatore calls "the Armco too close to the cars." (Thank you, Flavio.) But in 2006, we had something else as well. The engine had an idle issue which generated a lot of heat—not great at Monaco, where the speed can be quite slow at times. During Thursday practice, a small fire by the side of the engine on Kimi's car burned some wires and bodywork. There was a fair bit of thrashing to make some suitable heat shields in time to get Kimi out for the second practice; even Ron Dennis was in there, cutting solid rivets to length for Gavin Beresford and the rest of us to stitch something together. I wanted to do something about getting cool air into the "hot" area of the engine, but some people thought that wouldn't work. I thought it was a mistake not to have at least tried something.

There are always surprises at Monaco, and this year was no different when Michael Schumacher stopped at Rascasse with the nose of his Ferrari a couple of centimeters from the Armco. Oh, and the engine "stalled" as well! This happened on the last lap of qualifying, just as Alonso was on a quick lap. It meant yellow flags and no pole position for Fernando.

Michael Schumacher didn't get away with it this time. The word *deliberately* was racing up and down the pits soon after his purported misfortune. He was sent to the back of the grid, with Alonso taking Schumacher's place on pole. In the race, Kimi chased Alonso's leading Renault until the safety car appeared on lap 49. The leaders came into the pits and Kimi's stop was fine. Unfortunately, he followed someone slowly down the pit lane and then came out just behind the safety car, which meant going slowly for two laps. The heat/fire demon struck again on the left-hand side, which meant second place burned and melted onto the exhaust pipes.

JPM was more fortunate, as he came out of his stop to a clear track and was able to go up the hill quickly enough to cool things down. He would finish second behind Alonso. But thinking about Kimi's problem, it pissed me off more than others.

Kimi's dramas, albeit less damaging, continued at the British Grand Prix. On the last run in qualifying the right-hand Helga's horn (our name for the aerodynamic "horn" on each side of the engine cover) fell off, as well as the "cat flap" for the refueling hatch.

The car was working much better, thanks to a few more upgrades, which helped Kimi to the outside of the front row, alongside Alonso. (Mark Slade had been holding his breath, having added a bit more downforce to the car setup, which I thought had merit based on something we had done before with Mika.) The race was what you could call a walk in the park for Alonso, with Kimi finishing third after a great tussle with Michael Schumacher. JPM was over half a minute behind in sixth place, but not even those points would help us from falling even further behind Renault and Ferrari in the Constructors championship.

It wasn't much better for us at the Canadian Grand Prix, where Alonso, Michael Schumacher, and Kimi repeated the Silverstone result. We might have made it a better show if there hadn't been a problem with Kimi's clutch on both pit stops, which lost him a lot of time. He had more fuel than Alonso at the start and he did set fastest lap in the race.

JPM managed to have two shunts early on in the race, the second one finishing him off. The first triggered a fair bit of leaping about when he needed a nose, tires, and fuel. It didn't help that Phil Prew, his race engineer, was not on the pit wall timing stand dealing with

JPM's radio, having gone to the garage for a few minutes. This meant Ron Dennis was on the radio instead. Not ideal.

If we thought qualifying at the Indianapolis Grand Prix was bad a week later, the race was even worse. Kimi and JPM started from 9th and 11th before Montoya went into the back of Raikkonen at the second corner and put both of them out of the race. Well done! This is definitely not what I would really like to say. The expression on the face of the chairman of DaimlerChrysler (at that time, Mercedes' parent company) pretty much said it all.

Even the journey home had some turmoil. The flight out of Indy to Chicago was late, and it was a good thing that British Airways had three flights from Chicago to Heathrow. The first one had a bird strike in one of its engines; the second had some problem with cracks in the windscreen. We made the third flight thanks to the nice lady at BA who kept changing our boarding passes to suit.

JPM's collision at Indianapolis turned out to be the final straw in his relationship with McLaren, and he left to start a new life in NASCAR with Chip Ganassi Racing. JPM is a talented race driver, but he seemed to flush a fair bit of that down the loo on a few occasions, especially at times when his talent could have been very helpful. I guess there were other things on his mind.

His place for the French Grand Prix was taken by Pedro de la Rosa (PDR), who qualified seventh at Magny-Cours to line up directly behind Kimi. Pedro did a reasonable job—his testing having helped a lot—to finish seventh, a couple of places behind Kimi.

The gap between our two drivers was much greater during qualifying at Hockenheim, mainly because Kimi's pole position came from not having the correct amount of fuel in the car, making it lighter than it should have been. There had been a radio communications error in connection with the words *laps* and *kilos*. I know the two words don't sound alike; perhaps it was just the number that was heard. Either way, it was not a PR stunt for the German GP, which turned out to be a Schumacher show, as he won ahead of Ferrari teammate Felipe Massa. Kimi took third after being on a three-stop strategy, hindered by a slow pit stop, blistered tires, and a hydraulic issue.

PDR had a fuel-line connection problem inside the fuel tank that caused him to stop on the second lap. When the car got back to the factory, it took a while to understand how the problem had manifested itself, and why it happened at the start of the race rather than in practice or qualifying, as a missing part of the connector could not be found. Of course, the fact that it was missing could have been the reason. It was fixed in time for the Hungarian Grand Prix, where Kimi took pole and led from the start, and PDR, having qualified fourth, jumped into the second spot after four laps. Kimi was one of the first to stop on lap 17, at which point things were just about to turn to shit. Kimi was looking in his mirrors to let Pedro, who was doing three stops, go by when he ran into and then over Tonio Liuzzi's Toro Rosso. PDR managed to miss the flying collection of parts and carried on.

The order at the front then changed quite a bit, as Alonso lost a front wheel after his pit stop, allowing Button to move into the lead. Meanwhile, Michael Schumacher was doing one of his usual things, banging wheels and cutting across the chicane and not giving the place back to PDR. Did anyone in the FIA warn or punish Michael then or after the race? Of course not. Pretty disgusting, really!

A short time later, Schumacher ran into the back of Nick Heidfeld after the BMW had passed the Ferrari. Why was Schumacher not punished for these misadventures? Did everyone think they could get away with this sort of thing? It wasn't great for an endeavor that is meant to be a "sport" with rules of some kind. None of this affected Jenson Button on the way to his first win, while PDR did a great job finishing second, which wasn't bad considering that by mistake, he still had quite a bit of fuel in his car.

Kimi was in the wars again in Turkey, where trouble started when Alonso got squeezed by the two Ferraris, producing a chain reaction with cars going everywhere. Although PDR did get hit, he made it through the mess. Kimi got hit several times, the last one puncturing a rear tire and doing damage to the car's floor.

With part of it falling off, there was no point in trying to continue. There were pieces of carbon everywhere but no safety car, which we all thought was kind of strange. But it didn't stop Massa from winning his first race, with PDR coming home fifth on a one-stop strategy.

With the Italian Grand Prix next, that meant the usual pre-race test at Monza. At one point, someone had set up the tires in their heaters just behind the battle stations. This wasn't a great move, as it was already 95 degrees Fahrenheit (35 degrees Celsius) in the garage—hot enough to cook the computers as well as the people trying to use them.

Come qualifying we had a classic stitch-up of Alonso by the FIA when they claimed he had "impeded" Massa—who happened to be driving a Ferrari, of course. As someone pointed out, if the Ferrari driver thought he was close enough to be slowed down, perhaps his Super License should be reconsidered. At least the Italians were pissed-off when Kimi took pole position! This set up a race-long fight which Michael Schumacher eventually won. Schumacher was intending to announce his retirement on the podium, but the press release went out during the race, spoiling the surprise. Kimi backed off near the end to save the brakes and engine, while PDR's engine had failed in the middle of the race.

It was Kimi's turn to retire after running second in the early stages of the Chinese Grand Prix. The engine throttle on one side started acting up, sticking in various positions—sure as hell not what you wanted. So there we were in a good track position with a fair amount of fuel, only to then drop out. After the race, the engine people found a tiny washer that was part of the throttle control system getting caught up every so often. You couldn't make it up, could you? People just need to learn to do a better job when there is a lot going on.

The only good thing to say about Suzuka—where Kimi came in 5th and Pedro 11th—was that both cars finished, helping the workload for Brazil, where the cars were going straight from Japan.

As we've seen, Sao Paolo and Interlagos have a lot of things that other race tracks don't have. Some you might talk about, but others—such as the topless and bottomless clubs, with a fair bit of pornography thrown in, along with the transvestites—well, it's probably better not to continue the list! The main thing is the passion of the Brazilian people, a great deal of which was created by Ayrton Senna and others before him, such as Emerson Fittipaldi and Nelson Piquet. But there's no doubt that Ayrton increased that passion by several degrees. This is what's important about Interlagos—it doesn't matter that a guy is painting the metal wire fence with his bare hands and a rag, or that the electrical guys are checking the wires in the garage with their fingers. The point is, Interlagos remains a damn good race track.

The trip from the Sao Paolo airport to the hotel seemed to take nearly as long as our flight via Amsterdam. You could say we saw a great deal of Sao Paulo that we had never seen before—so much that the other guys on the flight had showered, changed, and were going out to dinner when we arrived.

Fifth and eighth places for Kimi and PDR hardly signified a good result, but second place for Alonso was enough to give him the championship for the second year in succession. Massa, the boy from Sao Paulo, won, and the passion in the grandstands flowed onto the track. It had been quite a long time since a Brazilian had won here, and Massa took a Brazilian flag from a spectator, which was fantastic for him. Was there a stink from the FIA about this? I don't think so. There had been a rule implemented by the FIA to stop this sort of thing from happening at the end of races, for safety reasons. This is not meant to take away from the win from Massa, who is a very nice guy with a great deal of passion for his home country.

Alonso and Schumacher shaking hands before the Brazilian Grand Prix, where Alonso's second-place finish was enough to give him a second World Championship. (LAT PHOTOGRAPHIC)

Third place for McLaren in the Constructors championship marked the end of a somewhat fraught, up-and-down season, with reliability issues and inconsistent performances.

You may have noticed that for someone with my experience, there are a great many aspects of motor racing that are the same over and over again, with a few things thrown in to spice things up. The genuinely hard part is not to let it get to you. There are some very good bits, some very sad ones, and a lot that are just plain frustrating almost every race weekend. There are times when you can be disappointed, disgusted, appalled, and mystified by some people's egos. The focus and dedication needed to solve these issues, along with working with some very good people, is what keeps you from tearing off your clothes and running naked across the nearest field.

# 2007: The Champ and the Challenger: Alonso and Hamilton

n 2007, when the FIA made changes to freeze the engine rules, someone at Mercedes had the foresight and guts to find the funding, along with a few new people who knew what they had to do.

This involved lots and lots of work, and the outcome was a much better engine for 2007. I thought it was one of the best things that had happened in a long time. Some people didn't think it was a good rule because it meant you couldn't fiddle around with the engine. But the truth was, you could if you needed to by making the engine more "reliable." As long as you have something good to start with, you have a better chance of having reasonable reliability.

The Kid was gone, along with his cohort, Mark Arnall. Raikkonen was replaced with two-time World Champion Fernando Alonso, a very, very good race driver who knows how to win races, but who also had (as we were going to find out) a small weak spot.

Also new to the team was Lewis Hamilton, who had been looked after by Ron Dennis and McLaren from karts upwards. Lewis could have driven in the last couple of races of 2006, but someone had talked him out of it. He did a short test at Silverstone and didn't act like the guy you thought he should be. Of course, it's possible that he was just being careful. Strange, because at one of the early tests in 2007, he was quick right away, just as one would have expected from his past record.

There was also a strange thing that happened when both drivers were present at the launch of the new Mercedes McLaren SLR Roadster. When it was rolled out, the car had a No. 2 on it. One would have thought that with the two-time F1 World Champion present, it would have carried a No. 1, the same as his MP4/22A. I think someone else (probably Spanish!) thought that as well. Perhaps it was meant to mean two World Championships? Probably not . . .

With a race in Abu Dhabi planned for the future, Bernie Ecclestone had set up a demo on the city streets with several of the teams. I went to Abu Dhabi, along with Guy Rogers, one of the race team gearbox guys, and the demo/test team (all a good bunch), plus Simon Moule and Steve Brodie from Mercedes HPE. It was interesting for me to see how the other teams dealt with this sort of thing. A couple of them did quite a few demos and I made a bunch of notes and took some photos, which I later gave to Steve Hallam.

Alonso showed up to drive the car. He and Ron Dennis had just flown in that morning. It was an interesting place and the demo went off okay, except for a couple of people spinning their cars around and stalling, which disrupted the show a bit and did not please Mr. Ecclestone.

There was also a show put on in downtown Valencia, with both Alonso and Hamilton using the 2006 cars, but with the new red-and-silver color scheme reflecting our new sponsor, Vodafone. The proper testing of the new car began at the Valencia race track a couple of days later. Hamilton shunted the MP4/22A03 badly enough at the second Valencia test to have it sent back to the factory for repairs. We had now completed the usual tests in Barcelona, plus a long test in Bahrain, which we had not done before.

There was some interest at this time in a movie about Bruce McLaren, and it was in the early stages of being put together in New Zealand. The man behind the intended film was Barrie Osborne, the producer of *The Matrix* and the Lord of the Rings films.

I received several inquiries from Barrie regarding my thoughts on working with Bruce in the early days of the team. Since he was going to be at Abbey Road in London, the recording studio made famous by the Beatles, to record the musical score for his new film, *The Water Horse*, he asked me to come up and have a chat. Barrie was a very interesting guy and asked a lot of straight, commonsense questions regarding Bruce and motor racing in general. Before I left, we went into a very large studio to listen to some of the background music being recorded for his movie.

What an experience to go into Abbey Road and be shown around! You may think it a strange comment to make, but to me, it seemed like you could "feel" the music while being shown around various recording rooms where some great songs were once made.

It was back to more-familiar music as practice got under way for the first race of 2007 in Melbourne. Raikkonen (who had replaced the retiring Schumacher at Ferrari) took pole, with Fernando second and Lewis qualifying fourth for his first grand prix.

At the start Hamilton jumped into second place by running around the outside of Alonso as he fended off Kubica's Renault at the first corner, only to later lose the place to Fernando when he ran a couple of laps longer at the second pit stop. But you could say a point had been made—and it hadn't gone unnoticed, particularly by Alonso.

Raikkonen won his first race for Ferrari, but there were some issues with his car's "bib," a part of the floor that sticks out from the bottom of the chassis just below the driver. The question concerned the way the bib was mounted and whether it was stiff enough. Yet the car still ran in the race and won. Hmmm . . . The flexibility of the bib would have offered an aerodynamic advantage similar to ground-effects bodywork. Shortly thereafter the FIA issued a clarification on the stiffness of the bib and how it would be measured.

We stayed in Melbourne for a few days before going up to Kuala Lumpur and the Sunway Lagoon Hotel. We spent the day by the pool after we arrived before going out to the track to get set up for what would be an epic test. Some of the guys worked on race-car rebuilds while the rest of us worked on testing. There were new parts coming out from England almost every day. De la Rosa started the test and Lewis took over before handing back to Pedro for a day and a half—when it rained. When Pedro returned to the cockpit, he immediately thought there was something wrong compared to when he had driven the car a few days before. The setup was put back to where it had been when de la Rosa had finished running, and he was a lot happier.

Paul Barnes, one of the new embedded systems guys, had an opportunity to run the car system monitor on the chassis side, which gave me more time to look at the colored lines and help resolve a couple of things with Ed Gibson, one of the electronics engineers, regarding the fuel system. Paul did a very good job, and this gave him confidence in dealing both with the system monitor and the car.

Dave Redding and Steve Hallam had decided we should get away from the track no later than 1:00 a.m. each night. It turned out to be a bit later every time, except for the last night of the test. Just to make you feel better, it was usually about 92 degrees Fahrenheit (33 degrees Celsius) and 70 percent humidity on the way back to the hotel in the early hours.

On the Friday night of race weekend someone was heard to say, "We have a rather large factory that should be doing this—but, then again, it would take them two weeks and probably wouldn't fit, so we're going to do it tonight." They finished at about 3:00 in the morning. The comment was prompted by some parts that we had sent back to the factory for modification—except that they were sent back to us with nothing having been done.

The race started okay, with the usual dodging and weaving at the first and second corners. Alonso (second on the grid) came out in the lead with Hamilton (fourth) following Fernando, after they both got the jump on Massa's pole-position Ferrari. Massa had a couple of goes trying to get by Hamilton, but they didn't work. I guess Felipe hadn't watched any of Lewis's 2006 GP2 races. The order stayed the same, at least for our guys, until the finish. It was very satisfying to finally have a one-two, particularly after all the hard work during that epic test the week before the race.

Both drivers said it had been a hard race because of the heat and humidity. The liquid in the drinks bottles had been as hot as old morning tea, and tasted about the same.

We left Kuala Lumpur on Monday and flew straight to Bahrain, getting to the hotel just in time for a sandstorm. That was appropriate in some ways, because there would soon be the beginnings of another kind of storm brewing on one side of the garage at the Sakhir track.

Qualifying was more or less to the 2007 pattern, in that as Massa took pole, Lewis was second, with Fernando, running a bit more fuel, fourth-fastest behind Raikkonen's Ferrari. In the race Massa won, but Lewis, pleased with the handling of his car, was able to stay with the Ferrari and finish second. Fernando had not been happy with his car more or less from the start, and knew he was in for a long, hard race.

During a three-week break before the next race, we did a film shoot at Silverstone for Mercedes using the MP4/22 and a DTM car, made all the more interesting when the clutch acted up on the F1 car.

A lot of people showed up in Barcelona to see Alonso, but the Spanish Grand Prix didn't quite work out the way they, or Fernando, wanted. The race to the first corner, one of the longest in Formula One, didn't go to plan, as Massa and Alonso—starting from the front row—were side by side. It was Fernando who fell off and came back on the track, just missing several other cars. The fans were not pleased, and neither was he. And to make things worse, he would eventually finish third behind Massa's winning Ferrari and his

Hamilton battles with Alonso at the 2006 season's last race in Brazil. It was Alonso's final race with the McLaren team. (LAT PHOTOGRAPHIC)

teammate, Lewis.

This put Hamilton into the lead of the championship, which was quite impressive. All of this had the British press leaping about. The hype was getting close to the point of making one sick, and getting closer to causing some damage. (Stay tuned; that's coming up next.)

At Monaco, Hamilton didn't get off to a good start during Thursday practice when he had a shunt at St. Devote that was bad enough to require a chassis change.

It was helpful to have the free day on Friday, which gave Paul "Taff" James, the number-one mechanic on Hamilton's car, and his guys a reasonable amount of time to do the job. Certainly everything was put right for qualifying, as Fernando took pole, with Lewis alongside. Raikkonen would start from the back of the grid after a strange kind of shunt at the exit of the swimming pool. He must have had some understeer and the front decided to grip just at the wrong time, because he hit the Armco well before the corner apex.

That helped set up the evening for an even better dinner at the Pizzeria Monegasque, where we stopped on the way back to the hotel. It was a treat to see George Lucas, who had been coming to Monaco for several years and always stopped by for dinner and to say hello. There was a pretty good group of us: Dave Redding, Phill Asbury, Ed Gibson, journalist David Tremayne, my girlfriend Jane Nottage, Joe Saward, and a late-arriving Neil Oatley. It was Roy Reader, one of our truckies, who found the place sometime in the 1970s.

Fernando led Lewis for the whole race, although there was a point when Hamilton, who had more fuel, might have gotten ahead. But he did not really speed up at that crucial point, and then made his pit stop a couple of laps earlier than planned.

Monaco is a tough place to win, and Alonso was driving to save the car, so going quicker was not a problem. But Hamilton was right on his ass (not clever!), with Massa about a minute behind. There was a lot of radio traffic from Lewis, wanting Fernando to get out of the way. It was pointed out that Alonso was driving at a reasonable pace at that point in the race, and that Lewis should back away from him to avoid any contact, since we were first and second. It was near the end of the race, and this was no time to screw around. There was some more radio traffic, and in the end Lewis sort of got the message.

The first three did the usual business on the podium and were then carted off to the media center, which was where the trouble gained momentum. Lewis had talked about the fuel in his car, the pit stop, and why he wasn't allowed to pass his teammate, saying such things as, "I've only got a number two on my car; he's got a number one on his." Someone should have pointed out that was because the other guy—the two-time World Champion—had *earned* the number 1. The mind boggled . . .

The atmosphere quickly became somewhat poisonous as the (mainly) British press, led by the usual suspects from the nationals, set about suggesting that McLaren had manipulated the race so that Alonso could win. This whole scene had probably been set off by Hamilton not thinking about what his oral runoff could cost the team, who were doing nothing more than hoping both of their cars finished. Teamwork has never been high on the list of priorities for quite a few drivers, who sometimes forget the fact that there is no "I" in the word *team*.

As Alonso sat throughout the press attack, with another nail hammered into his fragile psyche, he was probably becoming more convinced that his future did not lie with the "English team." Either way, the McLaren press officer emerged, saying the media center had been "like a bear pit," or words to that effect.

The subsequent suggestion in the media that McLaren had manipulated the race led to issues with the FIA—just what you don't need, and a waste of valuable time, as everyone had to go poring through the information requested. Not very clever, really. If anyone was being manipulated, it was the press, as they would come to realize later on.

The mood, certainly among the Brit Pack media, was very different in Montreal when Lewis won his first grand prix—the first of many, you suspected. Fernando did not have such a happy time after qualifying second to Lewis on pole, and then getting it all wrong trying to take the lead into turn one. He didn't make the corner, but managed to keep going.

This happened several times, and then he was caught out by the safety car in that he had to stop for fuel before the pit lane was open. Not a clever rule, as your fuel consumption is not based on when the pace car *might* come out. This cost Alonso a 10-second stop-go penalty to add to everything else that was not going very well. The off-road excursions seemed out of place for someone as talented as Fernando, and he was not at all happy with seventh place when his teammate was on top of the podium.

Now that he had the flavor of winning, Lewis did it again a week later at Indianapolis. We had a race-long battle between the two of them. At one point Alonso was coming down the long pit straight with his car right up to the pit wall in an attempt to point out that he was actually quicker than Hamilton. If it hadn't been for a slight glitch on his out lap after one of the pit stops, Fernando might well have gotten ahead.

Either way, the one-two finish was a great effort from the drivers, the Mercedes HPE engine people, and the whole team. As an added treat for me, my longtime friends, Paul

Wuori, Larry Cronin Jr., and his son Tucker were there as well.

Packing up having gone quite a bit faster than usual, Dave Ryan organized food and drinks in the Hilton when we all got back. Needless to say, a good time was had by all. A late-running flight from Indy to Chicago, followed by the Chicago-to-Heathrow flight arriving two hours behind schedule at the new Terminal 5, reinforced the thought that the race was a hell of a lot better than the journey home.

The Ferraris were back on the pace for the French GP and Fernando's problems were compounded by a failed bearing and gearbox at the start of Q3. It took more than an hour of really serious effort to change both. Not getting out in Q3 and replacing the gearbox as well as the engine meant he faced a start from 10th place. Lewis, meanwhile, had qualified 2nd alongside Massa.

The race was won by Raikkonen, as he managed to get past Massa in traffic. Hamilton hung on to third, a long way behind the two Ferraris. Alonso, stuck in traffic for most of the race, finished seventh. And just to round things off, the charter flight from Clermont-Ferrand to Luton was late, which meant we arrived home at about 2:00 a.m. on Monday morning, knowing the British GP was the following weekend. And then, as if there wasn't enough going on, a big story broke connecting McLaren with Ferrari technical drawings. This was to be the start of something that was more than just a mess, and would run for most of the summer.

While all this was kicking off in the Silverstone paddock, the guys in the garage concentrated on what we were there for. They did pretty well, as Lewis took a very popular pole position for his first home grand prix, with Fernando qualifying third behind Raikkonen.

Lewis led the race until the first pit stop, where he had a small problem with the lollipop at the getaway, all of which allowed Raikkonen into the lead. Fernando took his turn in front, but in the end had to give way to Raikkonen because the Ferrari had more fuel and was running a longer stint. Lewis got on the podium—as he had done at every race in his F1 career so far—but you could see he really would have liked to have won his first home GP. One way or another, it had been a pretty tense weekend, and it was good to leave by the back gate, take the old road most of the way back to the M25, and get home by about 8:30 p.m. Quite a change for race night!

With the drama at Silverstone centered on the paddock, it shifted to the track for most of the weekend at the Nürburgring. A wheel-gun maintenance problem caused Lewis to have a shunt during Q3, which put him down to 10th on the grid. Fernando was eight places

Lewis Hamilton celebrates after his apparent win at the 2007 Belgian Grand Prix. He'd later learn that a 25-second penalty would give his victory to Ferrari's Felipe Massa. (LAT PHOTOGRAPHIC)

Kimi Raikkonen in the garage before the 2007 Brazilian Grand Prix. His resourceful race engineer Mark Slade is in the background. (LAT PHOTOGRAPHIC)

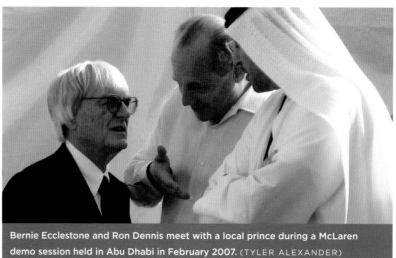

Bernie Ecclestone and Ron Dennis meet with a local prince during a McLaren demo session held in Abu Dhabi in February 2007. (TYLER ALEXANDER)

further forward on the front row.

A lot of that became academic when rain started to fall not long after the start. Lewis had a puncture and stopped for tires, then fell off in the worsening conditions and got himself stuck in the gravel at the first corner. Pat Fry told him to stay in the car and keep it running, which he did. The nice marshals got the crane to lift the car out of the gravel and set it down on the race track. Lewis, with his seat belts still done up and the engine running, selected first gear and drove away. Just brilliant—good call, Mr. Fry.

When the race was finally stopped, there was a fair bit of confusion getting the cars lined up correctly on the grid. In the midst of all this, and with time running out, Dave Redding arrived at Alonso's car looking for a tool that could remove the rocks that had become jammed in the starter motor entry hole in the floor of Hamilton's car. He finally managed to overpower these rocks just in time for the restart once the rain had stopped.

This being the Nürburgring, of course, it wasn't long before the rain returned and brought more pit stops for wet tires. Alonso found himself second to Massa, but four laps from the finish, Fernando decided it was "time" and went down the inside of the Ferrari with a bold move. There was no way Massa was going to recover from the shock, and Alonso took his third win of the season. Hamilton was out of the points in ninth, having had more things go wrong than one would have thought possible in a single race.

As Mark Slade said afterward, "Well, we have a wet setup; now all we need is a dry one." Raikkonen had failed to finish, so Lewis and Fernando were leading the championship with just two points between them. But when we got to Hungary a couple of weeks later, it seemed our guys were intent on fighting each other rather than the opposition.

Qualifying was going okay until Q3. In 2007, Q3 was all about burning off fuel and making sure your car was as light as possible for a final lap on fresh tires. Each team, however, would split their options by having one driver go flat out to burn off a lot of fuel, while the other, doing the same number of laps, would go slower, use less, and yet be credited with the same amount of fuel (based on the number of laps completed) when the car was prepared for the first phase of the race. That way, the second driver would be able to run longer in the first phase of the race, an advantage which would offset being a bit slower than his teammate because he'd had more fuel on board in Q3.

The other reason for having different strategies, with one driver going slower than the other during Q3, was that it helped us operationally in the pits by not having both drivers come in at once for their final set of tires. That was the theory, anyway.

In Hungary, Hamilton was supposed to be the driver who would save fuel, but when he got to the end of the pit lane first at the start of Q3 and showed no sign of letting his teammate by, Alonso's fuse was lit. After Alonso made his pit stop for the second set of tires and was told to go, he just sat there.

Hamilton, meanwhile, had arrived for his tires and had to wait. Alonso stayed long enough to prevent Hamilton from completing another qualifying lap. Alonso's final lap was quick enough for pole position, which was his response to feeling that he had been stitched up by Hamilton. Lewis was allegedly discovered hiding in a steward's office late in the evening, trying to find out what was going on. The steward was pretty surprised to discover the driver leading the World Championship hiding behind his sofa, refusing to come out. He had to conduct a conversation with said driver crouched between the sofa and the fridge. The situation had just turned into a farce.

A comment from Alan Jones summed up Alonso's qualifying performance, "Pretty impressive lap when you're that pissed-off. I wouldn't have made it around the second corner." It was not a clever thing to do on Alonso's part, but it had nothing to do with the team per se. It was a personal thing between two drivers, one of whom didn't stick to the plan.

Of course, the controlling arm of the FIA took up the charge, taking many hours during the stewards' inquiry to tell Alonso he had to start sixth, and then providing no explanation whatsoever about why McLaren would not be able to score any Constructors championship points. The guys on the team simply wanted to know what the hell was going on—and why there was so much fallout from what was just a scrap between the two drivers.

Lewis, now on pole position, drove very well and held off Raikkonen for most of the race; Fernando came home fourth. The win may have edged Hamilton seven points clear of Alonso, but there didn't seem to be much time to appreciate that as the tension increased over the so-called "Spygate" affair, which involved Ferrari's former chief mechanic Nigel Stepney and McLaren engineer Mike Coughlan. The controversy centered on claims that sensitive Ferrari technical drawings had been given to McLaren.

The mood was not helped by the McLaren/Ferrari thing bringing out a side of Alonso that was not pleasant, as he allegedly attempted to warn Ron Dennis on the Sunday morning of the Hungarian Grand Prix.

Meanwhile, everyone was looking for Nigel Stepney (one of the two main culprits in the Ferrari drawings mess), the former Ferrari man allegedly on a beach in the Philippines. Not a bad idea, really.

The two free weekends between Hungary and Turkey had done nothing to stop the media stirring up the tension between our two drivers. Ron Dennis had tried to dampen things by getting the two guys together in our Istanbul hotel before going to the track. On the surface, everything looked okay—only for Alonso to tell BBC Radio 5 Live that he'd given McLaren half a second in the car since he had first driven it and he didn't think the team was giving it back—whatever that meant. He forgot to say that some of us had tried to talk to him and help, but he didn't seem to be listening.

Once we got down to the proper business of the weekend, our two guys found themselves on the dirty side of the grid. Lewis was second-fastest and Fernando fourth, with the two Ferraris, led by Massa, first and third.

Being on the dirty side seemed to be more of a problem at Istanbul Park than other places, maybe because of the short distance to the quite awkward first corner. The two Ferraris led all the way. Hamilton was third until the right-front tire let go as he went through turn eight, the very long left-hander. Lewis made it back to the pits for a new set of tires and finished fifth, a good effort at the end of a day that saw Fernando take third, with just 16 points now covering the first four drivers in the championship: Hamilton, Alonso, Massa, and Raikkonen.

A few of us stayed on Monday with the boys, changing the engines and doing various things. It rained hard in the afternoon, and it took about two hours to do a 45-minute return trip to the hotel, complete with a count of 17 shunts. Dave Redding did a great job driving in the mind-boggling traffic to get us back in one piece.

We noticed that the local people have it well planned: When the traffic stops, they are straight onto the road, selling water, fruit, candy, and who knows what else. And the entertainment wasn't over yet. The bus taking us to the airport at 5:15 a.m. on Tuesday morning ended up leaving the hotel late, as the substantial electric security gate wouldn't open to let us out.

The fact that we had to wear plain shirts with no McLaren logos while traveling between the hotel and the race track at Monza was a reminder that this was Italy, where the cheap, petty politics of racing had gotten even worse.

All of this was very distracting for the management, but we got on with preparing the cars—a job which took even longer than usual when, at 11:20 on Friday night, we started Alonso's car and found a problem with reverse gear. After removing the gearbox, the problem was quickly sorted. Loctite is wonderful stuff; it just needs to be applied in the

Ron Dennis congratulates Pat Fry for his clever pit work during the 2007 European Grand Prix at the Nürburgring. (TYLER ALEXANDER)

right place. Certainly all was well for qualifying—at least, on the track—when Fernando and Lewis took the top two places.

Politics returned when the Carabinieri showed up at the McLaren Brand Center. Were they looking for Ron Dennis, Martin Whitmarsh, the drawings, or just an espresso? The feeling was that they didn't know themselves; they had simply been told to go there by certain people to make a show. With the media busy in the press room concentrating on qualifying, it was not surprising when a few key team members received phone calls from inside the building to inform them that there were several Carabinieri floating around, and hinting where they might be found.

Of course, no one was led away in handcuffs, but a few espressos were consumed, a conversation with Martin ensued, and the police officers were seen leaving the Brand Center clutching McLaren caps and looking very happy.

Alonso looked the same when he won the race, with Lewis giving McLaren a one-two for the first time at Monza. It was almost too much for poor Ron, who, after a weekend of continuing politics, became a bit emotional when his team gave Ferrari a kicking on their home ground.

The Tifosi in the grandstands were not that pleased, but the McLaren people sure as hell were. A post-race photo of the team, along with a special trophy the team presented to Ron Dennis regarding the Constructors championship, said it all.

The Constructors championship became the talking point at Spa—mainly because McLaren had now been excluded from it and fined $100 million for its part in Spygate.

It seemed a very harsh penalty, particularly when the FIA admitted that there was nothing on the MP4/22 that was connected with Ferrari in any way. It was difficult to assume anything other than a clash of personalities between Ron Dennis and Max Mosley, the president of the FIA.

Meanwhile, McLaren's name had been tarnished. Hearing that Max Mosley had said McLaren had "polluted" the 2007 World Championship sounded a bit over the top, and appeared to be nothing more than a shameful comment that told you more about the person who said it than it did about McLaren.

This was way above the heads of everyone in the garage. All we could do was focus on winning this race and the Drivers championship.

Just to make things a lot worse for us, Ferrari dominated qualifying and the race, with Raikkonen winning from Massa. Our two drivers engaged in some first-lap dodging and weaving at the first corner and then ran wheel to wheel toward Eau Rouge, where Alonso came out in front and stayed there. It was pretty scary for a few moments.

The race may not have been very exciting, but the paddock sure as hell was. The air remained heavy throughout with the strong smell of mendacity. It was also here that the next phase of the spying scandal—which involved Renault being discovered with McLaren discs downloaded to their factory computers—came out in the open. However, according to the FIA, this was okay, because Renault confessed to having the information!

The only point-scoring that mattered was between Hamilton and Alonso at the top of the championship, with Raikkonen 11 behind, and Massa 7 points further back.

Because the Japanese Grand Prix had been at Suzuka for 20 years, Dave Ryan and Mike Negline were the only McLaren team members to have been to the Fuji race track before. The only thing most of us knew about Fuji was its place in McLaren history as the circuit where

James Hunt won the Drivers championship in 1976. It rained then, and it rained again on race day in 2007. In fact, it was so bad that the teams received a message from FIA's Charlie Whiting, reminding us of a new rule that said you had to start the race on "extreme" wet tires. It was a pretty obvious choice for everyone—except Ferrari, who fitted intermediates to their two cars on the second row of the grid. Hamilton, on pole, and Alonso were directly ahead of the Ferraris as the race started behind the safety car and stayed that way for about 20 laps. The Ferraris had stopped for the correct tires and dropped to the back of the field while the safety car was out.

Lewis led pretty much the whole race. Alonso got caught up in traffic after his pit stop and had a spin in turn one, but kept going. While lying fifth on lap 41, he had a large shunt at a point on the back of the circuit where there was water running across the track. He was pushing hard, and from the data it looked like he had changed gear at just the wrong moment, something he had not done before. Fernando was okay, but the car was a bit of a mess.

That brought the safety car out once more and led to an incident where Sebastian Vettel, lying third in a Toro Rosso, went into the back of Mark Webber's Red Bull, putting them both out. Webber then pointed the finger at Lewis, although it was difficult to see why.

There was a lot of disarray, not helped by the fact that it was pretty hard to see anything most of the time given the amount of water on the track. But Lewis came through it to score his first win in the wet, edging 12 points clear of Fernando and 17 ahead of Raikkonen, who came home third. Massa ruled himself out of the championship fight by finishing sixth.

If we thought the Japanese race was over and done with by the time we got to Shanghai, we were mistaken. The FIA began an investigation into Lewis's driving while leading the field behind the safety car at Fuji, and they managed to turn the screw by stringing the whole thing out over 24 hours. By which time, of course, the media was writing all sorts of stuff—exactly, you suspected, as the FIA had hoped. On this occasion, however, it was the FIA who came under attack, not just from the journalists, but also from former champions Damon Hill and Sir Jackie Stewart, who criticized the FIA and its president.

At the end of it all, Lewis was found to have done nothing wrong and could focus on taking another pole position, with Raikkonen alongside and Fernando fourth. If you did the math, Hamilton would become champion by winning this penultimate round. But we should have guessed that as with everything else in 2007, it was not going to be as simple as that.

Rain before the race on Sunday meant everyone was on wet tires for the start. Lewis led through the first pit stop and stayed on the same set of wet tires, since the track was now drying

At Monza, runner-up Lewis Hamilton soaks winner Fernando Alonso after their 1-2 McLaren finish in the 2007 Italian Grand Prix. (LAT PHOTOGRAPHIC)

and the worn wets would be ideal. But it all went wrong when a few spots of rain returned. Hamilton's tires were in worse shape than most. Despite trying to drive on the wetter parts of the track, Lewis found his car felt as if it were on ice. And Raikkonen was closing in on him.

You could see the state of Hamilton's rear tires on the TV screen. It looked like he should stop—but it was difficult to know what tires to fit. Would the track continue to dry and be good enough for slicks? Lewis was asked to stay out for another lap, and when a backmarker changed to slicks and set the fastest lap, it was obvious slicks were the answer. Lewis was called in.

The pit entry had a tight left-hand corner that was still very wet. With virtually no rear grip, Lewis got sideways coming in and ended up in a very small runoff area, where he got stuck in the gravel. Game over.

Having Raikkonen and Alonso finish first and second, the championship continued to be up for grabs as the three contenders prepared to go to Brazil, covered by just seven points.

The Friday-morning practice at Interlagos was canceled because of—you guessed it— heavy rain. Fortunately, with so much at stake, it was dry and hot on Sunday, with Massa, enjoying huge local support, starting from pole. Lewis was alongside, but that didn't last long at the start, as Raikkonen and Fernando found their way through. Hamilton had a go at getting ahead of Alonso but spun off and dropped several places. Now the pressure was really on.

As Lewis started his fight back, the gearbox decided to go into a neutral position; not ideal at all. There was a great deal of radio traffic about trying different things to fix it.

In reality, all he could really do was keep pulling on the shift paddle until it began working again. By the time that had sorted itself out, he was down in 18th place. Lewis climbed back to 7th, but it was never going to be enough, particularly when Massa made a slow(-ish!) second stop and Kimi found himself in the lead and on his way to the championship—winning it by just two points.

As we were packing up, word came through about three cars (which had finished fourth, fifth, and sixth) having raced with fuel that was colder than required when the samples were taken and checked. The stewards took several hours to decide that *maybe* the fuel was not the temperature that was reported. Was there an inability to read or understand numbers? Surely not!

If the temperature was not wrong, then why bring up this issue at all? Of course, if the three cars were excluded, it would elevate Lewis to fourth and make him World Champion. So it was better to do nothing. One would surely have to question the integrity of the stewards after something like this—or was it just suggested to them to take that route?

As expected, in November it was announced that Alonso would not return to McLaren, returning instead to Renault for 2008. It was sad that Alonso was leaving; he is pretty damn good when the wires touch. I guess he didn't feel he fitted in very well at McLaren, and he had some people with him who I thought did not help the matter at all. I wanted to talk to him and try to explain some things about that, but he wouldn't let me.

He had a good car with good people working on it who cared about him. This package was more than capable of winning. But in a BBC article Alonso claimed, "McLaren failed to give me enough backing in my first season with them." Saying this just before the last race, when the championship was up for grabs, seemed rather out of place to me!

It was quite sad, along with all the foolishness that went on around Hungary time—and I don't mean in the pit lane. There were times when you read about what was going on and wondered if it was real. Sometimes it was like a very talented F1 driver was behaving like a five-year-old who wasn't getting his way. And the intrigue surrounding the various drivers, teams, and the FIA seemed better suited to some afternoon soap opera.

# 2008: Going Out on Top: Hamilton's Championship Season

For 2008, Alonso was replaced by Heikki Kovalainen—another Finnish driver, and a very personable guy who can be quick at times. Heikki would be driving No. 23, with Lewis in No. 22, a public sign of our status after being stripped of championship points in 2007. Doubtless that pleased someone in a high place in Paris. As far as the team was concerned, it was business as usual, getting ready with the new car, MP4/23, for the season start in Melbourne.

The weekend started off okay, but on Friday evening there was a problem with reverse gear on the T-car. Having not had this kind of problem before meant taking a look at all the gearboxes we had brought to Australia.

Two were on the race cars and had to come off. It was a good thing that we had Phil Taplin present as an extra gearbox mechanic to join Steve Lord, the normal race team gearbox guy, plus Jonathan Mays, who was new. Pretty soon there were a bunch of gearboxes in various states of disassembly, the one from the T-car receiving the most attention.

A lot of time was spent trying to understand what had happened, where it happened, and why. While this was going on, Mike Negline was off somewhere in Melbourne getting

Lewis Hamilton celebrates from atop his car after winning the 2008 Chinese Grand Prix. My final season with McLaren would be a victorious one for Lewis and the team. (LAT PHOTOGRAPHIC)

parts machined to fix the problem. He returned in the middle of the night and the rebuild process got under way.

I helped Phil Taplin replace damaged seals inside the T-car gearbox case and then waited until the boxes were back together before doing the drum sensor setup. This meant that the guys, who had gone home and were coming back very early, could fit the gearboxes to the cars.

I and a few others got back to the hotel at about 5:00 a.m. I guess about three hours' sleep was better than some of the others managed. At least all this hard work paid off when Lewis took pole, with Heikki third, our cars split by the BMW of Robert Kubica.

Hamilton led all the way apart from two periods when Heikki took over as Lewis made his pit stops. While the timing of these stops was perfect for Hamilton, Kovalainen got caught out when the safety car appeared just as he was due to stop. Heikki rejoined further down the field after having to wait (as the rules now required) for the whole field to be bunched behind the safety car before entering the pits. He had a good go at getting past Alonso's Renault, and did so briefly near the end of the race, only to lose it when he hit the pit lane speed limiter button while trying to clear the oil off his helmet visor. Fifth place for Kovalainen was the end result.

Lewis, having already made his second and final stop, was looking good for the first 10 points of the season and was not troubled by Nick Heidfeld's BMW at the end of 58 laps. Lewis was pleased with the car—as you would be when you win—and it was a great boost for the whole team to start the season this way after all the political crap of 2007.

The race took its toll, with only seven cars running at the finish. Raikkonen was classified eighth, five laps behind because of an engine failure. Massa had retired after colliding with Coulthard's Red Bull. But the feeling was that Ferrari would bounce back. They usually do.

Sure enough, we got to Malaysia and the red cars were on the front row, Massa ahead of Raikkonen. Meanwhile, Heikki and Lewis ended up eighth and ninth on the grid, both having received five-place penalties for "impeding" one of the other cars at the end of Q3.

Normally in Q3, drivers would be running flat out, but because rain was threatening, quite a few drivers had put in their quick laps early on and were then conserving fuel toward the end. Although the rules may have allowed you to do this, they were making everyone look stupid on this occasion.

Massa led until the first pit stops. At that point Raikkonen got the jump on him, and Massa then added to his problems by spinning off. Lewis made a good start to hold fifth at the end of the first lap, but at the first pit stop, there was a problem with one of his front wheels. He dropped back quite a way, eventually finishing back in fifth. Heikki, meanwhile, had a very good race and finished third, adding more of those elusive points and keeping McLaren ahead of BMW on the table.

Kubica went one better in Bahrain when he qualified fastest in the BMW, bringing the expected run of headlines about a Pole being on pole for the first time. Massa was up there as usual, with Lewis third and Heikki directly behind him in fifth.

Hamilton had a problem with anti-stall at the start, dropped to 9th, and then ran into the back of his old buddy Alonso. This meant a stop for a new nose and front wing, dropping him a long way back, which is pretty much where he stayed, finishing 13th, one lap behind. Kovalainen wasn't without his moments either, having gotten himself into 4th, only to make a couple of small mistakes, finishing 5th. Massa scored his first points of the season by winning, but Raikkonen's 2nd place put him at the head of the championship. Kubica, having made a mess of his start, finished 3rd ahead of Heidfeld, this being enough to move BMW to the top of the Constructors championship.

Ferrari's run continued at Barcelona with Raikkonen taking pole, the Ferraris split by Alonso's Renault. (He'd had a light fuel load; this was Spain, after all!) Lewis was fifth, but Heikki, carrying a lot more fuel, did a great job to qualify sixth. Unfortunately, all that hard work would come to nothing. Just as Kovalainen took the lead during the first pit stop phase, he had a very large high-speed shunt caused by a front-wheel problem that buried the car into the tire barriers at the very fast Campsa corner at the top of the hill. It took the marshals a long time to extract the car and get Heikki out of the cockpit.

Gary Hartstein, the FIA doctor who had taken over from Professor Sid Watkins, had a good look at Heikki before he was taken off to the hospital for a more thorough checkup. After a couple of days he returned home with the McLaren race team doctor, Aki Hintsa. Fortunately the problem with the wheel was found and sorted. The chassis was written off (both pieces of it!) and, thankfully, Heikki was all right.

The Ferraris, led by Raikkonen, finished one-two, with Lewis ending a disappointing couple of races by getting onto the podium, all of which helped to keep him second in the championship to Kimi.

Heikki showed no lingering effects from the shunt when we arrived in Turkey two weeks later. He was on the front row but, once again, a really good effort with a car heavy with fuel would come to nothing. The dirty side of the track seems worse at Istanbul Park than other places. At the start Heikki was slowed by the amount of fuel he had on board, and only Raikkonen ran into him, causing a slowish puncture in the left-rear tire. There was a lot of chaos behind this, and the safety car was out before you could blink.

I could see from the telemetry data that the tire was losing pressure and told the pit wall people, who asked several questions ("Are you sure?!"). Dear, oh dear. They spoke to Kovalainen, who said he couldn't feel anything wrong. (Going slowly behind the safety car, I wasn't surprised.) I pointed out, this time rather loudly, what the pressure was. There was more radio traffic, but when they decided to tell Heikki to stop, he had just gone past the pit entry.

Big mistake! When you have critical sensors on the car, you have to believe them. When a colored line starts moving down the screen, you have to act straightaway and not have a meeting about it. Twelfth place and a lap behind at the end, Heikki had every right to look deeply disappointed.

Massa won, with Lewis (doing three stops) chasing him the whole way and finishing ahead of Raikkonen. That maintained Kimi's lead of the championship, with Massa and Lewis sharing second place, seven points behind.

Kovalainen was in trouble again at Monaco when on his last run on Saturday morning, he hit the wall with the right-rear while exiting the swimming pool corner. It was only the tire that was damaged, but to be safe the guys changed the whole right-rear corner, nicking it from his spare gearbox. It was quite a big job, but once again, everyone pitched in and the car was ready for qualifying. Heikki qualified fourth, but was disappointed by the 0.3-second gap between him and the next driver, particularly when the first three—Massa, Raikkonen, and Hamilton—were covered by 0.052 seconds.

It was raining a bit on the grid, but that became immaterial when Kovalainen was pushed to the pit lane for a replacement steering wheel. Basically I made a rather large balls-up with something on the system monitor that I had not seen before and couldn't delete. I sure as hell should have done something before it got too late. As Richard Ford said to me, I should have just shut the system monitor off when this window popped up. He was quite right, and I am still pissed-off with myself to this day—and really sorry for Heikki, who was stuck in traffic for the rest of the afternoon, but worked his way through and grabbed the last point for eighth place.

Lewis had managed to get himself between the two Ferraris at the start, but just as the rain increased slightly on lap six, he hit the barrier exiting Tabac and punctured a tire.

Luckily, he was close enough to the pits to come straight in, fill the car with fuel, take on new tires, and get back out without losing a position, thanks to the field having become strung out in the slippery conditions.

As it turned out, this would win Lewis the race by allowing him to be on the right tires at the right time, even with a late safety car taking away the good lead he had built up by lap 60.

Luck really was on Lewis's side, as the race finished at the two-hour limit, two laps short of the scheduled distance. Had he needed to do the full 78 laps, Lewis would not have made it because of a slow puncture.

With Kubica taking second and Massa third, Lewis was on top of the championship. Raikkonen finished out of the points after what might best be described as an eventful race: Among other things, he'd gone into the back of Adrian Sutil's fourth-place Force India.

It's always best for one driver not to criticize another for making a mistake. In Canada, it would be Lewis's turn to make a simple but catastrophic error while leading. Having been on pole—and very happy with the car—Lewis had pulled out a comfortable lead when the safety car appeared after 16 laps.

The pit stop was a bit slow, allowing Kubica and Raikkonen to get out ahead of him and then stop at the end of the pit lane because of a red light at the exit. Lewis didn't see the red light until it was too late and went into the back of the Ferrari. Rosberg's Williams then added to the chaos by hitting the back of Hamilton.

Kubica, relieved that Lewis had gone into the waiting Ferrari rather than the BMW, went on to score his first win and lead a BMW one-two as Heidfeld finished second. McLaren came away with no points after Heikki struggled into ninth place after having trouble with his tires for the whole race.

The knock-on effect of the Canadian mistake was that Lewis was given a 10-place penalty after qualifying 3rd at Magny-Cours. Things didn't improve in the race when he got a drive-through for missing a chicane when overtaking Vettel, a penalty that dropped him to an eventual 10th, out of the points. Heikki, meanwhile, fought his way from 10th on the grid (he'd been penalized for impeding) to 4th, and was pushing Jarno Trulli in the Toyota. Trulli was never easy to pass at the best of times, even though there was a good overtaking place at the end of the long straight. A one-two for Ferrari (won by Massa) put them even further ahead in the Constructors championship as we held third behind Sauber. Massa now led the Drivers stakes, 10 points clear of Hamilton, in fourth place. What Lewis desperately needed was another win to prevent the Ferrari guys from easing ahead as the season

Hamilton congratulates his new teammate Heikki Kovalainen after Heikki's first F1 win at the 2008 Hungarian Grand Prix. (LAT PHOTOGRAPHIC)

approached half distance. Silverstone would be the perfect place to do it—if we could.

There had been the usual large amount of work at the factory, with more updates that looked to be taking us in a positive direction. This seemed to pay off when Heikki claimed his first pole position by over half a second; Lewis had to accept fourth after going across some curbs.

Heikki probably would have been in line for his first win had it not rained on and off during the race—perfect conditions for Lewis. He showed his intentions by overtaking Raikkonen's Ferrari and Webber's Red Bull by the time the field got to the first corner. By the end of lap five, he had passed Heikki—and then just drove off into the distance.

In what had to be the best race he had driven so far, Lewis finished over a minute ahead of Heidfeld. Heikki, having spun off once, took fifth. With Massa finishing out of the points, we now had the Ferrari driver and Lewis tied at the top of the points table.

A LIFE AND TIMES WITH MCLAREN

It seemed to fit the 2008 story thus far when Lewis and Massa were together on the front row at Hockenheim. This helped to ease some of the muttering that had been going on in the garage since the Mercedes engine people had appeared at around 7:00 p.m. on Friday to ask for an extra air bottle to be fitted to the engine pneumatic system, to give it more volume. Practice had finished about four hours earlier and it was not a quick job, even though there were some parts already made. There was a rather large collective groan in the garage before the task was started. But pole position and third on the grid were the results when it was finished.

It looked even better when we were first and second just after the start. This lasted until the end of the long straight when Kovalainen hit the brakes about 75 meters earlier than normal and lost a few places, one of them to Massa.

This helped Lewis to earn a 1.8-second advantage at the end of the lap, a lead which he held through the first pit stop—despite having a moment when he nearly ran into the back of the safety car (a brand-new Mercedes!).

This was probably because Hamilton had been distracted by having enough time to check the big screens around the stadium and notice that more than half the field was taking the opportunity to make their second stops. He was reassured that he had enough fuel on board to get going once the safety car had disappeared, opening a gap large enough to allow his second stop without losing the lead. That assumption was okay, except for one thing: It did not allow for the safety car staying out for much longer than expected. The predictable result was that he did not have enough time to build the 23-second lead he needed, which left Lewis in fifth place when he rejoined after his second stop.

With 17 laps remaining, Lewis had to drive like hell to get back in the lead. Which he did. His win was a big plus—not just for McLaren, but also for Mercedes at the German GP. With Massa finishing third, that put Lewis four points in front.

Hard though it is to maintain a roll when you're on one, we seemed to be doing okay, as Lewis took pole in Hungary with Heikki alongside. But then the plot changed somewhat as Massa, starting third on the clean side of the track, made a very good start and ran around the outside of Lewis to take the lead at the first corner.

Our strategy guys immediately investigated Plan B, which said that by having Massa stop first, we could work out how much fuel went into the Ferrari, fuel Lewis longer, and get the jump on Massa at the second stop. That might have been okay had Lewis not flat-spotted the left-front tire, which may or may not have contributed to the puncture not long into lap 41.

Now Massa looked to be home and clear. But then his Ferrari engine disgraced itself

428

three laps from the finish—and Heikki was there to take the lead. There was a lot of chat on the pit wall about saying a few things to Heikki, but, fortunately, common sense prevailed and no one said anything. They all just held their breath until he crossed the finish line for his first win.

This not only brought a smile to Heikki, but also to Mark Slade, Dave Robson, and the guys working on his car: Jonathan Brooks, Dave Colman, Robert Musgrave, Mark Jones, and Jonathan Mayes. Lewis, meanwhile, had climbed back to fifth, good enough to edge his championship lead (now over Raikkonen, who had finished third behind Timo Glock's Toyota) to five points. And for the first time in quite a few races, McLaren had pushed BMW out of second place in the Constructors championship. We were 100 points to Ferrari's 111.

After we got home from Hungary, we had a really enjoyable evening with Mark Webber and his partner, Ann, at The Stag Inn, their pub/restaurant at Mentmore, near Aylesbury. The others tried various dishes, but I had to have the Mark Webber pizza, which I have to say was very good. Mark and Ann are good hosts and good friends, proper people who have a healthy disregard for the bullshit that circulates around Formula One. Like me, they are racing people.

The new circuit in Valencia, built beside the marina where the America's Cup sailboats were kept, turned out to be a less than thrilling place for racing. Looking at the closeness of lap times, you got the feeling that people were driving at about 90 percent, thanks to having more respect than usual for the track's concrete walls.

It didn't help when a sewer became blocked and the circuit people had to remove some large cast-iron covers that just happened to be located between our two trucks. As you might imagine, this made for a not very pleasant sight during the many routine journeys between the garage and the trucks.

Massa was on form again, leading from pole with Lewis hanging on to second with a good steady pace—probably the best he could hope for, since he was not feeling well all weekend. Heikki got up to third and then ran over the fuel man at his second pit stop. As if to get even, the engine failed shortly thereafter. Massa, back to second on the table, was six points behind Lewis.

If Valencia had been a fairly quiet weekend, Spa was to change all that with a bit more excitement, turmoil, and drama than one wanted, along with a few disgusting decisions by some of the usual people. The standard Spa weather was on its best behavior, at least for practice and qualifying, as Lewis took pole ahead of Massa, with Heikki third and Raikkonen fourth.

Lewis led off the line but Raikkonen was on a mission, barging his way past Massa and taking advantage of a spin by Lewis at the start of the second lap to snatch the lead as they climbed the hill to Les Combes. Kimi was genuinely quick, and Lewis was trying as hard as he could to stay with him. There wasn't much in it as we went through the two pit stops, Lewis telling us later that he was praying for rain because he saw that as his only chance of getting ahead of the Ferrari.

With about eight laps to go, Hamilton's prayers were answered. Raikkonen began to slow, and at the Bus Stop chicane, just before the pits, Lewis had a go at taking the lead. Needless to say, Raikkonen blocked, and Hamilton went across the grass and came out of the chicane just ahead of the Ferrari. As required by the rules, Lewis let Kimi through almost immediately.

On the run up to the La Source hairpin Hamilton had another go and got by on the inside. Except that as far as the stewards were concerned, this pass was against the rules. By now the rain was getting worse. As the leaders came across Nico Rosberg (recovering from an off), Lewis went to one side and Raikkonen to the other to retake the lead. Then he spun, and in an effort to catch Lewis again, Kimi stuffed it into the wall. Game over.

Lewis backed off and drove very carefully to win the race. One hell of a drive from him, especially during the last few laps in the pouring rain. Lewis didn't think there would be any penalty regarding the chicane incident, but the stewards felt differently, adding 25 seconds to Lewis's race time, effectively putting him third, with Massa now the winner. Nearly everyone in the pit lane, along with a few million others watching their TVs, thought that if there was a penalty, then there sure as hell was something very wrong. Knowing the players involved, some of us refrained from making comments.

It seemed Lewis was meant to wait until he had gone around the next corner (La Source) after the incident before attempting to retake the lead. Where the hell did that rule come from, anyway? It was nothing more than a crock of shit made to validate the thinking of those who perpetrated it.

In a previous race, a mistake that usually warrants a 10-second drive-through penalty was punished by issuing a fine, thus enabling the car that made the mistake to still win the race. And now it was the same car that was "given" the race win at Spa, thanks to Hamilton's surprise penalty.

Our thinking was that it would probably be better if the rules were made before the race rather than after it!

Hamilton with his father and bodyguard after winning the 2008 world championship at the season's final race in Brazil. (TYLER ALEXANDER)

We drove back to the hotel at the Brussels airport, where Steve Hallam, Dave Redding, and I went to the bar for the odd drop of medicine. Our phones were ringing a great deal of the time, with folks asking us what the hell was going on. The rest of the boys showed up a bit later and joined us for some calming liquid. We heard that the mother of the stewards' chairman, Alan Donnelly, had wondered how they could be so harsh to that nice young boy.

On Monday morning, while sitting on the plane in Brussels waiting to leave for Milan, a seasoned Italian journalist told me, "Tyler, what happened late yesterday is the end of Formula One as a sport." I thought it had probably started quite some time before that, ramping up in 2007 with what you might call the alleged theft of $100 million and the alleged corruption regarding some computer discs and the information on them.

The rain traveled south for the Italian Grand Prix and more or less stayed for the whole weekend at Monza. Tire choice in qualifying proved critical, with Mark Slade and Dave Robson getting it right, as they kept Kovalainen fastest until near the end. Then, just as Heikki was going out for his last run, Mark said something about being on pole. I thought, "Oh no!" Mark told me later that he realized he'd made a slight mistake; Vettel had snatched his first pole position in the Toro Rosso. Massa was 6th, but Lewis was even worse off in 15th, due to the wrong choice of tires in Q1.

When the rain continued on race day, most people started on extreme wet tires and changed to intermediates late in the race, just around the time of the second pit stops, which was helpful!

Vettel led the whole way; Kovalainen finished second. We couldn't help but think Heikki should have had a go at the Toro Rosso, as he was quite quick, but because of a problem with the brakes, he thought being prudent was a better bet. Lewis finished seventh after a very aggressive drive in less than ideal conditions. With Massa finishing just one place ahead, Lewis's championship lead was down to a single point. But we had closed Ferrari's Constructors lead to five points.

A night race in Singapore was a new venture for Formula One. Given that it was still 95 degrees Fahrenheit (35 degrees Celsius) and very humid during the night, you could only imagine what it would have been like to go racing in the middle of the day with the sun beating down. It did seem strange going into the track very late in the afternoon. The lighting was very good and caused no real problems, particularly in the pits, where it was so bright it helped you forget it was really the middle of the damn night.

Once again, the two main championship players, Massa and Hamilton, were on the front of the grid. Lewis made a reasonable start from the dirty side of the track, but Heikki, starting fifth, had a small coming-together with Kubica on the first lap, and finished it in seventh place. Massa was pulling away with Raikkonen pressuring Lewis when the story of the race was about to change dramatically, thanks to Nelson Piquet Jr. spinning his Renault into the wall and bringing out the safety car. This happened just after teammate Alonso had made his first pit stop, way ahead of everyone else.

Alonso went on to win the race. Later it was discovered that Piquet had crashed deliberately, allegedly under orders of Renault team principal Flavio Briatore and chief engineer Pat Symonds. Renault was handed a suspended disqualification from Formula One, while Briatore was banned from motorsport indefinitely and Symonds given a five-year suspension. Both punishments would be overturned later in a French court. Trouble is, well-executed plans can sometimes turn into something not very well executed and quite smelly.

With the time being right to stop, there was a fair amount of chaos in the pit lane—not just with some drivers having to wait behind their teammate for fuel and tires, but also because Massa drove off with the fuel hose attached!

Alonso won—with a large bit of help from his friends—while Lewis took third to go seven points clear of Massa.

Packing up in the early hours of the morning and getting about two hours' sleep before leaving for the airport wasn't great. When I got down to the hotel lobby, I noticed quite a few engineers were already there, which seemed a bit unusual. It seems they came back to the hotel, got cleaned up, changed into their travel gear, and went out for some noodles and beer at a place they had eaten at earlier in the week; not a bad plan under the circumstances. It was all part of the learning process in a race where everyone was living and working on European time despite being eight hours east of home.

It was back to proper local time for the Japanese Grand Prix at Fuji, where Lewis took pole, with Heikki third and Massa lining up directly behind him.

Unfortunately, that was the last thing that went well for us. Hamilton made a poor start but was so determined not to lose ground that he out-braked himself into the first corner, ran wide, and took Raikkonen and others with him. The chaos allowed Heikki into third place, which would only last for 16 laps because of an engine failure. Meanwhile, as Hamilton and Massa recovered, the Ferrari ran into the McLaren, spinning Lewis around. He would finish 12th, with Massa getting two points for seventh.

What the team and Lewis needed after a race like that was a quiet weekend, which is

Ron Dennis loves to win, so he looked pleased when I caught him on his mobile phone after Hamilton's championship-winning victory in Brazil. After my retirement I was honored when Ron awarded me the first McLaren Fellowship. (TYLER ALEXANDER)

exactly what we got for the penultimate round in China. Lewis took pole position and led every lap. Ferrari was never a threat, and had it not been for Raikkonen "assisting" his teammate with eight laps to go, Massa would not have finished second.

The points table read Hamilton, 94; Massa, 87. Translated, this now meant Lewis needed to finish fifth or better in Brazil to win the championship. Easier said than done, but you never know who might be looking after you.

Lyndy Redding had arranged a farewell dinner on the Sunday in between races for Steve Hallam, who was off to his new job in NASCAR with Michael Waltrip Racing. Sao Paulo would be his last grand prix with McLaren. We met at Gordon Ramsay's Maze restaurant in London, and it was genuinely very, very good. We were shown around the restaurant and parts of the kitchen, where Dave Ryan had a go at cooking a few steaks. The only inconvenient part was the 5:30 a.m. taxi to the airport on Monday morning.

There are a couple of people at McLaren who I should have mentioned a lot more of during this journey. One is Neil Oatley, who could best be described as the backbone of the development and car-building side of things. Neil and I have been friends since he came to work for us at FORCE in 1985. He has experienced a great number of ups and downs over the years, which we've talked about, and yet he has always been able to keep a steady grip on things.

The other is Dave Redding, usually called "Otis" by a great many of us. Dave has been at McLaren quite a while, despite leaving to help set up and run the Stewart F1 team in the late 1990s before returning to McLaren. Otis has always worked on the race and test teams doing a variety of things—and been damn good at all of them. Being multitalented on both the engineering and management sides, Otis has been able to turn his hand over the years to many aspects of running a race team.

So we were now off to Brazil for the final race of the 2008 season, where the Drivers World Championship title would be decided. No sooner had we arrived in Sao Paulo than we were eating again! This time, of course, it was the now-traditional Mercedes team dinner in Fogo de Chao, which was as good and as sociable as ever.

Perhaps not surprisingly, considering this was his home race, Massa was on pole. Lewis was fourth-fastest, with Heikki less than a tenth behind, our cars separated from Massa by Trulli's Toyota and Raikkonen in the other Ferrari. As always seems to happen at Interlagos, it started to rain quite hard with about 10 minutes to go before the start. There was a bit of fumbling going on about the rain and whether it was going to last. Meanwhile, the system

# Ron Dennis

While McLaren represents the cutting edge of modernity, we also have huge pride and respect for our roots. Very few people embody the blend of both those worlds as well as Tyler Alexander.

That he has retained an important role on our race team until his leaving speaks volumes for both his passion for the sport and his vast experience, adaptability, and intelligence. His is a legacy that has spanned every decade of this team's involvement in Formula One, and one that we will continue to cherish while missing his day-to-day involvement with the team.

Everyone within the McLaren Group and Vodafone McLaren Mercedes wishes him a restful and creative time in the future.

monitor got soaked and died, which meant I had to use the spare one at the last minute to download some new numbers.

But the real chaos would come very near the end of the race. Massa had led more or less all the way. Lewis, lying in fourth place, was doing all he needed to. Then the radar picked up some wet weather on its way. With five laps to go and the track becoming slippery, most people stopped for wet tires. Most people, that is, except the Toyotas. Suddenly, things took on a very different perspective.

Everyone in the garage was asking, "Where the hell is the rain that the radar said was going to be here several minutes ago?" The order was Massa, Alonso, Raikkonen, Glock, and Hamilton. Fifth place would be good enough. But then with three laps to go, Vettel passed Lewis, dropping him to sixth—and out of the championship.

Massa crossed the line to win the race and, at that particular moment, the 2008 World Championship. The crowd and the Ferrari pits went wild, as you would expect.

Meanwhile, the rain had finally arrived and Glock, on dry tires, slid wide in the last corner, allowing Lewis into fifth place. Holding his breath to keep the adrenaline under control, he climbed the hill and moved onto the long straight toward the finish line. The heart rate of those in the garage and on the "pratt perch" on the pit wall was rising rapidly.

Once he crossed the finish line, Lewis Hamilton, at 23, became the youngest World Champion in Formula One history. Being in the right place at the right time and not throwing it away sure as hell can do things for you when it really counts.

It didn't take long for most people in the paddock to cram into the McLaren garage, which is why the two system monitors used to run Hamilton's car walked out of the garage with some thieving bastards.

It was a very emotional end to the race and the season, for both McLaren and Ferrari. Lewis had done all he could, and so had Felipe, who did a remarkable job of controlling his feelings on the podium, giving us all a lesson in dignity.

Oh, and one small note regarding the end of the 2008 season: Brazil was my last official race with McLaren. Though it wouldn't be formally announced until the following spring, I was retiring. It had been 18 years since I'd joined McLaren International, and more than 40 since I'd joined Bruce and Teddy to help start the original team. On the one hand, 1964 seemed a long, long time ago. On the other, I thought of a great line that I remembered from when I was in high school, "The summer break seemed to go on forever, and when it was over it seemed like only yesterday."

# Epilogue: Farewell to Old Friends, and Life after Racing

**M**otor racing can be a bit like a train that never stops—except to throw people off! But there are some things in life—and in motor racing—which you can't buy: dedication, resilience, loyalty, focus, and, probably most important of all, trust. Motor racing is about compromise. I am a person who likes to get straight to the point and take action, which sometimes bites you in the arse. Sometimes people have other ideas too! Listening and talking to people should always be the first step toward success in any team.

I'm damn sure that the reason, or one of the reasons, I've made it this far is that I had help, in some shape or fashion, from all of the people I have worked with.

I have mentioned trust, but I probably didn't always realize how the various aspects of one word would come to actually mean so much, especially in the convoluted world of motor racing. Trust is essential to building the team—trust between the engineers, mechanics, and technicians, as well as in the relationship with the driver, who is of course counting on all those involved.

When you go racing you meet a lot of people along the way, some of whom become friends you can trust, and others you have misgivings about. There is another group, of

A few years after my retirement I signed copies of my book of photographs, *McLaren From The Inside*, at an event marking the team's 50th anniversary in September 2013. (TYLER ALEXANDER COLLECTION)

course, that you can't or just don't trust; sadly, this group tends to be the larger one, made up of people you might refer to as "so-called friends."

Fortunately, over the years, I have been lucky enough to meet a lot of good people who have become real friends. Some I have worked with and some were very tough competitors. In the grand scheme of things, respect for your competitors is always important, whether you like them or not (probably not if they are beating you!). But when it comes to needing something, which usually works both ways, respect can become quite important.

I have mentioned this before, but the small group of people doing the early McLaren

International gearbox gear-change project, and a few others, became (and remain) very much "trusted friends." Teddy Mayer and Professor Sid Watkins were a couple of very good friends of mine, and I have written a few words here about both of them.

On May 3, 2009, I was on my way to Teddy Mayer's memorial services at the Scranton Country Club in Pennsylvania.

On the way I stopped off to have dinner with Mario Andretti and Amy Hollowbush, his personal assistant, at one of his favorite restaurants, consuming a reasonable amount of wine from his own vineyard in Napa Valley. By now it was midnight—time to stop. The stories had been great, covering everything from motor racing today to speculation about where Colin Chapman might be right now. Mario is a great guy in so many ways: There's no mistaking those "magic" eyes of his, either in a restaurant or in a race car with a helmet on. This chat was only about our amusing thoughts, with no BS—the sort of thing that can only happen with the few "real" and good people in your life.

Teddy's uncle Bill Scranton gave a nice speech at the service. He finished with a bit of humor, pointing out that Teddy had only one basic fault. No matter what you were talking about, he said, Teddy knew more about it than you did, which usually pissed people off. The real problem was that Teddy was actually right a great deal of the time. Bill's final observation was that Teddy had to be the only person he knew who could piss off and charm someone in the same sentence!

I gave the following short speech at Edward E. Mayer's memorial services at the McLaren Technology Centre on February 7, 2009:

*Ahh . . . Mr. Mayer. EEM to some of us; Teddy to a great many others. Although Teddy could be difficult at times—and there were some people who may well have thought a great deal of the time—the reality was that his passion, enthusiasm, and contributions to the challenges of motor racing, which covered a great many years, far outweighed any of that.*

*From the first time I met Teddy in 1962 at the SCCA races in the States, to him asking me to help build, along with some other guys, a couple of cars for Bruce and Timmy to drive in the 1964 Tasman Series (built mostly on the dirt floor in the back of the Cooper F1 workshop), to giving me a check to go and buy the Zerex Special sports car from Roger Penske / John Mecom (which was at a race in Pensacola, Florida, while we were in Stowe, Vermont), I knew we would be friends.*

*While Teddy was sorting things out on the phone with Bruce in England, "Mugs" here drove to Florida with a car and trailer, picked up the car on Sunday after the race, and drove nonstop to New York. Teddy had sorted out the shipping of the car to England, and I followed on the morning flight the next day. Eoin Young picked me up and took me to the workshop, where the car was already being worked on by Wally Willmott and a couple of other guys, as we were racing it at Oulton Park the coming weekend. These days it's called "back-to-back" races; then it was just what you did.*

*All of this became the start of a small company called Bruce McLaren Motor Racing, and with Teddy's determination and Bruce's charisma, it grew into something rather a bit more than that.*

*When Bruce didn't come back from Goodwood that day and the factory dropped into a bleak hole, he had to do something. That something was to say that "we" had a Can-Am race in two weeks, so we'd best get on with it . . . and everyone did.*

*His work with Mr. Ecclestone and a few others changed a part of motor racing forever. I was a business partner and friend, with the same trust and respect between us for the odd 40 years, and I would guess that there are a number of us here today who would not be where we are if he hadn't looked after us or given us a kick in the ass every now and again. And that was Teddy!*

The days go by so quickly.

On September 12, 2012, we lost Professor Sid Watkins OBE. Mr. Ecclestone described him as "irreplaceable." That really was an understatement.

Talking to Sid, you could easily forget that he was a professor of neurosurgery at the University of London between 1972 and 1993. "The Prof" was known to say, "Take two aspirin and a large glass of single malt whisky—that will help sort you out."

In the 1970s Sir Jackie Stewart started encouraging the people who were running Formula One to improve safety. In 1978 Mr. Ecclestone suggested to Professor Watkins that he should be in charge of sorting out how and what should be done about Formula One safety at all the circuits.

Fortunately for a great many of us, Sid took up the challenge. He had the ability to fit in with all of us with his intelligence and great sense of humor, but we never forgot, of course, that he was the doctor.

He became friends with a great many of us—not just the drivers but also the team owners, mechanics, and engineers. To take for granted what Professor Sid Watkins did for the safety of Formula One would probably come under the heading of "a criminal practices act"!

Motor racing and particularly McLaren are still important in my retirement. On March 19, 2009, Ron Dennis made Neil Trundle, Ray "Tex" Rowe, and me founding members of the "fellowship" that recognizes selfless contributions to McLaren. To this day I retain my access to McLaren, so if I'm home on a Friday, I go over to the McLaren Technology Centre and have coffee with my friends. Sometimes this is the highlight of my week. Feeling a part of it and feeling appreciated by certain good friends helps to keep me sensible. In addition, I go to some of the races, taking photos of people, which also keeps me connected to motor racing.

Apart from this, I'm still an American living in England, and enjoying it (apart from the taxes!). I go to Mexico to snorkel and take underwater photos of the fish and turtles, as well as visiting friends there. Once a year I go down to Port Douglas, Australia, and out to the Great Barrier Reef, taking more underwater photos. There is also an annual fishing trip to Boston and Nantucket to see my friends Batt (Paul Wuori) and Larry Cronin Jr. On some weekends my friend Jane and I have dinner and often talk about the intricacies and complexities of motor racing, a world she is sometimes involved in as well.

There are days when I think that I haven't learned a thing and others when I know that some folks haven't learned anything at all! I guess I was lucky; there aren't many people who have the chance to do what they really like, and I had that chance. Although there are many things that aren't great in the overall kaleidoscope of chaos that you sometimes find in motor racing, I would do it all over again.

# Index

Page numbers in *italics* refer to photographs and captions

Japanese Grand Prix, 418, 433

Malaysian Grand Prix, 406, 423–424

Monaco Grand Prix, 408, 425–426

San Marino Grand Prix, 396

Singapore Grand Prix, 432–433

Spanish Grand Prix, 406

Turkish Grand Prix, 400, 415, 425

Matthews, Andy, 321

Mayer, Annie, 43

Mayer, Garrill, 11–12, 36–37

Mayer, Sally, 37, 123–124, 212

Mayer, Teddy
 BMMR, 9, 43, 47, 54, 73, 97–98, 106–108, 117, 148
 British Grand Prix, *187*
 Bruce McLaren's death, 97
 Caguas circuit, 25
 Canadian Grand Prix, *150*
 conflicts with John Barnard, 168–169
 Daytona Continental, 23
 Dutch Grand Prix, *128*, 156
 education, 11
 FORCE/Lola/Haas team, 172, 182, 183, 185–186, 189, 192, 195
 Formula Junior car, 23
 friendship with Ecclestone, 186
 friendship with Tyler Alexander, 21, 22, 84, 212
 hiring Johnny Rutherford, 115
 Hoosier Grand Prix, 24
 Indianapolis 500, 97, 102, 105, 112, *134*, 178–179
 Kent, Washington, 56
 Laguna Seca, 31
 management of Timmy Mayer, 11, 36
 Mayer Motor Racing, 173, 174, 176, *178*
 McLaren cars, 59, 146
 McLaren drivers, 127
 McLaren Engines, 91
 McLaren International, 149–150, 158, 165, 169
 McLaren North America, 138–139
 Meadowlands Grand Prix, *184*
 memorial service, 439–440
 Monaco Grand Prix, *147*

Monza, 194

Mosport, 43

rental house in Spain, 123

Riverside, 31

Sanair, 181

SCCA racing, 20

St. Jovite, 105

Tasman Series, 30–31, *46*

Timmy Mayer's death, 11–12, 36–37

turbocharged Cosworth DFV engines, 133

Tyrrell team, 25

Villa d'Este Hotel, Italy, 123–124

Zerex Special, 38, *39*, 43

Mayer, Timmy
 Bahamas Speed Week, 32
 Brands Hatch Guards Trophy sports-car race, 30
 Caguas circuit, 24–25
 championships, 21, 25
 Cooper Formula Junior car, 21
 death, 11, 36–37, *46*
 Hoosier Grand Prix, 24
 Laguna Seca, 24, 31–32
 military service, 21
 Rev-Em Racing, 21
 Riverside, 31
 SCCA racing, 20
 Tasman Series, 11, 30–31, 33–34, *35*, 36, *38*, *46*
 Tyrrell team, 25

Mayer, Timmy (Teddy's son), 43

Mayer Motor Racing Ltd. (MMR), 173, 174, *175*, 176–179, 181–182, 184

Mayes, Jonathan, 421, 429

McCall, Alan, 77–78, 94, 96

McCluggage, Denise, 106

McCoy, Wiley, 139, 140–141, 171, 173

McKenzie, Bob, 375

McKeon, Bill, 174

McLaren, Bruce. *see also* Bruce McLaren Motor Racing
 achievements, 98
 Aintree, 40
 Bahamas Speed Week, 48
 Belgian Grand Prix, 79, *81*
 BMMR, 22, 43, 73
 Brands Hatch, 44, 77, *78*

Bridgehampton, 69

Can-Am championships, 71, 90

Can-Am series, 57–58

Canadian Grand Prix, 65, 80, 81

car design skills, 91–92, 96

Cooper Formula One team, 30, 42

Daytona, 61–62

death, 40, 97–98

Elkhart Lake, 69

four-wheel-drive F1 car, 81–82

French Grand Prix, 80

friendship with Jackie Stewart, 40

Goodwood, 45, 66, 97

homes in England, 62, 64

Italian Grand Prix, 80

Laguna Seca, 69, 70, *71*

McLaren-Elva sports cars, 48

McLaren Engines, 91

McLaren M1B, 52, 54, *55*, 57

McLaren M2B, 59

McLaren M4B, 64

McLaren M6A Can-Am car, *63*, 66, 68

McLaren M7A, 77, *78*, *82*

McLaren M8A Can-Am car, 74, 75

McLaren M8B Can-Am car, *89*

McLaren M9, 82

McLaren M15 Indy car testing, 93

Michigan Can-Am, 90

Monaco Grand Prix, 58–59, 64

Mosport, 43, 47, 55, 57, *60*, 69

movie about, 404–405

Nassau Speed Week, 56

Oulton Park, 57

parties at The Castle, 44

respect for, 40

Reynolds Aluminum sponsorship, 87

Riverside, 24, *55*, 56, 70, 90

Sebring, 23, 61–62

Shelby American team, 61

Silverstone, 77

Spanish Grand Prix, 77

St. Jovite, 57

Tasman Series, *10*, 30–31, 33–34, 36, 51, 52

Texas Can-Am, 90

Tyler Alexander's automobile accident, 62, 64

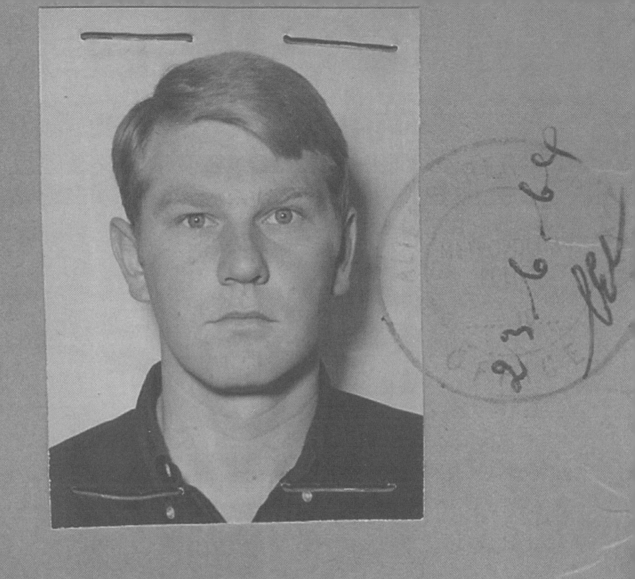

23-6-69

Signature of Holder

Tyler J. Alexander

Received the sum of 5s. 0d. for the issue of this certificate